ARIS AND PHILLIPS CLASSICAL TEXTS

I0593109

TERENCE

The Girl from Andros

*Edited with an Introduction,
Translation and Commentary by*

Peter Brown

LIVERPOOL UNIVERSITY PRESS

First published 2019 by
Liverpool University Press
4 Cambridge Street
Liverpool
L69 7ZU

www.liverpooluniversitypress.co.uk

British Library Cataloguing-in-Publication data
A British Library CIP record is available

ISBN 978-1-78962-010-8 hardback
ISBN 978-1-78962-011-5 paperback

Typeset by Tara Evans

Cover image: © The Bodleian Libraries, The University of Oxford.
                 MS. Auct. F. 2. 13, fol. 25v.

CONTENTS

PREFACE

I am grateful to Oxford University Press for permission to reproduce and adapt material from the Introduction and Notes to my translation of Terence's works in *Terence, The Comedies* in the Oxford World's Classics series. My translation is based on that one, though I have changed my mind about both large and small matters at quite a number of points.

I have printed the Latin text without the act- and scene-headings that are traditional in editions of Latin comedy. The scene-headings are found in the manuscripts, but they were almost certainly added to the text some time after Terence's death, and their inclusion tends to obscure the normally seamless continuity of the action on stage. The act-divisions are not found in the manuscripts but have been added by editors since the Renaissance, taking their hint from Donatus' commentary, which makes it clear that scholars in antiquity tried to impose a five-act structure on the plays (the structure recommended for tragedy by Horace at *Ars Poetica* 189–90 and exemplified in the surviving remains of Menander's Greek comedies). It is particularly absurd to impose such a structure on *The Girl from Andros*, in which the stage is empty at only two points (171/72 and 819/20). Since readers may well come across references to the text of Terence by act and scene (e.g. referring to line 500 as III.ii.20), I have included the traditional act- and scene-designations in the right-hand margin of the text.

In order to indicate the metrical structure of each line, I have printed the text with accents on the elements that carry the beat. For more details see the Introduction, section 8.9 (a); as I say there, the rhythm may well have been brought out by the pipe player in accompanied passages, and the audience were doubtless conscious of it as an underlying pattern in passages that were unaccompanied; but the actors presumably spoke or sang the words according to their natural rhythm. Thus the printed accents should not be interpreted as a guide to how the words were stressed in performance. (To avoid the danger of such misinterpretation, some editors prefer to indicate the rhythm by means of dots placed below the line, but I suspect most readers find these harder to interpret than accents.)

The Commentary includes basic help with the interpretation of the Latin text, normally by quoting from the relevant sub-heading in the Oxford

Latin Dictionary or from the relevant section of the Latin Grammar by B. L. Gildersleeve and G. Lodge or the relevant pages of H. Pinkster's Oxford Latin Syntax, vol. I. It probably provides more such help than is usual in this series, and I hope I have judged correctly the needs of students who know some Latin but are not familiar with Terentian idiom.

I have not included an apparatus criticus, but I do have a number of notes on the text in the Commentary (normally enclosed in square brackets), particularly at points where I print a text that is not found in any manuscripts, but also at points that have been the subject of recent discussion. I hope these notes will convey something of the sorts of decision that editors are required to make. The text of *The Girl from Andros* is more uncertain than that of Terence's other plays, doubtless mainly because manuscript A is missing until near the end (see Introduction, section 9), though the uncertainties rarely affect the meaning to any significant extent. I list at the end of the Introduction the main differences between my text and that of the Oxford Classical Text.

At a late stage Beppe Pezzini very kindly read through the entire volume; his comments have enabled me to make improvements on almost every page. Where you think you detect senile folly, you may reasonably assume that obstinacy led me to reject his advice at those points. I am also grateful to Alan Sommerstein and an anonymous reader for further helpful comments and to Karen Caines, Domenico Giordani, and David Sedley for bibliographical references.

I was introduced to Terence by Theo Zinn at Westminster School, tireless in his enthusiasm for Latin comedy, and I subsequently had the privilege of being taught by three of the greatest classical scholars of the twentieth century (and beyond): Eduard Fraenkel, Rudolf Kassel, and Robin Nisbet. I here express my gratitude for their support and encouragement.

Peter Brown

We are sad to have to record the death of Peter Brown in November 2018 while this book was in production. Liverpool University Press and Lesley Brown, Peter's widow, are extremely grateful to Beppe Pezzini for expertly seeing the work through the press.

INTRODUCTION

Terence (Publius Terentius Afer) was the outstanding comic playwright of his generation at Rome and, together with his predecessor Plautus, one of the founding fathers of European comic drama. He had written only six plays at the time of his early death, but they were quick to be acknowledged as classics and came to be included in the Roman school syllabus – indeed, they subsequently retained their place in the Latin syllabus throughout Europe, and they were studied wherever Latin was studied right down to the nineteenth century. Some 750 medieval manuscripts of Terence's plays survive, including some with famous miniature illustrations; and nearly 450 printed editions had been published before the year 1600. Plots portraying love affairs, confusion of identity, and misunderstanding were for centuries the dominant type of comic plot in the European dramatic tradition, and such characters as scheming servants and rediscovered children have long been standard ingredients of comic writing (not only for the stage). These elements go back to Greek New Comedy (see below, section 4), but it was Plautus and Terence who transmitted them to later generations.

1. Terence's life

'Publius Terentius Afer was born at Carthage and was a slave of the senator Terentius Lucanus at Rome. Because of his intelligence and good looks, his master not only gave him a liberal education but soon granted him his freedom as well.'[1] So begins the *Life of Terence* by Suetonius, written some 250 years after Terence's death in 159 BCE[2] but showing knowledge of earlier writers who had discussed the author. Suetonius records discussion by these earlier writers of the identity of Terence's powerful backers at Rome, the nature of their relationship with him, and their treatment of him. There are allegations that they were attracted by his physical beauty (he is said to have been of average height, slight build, and dark complexion), that they wrote sections of his plays, and that they failed to come to his help when he was reduced to poverty, leaving him to die in seclusion in a remote area of Greece. It is clear from Terence's prologue to *The Brothers* (15–21)

---

1 *Publius Terentius Afer Carthagine natus seruiuit Romae Terentio Lucano senatori, a quo ob ingenium et formam non institutus modo liberaliter sed et mature manu missus est.*
2 The date is given in section 5 of Suetonius' *Life*.

that he had such backers, and that he was accused already in his lifetime of relying on their help in the composition of his plays.[3] The story that he died in poverty in Greece conflicts with other accounts also recorded by Suetonius, and it is in fact more likely that he died relatively wealthy.[4] He is said to have been aged either 24 or 34 at the time of his death, and his prologues certainly represent him as a relatively young writer.

Unfortunately, ancient biographies are notoriously unreliable, and we have no way to check much of the information given by Suetonius. It is an intriguing idea that an author so central to the European cultural tradition was a slave from Africa (and that such an important Latin author came from Rome's great enemy, the city of Hannibal), but there may be no truth in it. In particular, Terence's Carthaginian birth and dark complexion may have been an incorrect deduction by later writers from his *cognomen* Afer ('the African'), though that does suggest at least some connexion with Africa. We know nothing of his alleged master Terentius Lucanus, and the nature of the discussions recorded by Suetonius does not encourage belief that their authors had much solid evidence for the playwright's life.

2. Chronology

The following chronology of Terence's plays is based on the production notices (*didascaliae*), compiled probably in the first century BCE and preserved in the manuscripts of the plays and in the commentary written by the grammarian Donatus in the fourth century CE. They are not entirely consistent, and their reliability has been questioned, but this is the generally accepted chronology.

166 BCE	Megalesian Games	*The Girl from Andros* [*Andria*]
165	Megalesian Games	*The Mother-in-Law* [*Hecyra*] (first attempt)
163	Megalesian Games	*The Self-Tormentor*
		[*Heauton Timorumenos*]
161	Megalesian Games	*The Eunuch* [*Eunuchus*]
161	Roman Games	*Phormio*
160	Funeral Games	*The Brothers* [*Adelphoe*]
	for Aemilius Paullus	and *The Mother-in-Law* (second attempt)
160	later in the year	*The Mother-in-Law* (third attempt)

---

3   Cf. also *HT* 22–24. For a discussion of the possible identity and significance of Terence's backers see D. P. Hanchey, 'Terence and the Scipionic *Grex*', in Augoustakis and Traill, 113–31.

4   See D. Gilula, 'How Rich was Terence?', *Scripta Classica Israelica* 8–9 (1989), 74–78.

The Megalesian Games were held at Rome in April each year in honour of the goddess Cybele; as part of the celebration, plays were performed outside her temple on the Palatine. The Roman Games were held each September in honour of Jupiter in the Circus Maximus. The Funeral Games in honour of Aemilius Paullus were held in the Forum in 160 BCE.

The Girl from Andros is the one play for which we do not have a *didascalia* in the manuscripts, but the information provided by Donatus clearly derives from one. It is generally accepted that this was Terence's first play, even by those who have questioned the conventional dating of some of the others (see below, the opening paragraph of section 6.1, '*The Girl from Andros*').

The prologue written for the third performance of *The Mother-in-Law* describes how the actors had had to abandon the two previous performances before completing them, because of the disruptive behaviour of the public (and the brief prologue written for the second performance similarly describes the fate of the first performance). Otherwise there is no evidence that any of Terence's plays had any difficulties, and we are told that *The Eunuch* was an unprecedented success.[5]

3. Rome in the 160s

The citizens of Rome in the 160s could reasonably feel themselves to have reached a pinnacle of power in the Mediterranean world: according to the Greek historian Polybius (who was contemporary with Terence and was in Rome when his plays were first put on), Rome had conquered 'almost the whole of the inhabited world in less than 53 years' from 220 (just before the outbreak of the Second Punic War, against Hannibal) to 167 (the year in which Aemilius Paullus and two other generals returned in triumph after the successful conclusion of the Third Macedonian War).[6] Terence's first play was put on in 166. The 160s themselves are an ill-documented decade for Rome, but Polybius tells us that the importation of Macedonian booty led to 'a great display of wealth, both in public and in private', and that in general this was a time when many Romans abandoned themselves to the sort of luxurious lifestyle that they traditionally associated with the Greek world.[7] This was a sign of their confidence in what their armies had

---

5   See Suetonius, *Life of Terence* 3, Donatus, *Eun. Praef.* 6, with H. N. Parker, 'Plautus vs. Terence: audience and popularity re-examined', *AJP* 117 (1996), 585–617.

6   Polyb. I.1.5.

7   Polyb. XXXI.25.3–7.

achieved, but it was also a source of tension within Rome itself: some were unhappy at the sapping of traditional Roman morality, and it is symptomatic that 161 (the year of *The Eunuch*) was marked both by sumptuary laws to limit public and private extravagance and by the expulsion of Greek rhetoricians and philosophers from Rome.[8] Greek culture was nothing new to the Romans, and since the end of the First Punic War in 241 there had been an explosion of Latin literature with Greek models, both in drama and in other fields; the years from 240 to 160 were the first Golden Age of Latin literature, and Greece was the acknowledged source of excellence in literature as in all the arts.[9] But it was particularly in this decade (if we can trust Polybius) that 'Greek' luxury joined Greek culture as a prominent feature of Roman life.

4. Latin Comedy and Greek New Comedy[10]

Terence's plays too are based on Greek models: his six comedies are all of the type known as *fabulae palliatae* ('plays in a Greek cloak [*pallium*]'), that is to say adaptations into Latin of Greek comedies written some 100–150 years earlier than the time of Terence. Four of the six are based on plays by Menander (one, *The Brothers*, with the addition of a scene from a play by Diphilus), two (*The Mother-in-Law* and *Phormio*) on plays by the less well-known Apollodorus of Carystus. In all but one case (*Phormio*), Terence has preserved the Greek title of the play. In writing this type of comedy, Terence was following in the footsteps of Livius Andronicus (first production 240 BCE), Naevius (active *c.* 235–204), Plautus (active *c.* 205–184), Ennius (239–169), and Caecilius (died 168): in his prologue to *The Girl from Andros* he invokes the precedent of Naevius, Plautus, and Ennius for his relatively independent approach to adaptation. This was not the only type of comic performance known at Rome, but it is the only type that happens to have survived in complete texts: twenty plays by Plautus and the six of Terence are in fact the earliest surviving complete works of Latin literature altogether (though not all of Plautus' twenty are entirely complete), together with Cato's *On Agriculture*, which probably dates from about 160. Since there was not an unlimited supply of Greek plays suitable for adaptation, the

8   Sumptuary laws: Gell. II.24.2–6; expulsion: Suet. *Rhet.* 1, Gell. XV.11.1.
9   See D. Feeney, *Beyond Greek: The Beginnings of Latin Literature* (Cambridge, Mass., 2016).
10   For a fuller discussion see P. Brown, 'Greek Comedy at Rome', in B. van Zyl Smit (ed.), *A Handbook to the Reception of Greek Drama* (Chichester, 2016), 63–77.

genre had a certain built-in obsolescence; and indeed its creative heyday ended before the end of the second century BCE, though plays by Plautus, Terence, and others continued to be performed for well over a century after Terence's death.

These plays show Greek characters in a Greek setting, and in general the authors are believed to have preserved at least the central elements of plot from their Greek originals while deviating from them to a greater or lesser extent. Very little remains of the particular Greek plays that Plautus and Terence adapted, but we know enough to be sure that they were normally not close line-by-line translators.[11] The Greek plays were regularly composed in five acts, separated by four interludes in which a chorus performed some kind of song-and-dance routine; the Latin authors abandoned this structure, writing for continuous performance (though no doubt with short pauses between some scenes) and eliminating the choral interludes. Like the Greek authors, Plautus and Terence wrote in verse, but they increased the proportion of text with musical accompaniment (see below, section 8) – with resulting effects that we can only guess at, since sadly the music has not survived. The Greek authors (as far as we know) never used more than three speaking actors in one scene; Plautus and Terence wrote many scenes requiring more, often thereby adding comic and dramatic effects not available to their Greek predecessors. Furthermore, in *The Girl from Andros*, *The Eunuch*, and *The Brothers* Terence imported material from a second Greek original, and we have evidence for the addition of further material of his own invention. For some of these changes we rely on the evidence of Terence's own prologues, for others on the commentary on his plays written in the fourth century CE by Donatus, a distinguished grammarian whose pupils included the future St Jerome; but this commentary does not survive in its original form, and Donatus is only sporadically interested in the original Greek plays.[12] Many scholars have thought to detect further changes by analysis of Terence's plays

---

11 Terence's claim at *Ad.* 11 to have translated one scene in *The Brothers* 'word for word' (*uerbum de uerbo*) points to a possible exception.

12 Donatus' commentary on the *Andria* is now best consulted in C. Cioffi (ed.), *Aeli Donati Quod Fertur Commentum ad Andriam Terenti* (Berlin and Boston, 2017). For the other plays, use P. Wessner (ed.), *Aeli Donati Commentum Terenti* (two vols, Leipzig, 1902, 1905). Wessner's third volume under the same title, subtitled *Eugraphi Commentum* (Leipzig, 1908), contains the far less useful commentary by Eugraphius (early sixth century), which focuses mainly on rhetorical analysis of the text and often does little more than paraphrase it. For Donatus, there is also an electronic edition with French translation and notes, ed. B. Bureau and C. Nicolas, available online at http://hyperdonat.huma-num.fr.

and comparison of their techniques with those of the surviving remains of Greek New Comedy. Overall, there has been, and will doubtless continue to be, much dispute over the extent and implications of the changes made by Terence.[13]

The type of comedy written by Menander and his contemporaries in the late fourth and early third centuries BCE is known as Greek New Comedy, to distinguish it from the rather different 'Old Comedy' written by Aristophanes and others a century earlier. New Comedy has been an area of particular interest in the last hundred years or so, when the rediscovery of texts written on papyrus has added considerably to our knowledge of it. Menander had been an extremely popular author in antiquity, but texts of his plays apparently ceased to circulate in about the seventh century CE; unlike those of Aristophanes, his plays did not survive into the Middle Ages, and he was essentially unknown to modern readers until the twentieth century, apart from a number of short passages that survived because they were quoted by other ancient authors. Even now we have perhaps eight per cent of his total output (and for other authors of New Comedy very little except scrappy fragments and short quotations); but we do have one complete play by him (first published in 1959), and substantial portions of several others. This material may be read in Maurice Balme's Oxford World's Classics translation (*Menander: The Plays and Fragments*, Oxford, 2001).

Typically, the plays of New Comedy (and their Latin adaptations) deal with personal relationships in fictional well-to-do families in a slave-owning, male-dominated society, above all with the love-life of boys in their late teens or early twenties and with associated tensions in their relations with their fathers. In this society, parents expect to arrange their children's marriages, and respectable citizen girls lead generally secluded lives; the accepted sexual outlet for citizen boys is provided by prostitutes (sometimes owned by pimps, sometimes free operators), whom they could never normally expect to marry. The action of the plays is enlivened by a number of stock characters, such as scheming slaves, parasites, prostitutes, pimps, and mercenary soldiers. Political references are rare; there are social tensions (between rich and poor, town and country, citizens and non-citizens, free and slave, men and

---

13   I have included discussion of the main points that have been made about this play in section 6 below and at some places in the Commentary. The classic discussion of Terence's use of his Greek models is that of Haffter 1953; see also Ludwig, J. Barsby, 'Terence and his Greek Models', in C. Questa and R. Raffaelli (eds), *Due seminari plautini* (Urbino, 2002), 251–77, and P. Brown, 'Terence and Greek New Comedy', in Augoustakis and Traill, 17–32.

women, parents and children), but they are not specific to one time or place, even though each play does have a specific setting in the Greek world. Many of the tensions are resolved at the end of the play, and societal norms tend to be reinforced; the plays do not advocate revolutionary programmes, though they may sometimes provoke uneasy thoughts about some aspects of society. Love (always heterosexual) is regularly shown triumphing over obstacles of various kinds, but the plays also portray the problems that arise from ignorance, misunderstanding, and prejudice. Because we are aware that such problems can arise in our own lives, we tend to sympathize with the predicaments in which the characters find themselves, even while we perceive them as comic because of our superior knowledge, enjoying the irony of the situation.

Complaints by members of the older generation about the extravagance of the young come to the surface from time to time in Terence's plays, and doubtless they had a particular resonance in the 160s. Above all in *The Brothers* we may reasonably see Demea (although he is no less Greek than the other characters) as representing traditional Roman attitudes, his brother Micio as representing more enlightened (or, alternatively, more effete) attitudes imported from Greece. In that way, the arguments between them certainly encapsulate arguments that were in the air while Terence was writing and that were associated with perceived tensions between Roman and Greek values. But beyond this we cannot easily detect more precise engagement with issues of the day in these plays.[14] It may be thought likely that the Roman spectators generally felt some distance between themselves and the Greek characters they were observing on the stage, but if so we cannot say how great the distance was. Athenian citizenship- and marriage-laws are central to the plays, and *Phormio* in particular depends on a detail of Athenian family law that had no equivalent at Rome. But this had not prevented the Greek originals from finding a large audience all over the Greek-speaking world outside Athens; and the presentation of characters, situations, and relationships is true to universal elements of human experience. Terence is notable for the consistency with which he preserves the Greek milieu (Plautus has many more references to Roman institutions and practices), but he does not remind his audience explicitly that they are Romans watching the antics of an alien world (Plautus also has more explicit references to the Greek world in which the plays are set).

---

14 For an attempt to show more precise engagement in the case of *The Brothers* see Leigh, 158–91.

Some scholars have seen Terence as a propagandist for Greek culture in a society not naturally sympathetic to it, as an author striving to show the Greeks as essentially civilized, humane, and admirable people. But some of the fathers in his plays are shown to be devious, hypocritical, or over-strict, and their sons are portrayed for the most part as somewhat feeble and aimless individuals, even if we feel that they will turn out well in the end. We are not invited to see the Greeks as intrinsically fit to be mocked (as Plautus sometimes invites us to see them), but nor are they held up as models for emulation. Rather, the Greek world depicted contains a variety of individuals such as one might expect to find in any society, some more admirable than others. In comparison with Plautus, not only does Terence portray the Greek milieu more consistently, but he also preserves more of the ethos of his Greek models (as far as we can tell, in the absence of those models), in terms of plot-construction, characterization, and style; the ironic humour and thought-provoking elements are also faithful to what we know of Greek New Comedy. This has been seen as constituting an attempt by Terence to educate his public in the refinements of Greek literature, but it may also be a sign that the Romans were naturally now more receptive to such subtleties. In any case, as we have seen, he adapted his Greek originals with some freedom and represented himself as the successor of Naevius, Plautus, and Ennius. In his prologues (see section 6.7 below) he defends his own practice against the criticisms of a rival playwright whom he accuses in his turn of taking too narrow a view of fidelity to the Greek plays. He does not represent himself as an ambassador for a new approach to Greek culture; he writes as a man who wishes to enjoy success, not as a man with a mission to educate.

Why, then, did Terence write *fabulae palliatae* (set in the Greek world) rather than *togatae* (set among non-Greek communities in Italy, but otherwise – as far as we can tell – having very similar plots to the *palliatae*)? Perhaps because it never occurred to him to do otherwise. *Palliatae* had been performed at Rome for over seventy years when he began writing, and it was in general characteristic of the Romans to take over established Greek forms of literature in such a way that they made explicit their dependence on Greek models; they had done the same with tragedy and epic already, since Livius Andronicus, Naevius, and Ennius had not restricted themselves to writing comedies; and they were to do it with didactic, pastoral, and lyric poetry later, in the works of authors such as Lucretius, Virgil, and Horace. Greek literature was the acknowledged standard of excellence; its importation into

Rome was the supreme cultural achievement, both a gesture of admiration and at the same time a form of cultural imperialism, a demonstration that it was possible to write such works in Latin too. *Togatae*, by contrast, were a recent innovation and did not provide an established tradition in which Terence could place himself.

5. Performance conditions and stage-directions[15]

Plays at Rome, as at Athens, were performed in daylight in the open air, and the action was supposed to take place out of doors. They were normally performed on wooden stages erected for the occasion. The first Roman theatre to last for any length of time was built by Pompey in 55 BCE, with a seating capacity estimated at 10,000. It has been calculated that the space available for the audience at the Megalesian Games – the occasion of the first performance of four of Terence's six plays, including *The Girl from Andros* – could have sat about 1,500 people in his lifetime.[16] The stage generally represents a street, fronted by at most three houses, and with side-exits/-entrances to left and right. On the stage stood an altar. Further details of the setting may well have been left to the audience's imagination. There was no drop-curtain between the stage and the audience, although at a later date we hear of a curtain lowered at the start of the performance and raised at the end. The actors were male, wore masks (or so most scholars believe; the ancient evidence is contradictory), and performed in Greek dress. Because of the open-air setting, characters are occasionally seen approaching at a distance, some time before they join those already on stage. The playwrights also make free use of conventions such as asides and overheard monologues.

According to Donatus, *The Girl from Andros* 'was performed by Lucius Atilius of Praeneste and Lucius Ambivius Turpio',[17] meaning that they were the actor-managers (*actores*) of the performing company. These two are regularly named together in the *didascaliae* (for all plays except *The Mother-in-Law*, where only Ambivius Turpio is named), but probably Ambivius

---

15   For a detailed discussion of performance conditions see G. Manuwald, *Roman Republican Theatre* (Cambridge, 2011), ch. 2, or (more discursively) C. W. Marshall, *The Stagecraft and Performance of Roman Comedy* (Cambridge, 2006).

16   See S. M. Goldberg, 'Plautus on the Palatine', *JRS* 88 (1998), 1–20. But T. P. Wiseman, *The Roman Audience* (Oxford, 2015), 55–59 (with refs at 207–209) argues that there was normally room for a 'big crowd' at all performance venues in Rome at this time, even for the Megalesian Games.

17   *Egerunt L. Atilius Praenestinus et L. Ambiuius Turpio* (Don. *Andria, Praef.* I.6).

directed the company in Terence's lifetime and Atilius was the director of later performances (though it is possible that he was the second actor in Ambivius' company).[18]

We know nothing about the size of a typical acting company at Rome. Eleven characters appear on stage in the course of *The Girl from Andros*, in addition to the prologue speaker and an unspecified number of slaves at the beginning of the first scene.[19] If some actors took more than one role each, the play could comfortably be performed by fewer than eleven actors. Five scenes have four named characters on stage simultaneously, all contributing to the dialogue; no scene has more, but in a company with only four actors not only would each actor have to take on more than one role but several roles would have to be shared between two actors. That would not be impossible, particularly with the use of masks, but it is perhaps unlikely that Terence would have chosen to construct his play in this way for such a company. A company with five actors could perform the play if Byrria and Crito were each played by different actors on their two appearances. Six actors could perform the play without having to split any roles. The following is suggested as a possible six-actor distribution: one actor for each of the three main parts, Simo (on stage for 538 lines), Davos (509), and Pamphilus (403), one actor playing both Charinus (189) and Chremes (245),[20] one both delivering the prologue (27) and playing Mysis (227), and one versatile actor playing Sosia (171), Byrria (57), Lesbia (17), Crito (72), and Dromo (5). But other arrangements would be possible, and overall it must be stressed that we do not know how many actors were in fact available to Terence.

Manuscripts of ancient dramatic texts contain no stage-directions. We have to work out from the words of the speakers where the play is set, the directions in which characters come and go, how the lines should best be delivered, what props are required – in short, all the details of stage business. This is a necessary part of the interpretation of the text as the script for a performance, and I have followed modern practice in adding to my translation at least the minimum indications of essential business that can be derived from the text. As with every element of a translation, some

---

18 On *actores* see P. G. McC. Brown, 'Actors and Actor-Managers at Rome in the time of Plautus and Terence', in P. E. Easterling and E. Hall (eds), *Greek and Roman Actors: Aspects of an Ancient Profession* (Cambridge, 2002), 225–37.

19 These slaves could be played by any otherwise unoccupied actors or by stage hands or other members of the company; if more were felt desirable, it would presumably have been possible to hire walk-on extras for half a day.

20 This requires a quick change of costume and mask off-stage at 952–57.

of these are inevitable deductions from the text, others are debatable matters of interpretation; and I have certainly not tried to prescribe every detail of blocking or lay down how every word is to be spoken. I am particularly conscious of having sometimes been quite arbitrary in deciding whether to indicate that a character utters a remark 'aside', 'to himself/herself', 'to the audience', or 'to the world at large'; it is a matter of judgement how best to deliver remarks that are not straightforwardly addressed to another character.

See further the note on 'Setting' in the Commentary, before the note on 28–171.

6.1. *The Girl from Andros*

As noted above at section 2, it is generally accepted that *The Girl from Andros* was Terence's first play. This is stated by Donatus in his Preface to the play (*Praef.* I.6 *Haec prima facta est*, 'This was the first of his plays to be written'), and also by Suetonius in his *Life of Terence* 3: 'He wrote six comedies. When he offered the first of them, *The Girl from Andros*, to the aediles, he was told to read it out first to Caecilius, who was having dinner when Terence arrived at his house. The story goes that, because he was not at all smartly dressed, he read the opening of the play sitting on a chair next to Caecilius' couch; but after a few lines he was invited to recline on the couch and dined together with him. He then read through the rest of the play, to the great admiration of Caecilius.'[21] Donatus gives 166 BCE as the date of the first performance (by naming the consuls of that year, Marcus Claudius Marcellus and Caius Sulpicius Galus [or Gallus]), which creates a problem for Suetonius' anecdote, since Caecilius is believed (on the evidence of St Jerome) to have died in 168: even if we are prepared to believe that the aediles (who were responsible for commissioning plays for performance at the Games that included such entertainments) sought the advice of an established playwright, we should expect them to have accepted Caecilius' enthusiastic endorsement of the play and commissioned it for immediate performance in (at the latest) 168; by 166 a different set of aediles was in post.[22] We could of course reject Jerome's evidence for

---

21   *Scripsit comoedias sex, ex quibus primam Andriam cum aedilibus daret, iussus ante Caecilio recitare ad cenantem cum uenisset dicitur initium quidem fabulae, quod erat contemptiore uestitu, subsellio iuxta lectulum residens legisse, post paucos uero uersus inuitatus ut accumberet cenasse una, dein cetera percucurrisse non sine magna Caecilii admiratione.*

22   Donatus names them as Marcus Fulvius and Manius Glabrio (*Andria, Praef.* I.6).

the date of Caecilius' death, but probably the story related by Donatus is a fiction designed to show that Terence was the natural successor of the leading comic playwright of the immediately preceding generation. But it does confirm that *The Girl from Andros* was believed to be his first play, and nothing tells against this, unless we take the plural 'prologues' in line 5 of the prologue to indicate that this is not Terence's first play with a prologue; few people have ever believed this,[23] though a number (unnecessarily, in my view) have believed the plural to show that this prologue was not written for the first performance of the play (see below, section 6.7). If Donatus can be believed, the play was a success.[24]

The three main characters are the Athenian citizen Simo, his slave Davos, and his son Pamphilus. Simo wishes Pamphilus to marry Philumena, the daughter of his friend Chremes, but Pamphilus is in love with another girl, Glycerium, and hopes that Davos will help him to avoid the marriage on which his father is so keen. Simo knows about Pamphilus' love for Glycerium, and he expects Davos to side with Pamphilus and do everything possible to thwart the proposed marriage, but he is determined to get Pamphilus to agree to it and has thought of a devious plan to bring that about. The heart of the play is a battle of wits between Simo and Davos,[25] but we also see the mental anguish of Pamphilus when he thinks he may be forced to abandon Glycerium, and we learn by report of Glycerium's own anguish and anxiety. In addition we see the anguish of another Athenian boy, Charinus, who is in love with Philumena and does not want to lose her to Pamphilus. Thus both boys hope for the same outcome, that Pamphilus should not marry Philumena, but for very different reasons. The play is full of plotting and counter-plotting, justified and unjustified suspicions, misunderstandings and recriminations, hopes and fears: a lively blend of comic and pathetic scenes.

The action is set on the day which had been previously agreed by Simo and Chremes as the date for Pamphilus to marry Philumena; at that stage neither father knew anything about Pamphilus' love for Glycerium, and it was Chremes who had taken the initiative in suggesting the marriage (99–102). But it was also Chremes who had cancelled the arrangement when it became

---

23 Lefèvre, 74–76 cites Tanaquil Faber and Anne Dacier from the seventeenth century and L. Gestri from the twentieth.

24 Don. *Andria, Praef.* 1.8: *successu spectata prospero hortamento poetae fuit ad alias conscribendas* ('it was favourably received by its audience and encouraged the poet to write further plays').

25 This is well brought out by Gilula and Compagno. See also Lefèvre, 184–97.

known that Pamphilus' affections were engaged elsewhere (144–49). Simo now plans to act as if the wedding were going ahead anyway: he hopes thereby to get Pamphilus either to agree to it or to put himself in the wrong by refusing to do so; if Pamphilus does agree to the wedding, Simo is sure that he will be able to persuade Chremes to reinstate it in reality (155–67).

It does not take Davos long to work out that Simo's wedding preparations are a pretence (359–69). He therefore urges Pamphilus to agree to the wedding, since he is confident that Chremes will never consent to it; this should buy time for Pamphilus to find some way of securing his future with Glycerium, whereas if he openly refuses to marry he risks provoking his father into taking extreme measures (375–98). Pamphilus acts accordingly, but Davos' plan backfires when Simo succeeds in persuading Chremes to reinstate the wedding after all (533–604); Davos has been too clever by half, and Pamphilus has now put himself in a position where he cannot easily back down from the marriage.

Between Pamphilus' agreement and Simo's persuasion of Chremes, exactly half way through the play, Simo witnesses the arrival of a midwife at Glycerium's house and hears Glycerium crying out in the agony of giving birth; he also hears the midwife and Glycerium's slave Mysis discussing the fact that Pamphilus is the father of the baby (459–73). The audience have known since 215–19 that Glycerium was pregnant by Pamphilus, but Simo quickly persuades himself that the midwife's arrival and the offstage screams were part of a plot to discourage him from marrying his son off and that no birth has in fact taken place (469–80, 489–506). He has assumed from the start of the play that Davos would lay plans against him (159–64); he now assumes that Davos is behind this pretence, and he is pleased to think that he has seen through it. Just as Davos had (unknown to Simo) seen through Simo's plot, so Simo is confident that he has seen through Davos'. Unlike Davos, he is wrong, but as far as he is concerned there is no reason not to persevere with his plan of persuading Chremes to agree to the marriage; in that scene of persuasion he does not even mention the possibility that Glycerium has just given birth to Pamphilus' child, and for the time being the birth of the baby makes no difference to the development of the play's action. Once Simo has persuaded Chremes, the situation looks utterly bleak for Pamphilus, Charinus, and Glycerium; and Davos is the one responsible, since it was he who advised Pamphilus to agree to the marriage.

However, the baby plays a crucial part in Davos' next scheme, which does achieve its aim. He brings the baby out from Glycerium's house (fewer than 250 lines after it had been born!) and orders Mysis to lay it on the ground in front of Simo's house (721–31). When Chremes then appears on the scene, Davos is able to stage an argument with Mysis for Chremes' benefit in which he pretends to believe that the baby has been imported from elsewhere as part of a plot to dissuade Chremes from marrying his daughter to Pamphilus, since the alleged plot involves claiming that Pamphilus is the baby's father and in addition that Glycerium is an Athenian citizen (740–89). (Again, the audience have known since 220–24 that Glycerium claims to be an Athenian by birth who had been shipwrecked in infancy off the island of Andros and brought up there before moving back to Athens, where she now lives ostensibly as a foreigner but hopes one day to be able to prove her true birth.) Davos thus exploits the very suspicion into which Simo had fallen and tries to persuade Chremes of its truth; the additional information that Glycerium claims to be Athenian is even more of a deterrent for Chremes, since Pamphilus would certainly be expected to marry an Athenian girl who had given birth to his child. Davos represents all this as an elaborate plot, but Mysis (who is completely baffled by Davos' behaviour) insists that it is all true, and Chremes is clearly inclined to believe her. He storms into Simo's house at 789, and before long (820–41) the two fathers reappear, involved in an argument similar to their argument earlier in the play (at 533–74). For Chremes it is now out of the question for Pamphilus to marry his daughter, whereas Simo is convinced that the scene with the baby had been staged to put Chremes off – as indeed it had: this time Simo is quite right to suspect a plan orchestrated by Davos, though he is still wrong to doubt that Glycerium has really given birth to Pamphilus' child.

Would Simo once again have persuaded Chremes if their discussion had continued for longer? Of course there is no answer to such a question, but in any case events are now moving to a conclusion with which everyone will be happy, since an old man called Crito has arrived from Andros who is able to confirm that Glycerium is indeed an Athenian by birth who was shipwrecked off Andros in infancy. What is more, he is able to supply details of her family background which show her to have been the daughter of none other than Chremes (904–52)![26] There is now naturally no objection to Pamphilus' marrying her, so after all he does marry a daughter of Chremes, though not the one Chremes had originally hoped he would. That daughter,

---

26 Similarly in Plautus' *Cistellaria* Alcesimarchus' beloved Selenium turns out to be a daughter of Demipho, the very man whose (known) daughter his father wanted Alcesimarchus to marry.

Philumena, is now available for Charinus, and we can safely assume that they will marry too. The audience could have guessed that Glycerium's claims to Athenian birth would be confirmed by the end of the play, but there were no clues to precisely whose daughter she would turn out to be. They were thus unable to enjoy the irony of the situation at 740–89 where Chremes is unknowingly on stage with his own grandchild, witnessing an argument about whose child it really is and about the status of the woman who claims to be its mother (who is in fact his daughter). On the other hand, they were able to appreciate the irony earlier in the play of the fact that the child's other grandfather, Simo, refused to believe in its existence even while he heard it being born, since they have known all along that Pamphilus was its father.

Probably most readers have assumed that the play is named after Glycerium, since (although she is never seen and is heard emitting only one scream at 473) the happiness of all the characters hinges on her identification as the daughter of Chremes. Some, however, have thought it was named after a different woman, Chrysis, whose father had brought Glycerium up on Andros and who had herself come to Athens three years before the action of the play in search of a new life.[27] Chrysis has died before the play begins, but we learn about her in the opening scene before hearing of Glycerium, and she is there twice referred to as 'the Andrian woman' (*Andria*, 73, 85–86).[28] The audience might well assume at her first mention (69–79) that she is the Andrian girl of the title, and there is a memorable account later in the same scene (104–37) of her funeral, which was the occasion on which Pamphilus' actions revealed his love for Glycerium, thereby leading Chremes to cancel his proposed marriage to Philumena. We also hear from Pamphilus at 282–98 how Chrysis on her deathbed had entrusted Glycerium to his care, and it is her death that has motivated Crito to turn up towards the end of the play (796–99), since he is her heir and wishes to lay claim to her property. The death of Chrysis has thus been the catalyst both for the complications of the play and for their resolution, whether or not Terence (or Menander before him: see next section) regarded her as the title figure.

---

27 See T. B. Haber, 'The Woman of Andros: Who is She?', *The Classical Journal* 50.1 (1954), 35–39.

28 On the other hand, Davos refers to Glycerium as *haec Andria* at 215; *Andria* at 461 and 756 may well also refer to Glycerium, though that is not absolutely clear.

6.2. Terence and Menander

Terence's *Andria* was based on a Greek play of the same name by Menander.[29] Most scholars believe that in a 'recognition comedy' of this kind Menander would have used an omniscient divine figure to set out the background in a prologue speech early in the play and to give some pointers towards the outcome.[30] Menander's prologues (such as we know them) do not predict every detail of the ensuing action, and it might be felt that the identification of Chremes as Glycerium's father at the end of the play would fall rather flat if the audience had known it from the start. On the other hand, they would then have been able to appreciate the irony not only of the scene with the baby towards the end but also of the fact that throughout the play Pamphilus strives to avoid marrying into Chremes' family (see particularly 247: 'Is there no way for me to avoid having Chremes as my father-in-law?'). The fiercest opponent of the idea that Menander regularly used an omniscient prologue for this kind of plot was Karl Büchner,[31] who was right to point out the danger of circular argumentation if we reconstruct lost plays or missing portions of plays on the assumption that Menander was addicted to ironic effects. Nonetheless Menander often did exploit irony, and Büchner's arguments against supposing his *Andria* to have had a prologue are not strong.

That, however, leads to further questions about the relationship of Terence's play to Menander's. If Menander's play did have a divine prologue which Terence has omitted, what difference did that make to Terence's exposition of essential background information at the start of the play? And what do we learn from Terence's claim (in the completely different sort of prologue that he did write) that his play is based on *two* plays by Menander, *The Girl from Andros* (*Andria*) and *The Girl from Perinthos* (*Perinthia*)? To take the second question first, Terence says he has 'transferred what was suitable

---

29   Menander's *Andria* may also have formed the basis of a comedy by Caecilius of which one three-word fragment (meaning 'He hires a rotten ship') is quoted by Nonius. This would add some piquancy to the anecdote quoted at the beginning of section 6.1, but it seems unlikely, since *Eun.* 23–34 and *Ad.* 7–14 suggest that Terence would have risked being accused of blatant plagiarism if he had reworked an entire play that had already been adapted by a Roman playwright. The title transmitted by Nonius is not absolutely certain, and even if it is *Andria* some scholars would prefer to posit an otherwise unattested play of this name by a Greek playwright other than Menander as the basis of Caecilius' play.

30   On prologues and expository technique in Greek and Roman comedy see Hunter, 24–35.

31   Büchner, 42 n. 21, 48–52, 54–55. 98–100, 109, 111 on *Andria*; 484–98 on the general question.

into the *Andria* from the *Perinthia* and made his own use of this material'
(13–14), and he also says of the two Greek plays that 'the man who knows
either of them properly will know both of them: they're not so different in
plot, but they *are* written in different words and style' (10–12). He gives
no further details but devotes most of his prologue to replying to those who
have criticized him for combining two Greek plays in this way. More detail
is supplied by Donatus in his commentary on Terence's play. On line 10
Donatus says 'The first scene of the *Perinthia* is written in almost the same
words as the *Andria*; otherwise they are different, except for two passages,
one of about eleven lines, the other of about twenty, which come in both
plays' (he does not say whether Terence has reproduced either of these
passages).[32] That tells us nothing about what Terence has imported from the
one play into his adaptation of the other, and it seems rather at odds with
Terence's claim about the similarity of Menander's two plays. Furthermore,
Donatus' claim about the opening scene needs to be qualified in the light of
his further remark on line 14 that Terence 'is aware that his first scene has
been transferred from the *Perinthia*, where the old man talks with his wife
just as he does with his freedman in Terence; but in Menander's *Andria*
the old man is on his own'.[33] The opening of Terence's play is essentially a
monologue by Simo expounding his plan, broken up by brief interruptions
from his freedman Sosia; it is easy to imagine that much the same speech
could have been delivered either as a monologue without interruptions or
with interruptions by a wife instead of a freedman. Donatus does not point
out that in Terence's play the bulk of the opening twenty lines is devoted to
establishing the character of the freedman and of his relationship with his
ex-master, none of which can have come in either of Menander's plays. In
other words, Terence must have composed the first twenty lines of his first
play entirely out of his own head, unless (as some have done) we suppose him
to have been so incapable of original composition that he must have derived
them from yet another Greek play.[34] (He must in any case have composed
the prologue out of his own head: see below, section 6.7.) Terence must
also have added the instruction to Sosia at the end of the scene (169–70) to

---

32   *Prima scaena Perinthiae fere isdem uerbis quibus Andria scripta est, cetera dissimilia
sunt exceptis duobus locis, altero ad uersus XI, altero ad XX, qui in utraque fabula positi sunt.*
33   *Conscius sibi est primam scaenam de Perinthia esse translatam, ubi senex ita cum uxore
loquitur ut apud Terentium cum liberto. At in Andria Menandri solus est senex.*
34   G. Rambelli, 'Il prologo e la prima scena dell' "Andria"', *SIFC* n.s. 16 (1939), 79–104
suggests at pp. 102–103 that they have been imported from a later scene in the *Perinthia*.

'terrify Davos, and keep an eye on what my son's up to and what plans he's hatching with him', though if this leads us to expect that Sosia will play a significant part in what follows we shall be disappointed, since we never see him or hear about him again; he is what is called a 'protatic' character, whose function is to help in setting the scene at the start of the play.[35]

If Menander's two plays had divine prologues, the expository material was presumably shared between them and the opening scenes in ways that we can only guess at. However, to return to the first question above, the only details of background information that *Terence's* audience have not learnt about by the end of the opening scene and which may well have been provided by a prologue figure in Menander's play(s) are the further details concerning Glycerium's Athenian background and the fact that she is pregnant by Pamphilus. As we have noted, it is only at the end of Terence's play that we learn that she is a daughter of Chremes. Terence has, however, ensured that we learn as much as we otherwise need to know at the earliest possible opportunity, in the mouth of Davos at 215–25. Davos himself regards her claims about her background as a very implausible fiction, but the audience will be well aware that Terence would not have made him report them at all if they were not going to turn out to be true (cf. 220n.). Almost all scholars have accepted Hans Oppermann's claim that Terence transferred the essence of this material from the prologue of Menander's play(s) and put it into Davos' mouth at this point, thus telling the audience almost everything they need to know and yet allowing Davos to remain in character.[36]

Davos is of course in no position to tell us about Crito, whose arrival towards the end of the play has not been foreshadowed in any way. Nor does he or anyone else tell us about Charinus, Pamphilus' rival for the hand of Philumena, before Charinus himself appears at 301 together with his slave Byrria. In both cases we have no difficulty in working out who they are and how they fit into the plot, and we need not suppose that Menander would have felt any necessity to give his audience advance notice of their arrival. In the case of Charinus and Byrria, indeed, there is good reason to think that he did not do so (at least in his *Andria*), since Donatus tells us (on line 301) that these characters have been added to the play by Terence and 'do not come in Menander'.[37] This has been taken to mean either that

---

35 Such characters are found also at the beginning of *The Mother-in-Law* and *Phormio*; for further details see Maltby 2012 on *Ph.* 35–50.

36 H. Oppermann, 'Zur Andria des Terenz', *Hermes* 69.3 (1934), 262–85, at pp. 264–69.

37 *Has personas Terentius addidit fabulae (nam non sunt apud Menandrum), ne* παθητικόν

they did not come in Menander's *Andria* but have been imported from the *Perinthia* (or perhaps from some other Greek play) or (as with Sosia) that Terence has entirely invented their parts.[38] Charinus and Byrria add a considerable dramatic dimension to some scenes, as we shall see, and as a minimum Terence must have had to make their lines dovetail with the plot of the *Andria*.

Donatus does identify one brief passage as coming from a third source, at 959–61, where Pamphilus says 'The reason I believe that the life of the gods is everlasting is because pleasure is permanently theirs; I've won immortality if no sorrow intervenes in my joy!' Donatus comments that Terence 'has transferred this whole sentence from Menander's *Eunuch*',[39] a play that Terence was to take as the primary source for his adaptation five years later.[40]

On 891 Donatus comments that the stylistic intensity of the passage has been created by Terence and not reproduced from Menander,[41] and he mentions Menander at a further ten points, to report how Menander expressed a number of small details in Greek (without specifying from which play he is quoting).[42] At these places Donatus is probably reproducing material from an earlier commentator who had been able to compare Terence's text with

---

fieret Philumenam spretam relinquere [read *relinqui*?] *sine sponso, Pamphilo aliam ducente* ('Terence added these characters to the play – for they do not come in Menander – so that it would not be upsetting that Philumena is rejected and left without a fiancé when Pamphilus marries another girl'. [παθητικόν ('upsetting') is Rabbow's conjectural correction, accepted by Wessner, of the meaningless sequence of Greek letters found in manuscript A of Donatus; Cioffi leaves the sequence uncorrected.] We do not have to accept the motive that Donatus attributes to Terence: since we never see Philumena or hear anything about her feelings, it is unlikely that the audience would have minded if she had been quietly forgotten about at the end of the play, and it is more likely that Terence added Charinus in order to create extra comedy and increase the complication of the plot.

It may be worth noting that on line 977, in discussing the fact that Terence's play contains the loves of two boys and ends with the promise of two weddings, Donatus says that this is 'beyond what was laid down by Menander, whose comedy he was translating (*extra praescriptum Menandri, cuius comoediam transferebat*)'; he shows no awareness there that one of the boys could have been imported from the *Perinthia* or indeed that Terence was following more than one model at any stage.

38 For a survey of views see Lefèvre, 58–63.
39 *Hanc sententiam totam Menandri de Eunucho transtulit.*
40 Not everyone takes Donatus at his word, though Fraenkel, 348–49 n. 12 defends him.
41 *Mira grauitate sensus elatus est; nec de Menandro, sed proprium Terentii.*
42 Don. on 204, 406, 473, 483, 592, 611, 726, 794, 801, 919, all quoted in PCG VI.2, pp. 62–67.

its Greek model at first hand; Donatus himself does not have such questions consistently in view, and his aim is above all to elucidate the Latin text; nor is it always clear why he quotes or refers to Menander's play at all.[43]

Apart from his comments on lines 10 and 14, Donatus nowhere explicitly cites Menander's *Perinthia*, for which our main additional source of information is a fragment of papyrus in which a slave called Daos (the Greek name of which *Dauos* is the Latinized version), who has taken refuge at the altar on stage, is threatened with being smoked out by a bonfire that is prepared round the altar.[44] This is a part of the play that Terence has not reproduced; it has been suggested that Simo's instructions to have Davos taken indoors and tied up at 860–65 could be a faint echo of that scene, but they have little in common with it. At some stage in the play Daos has boasted that it is an easy matter for a slave to trick a master who is 'easy-going and empty-headed' (*Perinthia* fr. 3 Arnott); in the papyrus fragment his master taunts him with this as the bonfire is built up around the altar. This suggests that the *Perinthia*, like Terence's play, may have featured a battle of wits between a master and his slave, but we cannot reconstruct the details of how that battle developed. It may be worth noting that Terence's Davos nowhere says that it will be easy to trick Simo; indeed at 211 he says 'it's not easy to put one over on *him*'.[45] So the dynamics of their interaction may have been quite different in the two plays.

In addition to the papyrus fragment we have ten brief fragments quoted from the *Perinthia* by various ancient authors;[46] some could be seen as corresponding to something in Terence's play, though none inevitably does so, and between them they tell us very little about Menander's play. The most discussed fragments of the play in this context have been frs 4 and

---

43 Further fragments of Menander's *Andria* are quoted by Photius (Menander fr. 40 K-A, apparently the Greek lying behind line 484) and Stobaeus (fr. 49 K-A, which appears not to correspond to anything in Terence's play: 'Love, it seems, casts a shadow over everyone, both the sensible and the ill-advised [τὸ δ' ἐρᾶν ἐπισκοτεῖ / ἅπασιν, ὡς ἔοικε, καὶ τοῖς εὐλόγως / καὶ τοῖς κακῶς ἔχουσιν].').

44 See Arnott, 480–87. It has been tentatively suggested that this scene is illustrated in a number of surviving works of art (painted friezes, terracotta reliefs, a mosaic and a sculpted relief) dating from about 150 BCE to 50 CE: see T. B. L. Webster, *Monuments Illustrating New Comedy* (3rd edn, revised and enlarged by J. R. Green and A. Seeberg, *BICS* Supplement 50, 1995), 91–92.

45 See Mazzarino, 49–54.

46 See Arnott, 486–97. Fr. 10 is cited as coming from Menander's 'first *Perinthia*', which suggests that he may have written more than one play with this name – a further complicating factor, were we to wish to use these fragments in reconstructing the *Perinthia* used by Terence.

6 Arnott (= 4 and 2 S). Fr. 4 is quoted and discussed in the note on 228–33. Fr. 6 says 'The slave-boy came in bringing sprats'.[47] This could well correspond to Davos' words at 368–69 when he is outlining how he came to the conclusion that no wedding preparations were in train: 'I even bumped into one of Chremes' slave-boys as I was coming away from there; he was bringing an obol's worth of vegetables and teeny little fish for the old man's dinner.' Although we cannot be certain of the context (which could concern the serving of food at a meal rather than its purchase), it is very tempting to take this fragment as showing that Menander's *Perinthia* did include the notion that the plan to hold a wedding today was a pretence and that one character saw through it partly because he observed the paucity of the provisions being bought for one of the relevant households.

Overall, the surviving fragments of the relevant Greek plays do not get us very far in identifying how Terence used them in writing his own play, and the information provided by Donatus is less helpful than we might have hoped. If we can accept that Charinus and Byrria have been imported by Terence (whether from a Greek play or out of his own head), i.e. that there was no rival suitor for Philumena's hand in Menander's *Andria*, then Terence has added some notably comic moments to the play, for instance in the dialogue of Charinus and Byrria with Pamphilus at 323–36. One of the dramatic highlights of the play comes at 412–31 when Byrria as an eavesdropper witnesses Pamphilus agreeing to his father's wish that he should marry Philumena; since Byrria does not know that this is part of a scheme suggested by Davos, he naturally assumes that Pamphilus has gone back on his assurance to Charinus that he will do his utmost to avoid having to marry the girl. This leads directly to a scene of bitter reproach of Pamphilus by Charinus at 625–62, at a time when Pamphilus' position seems particularly hopeless because Davos' plan has backfired. The drama contributed by Charinus and Byrria consists essentially of reactions to events in the play; Charinus never does anything that impinges on Pamphilus' fortunes, though it makes a considerable difference to Charinus whether Pamphilus is or is not going to marry Philumena. Nonetheless, the addition of this pair of characters has added moments of great entertainment (both comic and pathetic) for the audience. Charinus functions very much as a foil to Pamphilus, giving us a different perspective on the events of the play;

---

47 τὸ παιδίον / εἰσῆλθεν ἑψητοὺς φέρων. ἑψητοί were small fish for boiling or frying, not necessarily already cooked: see D. W. Thompson, *A Glossary of Greek Fishes* (London, 1947), 73.

and to a lesser extent Byrria can be seen as a foil to Davos, equally loyal to his young master but with no scope for devising a plot.[48]

Byrria's eavesdropping scene is the first of five points in the play at which there are more than three speaking actors on stage. This in itself is almost certainly a sign of Terentian adaptation, since we do not know of any scene in Menander that requires more than three; and the addition of an eavesdropper provides obvious scope for showing a character reacting to what the other characters in the scene are doing; see the end of the note on 404–31.

It has been noted that a papyrus fragment of Greek comedy (PCG *adesp.* 1007, fifty incomplete lines) shows a slave called Daos in conversation with a boy who has been engaged to marry a citizen girl but is in love with a non-citizen girl, followed by a monologue for Daos which has something in common with Davos' monologue at *Andria* 206–27, after which a character called Simon appears giving orders for a sacrifice to be performed. That play clearly had some motifs in common with the *Andria*, though the fragment also contains details that correspond with nothing in our play.

6.3. Simo

Some scholars have tried to reconstruct Menander's two plays on the basis of an alleged split in the character of Simo between an understanding and loving father (supposed to derive from the *Andria*) and a more tyrannical and domineering one (supposed to derive from the *Perinthia* and to be shown in the papyrus fragment from the end of that play, which shows the old man threatening the slave with brutal treatment).[49] It cannot be denied that Simo's motivation is quite complex. On the one hand, he wants his son to settle down, and he believes that forcing him to marry will help him to do so (as he says to Chremes at 538–62). On the other hand, he also seems

---

48 Four of Terence's other five plays (all except *The Mother-in-Law*) portray two boys in love with different girls, and Terence has become famous for the so-called 'duality method' of his plot-construction (discussed by Duckworth, 184–90). But Gilula rightly insists that that is not the main point of *The Girl from Andros*. In the case of the other plays there is no reason to doubt that both pairs of lovers derive from the original Greek play.

49 So V. Martin, 'Die Dramaturgie des Terenz in der "Andria"', *Das Altertum* 10 (1964), 234–49; Büchner, 79–82, M. Weißenberger, 'Der 'doppelte Simo': Zur Komposition der *Andria* des Terenz', in B. Zimmermann (ed.), *Griechisch-römische Komödie und Tragödie II (Drama* 5, Stuttgart, 1997), 105–18. Against this view see Sherberg, 97–102 (though she too sees Simo as a contradictory mixture of character-types), Posani, 39–40.

keen in the opening scene to engineer a situation in which (if all else fails) he will have reasonable grounds to criticize his son; that seems almost to have become an end in itself for him.[50] There is some evidence that he has been a tolerant father: at 262–63 Pamphilus is conscious that Simo has so far treated him leniently and allowed him to behave as he liked. But he has snooped on his son (83–91), and his deviousness in plotting against him now is more characteristic of a comic slave than of a citizen father. He claims to Davos at 186–87 that he does not wish 'to behave like an unreasonable father', but his peremptory instruction to Pamphilus to prepare to get married today (as reported by Pamphilus at 254–55) seems far from reasonable. It is particularly in dialogue with Sosia in the opening scene that Simo shows himself to have been cautious about confronting Pamphilus directly over his involvement with Glycerium and at the same time searching for an acceptable reason to rebuke him: see 137–43, 149–58. But I am not convinced that this complexity in his character must result from combining two different fathers from different Greek plays. After the opening scene Simo is more straightforward: he is determined not to be outwitted by Davos and also determined that his son should marry Chremes' daughter. The former trait leads him to suspect a plot against him where none exists, and the latter leads him to be peremptory towards his son and unwilling to accept any reluctance displayed by Chremes. His cruel punishment of Davos at 861–65 is provoked by the situation in which he finds himself, with Pamphilus continuing to frequent Glycerium's house (851) and an apparent plot to pass off Glycerium as an Athenian citizen (858–59); this is the last straw for Simo, and it is not surprising that he reacts violently. There is no inconsistency here: just as we need not suppose that the master in the *Perinthia* showed the sort of anger throughout the play that he manifests at the end (in the papyrus fragment), so we should not be surprised that anger leads Simo to extreme behaviour at the end of Terence's play.

---

50   Scafuro, 354–77 is good on this aspect of Simo's character and on the hypocrisy of his self-presentation at various points, though she plays down the fact that what he wants above all is that Pamphilus should marry Chremes' daughter (cf. 165–67, 526–27). See also Anderson 2004 on how 'we learn a lot that is unflattering and important about Simo' (p. 18) from his dialogue with Sosia in the opening scene. Scafuro, 364–65 makes interesting comparisons between *The Girl from Andros* and Menander's *Samia*, including n. 50 on similarities between Simo and Demeas in that play.

6.4. Davos' plans

A more recent attempt to assign different elements of Terence's play to each of Menander's plays is based on the planning of Davos. Terence's *Girl from Andros* shows Davos initiating two schemes, (1) that Pamphilus should agree to the proposed marriage with Chremes' daughter, confident that there is no plan for it actually to take place, (2) that Chremes should learn that Pamphilus and Glycerium are the parents of a newborn baby and that Glycerium may well be an Athenian citizen. The second scheme starts by getting Mysis to put the baby on the ground in front of Simo's house; Davos may have intended Simo to be the one to see the baby lying there, but he adapts rapidly to the fact that it is Chremes who appears at this point.[51] Eckard Lefèvre suggests that Menander's *Andria* and *Perinthia* each had only one of these schemes and that Terence has combined them in order to magnify Davos' role as a schemer (although the first scheme backfires).[52] His main argument is based on lines 507–16, where Davos predicts to Simo that 'a baby will soon be brought out here in front of the door' because 'if they can't get you to see a baby, the wedding won't be put off'. Lefèvre believes that these lines have been added by Terence to link the two plots in a way which makes no sense dramatically. He points out that at this stage Davos has no reason to doubt the success of his first plan, and that later, at 615, 622, etc. (when he knows his first plan has failed), he has no idea what his second plan will be; only at 704 does he think of a new plan. We never learn exactly what the new plan was to be, since he abandons it on seeing Chremes arrive at 732–33, but before seeing Chremes (at 722–31) he has brought the baby out from indoors and ordered Mysis to put it on the ground in front of Simo's house. In other words, the display of the baby in front of Simo's house was clearly part of the new plan, a plan that (according to Lefèvre) Davos had not conceived at 507–16 although he predicts it there.

Even if Lefèvre is right that Terence has added lines 507–16 at the expense of the coherence of the plot, it does not follow that Menander's *Andria* did not contain both of Davos' schemes: Terence may simply have wished to whet his audience's appetite for one of the play's most striking scenes by giving advance notice of it. In any case, the incoherence introduced by the lines is not as great as Lefèvre alleges. It is not in itself implausible that Davos lays the ground for a second plan before learning that his first plan has

---

51 See 507–16, 732–36.
52 Lefèvre, 63–68, 82–85.

turned out disastrously, since (as he explained to Pamphilus at 397–98) the first plan was designed only to buy time, in the hope that 'in the meantime something lucky will turn up'. If Davos appears to have no new plan in mind between 615 and 704, it could be at this later stage that Terence has added to the tension by making Davos temporarily forget what he had been planning to do next (perhaps under the pressure of the urgent new situation that has there arisen, if we feel the need to provide a psychological explanation). Lefèvre thinks it unlikely that Menander would have given Davos both plots in one play; as far as I can see, that is an entirely arbitrary assumption.

6.5. Balancing scenes

To return to consideration of Terence's play as it stands, one notable feature of its structure is the number of balancing scenes that it contains, some of them created by the addition of Charinus, others showing balances involving other characters.[53] The first time we see Pamphilus, he is complaining in a soliloquy about his father's inhumane treatment of him (236 *Hoccinest humanum factu aut inceptu?*, 'Is this what a human being would do or start on?'); later in the play Charinus enters with a soliloquy complaining about Pamphilus' betrayal of him, starting with the same word (625 *Hoccinest credibile aut memorabile*, 'Can I believe this? Can it be true?'). But already on Charinus' first appearance we can see a balance between the two boys: at 236–98 Pamphilus has lamented the fact that his father wants him to marry Philumena but has then assured Mysis that he will not desert Glycerium; that is immediately followed by the arrival of Charinus, lamenting the very same fact but for a very different reason, since he himself *wants* to marry Philumena. Pamphilus then assures Charinus, as he had assured Mysis, that he himself has no desire to marry her (301–35). After this first meeting between the two boys Davos arrives with the good news that he has worked out that the marriage cannot really be taking place (338–69), after which he advises Pamphilus to agree to the marriage in order to call Simo's bluff (375–403). When the boys next meet, the disastrous results of that advice have become clear. Once again it is Pamphilus who enters first, complaining that Davos has ruined him (607), then Charinus complaining that Pamphilus

---

53 This aspect of the play's construction is well discussed by Glücklich, 130–42, stressing that its effect is often to give differing perspectives on the same events. I am less convinced by his argument at pp. 141–42 for a symmetrical grouping of scenes round the central passage 459–531, the sequence of scenes in the first half being mirrored by corresponding scenes in reverse order in the second half.

has betrayed him (625). Once again Davos comes up with a plan, though this time he does not tell either of the boys what it is (702–707). We can thus see a number of different balances and contrasts in the scenes that involve Charinus, who (as I have said) acts as a foil to Pamphilus.

The other main balance is in the scenes between Simo and Chremes. At 533 Chremes enters to remonstrate with Simo but is persuaded by him to let the wedding go ahead; Davos then appears from Simo's house, urging Simo not to delay in sending for the bride (which Davos thinks he can safely do, since he believes no wedding is really being planned), and then receiving the bombshell of learning that after all the wedding *is* to take place. At 820 the two fathers enter together, with Simo again trying to persuade Chremes to let the wedding go ahead (since Chremes has changed his mind again in the meantime, for very good reason). In the middle of their discussion it is again Davos who enters (this time from Glycerium's house); he again briefly tries to keep up the pretence that all is ready for the arrival of the bride (846–48), but this time it is Simo who is in for a shock as he learns that Pamphilus too is in Glycerium's house and that an old man has turned up who claims that Glycerium is an Athenian citizen. Once again the balance brings out the contrast.

We could also mention that in the middle of the play (459–523) Simo witnesses the arrival of the midwife and hears Glycerium giving birth but quickly persuades himself that this is all part of a plot orchestrated by Davos to disrupt the marriage plans, whereas at 740–89 it is Chremes who actually sees the baby but witnesses Davos claiming in a staged argument with Mysis that the baby is not really Glycerium's but part of a plot to disrupt the marriage plans (and this time Davos himself really is trying to disrupt those plans). For those rereading the play, or seeing it for the second time, there is the added irony that the baby is the grandchild of both Simo and Chremes, but (as noted above) that is not something that the first audience were in a position to appreciate in the case of Chremes.

The battle of wits between Simo and Davos is fought out in a number of balancing scenes. In the first of them, at 172–205, Simo threatens Davos with punishment if he tries in any way to disrupt the wedding; in the last, at 842–71, he sends him off to be punished. In their second encounter, at 432–58, Davos enjoys the superior position of the slave who has seen through his master's deception and knows that the wedding plans were a pretence; he encourages Simo to believe that Pamphilus really has decided to settle down and marry Philumena, while Simo remains suspicious. When they next meet, at 581–

604, Davos enters hoping to continue enjoying the same position of superior knowledge but is very quickly disillusioned by Simo; Simo himself does not realize that *he* has now called *Davos'* bluff, but the audience can appreciate the reversal in Davos' fortunes. Davos is left to reflect on the awkwardness of his situation at 599–606, just as he was left to reflect on the difficulties ahead of him at 206–25 after his first encounter with Simo.

In addition there are two scenes in which Pamphilus assures Mysis of his devotion to Glycerium (267–98, 692–701); and Pamphilus also expresses very similar feelings about his relations with his father in overheard monologues at 262–64 (overheard by Mysis, culminating in *Incertumst quid agam*, 'I can't decide what to do') and 612–14 (overheard by Davos, culminating in *Nec quid nunc me faciam scio*, 'I don't know what to do with myself now').

It has even been suggested that Terence sometimes brought out the balance between scenes by giving each scene exactly the same number of lines. Thus 301–37 and 338–74 (Act II scenes i and ii in the traditional numbering) each has 37 lines, 432–58 and 581–606 (II.vi and III.iv) each has 27 lines.[54] This is based on the scene-divisions found in the manuscripts,[55] which are generally agreed to be post-Terentian and may or may not coincide with what Terence or his audience would have felt to be self-contained dramatic units; to my mind, for instance, it would be more natural to mark III.iv as ending at 604 than at 606, with the appearance of a new character underlined by a change from iambic to trochaic metre at 605, but the manuscripts generally mark a new scene as starting when a new character first speaks rather than when he or she is first seen. The approach also takes no account of differing line-lengths, which would make a difference to the time it would take to perform some scenes containing the same number of lines.[56] We may, however, accept that dramatic units will seem more strikingly to balance one another if they are of roughly comparable length.

---

54 P. Kruschwitz, 'Verszahlresponsionen bei Terenz', *Philologus* 145.2 (2001), 312–23: pp. 316–18 on the *Andria*. See also Kruschwitz 2004, 43–45. In addition, Kruschwitz sees significance in the fact that I.iii, III.i and V.i each has 22 lines and are linked by the theme of Glycerium's baby; but that theme is not equally prominent in all three scenes, whereas it is very prominent indeed in IV.iii–iv, scenes which do not fit his numerical scheme.

55 In fact the manuscripts do not mark a new scene as starting after 374; editors have followed Donatus in doing so.

56 I should make clear that Kruschwitz does not claim that the spectators would notice that balancing scenes had the same number of lines; he sees it rather as an insight into Terence's artistry.

6.6. Interpretation and Metatheatre

(a) A. W. Gomme wrote that 'What is at bottom wrong with the *Andria*, the *Heautontimorumenus*, and the *Eunuchus* [...] is that, unlike the three later plays and still more unlike those of Menander, they are not *about* anything. There is much good writing [...] but we are not interested in any one.'[57]

Others, however, have found themes of some significance in the play. Thus Terry McGarrity seeks thematic unity in the notions of responsibility and duty, particularly the duty of a father; his focus is above all on the portrayal of Pamphilus, whom he sees (implausibly, to my mind) as maturing into accepting the duties of a *paterfamilias* by the end of the play, but he also discusses Simo's role in Pamphilus' upbringing and the development of the relationship between father and son.[58]

Sander Goldberg gives more weight to Simo as the dominant figure and sees the play as showing 'a relationship between a father and son as it is revealed under stress';[59] he regards 'the great confrontation of Simo and Pamphilus' at 872–903 as the play's 'greatest scene'.[60]

Robert Germany also attaches importance to Simo's denunciation of his son in that scene, citing it in support of his claim that 'the ethos of *Andria* as a whole is not exactly comic'; he also adduces Simo's account of Chrysis' funeral in the opening scene and Pamphilus' account of her deathbed request at 282–98. More generally he argues for the play's 'ongoing flirtation with the boundaries of what is possible in comedy', with Simo 'much more like the stock character of the tricky slave than a typical comic father', with Davos 'cast as a blocking figure, a function more typical of the comic father',[61] with a midwife who turns out to be sober after we have been led to expect her to be drunk, and with Charinus as a rival lover who is not really a rival at all, 'a perfect illustration of what I take to be the central preoccupation of

---

57 A. W. Gomme, 'Menander', in *Essays in Greek History and Literature* (Oxford, 1937), 249–95, at p. 284.

58 T. McGarrity, 'Thematic Unity in Terence's *Andria*', *TAPA* 108 (1978), 103–14.

59 Goldberg 1981–82, 142. S. Lape, 'The Terentian Marriage Plot: Reproducing Fathers and Sons', *Ramus* 33 (2004), 35–52 also focuses on the father-son relationship (in the *Andria* and other plays) as revealing at a time of crisis 'that the young men in these plays are caught in a conflict of roles or identities created by the idiosyncrasies of Roman social kinship' (p. 36).

60 Goldberg 1981–82, 139–41, 143 n. 8.

61 This is overstated, since Davos acts throughout in the interests of his young master's love life, as one expects a comic slave to do, and Simo does attempt to block his son's love affair.

Andria'.[62] It is not clear to me why he speaks in this context of an 'ethical paradox' and 'ethical surprise', but there certainly are elements of paradox and surprise in the play.

All these scholars point to things that are undoubtedly there in the play, but none conveys the richness of what it has to offer, which I try to summarize in the final paragraph of this section [(c) below], though Germany's wider-ranging approach comes closer to that than the others.

(b) One way in which Terence has long been seen as playing games with his audience is by introducing metatheatrical touches, most notably in the scene where Simo suspects Davos of engineering a plot against him by arranging for Mysis, the midwife, and Glycerium to put on an act for his benefit, and in the later scene where Davos does himself put on an act for Chremes' benefit, with the unwitting assistance of Mysis, who is not putting on an act at all. In the former scene Simo is suspicious of the timing of Glycerium's off-stage cries (474–76), and he also criticizes the implausibility of the fact that the midwife comes out of Glycerium's house giving instructions to those indoors (481–94) rather than giving her instructions while still inside the house. This is to criticize a standard dramatic technique of New Comedy; see 490–91n. At the end of the latter scene Mysis complains that Davos should have told her in advance what he was up to; he replies (794–95) 'Do you think it makes a small difference whether you do everything instinctively and naturally or according to a careful plan?', suggesting that a spontaneous performance will be more effective than a prepared one, that improvisation is superior to rehearsed play-acting. We need not suppose that Terence and his cast would have agreed, but the audience are reminded that they are watching actors performing for their benefit. They may also have been reminded of this earlier, when they saw Davos at 417–18 giving acting instructions to Pamphilus ('Pretend to be surprised! Turn to look at him!') and then commenting aside on Pamphilus' performance ('Perfect!').

As noted above, Simo has assumed from the start that Davos would plot against him. This is partly because he believes him to have 'an evil mind, an evil heart' (164), but partly because he *expects* a slave to plot against his master when the master's son is having an affair, as he explains to Davos at 582–84. This expectation surely derived from watching too many comedies![63] At 916–17 Simo suspects that Crito is also part of the plot: 'Has

---

62   Germany, 239–42. The bulk of Germany's chapter is concerned with trying to establish links between Terence's prologue and the play that follows it; see below, section 6.7.

63   A character in an unknown play by Caecilius refers more explicitly to the comic theatre

it just '*turned out*' so conveniently that he *turned up* today – on the very day of the wedding – and never before this?'[64] Once again he is wrong to be suspicious of the neat coincidence, but the playwright who makes him voice his suspicion draws our attention to the importance of coincidence in his play. Similarly, when Davos at 221–25 dismisses as an implausible fiction (*Fabulae*, 224) the story about Glycerium's Athenian background and shipwreck off Andros, we may smile at his suggestion that a standard story-pattern of New Comedy is implausible, a point rubbed in by the fact that *fabulae* can mean 'plays'.[65] Ortwin Knorr sees it as 'one of the most important themes of the play that virtually everything that one of the play's characters rejects as unrealistic because of its obvious theatricality turns out to be true'.[66]

(c) These last points might not have sufficed to make Gomme interested in the characters, and Simo's initial plan is perhaps so absurd that it becomes hard to engage with the play at all. However, if we are willing to suspend our disbelief about that, there is much in the play to attract our interest and provoke our thoughts, not only about dramatic conventions and expectations but about the way in which chance events such as the arrival of Crito can cut through the most carefully laid plans, about the difference between reasonable scepticism and excessive suspicion, about the precarious position of an apparently foreign woman in a male-dominated society that jealously guards its rights of citizenship, and about father-son and father-daughter relationships in a society where fathers expect to plan the marriages of their children. We might also reflect on relations between masters and slaves, since that is the theme of the dialogue between Simo and Sosia in the first twenty lines of the play, and *The Girl from Andros* is one of only two Roman comedies in which a slave is actually sent off for punishment; see on 28–171, 842–65. It is also worth noting the skill with which the slave Mysis handles the young citizen Pamphilus; see on 234–300. Pamphilus' dilemma over whether to obey his father or stand by Glycerium (260–64) is one that we can all sympathize with, as is the upset of both Pamphilus and

---

in this context: 'today you have most elegantly manipulated and fooled me more than all the stupid old men of comedy' (256–57 Guardi = 243–44 Ribbeck, discussed by Wright, 110–12).

64   *Itane adtemperate euenit, hodie in ipsis nuptiis / ut ueniret, antehac numquam?* (*euenit* alludes to Crito's *euenit* at 907, the only explanation that he has offered of his arrival in this scene.)

65   See the notes on 220, 747, 925. On metatheatrical elements in the play more generally see also Moodie.

66   Knorr, 169.

Charinus when it looks as if they will lose the woman they love. Above all, however, the play is a theatrical *tour de force*: the scene with the baby on stage is a comic highlight, and the constantly shifting fortunes of the plots of Simo and Davos, with all their implications for the other characters, keep us both entertained and engaged. That's not bad for a young man's first play.[67]

6.7. The Prologue

Each of Terence's plays is preceded in the manuscripts by a prologue, written by Terence to be delivered by one of the actors before the start of the play proper (two prologues for *The Mother-in-Law*, for the second and third performance respectively). These prologues cannot represent anything that Terence found in his Greek originals, since they are entirely concerned with Terence himself and the Roman theatre of his day: they defend him against criticisms, attack his critic or critics in their turn, and plead for a fair hearing for Terence's own play. The criticisms against which they defend him are sometimes quite general but sometimes (as in *The Girl from Andros*) concern the play about to be performed. In this prologue it is notable that Terence's critic starts as 'a malicious old author' (6–7) but immediately becomes a plurality of critics from line 8 onwards, no doubt for rhetorical effect. The prologues are forensic pieces, written in verse like the plays themselves, but in a more formal style, with a great deal of antithesis and word-play. The prologue to *The Girl from Andros* can be analysed as having the structure of a law-court speech, with an introduction (1–7), statement of the point at issue (8–16), rebuttal of the charge (17–21), threat of a future counter-charge (22–23), and peroration (24–27). Striking stylistic features include the alliteration in lines 1 and 3, the emphatic repetition of *male-* in *maleuoli … maledictis* (6–7; cf. 23 *maledicere, malefacta*), the carefully balanced structure of lines 10 and 20–21 (with *neglegentiam* and *diligentiam* each at the end of its line), the repetition of *dissimili* (11–12) and *accusant* (18–19), the word-play *intellegendo … intellegant* (17) and *cognoscite … pernoscatis* (24–25), and the balance of *spectandae* and *exigendae* in 27. Some of the language would also be at home in a forensic context: *maledictis* (7, cf. 23), *fatetur* (14), *uituperant* and *disputant* (15), *accusant* (18, 19),

---

67 In spite of its title, the paper by L. Richardson Jr, 'The Moral Problems of Terence's *Andria* and Reconstruction of Menander's *Andria* and *Perinthia*', *GRBS* 38 (1997), 173–85 has very little to say about moral problems; its main contribution is a speculative reconstruction of Menander's two plays on pp. 181–85.

malefacta (23), and all the words in line 24. It is possible that Terence has quite misrepresented what was really at issue between him and his critics; but we are in no position to assess that. On the rhetorical nature of Terence's prologues see Goldberg 1986, 40–60, with references to earlier discussions; Goldberg discusses the prologue to *The Girl from Andros* on pp. 47–54.

As in several of the prologues written to introduce Plautus' plays (*Asinaria, Captiui, Casina, Menaechmi, Poenulus, Pseudolus, Truculentus*), the speaker is neither a character in the play nor an omniscient divinity; he is given no personality at all beyond his function as an advocate for the playwright. Nonetheless, as Dwora Gilula notes, 'his role calls for some versatility: he has to narrate, argue, plead, threaten, warn, and also calm and win over the audience' ('The First Realistic Roles in European Theatre: Terence's Prologues', *QUCC* 62 [1989], 95–106, at p. 100). Line 6 suggests that the prologue is expected to provide some details of the plot, as most of the Plautine prologues do. However, the *Asinaria* prologue gives no plot details, and the prologue to *Trinummus* (spoken by the personification of Luxury) tells us only at 12–15 that one of the stage houses is inhabited by a young man who has squandered his family fortune and at 16–17 explicitly refuses to give any further details of the plot (cf. also the fragmentary *Vidularia* prologue, lines 10–11, and Ter. *Ad.* 22–24). Those prologues too suggest an expectation that a prologue will say something about the plot. Terence was not the first to defeat that expectation (and not all of Plautus' plays have a prologue at all), but he was as far as we know the first to do so consistently.

We learn from the opening of the prologue to *The Self-Tormentor* that prologues were normally delivered by young men, and there is no reason to doubt that that was the case here; *The Self-Tormentor* and *The Mother-in-Law* (at its third performance) were exceptional in having prologues delivered by an older man, the leader of the company of actors. The speaker does not identify himself, but his function was perhaps immediately clear to the audience, since the prologue for the third performance of *The Mother-in-Law* starts 'I am dressed as the prologue-speaker, but I come to you to plead a case'; this suggests that there was a standard costume for the prologue-speaker (when not speaking as a character in the play or a divinity of some kind), but we know nothing about it. The speaker probably did not wear a mask, since lines 1–2 of *The Self-Tormentor* suggest that the spectators could tell immediately whether he (the speaker himself) was young or old. (On the depiction of prologue-speakers in the illustrated manuscripts of Terence see G. Guastella, in A. J. Turner and G. Torello-Hill (eds), *Terence between*

Late Antiquity and the Age of Printing [Leiden, 2015], 207–10; we cannot tell what these depictions were based on.) As noted above, all of Terence's prologues are designed 'to plead a case' on behalf of the playwright.

With the exception of those for *The Mother-in-Law*, the prologues appear to have been written for the first performance of the play in question. In the case of *The Girl from Andros*, however, several scholars have believed that our prologue was written for a later performance, though still by Terence himself and thus not very long after the first performance. This has been based above all on the use of the plural *prologis* in line 5 (suggesting that this is not Terence's first prologue), but also on the fact that Terence's critics clearly already know something about the play and on the self-confident tone adopted (felt to be unlikely for a beginner); see Lefèvre, 73–78. None of these arguments is compelling: *prologis* is easily understood as a rhetorical plural; Terence's critics know only that he claims to have used two plays by Menander, something which could easily have been known before the first performance;[68] and since when have brilliant young men lacked self-confidence at the start of their careers? In contrast, lines 24–27 seem entirely appropriate for the first production of a first play. (An alternative view has been that *The Girl from Andros* was not Terence's first play after all; see above, the end of the first paragraph of section 6.1.)

In spite of what he implies in lines 5–7, nothing obliged Terence to reply to criticisms by composing prologues. It was his decision to do so, and he must have welcomed the opportunity to promote himself and his play; as Goldberg says (1986, 59). 'The quarrel with Luscius is used as a device to pique their [the audience's] interest'. He may also have enjoyed placing himself in a literary tradition, since Aristophanes in some of his parabases had conducted feuds with rival playwrights, and more recently (but in a different genre) Callimachus had opened his *Aitia* with a polemical prologue in which he replied to critics and proclaimed his own artistic principles, including references to some predecessors. Callimachus was not at the start of his career when he wrote that, but he does at one point say what instructions he had received from the god Apollo 'when I first put a writing-tablet on my knees' (lines 21–22 Pf). Line 1 of Terence's prologue could

---

68   In fact it would probably not have been impossible for them to know more: the prologue to *The Eunuch* (lines 19–26) shows that it was (at least on that occasion) possible for an outsider to spy on a rehearsal before the play's first performance and perhaps also to see a copy of the text in advance. The prologue to *The Brothers* (1–5) introduces us to another case in which criticism of the play has been voiced before its first performance.

be seen as echoing that, though the context is quite different and Terence's aim to 'please the public' might not have won Callimachus' approval. For these precedents see Hunter, 30–33 (stressing particularly Aristophanes), Sharrock, 77–83. Rivalries between various further types of Greek author are discussed by M. Pohlenz, 'Der Prolog des Terenz', *SIFC* n.s. 27/28 (1956), 434–43, stressing particularly the importance of Isocrates for the development of a self-standing polemical prologue.

It would be interesting to know whether the prologues were included in subsequent performances of the plays, even after Terence's lifetime; if they were not, it is perhaps surprising that they have survived at all. Later audiences could well have savoured the forensic style and the evocation of earlier literary feuds, but one might wonder how interested they would have been in Terence's spats with unnamed critics once the freshness of the immediate context had faded. Some scholars, however, have seen the prologues as anticipating the plot of their play in subtle ways and thus as being more closely bound up with the play than might appear at first sight. In the case of *The Girl from Andros*, E. Gowers, 'The Plot Thickens: Hidden Outlines in Terence's Prologues', *Ramus* 33 (2004), 150–66, at pp. 151–55, suggests that Glycerium's fortunes as a young woman treated with suspicion and hostility by the older generation but finally winning acceptance parallel Terence's account of his first play subjected to hostile criticism by an older rival but (he hopes) finally being approved. She also sees a parallel between the two Menandrian plays used by Terence in composing his own play, each with its own 'words and style' (line 12), and the two girls on whom Terence's play centres, Glycerium and Philumena, each with her own very different style – in spite of which 'the man who knows either of them properly will know both of them' (10), since Glycerium turns out to be Philumena's long-lost sister. However, this glosses over the fact that the 'plots' of the two girls, unlike the plots of Menander's two plays according to line 11, are utterly different. (Gowers' main concern otherwise is to detect parallels between the fortunes of Glycerium and those of Terence himself according to Suetonius' *Life of Terence*, but this has nothing to do with what is said in the prologue to this play.) Moodie, 158–64 builds on Gowers in seeing a parallel between Terence's rival and Simo as 'blocking characters who stand in the way of a young man's dreams and want to control the creative powers of a poet-like figure' (pp. 158–59), with Davos as the poet-like figure paralleling Terence in the prologue, both essentially passive or reactive but using their knowledge of comic traditions by building on those traditions 'in a nimble and erudite way' (p. 159). Again, this glosses over significant differences: Terence's rival does not lay devious traps for him but voices his criticism openly; and Davos is rather less in control of the events of the play than Terence, though it is true that he is nimble in adapting to situations. Germany argues for a yet more thoroughgoing interrelationship of prologue and play, under three headings. (1) He sees details of the technique and content of the exposition of the facts in the opening scene as paralleling details in the prologue (but he is probably wrong to think that the speaker of the prologue is an old man and thus equivalent to Simo [see above], and the claim that Chremes is the equivalent of the 'malicious old author' [lines 6–7] is strange). (2) He argues that the terms 'carelessness' (*neglegentia*) and 'undistinguished carefulness' (*obscura diligentia*) in lines 20–21 (his own translation of the latter term on p. 229 is 'cryptic attentiveness') can be applied to characters in the play, with Chremes, Charinus, and Byrria exemplifying *neglegentia* while Simo, Pamphilus, and Davos display *diligentia* (Moodie, 159 top had already ascribed *obscura diligentia* to Simo). However, while there are indeed contrasts between the various characters, those contrasts are not well brought out by trying to force them into the straitjacket of the terms in question. The Chremes of 99–102, 144–49, 533–35, and 563–66 can hardly be said to show a 'laissez faire approach', nor does he display 'easygoing credulity' at 940–42 (both expressions quoted from p. 235). Similarly, the Charinus of 301ff., 373–74, and 625ff. is not well described as 'lackadaisical' (p. 239).[69] (3) As noted above (section 6.6), Germany regards various paradoxical elements in the play as encapsulating its 'central preoccupation'; he finds a similar paradox in the prologue in the expression 'achieve with their learning that they've learned nothing' (line 17). This line is less central to the prologue than some of the paradoxical elements are to the play itself, though Germany could perhaps have strengthened his case by adding that many would find it paradoxical to proclaim a preference for *neglegentia* over *diligentia*. Overall, I am not yet convinced that an audience seeing the play without the prologue would be missing much,[70] though for a possible further metaphorical link between prologue and play see on 1 *animum ... adpulit*.

On the likelihood that Menander's *Girl from Andros* and *Girl from*

---

69   The uses of *neglegentia* at 71 and *neglegenter* at 253 do not strengthen Germany's case, though he could perhaps have done something with *neglegentem* at 397; *diligentia* does not recur in the play.

70   In 'An Interpolated Line of Terence at Cicero, *De finibus* 2.14', *CQ* 47.2 (1997), 583–84 I suggested that whoever interpolated *HT* 53 at Cic. *De fin.* 2.14 regarded that and not line 1 as the opening of the play.

Perinthos both included an expository prologue to provide some details of the background to the plot and some foreshadowing of its outcome, and on the consequences for Terence's play of his non-inclusion of such a prologue, see above, pp. 16–18.

6.8. Reception[71]

The *Andria* was the first ancient Latin comedy to be performed in the Renaissance, at Florence in 1476, and the first to be translated into English, in the 1520s. It was translated into Italian by Ariosto and Machiavelli, and into German by the sixteen-year-old Felix Mendelssohn in 1825, at the same time as he was composing his Octet. It was regularly performed at Westminster School in the eighteenth and nineteenth centuries and through to the 1930s, at a time when the Westminster Latin Play was one of the great social events of the year in London. In 1722 in London Richard Steele's hugely successful sentimental comedy *The Conscious Lovers* was based on the *Andria*, as were a large number of less well known plays, from Giovanni Armonio's *Stephanium* of about 1500 (a combination of the *Andria* with four plays by Plautus, in Latin) to the anonymous German play *Die Engländerin in Berlin* ('The English Girl in Berlin') of 1777, which is closely modelled on Terence's play though updated and transposed to a new setting. Nicolai Abildgaard, one of the leading Danish artists in the late eighteenth and early nineteenth century, painted four scenes from the *Andria*, now in the Royal Collection of Paintings in Copenhagen, as a wedding present for his second wife. Thornton Wilder's short novel *The Woman of Andros* had some success when it was published in 1930; it follows Terence's play closely in some respects, but it transforms it into something far more sentimental and melancholy. The main character is Chrysis, who dies two thirds of the way through the book, and at the end Glycerium dies in childbirth, together with her baby. There are no plots, no counter-plots, no Davos to act as a foil to Simo, no rival for the hand of Philumena – in short, none of the elements that create the potential for comedy.

The play's greatest influence has probably been as a source of quotations, such as *hinc illae lacrumae* ('That's what those tears were for', line 126), *Dauos sum, non Oedipus* ('I'm Davos, not Oedipus', line 194), or *amantium irae amoris integratio est* ('when lovers feud, their love's renewed', line 555). The last of these was used as a chapter heading by Thackeray in

71   For fuller details see Brown 2014.

Vanity Fair and by Trollope in both *Framley Parsonage* and *Phineas Finn*; it was also quoted by Benjamin Disraeli in his maiden speech in the House of Commons in 1837 and by Winston Churchill in a telegram to President Roosevelt towards the end of the Second World War ('one of my very few Latin quotations', as he said).[72]

7. Language and style

It is above all for his style that Terence has been read in the many centuries since his death.[73] Although criticized as 'thin and lightweight' in Terence's own lifetime,[74] it has since been more generally admired for its elegance and clarity. Terence was the first Latin writer to reproduce the sometimes elliptical style of natural conversation (cf. 635n., and a number of other notes where ellipses are explained). It is not a low colloquial style, but its clipped constructions have a realistic ring which is generally absent from Plautus. Not all passages are written in this style: some sections are more ornate and repetitive, and this is particularly true of the prologues (see the first paragraph of section 6.7). But it is the clipped conversational style that is most distinctively Terentian. There is a general tendency in both Plautus and Terence for the more ornate features to be found in passages with musical accompaniment,[75] but they can also be found in unaccompanied senarii (see section 8 for details of Terence's metres): the second paragraph of 234–300n. draws attention to the presence of such features in Pamphilus' mouth both in 236–64 (accompanied) and in 270–98 (unaccompanied).

Early Latin differed from Classical Latin in some respects in terms of morphology, spelling, and syntax. Our manuscripts of Terence's plays were

---

72 Alan Sommerstein points out that the poem 'In going to my naked bed', composed and set to music by (probably) Richard Edwards (1525–66), has a refrain 'The falling out of faithful friends renewing is of love'.

73 He has also been read for the moral sentiments occasionally uttered by his characters. Some readers, however, have perceived immorality in his plots, concerned as they often are with young males seeking sexual gratification, and debate about that has featured prominently at various stages in the reception of his plays (see P. Brown, 'The Eunuch Castrated: Bowdlerization in the Text of the Westminster Latin Play', *IJCT* 15 [2008], 16–28).

74 See the prologue to *Phormio*, line 5: *tenui esse oratione et scriptura leui* ('thin in language and lightweight in writing'). Cicero and Caesar took a more positive view in epigrams quoted in Suetonius' *Life of Terence* 7; Caesar's designation of Terence as a 'lover of pure language' (*puri sermonis amator*) has been particularly influential, though Caesar also laments a lack of *uis* ('force') in his writing.

75 See Haffter 1934, particularly pp. 114–25.

written many centuries after his death (see section 9) and cannot be relied on to present the text exactly as he wrote it. Editors generally compromise between restoring archaic features and accepting the text as presented by the manuscripts. For the most part I have followed K-L e.g. in printing *quoius, quoi, quor*, and *quom* for *cuius, cui, cur*, and *cum* (the conjunction) throughout. Such matters are normally discussed in the Commentary as they arise, but note in addition that the Classical sequence *uu* is printed as *uo* (thus *Dauos, seruos, suos, suom, uolt*, not *Dauus, seruus, suus, suum, uult*), that prefixes are sometimes not assimilated to stems (thus *adpulit, adtendite, inmemoris, ecfertur, inmortalitas*, not *appulit, attendite, immemoris, effertur, immortalitas*), and that *uoster* and *reuortar* are written for *uester* and *reuertar* (cf. on 42 *aduorsum*); *paullum* and *paullulum* are written for *paulum* and *paululum, periclum* for *periculum, lubet* and *lubido* for *libet* and *libido, carnufex, lacrumae, facillume, maxumus, optumus*, and *pessumus* for *carnifex, lacrimae, facillime, maximus, optimus*, and *pessimus*.

There is an excellent account of Terence's language and style in Barsby 1999, 19–27, and a very full summary of linguistic and stylistic features of the *Andria* in German in Thierfelder, 26–42 (language) and 42–51 (style). For a briefer summary, illustrated from *Phormio*, see Palmer, 89–94. Shipp, 44–55 discusses stylistic features of the *Andria*. Karakasis offers a fuller study of Terence's language, and there is an overall account of 'The Language of Roman Comedy' by W. de Melo in J. Clackson (ed.), *A Companion to the Latin Language* (Chichester, 2011), 321–43.

8. Music and Metre

8.1. Latin comedies are written entirely in verse and have the structure of a modern musical, with alternating passages of speech and song. In the case of *The Girl from Andros*, in addition to the spoken prologue, 51% of the lines of the play proper are spoken (representing somewhat less than 50% of the time taken to perform the play, since the spoken lines are shorter than nearly all of the sung ones). The spoken lines are **iambic senarii**, the ancient equivalent of blank verse but with six, not five, beats per line. The sung lines are almost all longer iambic or **trochaic** lines, with a handful of shorter lines in these rhythms (altogether 23% iambic, 24% trochaic); in addition there are two passages in so-called 'lyric' metres, with four lines of **bacchiacs** at 481–84 and twelve lines of **cretics** preceded by a **dactylic** line at 625–35, 637–38. (See below for a definition of all these metrical terms.) The dactylic line is unique in Latin comedy, but the other metres are all found in Plautus. Plautus, however, typically has a smaller proportion of spoken lines and a larger proportion in 'lyric' metres. There is thus less metrical variety, and less music altogether, in this play than in almost all of Plautus' surviving plays; the same is true of Terence's other plays. But the musical element is still quite considerable, and one distinctive feature of Terence's use of the accompanied iambic and trochaic metres is that he sometimes shifts rapidly between them (e.g. at 234–55) rather than composing in blocks of one metre at a time as Plautus had generally done (though Terence does also compose in such blocks, e.g. the blocks of trochaic **septenarii** at 319–83, 820–60, 896–928) – accompanied passages incorporating rapid changes of metre are more characteristic of Plautus' use of 'lyric' metres. Terence also switches between accompanied and unaccompanied lines more frequently than Plautus. Moore 2013 goes through the play discussing the effect of the choice of metre in each scene and of the change from one metre to another, above all stressing the originality of Terence's flexibility in this respect and the fact that metrical changes are often linked to shifts in the thoughts and emotions of the characters; he also singles out Terence's innovative use of the iambic **octonarius**, which is much rarer in Plautus. Overall Moore proclaims this play as 'a musical tour de force unique in Roman Comedy' (p. 112). I have incorporated some of his conclusions in the introductory note to each section of the Commentary. There are clear accounts of the pattern of each metre in T. J. Moore, 'Meter and Music', in Augoustakis and Traill, 89–110, at 89–94, and in M. Deufert, 'Metrics and Music', in Fontaine and Scafuro, 477–97. Barsby 1999, 290–304 gives more detail on some matters, particularly on questions of prosody. For a full account of the musical element in Latin comedy see Moore 2012. The most detailed and authoritative study of the metres of Plautus and Terence is that of Questa (in Italian).

8.2. The sung passages were accompanied on the *tibia*, a reed-pipe most closely resembling the oboe among modern orchestral instruments. We do not have the music, but we believe that it underpinned the words rather than consisting of 'numbers' with catchy tunes; the effect was probably similar to that of the passages of accompanied recitative in seventeenth- and eighteenth-century Italian opera. According to Donatus (*Andria, Praef.* I.6) 'the music was composed by Flaccus the son of Claudius on equal pipes, right or left';[76] 'son' is probably a mistake for 'slave'. The terminology of types of pipe is hard to interpret (see Moore 2012, 56–63), but Flaccus is named as the composer of the music for all of Terence's plays.

8.3.

(a) The metrical pattern is established not (as in English verse) by the accentuation of the words but by the 'weight' (or 'length' or 'quantity') of the syllables in the line. Each line contains a certain number of '**feet**', and in iambic and trochaic lines a foot has two '**elements**'. An iambic foot in its purest form consists of a '**light**' (or 'short') syllable followed by a '**heavy**' (or 'long') one, conventionally indicated by the symbols ˘ and – respectively; each syllable represents one element. An **iambic senarius** consists of six such feet (twelve elements), a **septenarius** of seven and a half (fifteen elements), an **octonarius** of eight (sixteen elements). A **trochaic** foot is the reverse of an iambic one, i.e. – ˘ instead of ˘ –. A trochaic **septenarius** has seven and a half feet, an **octonarius** has eight. There are also shorter lines in each of these rhythms: **acatalectic quaternarii** have four feet (eight elements), **catalectic** quaternarii have three and a half (seven elements) – 'catalectic' means 'ending with a half foot rather than a complete foot' (or more literally 'stopping short'), so the iambic or trochaic septenarius is also a catalectic line; 'acatalectic' means 'not stopping short'. Of the 'lyric' metres, the pure form of the **bacchiac** is ˘ – –, of the **cretic** – ˘ –, of the **dactyl** – ˘ ˘. A '**cretic colon**' consists of a cretic with two extra syllables either preceding or following it; line 635 consists of two such colons. The traditional terminology in all of this is a mixture of words that are Latin-based ('element', 'quaternarius', 'senarius', 'septenarius', 'octonarius') and words that are Greek-based (the others).

(b) At most points in the line a heavy syllable can substitute for a light one, and two light syllables can take the place either of a single light syllable or of a heavy one (a phenomenon known as '**resolution**'). Thus each of the first five feet of an iambic senarius can be ˘ – (**iamb**), – – (**spondee**), ˘ ˘ ˘ (**tribrach**), ˘ ˘ – (**anapaest**), – ˘ ˘ (**dactyl**), or ˘ ˘ ˘ ˘ (**proceleusmatic**), i.e. the first, third, fifth, seventh, and ninth elements can be either ˘, ˘ ˘, or –, while the second, fourth, sixth, eighth, and tenth can be either ˘ ˘ or –. The first element of the sixth foot, however, must be a single light syllable, and the second element (the final element in the line) must also be a single

---

76 *Modos fecit Flaccus Claudi filius tibiis paribus dextris uel sinistris.* Cioffi deletes both *filius* and the last three words.

syllable but can be either heavy or light. Similar substitutions are possible in the other metres (though dactyls always start with a heavy syllable). Very occasionally (normally before a clear break such as a change of speaker) a single light syllable is found where a heavy syllable would be expected, a phenomenon known as *breuis in longo* ('a short in place of a long'). So the final syllable of 267 *Pamphile*, 437 *dicere*,[77] 930 *Iuppiter* (all followed by a change of speaker).

(c) The rhythmical beat falls on the element in each foot that is heavy in the pure form of the rhythm, i.e. on the first element in a trochaic or dactylic foot and the second element in an iambic one; in bacchiacs it is thought to fall on the second and third elements, in cretics on the first and third.[78] This beat often coincides with the natural word-accent (by which a stress falls on the penultimate syllable if that is heavy, or if the word has only two syllables, otherwise on the antepenultimate), but not always. Actors presumably spoke or sang the words according to their natural rhythms, i.e. they did not bring out the metre by stressing syllables that they would not have stressed in normal speech. But they and the audience would have been conscious of the underlying metrical pattern, which may well have been brought out by the pipe player in accompanied passages.

8.4. The freedom to substitute or resolve gives a wonderful flexibility to the rhythm, but it can sometimes make it quite hard to see how a line is to be scanned. However, there are some restrictions on the apparent anarchy that results, most notably the following four, the first three of which help to ensure that we do not lose sight of the basic rhythm. (It is normally possible to scan the lines without knowledge of the following rules, simply by looking out for the requisite number of beats, but knowledge of the rules can sometimes help to resolve difficulties of scansion or to establish the text.)

Hermann-Lachmann's law (named after the scholars G. Hermann and K. Lachmann): if an element consists of two light syllables (is 'resolved'), they should not be the final syllables of a trisyllabic or longer word. This law does not apply in the second element of a line or half-line.

Ritschl's law: if an element consists of two light syllables, there should not be word-break between them, unless the first of the two is a monosyllable or an elided disyllabic word. This law is not always strictly observed: it is

---

77 See on 125 *Attat* for a possible alternative explanation of this case.
78 Some scholars, including Questa, deny the existence of a rhythmical beat altogether, and this has been a much debated issue. For a discussion see Moore 2012, 157–63.

ignored in the second element of 77 (-*nus et*), 439 (-*ter hu-*),[79] and 809 (-*per e*-), but also in the third element of 322 (-*cis ho-*) and 965 (-*lus u*-), the fourth element of 23 (-*re ma-*) and 535 (-*re tu-*),[80] the fifth element of 301 (-*a Da-*), the sixth element of 598 (-*tur u-*), and the seventh element of 522 (-*cis et*).[81]

Meyer's law: if a word of more than one syllable ends at the end of the second or fourth foot of an iambic senarius (or at comparable places in longer iambic or trochaic lines), that foot must be a pure iamb. Exceptions are allowed if the word-break is followed either by a monosyllable (as at 957 *aliquis me*) or by a word of four syllables filling four elements (as at 7 *maledictis respondeat*).[82]

Bentley-Luchs' law (named after R. Bentley and A. Luchs): if an iambic line or half-line, or a catalectic trochaic line, ends with an iambic word, the preceding foot (or the equivalent elements in a trochaic line) may not be formed by an iambic word or the iambic end of a longer word.[83] The reason for this law is that otherwise the line might seem to be coming to a premature end before the final iambic word.

8.5.

(a) In the iambic senarius there is regularly a break between words (a 'caesura') after the fifth element, less commonly after the seventh; very occasionally there is instead a break after the sixth element,[84] in which case (i.e. if the break comes between feet rather than within a foot) it is often called a '**diaeresis**' rather than a 'caesura'. This is a matter of word-patterning and is not necessarily related to a break in sense (though it often is, particularly in Plautus). Line 767 is unusual in having no word-break at any of these points. In the case of a line like 717, where a caesura would

---

79   See also on 377 *ipsus sibi esse*.

80   See also on 950. In 217 synizesis at the beginning of *eorumst* ensures that the law is observed in the fourth element.

81   It is perhaps ignored in the tenth element of 713 (-*quid a-*), the second element of a half-line, but *siquid* should perhaps rather there be treated as two words.

82   It is also worth noting that the third and seventh elements of a senarius are significantly less often heavy or resolved than are the first, fifth, and ninth elements. This suggests (as does Meyer's law) some attempt to reproduce the structure of the equivalent Greek metre (the iambic trimeter), in which the third and seventh elements are never heavy, though these elements are nonetheless more often heavy than light in Latin comedy.

83   The exceptions at 89, 749, and 762 form part of an allowable pattern discussed by Questa, 375–76.

84   At 44, 64, 801, and perhaps also 745 and 774 (Questa, 334); also at 154, 167, and 447, unless we accept a caesura before *est*.

come after *esse* if it were not elided, it is customary to accept the line as having a 'quasi-caesura'.

(b) Septenarii and octonarii (both iambic and trochaic) regularly have a word-break after either the eighth or the ninth element (after the tenth in 821 and 907)[85]; if after the eighth or tenth it is often called a 'diaeresis'. If the word-break in iambic verses comes after the eighth element, the fourth foot is treated like the last foot of the senarius: the seventh element must be a single light syllable, and the eighth element must also be a single syllable but can be either heavy or light. Thus a light element is found as the last syllable of the word in 584 *filius*, 705 *cedo* (in both cases followed by a change of speaker), 957 *Pamphilus*.

8.6. In determining whether a syllable is heavy or light, the following rules apply:

(i) A syllable is heavy if it contains a naturally long vowel or a diphthong, or if it ends in a consonant.

(ii) A syllable ends in a consonant if two or more consonants follow its vowel, as long as at least one of them is in the same word: the first consonant is regarded as 'closing' that syllable, while the next consonant opens the succeeding one. This does not apply if the vowel is the last letter of a word, nor if the consonant combination is a so-called 'mute and liquid' combination such as *br*, *cr*, *gr*, *pr*, or *tr* and both consonants come within the same word (unless they belong to the different parts of a compound word such as *ab-ripi* at 786): in these circumstances both consonants are regarded as opening the following syllable, and a syllable preceding them is light if its vowel is naturally short. This is a strict rule in Early Latin; later it became optional whether to treat such syllables as heavy or light. The following are examples of light syllables before a 'mute and liquid' combination in this play: the first syllable of *patri* (112, etc.), *supra* (120), and *probro* (881); the second syllable of *integra* (72) and *obsecro* (232, etc.).

(iii) A syllable is light if it contains a naturally short vowel followed by a single consonant, either within the same word or at the start of the next word; in that case the consonant is regarded as belonging to the following syllable, even if there is word-break after it. Thus *facite* is treated as *fa-ci-te*, and *quid est* is treated as *qui-dest*. A syllable is said to be 'open' if it ends in a vowel.

---

85   See Questa, 361.

(iv) *h* does not count as a consonant; *x* and *z* count as double consonants.

(v) Some vowels in the final syllable of a word that are naturally short in Classical Latin are long in Plautus and perhaps also in Terence, e.g. 638 *pudēt*, 682 *concrepuīt*. For more details see Barsby 1999, 298. The light final syllable of *habet* (83, 160), *memor* (281, 282), *fuit* (294), and *sequar* (819) could be the result of iambic shortening (see 8.8 (a) below), as noted by Questa, 96–97, 184.

8.7. If a word ends in a vowel or *–m* and the next word starts with a vowel or *h*, the final syllable of the first word is '**elided**', i.e. it does not count at all for scansion purposes (although it almost certainly did not disappear entirely in pronunciation). This regularly happens even across a change of speaker. On the other hand, at 593, 665, and 895 (if the text is correct) such a vowel remains unelided (in '**hiatus**') before a change of speaker.
8.8.

(a) In defiance of the above rules, a heavy syllable may (in Early Latin) be lightened by a process known as '**iambic shortening**' if it is the second syllable in an iambic sequence: the light (or 'short') first syllable is said to lighten (or 'shorten') the second one and is referred to as *breuis breuians* (the 'shortening short' syllable). This phenomenon is quite common and is found in cases where the two light syllables belong to the same element and where the syllable to be lightened does not carry the natural word-accent. (In general the word-accent plays no part in the rules for scansion, but it is clearly relevant here. On the other hand, see on 237 *illud* for the lightening in some circumstances of the first syllable of *ille*, *ipse*, and *iste*, and on 391 for the lightening of the first syllable of *omnis*.) The second syllable of *bene* and *male* was in fact so often lightened by iambic shortening in everyday speech that the final vowel is treated as a short vowel in all surviving Early and Classical Latin; the same is overwhelmingly true of the second syllable of *ego*, *mihi* (though it is long at 112), *tibi*, and *sibi*.[86] Examples of iambic shortening in the first hundred lines: 42 *id*, 43 *hoc*, 52 *erat* (second syllable), 65 *ut*, 66 *inuidia* (first syllable), 91 *Enimuero* (second syllable), 95 *scias* (second syllable).

(b) Another peculiarity of Early Latin (still found in Lucretius and at Catullus

---

86 The final vowel of *ego* could be long at 702, as could that of *tibi* at 684 and 703, but in these cases the syllable could be a light syllable at the central break in the line (see above, section 8.5 (b)). *Ego* could also have a long final vowel at the beginning of 864, making that line an iambic octonarius; a few editors have favoured this.

116.8) is that the consonant *s* **following a short vowel at the end of a word can be disregarded before a following consonant** ('sigmatic ecthlipsis': Pezzini, 193–234), thus making the final syllable of the word 'open' rather than 'closed'; at 599, for instance, the metre requires that the line end *Nullu' sum*, at 619 *fretu' sim*.[87] In practice it is often impossible to tell whether a light final syllable of this kind has been lightened by disregarding the final *s* or by iambic shortening; so *satis* (131, 150, etc.), *prius* (239, 311, etc.), *patris* (262), *magis* (308, 698, 774),[88] *opus* (337, 424, etc.), *Erus* (412, 423), etc.

(c) A similar problem often arises in possible cases of '**synizesis**', the process by which two vowels which do not form a diphthong, such as the first two vowels in *fuisse* (42), *eorum* (64, 576), or *meorum* (453), coalesce to function essentially as a diphthong (making *fuisse*, *eorum*, and *meorum* words of two syllables rather than three).[89] If an iambic word such as *meos* is found filling one element, it is normally impossible to tell whether the element is a heavy syllable as the result of synizesis or resolved thanks to iambic shortening. So 49 *eo*, 63 *eis*, 95 *suae*, 168 *tuomst*, 185 *Meum*, 237 *deum*,[90] 325 *fuit*, 353 *ait*, 487 *Deos*, etc. In such cases, for the sake of consistency, I have followed the practice recommended by Questa, 178–80 of indicating synizesis rather than iambic shortening in the text, though I am not confident that there are strong reasons for preferring this solution.[91]

(d) One final phenomenon to look out for is '**prosodic hiatus**', by which a syllable (usually a monosyllable) ending in a long vowel, a diphthong, or -*m* may remain unelided and be treated as light before a word starting with a vowel or *h*; so 182 *ne*,[92] 191 *qui*, 639 *cum*, 947 *di*, etc.

---

87 At 203 the metre requires *passu' sim* in the middle of the line, and it probably also requires *ueritu' sum* at 582; see Pezzini, 223–24 on these and the two cases cited in the text above.

88 Some editors prefer to print the alternative form *mage* at these places, although there is no warrant for that in the manuscripts.

89 In addition the final syllable of *eorum* and *meorum* is elided in 64 and 453.

90 But at 246 *deum* scans as two syllables of which the second is elided.

91 At 781 and 971 *eam* is an elided monosyllable, unless the first syllable of *uxorem* is lightened by iambic shortening (in which case *eam* is two syllables of which the first is elided). So too 242 *suam*, 378 *tuom*, 510, 939 *tuam*.

92 Alternatively, *ne* here is elided and the line is a self-contained trochaic septenarius in a run of iambic octonarii; some editors have taken it thus. Prosodic hiatus before a long vowel is unusual but probably allowable. [To avoid it but keep the iambic metre Bentley read *ut ne* (cf. 259n.), which is another possible solution.]

8.9.

(a) As noted in the Preface, I have indicated the rhythm in the text by printing accents on the elements that carry the beat.[93] The accent is marked on the first syllable of a resolved element and on the second vowel of a diphthong (or the third in the case of a word like *tuae* or *eius* when it is scanned as a monosyllable: see above, section 8.8 (c), and on 93 *eiusmodi*). There is never an accent or a metrical marking on an elided syllable; thus (e.g.) 458 *ĕm* remains unelided (cf. 8.8 (d) on prosodic hiatus), as does the second syllable of *Chremĕ* at 895, whereas *Hem* at 270 carries no accent or metrical marking and should be elided.

(b) I have indicated the metre to the right of the text, using the abbreviations shown in the following scheme:

*ia.4^*	iambic catalectic quaternarius (line 485)
ia.4	iambic acatalectic quaternarius (176, 240, 244, 252, 537)
ia.6	iambic senarius (486 lines)
ia.7	iambic septenarius (299–300, 575–81, 684–715)
ia.8	iambic octonarius (176 lines)
*tro.4^*	trochaic catalectic quaternarius (246, 517, 605, 636)
tro.4	trochaic acatalectic quaternarius (638a)
tro.7	trochaic septenarius (218 lines)
tro.8	trochaic octonarius (245, 247, 301, 305, 307, 607–608)
ba.4	bacchiac quaternarius (i.e. four bacchiacs: 481–84)
cre.3	cretic ternarius (i.e. three cretics: 637–38)
cre.4	cretic quaternarius (i.e. four cretics: 626–34)
cre.co.	cretic colon (635 consists of two)
da.4	dactylic quaternarius (i.e. four dactyls: 625)

9. Manuscripts

Unfortunately, the best manuscript of Terence (designated A in the apparatus of scholarly editions, probably written in the fifth century CE) lacks almost all of the *Andria*. It offers a few letters from the beginning or end of most of lines 787–865; it starts to offer a more complete text from 888 onwards, though 903–11 are missing altogether and many other lines are incomplete; 916–81 are complete or nearly so.

---

93 Sometimes, particularly in the longer lines, more than one scansion is possible. I did not always have strong reasons for preferring the scansion marked.

This play is unusual in that parts of it are found in two fragmentary papyrus texts roughly contemporary with A. The Vienna papyrus (P. Vindob. inv. L 103) has the beginnings of lines 489–99, the ends of 513–21, the beginnings of 540–54, and the ends of 573–82; for a full account see Danese. The Oxyrhynchus papyrus (P. Oxy. 2401) has lines 602–68 and 924–79a, many of them complete or nearly so; see *The Oxyrhynchus Papyri*, vol. XXIV (London, 1957), 110–23.

The remaining manuscripts date from the ninth century onwards; well over 700 have been catalogued, though not all contain the *Andria*. They are thought all to derive from a tradition separate from A and originally to have formed two sub-groups known as the γ and δ groups. However, much cross-contamination has taken place in the process of copying and correcting, and a third sub-group of 'mixed' manuscripts has also been identified.

The most up-to-date apparatus for the *Andria* is that of Posani, who follows K-L in citing the following manuscripts in addition to A and the two papyri: PCEVεη (from the γ group), DGLpV (from the δ group). I occasionally refer to some of these manuscripts in the textual notes in the Commentary; for details of them see pp. 73–74 of Posani's edition or B. Victor, 'The Transmission of Terence', in Fontaine and Scafuro, 699–716.

The manuscripts divide the play into scenes, normally marking a new scene at the point where a character who has just entered starts to speak (but e.g. at 432 a new scene is marked for two characters who remain on stage after others have departed). They mark the new scene by inserting a heading which lists the characters who are to speak in it (from left to right across the page) and sometimes also indicates the role that each character performs (e.g. *senex* ['old man'], *adulescens* ['young man']). In some γ manuscripts there is also an illustration at this point to show the named characters in action. It is normal in modern editions to print the names of the characters in the same way and also to indicate the number of the scene that follows (further dividing the play into acts, each containing several scenes), but I have explained in the Preface why I prefer not to do this. In particular, marking the start of a new scene might seem to indicate that the previous scene has been rounded off, but that is clearly not the case e.g. at 532–33, 580 (where the new scene is marked as starting half way through the line), or 871–72. (See also the last paragraph of section 6.5 above.)

The illustrations may well offer evidence for what some kinds of theatrical performance looked like several hundred years after Terence's death (the date of the original series from which they derive is debated but is generally thought to have been about 400 CE), but such performances were not necessarily of Terence's comedies, and in any case the illustrations are sadly not evidence for the time of Terence himself. There is a brief discussion by S. Nervegna, 'Graphic Comedy: Menandrian Mosaics and Terentian Miniatures', in Fontaine and Scafuro, 717–34, at 727–31.

The manuscripts indicate changes of speaker within scenes and identify the speaker of each utterance. It is generally agreed that these indications and identifications derive from interpretation of the text, not from any independent ancient evidence. Editors should therefore feel free to ignore them and to work such things out for themselves.

I list here the main differences between my text and that of K-L. I have not included minor differences of spelling or punctuation. I differ from K-L in starting each sentence with a capital letter, in using 'u' instead of 'v' (though in capitals I have used 'V' before a vowel), and in not substituting an apostrophe for 's' at the end of a word before a following consonant except in the four cases where it is certainly or probably required by the metre [203, 582, 599, 619; cf. above, 8.8. (b)]; K-L use the apostrophe wherever sigmatic ecthlipsis is metrically possible, even when it is not required.

	This edition	**K-L**
11	sunt dissimili ... sed	dissimili sunt ... et
52	liberius uiuendi erat potestas	†liberius vivendi fuit potestas†
87	nam hi tres tum eam	†nam î tres tum simul†
90	comperiebam	comperibam
121	Quae quom	quia tum
171	SO. I prae, sequor	(SI.) i prae, sequar
189	adfert	defert
201	intellextin	intellexti
205	dices	dicas
208	*deleted*	*not deleted*
213	si lubitum fuerit	aut si lubitum fuerit
235	turbae tristitia	turba tristitiae
248	Em	hem
289	dextram oro et	dexteram et
308, 698, 774	magis	mage
325	Aha	ah
343	adloqui	conloqui

	This edition	**K-L**
345	Euge	eugae
346	PA. Interii	CH. interii
347	CHA. Mea quidem	PA. mea quidem
361	Quorsum	quorsu'
369	ferre	fere
378, 377	*in this order*	377, 378
390	certa ei consilia	certa consilia
434	Aegre	aeque
438, 656, 700	hae	haec
451	opsonatus	opsonatum
461	haec? Quid narras? DA. Itast.	haec. DA. quid narras? ita est.
483	post	poste
485	reuortar	revortor
489	quis non credat	quis credat
496	ueritu's	veritus
500	intellexti hoc adsimulari	intellexti adsimularier
506	Intellexeris	intellexti
533	(SI.) optato aduenis	CH. optato advenis
557	contumeliis.	contumeliis,
577	suadet	persuadet
579	uerba audies. Heus, euocate	audies verba. evocate
592	audiam	audio
596	gnatum mihi corrigere	corrigere mihi gnatum
599	itidem	idem
607	illest	illicst
610	Ergo	ego
	id numquam	numquam id
611	scio fore me	scio me
613	ipse	ducere
	fiducia	audacia
615	producam	productem
633	*deleted*	*not deleted*
638	opust	opus
665	ais, scelus?	ais? scelus,
669	CHA. Scio	PA. scio
688	ait te	te ait

	This edition	**K-L**
703	DA. Scio quid coner; hoc ego	(PA.) scio quid conere.
		DA. hoc ego
705	Dies hic mi	dies mi
712	ad me ut uenias	ad me venias
723	malitia	memoria
728	iurato	iurandum
785	Em	hem
817	DA. O optume hospes!	MY. o optume hospes! pol
	MY. Pol	
825	lubes	lubet
850	Modo ĭntroiui	modŏ introii
857	ueritas	severitas
858	adportas	adportat
864	(SI.) Ego iam	DR. ego iam
931	audiuere	tum audire
936	Postilla hinc	† postilla nunc
940	scrupulus mi etiam unus	mi unus scrupulus etiam
941	istud	istuc
944	egomet	ego
945	Pasibula? Ipsast	ipsa east
957–58	me forsitan / putet non	fors me putet / non
962	quoi nunc	nunc quoi
971	ille	illic
972	uoluit uigilans	vigilans voluit
973	es ... di?	est ... di.
979	auferant eam	auferant. em
980	PA. Ne exspectetis	(DA.) ne exspecteti'
981	(PA.) Plaudite!	CANTOR. plaudite!
989a	copiam hanc	copia ac
992a	†id quod abs te expecto†	id <quod volo> / quod <abs te expecto et summo studio> abs te expeto

ABBREVIATIONS AND BIBLIOGRAPHY

The Bibliography contains items mentioned more than once in the Introduction and/or Commentary, where they are referred to simply by the name of the author, with date where necessary to distinguish different publications by the same author. If an item is mentioned only once, full details are given in the text.

* indicates an edition. Editions of authors other than Terence are normally referred to in the Commentary by the name of the editor or commentator without full publication details.

GL   Gildersleeve, B. W. and Lodge, G., *Latin Grammar* (3rd edn, London, 1895): numbers refer to sections, not pages.

GS   Gomme, A. W. and Sandbach, F. H., *Menander: A Commentary* (Oxford, 1973)

K-A   Kassel, R. and Austin, C. (eds), *Poetae Comici Graeci* (Berlin and New York, 1983–2001), also referred to as PCG

*K-L   Kauer, R. and Lindsay, W. M., *P. Terenti Afri Comoediae* (2nd edn, Oxford, with additions to the critical apparatus by O. Skutsch, 1958)

OLD   Glare, P. G. W. (ed.), *Oxford Latin Dictionary* (Oxford, 1968–82)

PCG   See K-A

TLL   *Thesaurus Linguae Latinae* (Leipzig, 1900–)

Adams, J. N. (1984) 'Female Speech in Latin Comedy', *Antichthon* 18, 43–77.

Anderson, W. S. (2003–2004) 'Terence and the Roman Rhetorical Use of the *Andria*', *LICS* 3.2, 1–9.

Anderson, W. S. (2004) 'The Invention of Sosia for Terence's First Comedy, the *Andria*', *Ramus* 33, 10–19.

*Arnott, W. G. (ed.) (1996) *Menander*, vol. II (Loeb Classical Library, Cambridge, Mass. and London).

Augoustakis, A. and Traill, A. (eds) (2013) *A Companion to Terence* (Malden, MA, Oxford, and Chichester).

Austin, J. C. (1921) *The Significant Name in Terence* (Urbana, IL).

Bain, D. (1977) *Actors and Audience: A Study of Asides and Related Conventions in Greek Drama* (Oxford).

Barrios-Lech, P. (2016) *Linguistic Interaction in Roman Comedy* (Cambridge).

*Barsby, J. (ed. and comm.) (1999) *Terence, Eunuchus* (Cambridge).

*Barsby, J. (ed.) (2001) *Terence*, vol. I (*The Woman of Andros, The Self-Tormentor, The Eunuch*: Loeb Classical Library, Cambridge, Mass. and London).

Beare, W. (1964) *The Roman Stage* (3rd edn, London).

Bennett, C. E. (1910, 1914) *Syntax of Early Latin* (2 vols, Boston).

*Bentley, R. (ed.) (1726) *Publii Terentii Afri Comoediae* (Cambridge).

*Bothe, F. H. (ed.) (1806) *Publi Terenti Afri Comoediae* (Berlin).

Brown, P. G. McC. (2012) 'Terence, *Andria* 236–300, and the Helpfulness of Donatus' Commentary', in R. López Gregoris (ed.), *Estudios sobre teatro romano: el mundo de los sentimientos y su expresión* (Zaragoza), 23–45.

Brown, P. G. McC. (2014) 'Interpretations and Adaptations of Terence's *Andria*, from the Tenth to the Twentieth Century', in Papaioannou, 241–66.

Bruder, H. W. (1970) *Bedeutung und Funktion des Verswechsels bei Terenz* (Zurich).

Büchner, K. (1974) *Das Theater des Terenz* (Heidelberg).

Compagno, B. (2002) 'L'*Andria* e la parodia della *fabula*', *Pan* 20, 49–55.

Danese, R. M. (1990) 'Revisione del PVindob L 103 (Terenzio), *SCO* 39, 133–57.

de Melo, W. D. C. (2007) *The Early Latin Verb System: Archaic Forms in Plautus, Terence, and Beyond* (Oxford).

Denzler, B. (1968) *Der Monolog bei Terenz* (Zurich).

Duckworth, G. E. (1952) *The Nature of Roman Comedy* (Princeton, repr. Bristol, 1994).

*Dziatzko, C. (ed.) (1884) *P. Terenti Afri Comoediae* (Leipzig).

Fabre, G. (1981) *Libertus: recherches sur les rapports patron-affranchi à la fin de la République romaine* (Rome).

*Faernus, G. (ed.) (1565) *Terentii Comoediae* (Florence).

Fantham, E. (1972) *Comparative Studies in Republican Latin Imagery* (Toronto).

*Fleckeisen, A. (ed.) (1857, 1898) *P. Terenti Afri Comoediae* (edns 1 and 2, Leipzig).

Fontaine, M. and Scafuro, A. C. (eds) (2014) *The Oxford Handbook of Greek and Roman Comedy* (Oxford).

Fraenkel, E. (2007) *Plautine Elements in Plautus*, translated by T. Drevikovsky and F. Muecke (Oxford), a translation of *Plautinisches im Plautus* (Berlin, 1922).

Germany, R. (2013) '*Andria*', in Augoustakis and Traill, 225–42.

Gilula, D. (1991) 'Plots are not Stories: the So-called "Duality Method" of Terence', in H. Scolnicov and P. Holland (eds), *Reading Plays: Interpretation and Reception* (Cambridge), 81–93.

Glücklich, H.-J. (1966) *Aussparung und Antithese. Studien zur terenzischen Komödie* (Heidelberg).

Goldberg, S. M. (1981–82) 'The Dramatic Balance of Terence's *Andria*', *Class. et Med.* 33, 135–43.

Goldberg, S. M. (1986) *Understanding Terence* (Princeton).

*Goldberg, S. M. (ed. and comm.) (2013) *Terence, Hecyra* (Cambridge).

*Guyet, F. (1657) *Francisci Guieti in Comoedias VI. Terentii Commentarii*, included in *Publii Terentii Carthaginiensis Afri Vi. Comoediae cum Annotationibus Jo. Henrici Boecleri* (Strasbourg).

Haffter, H. (1934) *Untersuchungen zur altlateinischen Dichtersprache* (Berlin).

Haffter, H. (1953) 'Terenz und seine künstlerische Eigenart', *MH* 10, 1–20, 73–102 (repr. as a book, Darmstadt, 1967).

Handley, E. W. (1970) 'The Conventions of the Comic Stage and their Exploitation by Menander', in E. G. Turner (ed.), *Ménandre* (Geneva), 1–42.

Hersch, K. K. (2010) *The Roman Wedding: Ritual and Meaning in Antiquity* (Cambridge).

Hunter, R. L. (1985) *The New Comedy of Greece and Rome* (Cambridge).

Kamen, D. (2013) *Status in Classical Athens* (Princeton and Oxford).

Karakasis, E. (2005) *Terence and the Language of Roman Comedy* (Cambridge).

*Kauer, R (ed. and comm.) (1930) *P. Terentius Afer, Andria* (Bielefeld and Leipzig).

Knorr, O. (2007) 'Metatheatrical Humor in the Comedies of Terence', in Kruschwitz, Ehlers, and Felgentreu, 167–74.

Kruschwitz, P. (2004) *Terenz* (Hildesheim, Zurich, New York).

Kruschwitz, P. (2010) 'Alles nur ein Missverständnis: zu Erklärung und gedanklicher Struktur von Terenz, *Andria* 954–956', *Hermes* 138.3, 370–76.

Kruschwitz, P., Ehlers, W.-W., and Felgentreu, F. (eds) (2007) *Terentius Poeta* (Munich).

Lefèvre, E. (2008) *Terenz' und Menanders* Andria (Munich).

Leigh, M. (2004) *Comedy and the Rise of Rome* (Oxford).

Lindsay, W. M. (1922) *Early Latin Verse* (Oxford).

Lindsay, W. M. (1925) 'Notes on the Text of Terence', *CQ* 19.1, 28–36.

Lowe, J. C. B. (1997) 'Terence's Four-Speaker Scenes', *Phoenix* 51.2, 152–69.

Luck, G. (1964) *Über einige Interjektionen der lateinischen Umgangssprache* (Heidelberg).

Ludwig, W. (1968) 'The Originality of Terence and his Greek Models', *GRBS* 9, 169–82.

MacDowell, D. M. (1978) *The Law in Classical Athens* (London).

Maltby, R. (1979) 'Linguistic Characterization of Old Men in Terence', *CP* 74, 136–47.

Maltby, R. (1985) 'The Distribution of Greek Loan-words in Terence', *CQ* 35, 110–23.

*Maltby, R. (ed., transl., and comm.) (2012) *Terence, Phormio* (Aris & Phillips).

*Marouzeau, J. (ed.) (1942–49) *Térence* (3 vols, Paris).

Martin, R. H. (1964) 'Three Notes on Terence's *Andria*', *CR* 14.1, 3–4.

*Martin, R. H. (ed. and comm.) (1976) *Terence, Adelphoe* (Cambridge).

Mazzarino, A. (1947) *Da Menandro a Terenzio. Sulla composizione dell' 'Andria'* (Rome, repr. Messina, 1966).

Moodie, E. K (2009) 'Old Men and Metatheatre in Terence: Terence's Dramatic Competition', *Ramus* 38.2, 145–73.

Moore, T. J. (2012) *Music in Roman Comedy* (Cambridge).

Moore, T. J. (2013) '*Andria*: Terence's Musical Experiment', in T. J. Moore and W. Polleichtner (eds) *Form und Bedeutung im lateinischen Drama / Form and Meaning in Latin Drama* (Trier), 87–114.

Mouritsen, H. (2011) *The Freedman in the Roman World* (Cambridge).

Müller, R. (1997) *Sprechen und Sprache: Dialoglinguistische Studien zu Terenz* (Heidelberg).

Otto, A. (1890) *Die Sprichwörter und sprichwörtlichen Redensarten der Römer* (Leipzig, repr. Hildesheim, 1964).

Palmer, L. R. (1954) *The Latin Language* (London).

Papaioannou, S. (ed.) (2014) *Terence and Interpretation* (Newcastle upon Tyne).

Penwill, J. L. (2004) 'The Unlovely Lover of Terence's Hecyra', *Ramus* 33, 130–49.

Perutelli, A. (2013) *Studi sul teatro latino* (Pisa).

Pezzini, G. (2015) *Terence and the Verb 'To Be' in Latin* (Oxford).

Pinkster, H. (2015) *The Oxford Latin Syntax*, vol. I (Oxford).

*Posani, M. R. (ed.) (1990) *Terenzio, Andria* (Bologna).

Questa, C (2007) *La Metrica di Plauto e di Terenzio* (Urbino).

Rambelli, G. (1936) 'Due scene dell'"Andria"', *SIFC* 13, 130–60.

Richlin, A. (2017) *Slave Theater in the Roman Republic: Plautus and Popular Comedy* (Cambridge).

Ritschl, F. (1866–79) *Opuscula Philologica* (5 vols, Leipzig, repr. Hildesheim and New York, 1978).

Scafuro, A. C. (1997) *The Forensic Stage: Settling Disputes in Graeco-Roman New Comedy* (Cambridge).

Sharrock, A. (2009) *Reading Roman Comedy: Poetics and Playfulness in Plautus and Terence* (Cambridge).

Sherberg, B. (1995) *Das Vater-Sohn-Verhältnis in der griechischen und römischen Komödie* (Tübingen).

*Shipp, G. P. (comm.) (1960) *P. Terenti Afri Andria* (2nd edn, Oxford, repr. Bristol Classical Press, 2002).

Skutsch, O. (1957) 'Der zweite Schluss der Andria', *Rh. Mus.* 100.1, 53–68.

*Spengel, A. (ed. and comm.) (1888) *Die Komödien des P. Terentius, I: Andria* (2nd edn, Berlin).

*Thierfelder, A. (ed.) (1960) *P. Terentius Afer, Andria* (Heidelberg).

Treggiari, S. (1969) *Roman Freedmen during the Late Republic* (Oxford, repr. 2000).

Treggiari, S. (1991) *Roman Marriage* (Oxford).

*Umpfenbach, F. (ed.) (1870) *P. Terenti Comoediae* (Berlin).

Vérilhac, A.-M. and Vial, C. (1998) *Le mariage grec du VIe siècle av. J.-C. à l'époque d'Auguste* (Athens).

Victor, B. (1989) 'The *alter exitus Andriae*', *Latomus* 48, 63–74.

Victor, B. (1993) 'Remarks on the *Andria* of Terence', *HSCP* 95, 273–79.

Victor, B. (1996) 'Four Passages in the *Andria* of Terence', *EMC/Classica Views* n.s. 15, 371–77.

Victor, B. (1999a) '*Numne*', *EMC/Classical Views* n.s. 18, 79–82.

Victor, B. (1999b) 'Further Remarks on the *Andria* of Terence' *HSCP* 99, 269–73.

Victor, B. (2007) 'New Manuscript Sources of the Terence-Text', in Kruschwitz, Ehlers, and Felgentreu, 1–14.

Victor, B. (2010) 'Terence's Greek: Observations on Certain Cruxes in his Comedies', *BICS* 53.2, 45–54.

Victor, B. (2015) 'In Terentium', *CP* 110.4, 301–12.

Wackernagel, J. (2009) *Lectures on Syntax with Special Reference to Greek, Latin, and Germanic*, edited with notes and bibliography by D. Langslow (Oxford), a translation of *Vorlesungen über Syntax* (2nd edn, 2 vols, Basel, 1926, 1928).

Wright, J. (1974) *Dancing in Chains: The Stylistic Unity of the Comoedia Palliata* (Rome).

Zelnick-Abramovitz, R. (2005) *Not Wholly Free: the Concept of Manumission and the Status of Manumitted Slaves in the Ancient Greek World* (Leiden and Boston).

TERENCE

THE GIRL FROM ANDROS
[ANDRIA]

First performed in Rome at the Megalesian Games, April 166 BCE

PERSONAE

SIMO senex
SOSIA libertus
DAVOS seruos
MYSIS ancilla
PAMPHILUS adulescens
CHARINUS adulescens
BYRRIA seruos
LESBIA obstetrix
(GLYCERIUM uirgo)
CHREMES senex
CRITO senex
DROMO seruos

C. SULPICI APOLLINARIS PERIOCHA

Sorórem fálso créditám meretrículaé   *ia.6*
genere Ándriaé, Glycérium, uítiat Pámphilús,
grauidáque fácta dát fidem úxorém sibí
fore hánc. Năm áliam páter eí despónderát,
gnatám Chremétis, átque ut amórem cómperít   5
simulát futúras núptiás, cupiéns suús
quid habéret ánimi fíliús cognósceré.
Dauí suásu nón repúgnat Pámphilús.
Sed éx Glycério nátum ut uídit púerulúm
Chremés recúsat núptiás, generum ábdicát.   10
Mox fíliám Glycérium inspérato ádgnitám
hanc Pámphilo, áliam dát Charíno cóniugém.

CHARACTERS (in order of appearance)

SIMO, an Athenian male citizen
SOSIA, an ex-slave (male) in Simo's household
DAVOS, a male slave in Simo's household
MYSIS, a female slave in Glycerium's household
PAMPHILUS, son of Simo, in love with Glycerium
CHARINUS, a young Athenian male citizen, in love with Philumena
BYRRIA, male slave of Charinus
LESBIA, a midwife
CHREMES, an Athenian citizen, father of Philumena
CRITO, a male citizen of Andros, cousin of Chrysis
DROMO, a male slave in Simo's household
Further (non-speaking) slaves from Simo's household at the beginning of the opening scene

GLYCERIUM's voice is heard from her house at 473. She is a teenage girl who was shipwrecked on Andros as a small child and brought up in the family of Chrysis (who has died before the play opens). She now lives next door to Simo.

PHILUMENA (daughter of Chremes) does not appear, nor does ARCHYLIS, a female slave in Glycerium's household who is addressed at 228 and 481.

PLOT SUMMARY BY GAIUS SULPICIUS APOLLINARIS

Glycerium, wrongly believed to be the sister of a prostitute who was by birth from Andros, is seduced by Pamphilus; when she becomes pregnant he promises that she will become his wife. Now his father had engaged another girl to marry him, the daughter of Chremes, and when he discovers his affair **[5]** he pretends that the wedding is going ahead, since he wishes to ascertain what his son has in mind. On Davos' advice Pamphilus does not resist. But when Chremes has seen the baby born to Glycerium he refuses to allow the wedding and rejects Pamphilus as his son-in-law **[10]**. In due course, when Glycerium has unexpectedly been recognized as his daughter, he gives her to Pamphilus as his wife, giving his other daughter to Charinus.

PROLOGUS

Poéta quóm primum ánimum ad scríbendum ádpulít,   *ia.6*
id síbi negóti crédidít solúm darí,
populo út placérent quás fecísset fábulás.
Verum áliter éueníre múlto intéllegít;
nam in prólogís scribúndis óperam abútitúr,   5
non qui árguméntum nárret séd qui máleuolí
ueterís poétae máledictís respóndeát.
Nunc quám rem uítio dént, quaeso, ánimum adténdité.
Menánder fécit Ándriam ét Perínthiám.
Qui utrámuis récte nórit ámbas nóuerít: 10
non íta sunt díssimili árguménto, séd tamén
dissímili orátióne súnt factae ác stiló.
Quae cónuenére in Ándriam éx Perínthiá
fatétur tránstulísse atque úsum pró suís.
Id ĭstí uitúperant fáctum atque ín eo dísputánt   15
contáminári nón decére fábulás.
Faciúntne intéllegéndo ut níl intéllegánt?
Qui quom húnc accúsant, Naéuiúm, Plautum, Énniúm
accúsant, quós hic nóster aúctorés habét,
quorum aémulári exóptat néglegéntiám   20
potiús quam istórum obscúram díligéntiám.
Dehinc út quiéscant pórro móneo et désinánt
maledíceré, malefácta né noscánt suá.
Fauéte, adéste aequo ánimo et rém cognóscité,
ut pérnoscátis écquid speī sit rélicuóm,   25
posthác quas fáciet de íntegró comoédiás
spectándae an éxigéndae sínt uobís priús.

PROLOGUE
[Spoken by a young actor]

When the author first turned his mind to writing, he thought the only task he was set was that the plays he'd written should please the public. But he's learning that it turns out quite differently: he's expending his energy in writing prologues **[5]** – not to tell the plot, but to reply to abuse from a malicious old author.

And now please pay attention and learn what it is that they criticize. Menander wrote *The Girl from Andros* and *The Girl from Perinthos*. The man who knows either of them properly will know both of them **[10]**: they're not so different in plot, but they *are* written in different words and style. He admits that he has transferred what was suitable into *The Girl from Andros* from *The Girl from Perinthos* and made his own use of this material. They criticize him for doing that, and in doing so they maintain **[15]** that plays should not be 'contaminated'. Is this what they achieve with their learning – that they've learned nothing? When they accuse this man, they're accusing Naevius, Plautus, and Ennius: they are the men our playwright here takes as his authorities, and he'd much rather try to match their carelessness **[20]** than the undistinguished carefulness of his critics. So I advise them to keep quiet in future, and stop abusing him; otherwise, they'll learn about their own abuses!

Give us a favourable hearing: pay attention, be fair, and examine the evidence; find out for certain if he shows any promise for the future **[25]**, and whether you ought to give a showing to the fresh plays he'll write after this, or whether you should drive them off the stage in advance.

SIMO Vos ístaec íntro auférte, abíte. Sósiá,   **[I.i]**   *ia.6*
adés dum: paúcis té uoló. **SOSIA** Dictúm putá:
nempe út curéntur récte haec? **SI.** Ímmo aliúd. **SO.** Quid ést   30
quod tíbi mea árs effícere hoc póssit ámpliús?
SI. Nil ístac ópus est árte ad hánc rem quám paró,   [5]
sed eís quas sémper ín te intéllexí sitás,
fide ét tacitúrnitáte. **SO.** Exspécto quíd uelís.
SI. Ego póstquam te émi, a páruolo út sempér tibí   35
apúd me iústa et clémens fúerit séruitús
scis. Féci ex séruo ut ésses líbertús mihí,   [10]
proptérea quód seruíbas líberálitér.
Quod hábui súmmum prétium pérsoluí tibí.
SO. In mémoria hábeo. **SI.** Haud múto fáctum. **SO.** Gaúdeó   40
si tíbi quid féci aut fácio quód placeát, Simó,
et ĭd grátum fuĩsse aduórsum te hábeo grátiám.   [15]
Sed hŏc míhi moléstumst: nam ístaec cómmemorátió
quasi éxprobrátióst inmémoris béneficí.
Quin tu úno uérbo díc quid ést quod mé uelís.   45
SI. Ita fáciam. Hoc prímum in hác re praédicó tibí:
quas crédis ésse has nón sunt uérae núptiaé.   [20]

The play is set at Athens. The scene shows the exterior of three houses fronting a street, those of CHARINUS, *of* SIMO, *and of* GLYCERIUM *(from left to right respectively, as seen from the audience); in front of the central house stands an altar, with foliage spread on top of it. To the audience's left the street leads to the main square (the forum); to the right it leads to the harbour (from which* CRITO *comes at 796) and to the houses of* LESBIA *and* CHREMES.

[SIMO *and* SOSIA *enter from the left, accompanied by some slaves from* SIMO'*s household carrying the provisions which they have just bought.*]

SIMO   [*to his slaves*] You take that stuff indoors: off you go! [*The slaves go into his house;* SIMO *turns to* SOSIA.] Sosia, come here, will you? I want a few words with you.

SOSIA   Take it as said; you mean you want these things to be properly seen to.

SIMO   No, it's something else.

SOSIA   What is there [30] that my skill could achieve for you beyond that?

SIMO   That's not the skill I need for what I'm planning now; I need the ones I've always known you to possess, loyalty and discretion.

SOSIA   I'm all ears: what do you want?

SIMO   Ever since I bought you, from your childhood onwards, you know [35] how fair and mild your slavery in my household always was. I turned you from my slave into my freedman, because in your slavery you behaved like a free man; I gave you the greatest reward it was in my power to give.

SOSIA   I never forget it.

SIMO   And I don't regret doing it. [*Pause.*]

SOSIA   I'm glad [40] if I've done anything or do anything that you like, Simo; and I'm pleased that it's given you pleasure. But this is what troubles me: your reminding me looks like a reproach for not remembering your kindness. Why don't you tell me in one word what it is you want of me [45]?

SIMO   I'll do so – and to start off with, the first thing I'll tell you about the matter is this: you think this wedding is really going to happen; but it isn't.

SO. Quor símulas ígitur? **SI.** Rem ómnem a príncipio aúdiés:
eō pácto et gnáti uítam et cónsiliúm meúm
cognósces ét quid fácere in hác re té uelím.   50
Nam is póstquam excéssit éx ephébis, Sósia, ét
libérius uíuendi érăt potéstas, (nam ánteá   [25]
qui scíre pósses aút ingénium nósceré,
dum aetás, metús, magíster próhibebánt? **SO.** Itást.)
SI. quod plérique ómnes fáciunt ádulescéntulí,   55
ut ánimum ad áliquod stúdium adiúngant, aút equós
alere aút canés ad uénandum aút ad phílosophós,   [30]
horum ílle níl egrégie praéter céterá
studébat ét tamen ómnia haéc mediócritér.
Gaudébam. **SO.** Nón iniúriá: nam id árbitrór   60
adpríme in uíta esse útile, út nequíd nimís.
SI. Sic uíta erát: facile ómnis pérferre ác patí;   [35]
cum quíbus erát quomque úna eīs sése déderé,
eōrum óbsequí studiís, aduórsus néminí,
numquám praepónens se íllis – íta ŭt facíllumé   65
sine īnuídia laúdem inuénias ét amicós parés.
SO. Sapiénter uítam instítuit: námque hoc témporé   [40]
obséquium amícos, uéritás odiúm parít.
SI. Intérea múlier quaédam abhínc triénniúm
ex Ándro cómmigráuit húc uicíniaé,   70
inópia et cógnatórum néglegéntiá
coácta, egrégia fórma atque aétate íntegrá.   [45]
SO. Eī, uéreor néquid Ándria ádportét malí!
SI. Primo haéc pudíce uítam párce ac dúritér
agébat, lána ac téla uíctum quaéritáns.   75
Sed póstquam amáns accéssit prétium póllicéns
unús et item álter, íta ut ingéniumst ómniúm   [50]
hominum áb labóre prócliue ád lubídiném,
accépit cóndiciónem, dehīnc quaestum óccipít.
Qui tum íllam amábant fórte, ita út fit, fíliúm   80
perdúxere ílluc, sécum ut úna essét, meúm.
Egomét contínuo mécum: "Cérte cáptus ést: [55]
habet". Óbseruábam máne illórum séruolós
ueniéntis aút abeúntis; rógitabam: "Heús, puér,

SOSIA   Then why are you pretending?

SIMO   I'll tell you the whole story from the beginning; that way you'll find out what my son's been up to, what I have in mind, and what I want you to do in all this **[50]**.

Well then, when he'd finished his military service, Sosia, and was able to live more as his own master – after all, how could you know his character before that, or get to know what he was like, when he was restrained by his age, and fear, and his teacher? –

SOSIA   Quite.

SIMO   – he took an interest in what pretty well all young lads do **[55]**, I mean taking up some hobby like keeping horses or hunting-dogs or studying philosophy. He didn't take up any of these more than the others especially, but all of them in moderation. I was pleased.

SOSIA   And rightly so; I think **[60]** 'nothing in excess' is a particularly useful rule in life.

SIMO   This is what he was like: he was ready to tolerate everyone and put up with them; he gave himself over to whoever he was with, and devoted himself to their hobbies; he never argued with anyone and never put himself ahead of them. That's the easiest way **[65]** to win praise and find friends without making enemies.

SOSIA   [*sardonically*] He organized his life sensibly: these days you win friends by being obsequious, and enemies by being frank!

SIMO   Well, three years ago a woman from Andros moved into our neighbourhood here **[70]**; she'd been forced to leave home by poverty, and because her relatives had failed to look after her. She was young and extremely beautiful.

SOSIA   Oh dear, I'm afraid the Andrian woman's going to bring some trouble!

SIMO   To start with she lived a respectable life, frugal and hard; she earned her living by weaving wool **[75]**. But then lovers approached her, one after another, offering money. It's human nature to prefer pleasure to work: she accepted their terms, and after that she began in the trade. One day her lovers happened to take my son **[80]** along there to keep them company, as often happens. Immediately I said to myself 'He's caught for sure, he's had it!' Each morning I'd watch their slave-boys entering or leaving, and I'd ask them 'Hey! Boy! Tell me, please, who had Chrysis yesterday?' – That

dic sódes, quís heri Chrýsidem hábuit?" Nam Ándriaé   85
illi íd erat nómen. **SO.** Téneo. **SI.** Phaédrum aut Clíniám
dicébant aút Nicératúm; nam hi trés tum eám   [60]
amábant. "Ého, quid Pámphilús?" "Quid? Sýmbolám
dedít, cenáuit." Gaúdebam. Ítem alió dié
quaerébam: cómperiébam níl ad Pámphilúm   90
quicquam áttinére. Enĭmuéro spéctatúm satís
putábam et mágnum exémplum cóntinéntiaé.   [65]
Nam quí cum ingéniis cónflictátur eĭūsmodí
neque cómmouétur ánimus ín ea ré tamén,
sciăs pósse habére iam ípsum suaé uitaé modúm.   95
Quom id míhi placébat tum úno ore ómnes ómniá
bona dícere ét laudáre fórtunás meás,   [70]
qui gnátum habérem táli ingénio praéditúm.
Quid uérbis ópus est? Hác fama ínpulsús Chremés
ultro ád me uénit, únicám gnatám suám   100
cum dóte súmma fílio úxorem út darét.
Placuít: despóndi; hic núptiís dictúst diés.   [75]
SO. Quid óbstat quór non uérae fíant? **SI.** Aúdiés.
Ferme ín diébus paúcis quíbus haec ácta súnt
Chrysís uicína haec móritur. **SO.** Ó factúm bené!   105
Beásti: eī, métui a Chrýside! **SI.** Íbi tum fíliús
cum illís qui amábant Chrýsidem úna aderát frequéns,   [80]
curábat úna fúnus; trístis ínterím,
nonnúmquam cónlacrumábat. Plácuit tum íd mihí.
Sic cógitábam: "Hic páruae cónsuetúdinís   110
causa húius mórtem tám fert fámiliáritér:
quid si ípse amásset? Quíd hĭc mihí faciét patrí?"   [85]
Haec égo putábam esse ómnia húmani íngení
mansuétique ánimi offícia. Quíd multís morór?
Egomét quoque éius caúsa in fúnus pródeó,   115
nil súspicáns etiám mali. **SO.** Hém, quid id ést? **SI.** Sciés.
Ecfértur; ímus. Ínterea ínter múlierés   [90]
quae ibi áderant fórte unam áspicio ádulescéntulám

was the Andrian woman's **[85]** name.

SOSIA   I'm with you.

SIMO   They would say Phaedrus, or Clinia, or Niceratus – those three were her lovers at the time. 'Well, what about Pamphilus?' 'What? He paid his share and had his dinner.' I was pleased. I'd ask again another day; I discovered that Pamphilus **[90]** wasn't involved in anything at all. I thought he'd certainly had enough of a test and was a great model of self-restraint. After all, if a man tangles with characters of that kind and still isn't tempted by the opportunity, you can be sure that he's well able to take control of his own life unaided **[95]**. Not only was I glad about this, but everyone was unanimous in showering congratulations on me and praising my good luck in having a son with such a character. To cut the story short, Chremes was inspired by these reports to seek me out and offer his only daughter **[100]** as my son's bride with a very large dowry. I agreed, and engaged her to marry him; today was fixed for the wedding.

SOSIA   What's the problem? Why won't it take place?

SIMO   I'll tell you. A few days or so after that happened, our neighbour Chrysis died.

SOSIA   That's good news **[105]**! You've cheered me up: I was really afraid of Chrysis!

SIMO   Well, my son was then constantly in the company of her lovers, helping them plan her funeral. He was sad all the time, and occasionally he'd burst into tears. I was glad about that at the time, and I thought to myself 'He didn't know her very well **[110]**, but he reacts to her death as if she'd been a close friend; suppose he'd been in love with her himself! What will he do for me, his own father?' I thought all his behaviour showed him to have a sympathetic character and a gentle heart. But I needn't go on about it; for his sake I went along to the funeral myself **[115]**, still not suspecting anything was wrong.

SOSIA   What? Why do you say that?

SIMO   You'll discover. The corpse was carried out; we set off. As we went along, my eye happened to be caught by one young girl in particular among the women who were present. Her looks were – [*struggles to find the right word*]

formá – **SO.** Boná fortásse? **SI.** – et uóltu, Sósiá,
adeó modésto, adeó uenústo ut níl suprá.   120
Quae quóm mihi lámentári praéter céterás
uisást, et quía erat fórma praéter céterás   [95]
honésta ac líberáli, accédo ad pédisequás,
quae sít rogó. Sorórem esse áiunt Chrýsidís.
Percússit ílico ánimum: "Attát, hoc íllud ést,   125
hinc íllae lácrumae, haec íllast mísericórdiá!"
SO. Quam tímeo quórsum euádas! **SI.** Fúnus ínterím   [100]
procédit: séquimur; ád sepúlcrum uénimús;
in ígnem inpósitast; flétur. Ínterea haéc sorór
quam díxi ad flámmam accéssit ínprudéntiús,   130
satĭs cúm períclo. Ibi tum éxanimátus Pámphilús
bene díssimulátum amórem et célatum índicát: [105]
accúrrit; médiam múlierém compléctitúr;
"Mea Glýcerium," ínquit, "quíd agis? Quór te is pérditúm?"
Tum illa, út consuétum fácile amórem cérnerés,   135
reiécit se ín eum fléns quam fámiliáritér!
SO. Quid aís? **SI.** Redeo índe irátus átque aegré feréns;   [110]
nec sátis ad óbiurgándum caúsae. Dícerét
"Quid féci? Quíd commérui aut péccauí, patér?
Quae sése in ígnem inícere uóluit próhibuí,   140
seruáui." Honésta orátióst. **SO.** Recté putás:
nam si íllum obiúrges uítae qui aúxiliúm tulít,   [115]
quid fácias ílli quí dederít damnum aút malúm?
SI. Venít Chremés postrídie ád me clámitáns:
indígnum fácinus; cómperísse Pámphilúm   145
pro uxóre habére hanc péregrinam. Égo ĭllud séduló
negáre fáctum; ille ínstat fáctum. Déniqué   [120]
ita túm discédo ab íllo ut quí se fíliám
negét datúrum. **SO.** Nón tu ibi gnátum – ? **SI.** Ne haéc quidém
satĭs uéhemens caúsa ad óbiurgándum. **SO.** Quí, cedó?   150
SI. "Tute ípse his rébus fínem praéscriptí, patér."

SOSIA   [*supplying an inadequate one*] Good, perhaps?

SIMO   And her expression, Sosia – so modest! So charming! Incomparable
        [**120**]! Because it struck me that she was mourning more than the
        others, and because she looked more beautiful and noble than the
        others, I went up to the accompanying slave-girls and asked who
        she was. They said she was the sister of Chrysis. It struck me at
        once: 'Yes, that's what it was! [**125**] That's what those tears were
        for; that's why he was so upset!'

SOSIA   I can't bear to think what you're leading up to!

SIMO   Meanwhile the funeral procession continued; we were following
        the corpse. We reached the graveyard; she was put on the pyre;
        everyone wept. Then the sister I've mentioned came rather
        foolishly close to the flames [**130**] and was in some danger.
        Pamphilus was terrified; he'd been keeping his love well hidden
        and concealed, but now he betrayed it: he ran up to her and put his
        arms round her waist. 'Darling Glycerium,' he said, 'What are you
        doing? Why are you going to kill yourself?' And then it became
        obvious that they were established lovers [**135**]: she sank back
        into his arms, weeping – and so intimately!

SOSIA   What a story!

SIMO   I returned home furious and upset. But I didn't have enough
        grounds to criticize him. He'd have said 'What did I do? What
        have I done wrong, dad? What's my crime? She wanted to throw
        herself on the fire; I stopped her [**140**] and saved her life.' It's a
        reasonable answer.

SOSIA   You're right: if you criticize someone who helped save a life, what
        would you do to someone who caused damage or injury?

SIMO   The next day Chremes came to me, shouting that it was a disgrace
        – that he'd discovered Pamphilus [**145**] was treating this foreign
        girl as if she were his wife! I denied it hotly; he insisted it was
        true. Finally, the way things stood when I parted from him was
        that he refused to give his daughter in marriage.

SOSIA   Didn't you *then* give your son a – ?

SIMO   [*interrupting*] No, even that wasn't strong enough grounds to
        criticize him.

SOSIA   Why ever not [**150**]?

SIMO   [*imitating his son*] 'You've laid down the limits of this affair

Prope adést quom aliéno móre uíuendúmst mihí;   [125]
sine núnc meó me uíuere íntereá modó."
SO. Qui igitúr relíctus ést obiúrgandí locús?
SI. Si própter amórem uxórem nólet dúceré.   155
Ea prímum ab íllo animum áduorténda iniúriást.
Et núnc id óperam do út per fálsas núptiás   [130]
uera óbiurgándi caúsa sít, si dénegét;
simúl scelerátus Dáuos síquid cónsilí
habet, út consúmat núnc quom níl obsínt dolí;   160
quem ego crédo mánibus pédibusque óbnixe ómniá
factúrum, mágis id ádeo míhi ut incómmodét   [135]
quam ut óbsequátur gnáto. **SO.** Quáproptér? **SI.** Rogás?
Mala méns, malus ánimus. Quém quidem égo si sénseró –
sed quíd opust uérbis? Sín euéniat quód uoló,   165
in Pámphilo út nil sít moraé, restát Chremés,
quoi mi éxpurgándus ést; et spéro cónforé.   [140]
Nunc tuõmst offícium has béne ut adsímules núptiás,
pertérrefácias Dáuom, obsérues fíliúm
quid agát, quid cum íllo cónsilí captét. **SO.** Sat ést: 170
curábo. **SI.** Eámus núnciam íntro. **SO.** I praé: sequór.

SIMO Non dúbiumst quín uxórem nólit fíliús: **[I.ii]**   *ia.6*
ita Dáuom módo timére sénsi, ubi núptiás
futúras ésse audíuit. Séd ípse exít forás.
DAVOS Mirábar hóc si síc abíret, ét eri sémper lénitás   175   *ia.8*
uerébar quórsum euáderét.   [5]   *ia.4*
Qui póstquam audíerat nón datum íri fílio úxorém suó,   *ia.8*
númquam quoíquam nóstrum uérbum fécit néque id aegré tulít.   *tro.7*
SI. Át nunc fáciet néque, ut opínor, síne tuó magnó maló!

yourself, dad. It won't be long before I have to live to please someone else; just let me live life my own way in the meantime!'

SOSIA   So what room's left for criticizing him?

SIMO   If he won't marry because of his love **[155]**; that's the first misbehaviour of his that I could punish. And that's what I'm working on now: this fake marriage will provide real grounds for criticism, if he refuses it. And at the same time, if that rascal Davos has any schemes up his sleeve, he can use them up now, when his tricks can't do any harm **[160]**. I believe he'll strain every nerve and do anything he can – and more to be a nuisance to me than to help my son!

SOSIA   Why?

SIMO   Why? An evil mind, an evil heart! If I catch him – but I needn't waste words on that. However, if things turn out as I want **[165]**, and Pamphilus doesn't hold things up, that leaves Chremes: I'll have to get him to forgive Pamphilus – and I'm sure that'll happen. Now it's your job to make a good pretence of this wedding, terrify Davos, and keep an eye on what my son's up to and what plans he's hatching with him.

SOSIA   Say no more **[170]**; I'll see to it.

SIMO   Let's go inside now.

SOSIA   You go ahead; I'll follow.

[SIMO *and* SOSIA *go into* SIMO's *house. After a pause, deemed to be long enough for those inside to learn that preparations are on foot for a wedding today,* SIMO *re-enters from the house and addresses the audience.*]

SIMO   There's no doubt that my son doesn't want to marry: I could tell that Davos was frightened just now when he heard that the wedding was going to take place. [*Enter* DAVOS *from* SIMO's *house.*] But he's coming outside himself.

DAVOS   [*to himself, not seeing* SIMO] I *thought* it wasn't likely to come off like that! I was afraid all along what my master's mildness was leading up to **[175]**. – When he'd heard that the girl wasn't going to be married to his son, he never said a word to any of us, and he wasn't upset about it!

SIMO   [*aside*] But he'll say something now – and that'll mean a heavy punishment for you, I should think!

DA. Id uóluit, nós sic nécopinántis dúci fálso gaúdió, 180 *ia.8*
sperántis iam ámotó metu, ínteróscitántis ópprimí, [10]
ně ésset spátium cógitándi ad dísturbándas núptiás:
astúte! **SI.** Cárnuféx quae lóquitur? **DA.** Érus est néque prouíderám!
SI. Daue! **DA.** Hém, quid ést? **SI.** Eho dum ád me. **DA.** Quíd hĭc uolt?
 SI. Quíd ais? **DA.** Quá de ré? **SI.** Rogás?
Meum gnátum rúmor ést amáre. **DA.** Id pópulus cúrat scílicét. 185
SI. Hoccín agis án non? **DA.** Égo uero ístuc.
 SI. Séd nunc éa me exquíreré [15]
iníqui pátris est. Nám quod ánteh̄ac fécit níl ad me áttinét.
Dum témpus ád eam rém tulít, siui ánimum ut éxplerét suóm;
nunc híc diés aliám uitam ádfert, álios móres póstulát.
Dehinc póstuló siue aéquomst te óro, Dáue, ut rédeat iam ín uiám. 190
Hoc quíd sit? Ómnes quī amant gráuiter síbi dari úxorém ferúnt. [20]
DA. Ita áiunt. **SI.** Túm siquís magístrum cépit ád eam rem ínprobúm,
ipsum ánimum aegrótum ad déteriórem pártem plérumque ádplicát.
DA. Non hércle intéllegó. **SI.** Non? Hém? **DA.** Non: Dáuos súm,
 non Oédipús.
SI. Nempe érgo apérte uís quae réstant mé loquí? **DA.** Sané quidém. 195
SI. Si sénsero hódie quícquam in hís te núptiís [25] *ia.6*
falláciaé conári quó fiánt minús,
aut uélle in eá re osténdi quám sis cállidús,

DAVOS   What he wanted was for us to be led on unawares, just as we were [180], living in a fool's paradise, full of hope and free from fear; he wanted to catch us half-asleep, so that we'd have no time to think about how to prevent the wedding. Clever!

SIMO   [*still aside*] What's the villain saying?

DAVOS   [*hearing* SIMO] It's the master! I hadn't spotted him.

SIMO   [*calling to him*] Davos!

DAVOS   Yes, what is it?

SIMO   Over this way, will you?

DAVOS   [*to himself, as he obeys*] What does he want?

SIMO   Tell me, –

DAVOS   What about?

SIMO   Listen: people say my son's having an affair.

DAVOS   [*sarcastically*] That's a matter of public interest, I suppose [185].

SIMO   Are you concentrating or not?

DAVOS   I certainly am.

SIMO   Well, for me to look into that now is to behave like an unreasonable father. What he's done up till now is no concern of mine; while the time was right for that sort of thing, I let him satisfy his desires. But today's the day that ushers in a different lifestyle and requires different behaviour. So I require you, or, if it's proper to do so, I beg you, Davos, to make him come back now to the straight and narrow [190]. You know what I mean: boys who are having an affair always take it hard when they're made to marry.

DAVOS   So they say.

SIMO   And if anyone acquires a wicked teacher for that sort of thing, he starts with a mind that's sick but generally makes it take a turn for the worse.

DAVOS   I don't understand a word.

SIMO   Don't you? Really?

DAVOS   No; I'm Davos, not Oedipus.

SIMO   So you want me to say the rest explicitly, then?

DAVOS   Yes please [195].

SIMO   If I find out that you're trying any trickery today over this wedding, to stop it happening, or that you're wanting it to be shown how clever you are in that regard, I'll flog you with the whips and send

uerbéribus caésum te ín pistrínum, Dáue, dédam usque ád necém, *ia.8*
ea̅ lége atque ómine út, si te índe exémerim, égo pro té molám. 200
Quid, hŏc íntelléxtin? Án nondum étiam ne hóc quidem?
DA. Ímmo cállidé: [30]
ita apérte ipsám rem módo locútu's, níl circum ítione úsus és.
SI. Ubiuís facílius pássu' sím quam in hác re mé delúdiér.
DA. Bona uérba, quaéso! **SI.** Inrídes? Níl me fállis. Séd dicó tibí:
ne témere fácias. Néque tu haud díces tíbi non praédictúm. Caué! 205
DA. Enĭmuéro, Dáue, níl locíst segnítiae néque socórdiaé, **[I.iii]**
quantum íntelléxi módo senís senténtiám de núptiís.
[Quae sí non ástu próuidéntur, me aút erúm pessúm dabúnt.]
Nec quíd agam cértumst, Pámphilúmne adiútem an aúscultém serní.
Si illúm relínquo, eius uítae tímeo; sín opítulor, huĩus minás, 210 [5]
quoi uérba dáre diffícilest: prímum iám de amóre hoc cómperít;
me inténsus séruat né quam fáciam in núptiís falláciám.
Si sénserít, perií: si lúbitum fúerit, caúsam céperít
quo iúre quáque iniúriá praecípitem in pístrinúm dabít.
Ad haéc mala hóc mi accédit étiam: haec Ándriá, 215 [10] *ia.6*
si ista úxor síue amícast, gráuida e Pámphilóst.
Audíreque eõrumst óperae prétium audáciám
(nam incéptióst améntium, haúd amántiúm):
quidquíd peperísset décreuérunt tólleré.
Et fíngunt quándam intér se núnc falláciám, 220 [15]
ciuem Átticam ésse hanc: "fúit olim hínc quidám senéx
mercátor; náuem is frégit ápud Andrum ínsulám;
is óbiit mórtem"; ibi tum hánc eiéctam Chrýsidís
patrém recépisse órbam páruam. Fábulaé!
Mĩquidem hércle nón fit uéri símile, atque ípsis
　　　　　cómmentúm placét. 225 [20] *ia.8*
Sed Mýsis áb ea egréditur. Át ego hinc me ád forum út *ia.6*
conuéniam Pámphilúm, ne de hác re páter inprúdentem ópprimát. *ia.8*

you to work at the mill till you're dead, Davos! And these are your terms and prospects: if ever I release you from it, I'll do the grinding for you **[200]**! All right? Have you understood now? Or is even that not clear yet?

DAVOS   Yes, that's brilliant! You've put it quite explicitly now; you said it straight; you didn't beat about the bush.

SIMO   I wouldn't mind being cheated over anything else as much as this.

DAVOS   [*ironically*] Heaven forbid!

SIMO   Are you laughing at me? I can tell! But listen here: don't do anything silly! You won't be able to say you weren't warned. Watch out **[205]**! [*Exit left, leaving* DAVOS *alone on stage.*]

DAVOS   Well, Davos, there's certainly no room for sluggishness or sloth, as far as I understood the old man's views on the wedding just now. [If we're not smart in plotting against it, it'll be the ruin of me or my master!] I can't decide what to do, whether to help Pamphilus or listen to the old man. If I abandon him, it's his life I fear for; if I assist him, it's this one's threats **[210]** – and it's not easy to put one over on *him*: first of all, he's already found out about this love affair; he's got it in for me, he's watching to see that I don't play any tricks over the wedding. If he catches me out, I've had it: if he feels like it, he'll seize the excuse, right or wrong, to send me straight off to the mill!

And that's not the end of my troubles, because this girl from Andros **[215]**, whether she's his wife or his mistress, is pregnant by Pamphilus. And just listen to what a nerve they've got! It's the project of loonies, not lovers! They've decided to let the baby live, whatever it turns out to be! And now the pair of them are making up some bogus story **[220]** that she's a citizen of Attica: 'Once there was an old man from here in the import-export business; he was shipwrecked off the island of Andros; he lost his life' – and then she was washed ashore and taken in by Chrysis' father as an orphan child! Rubbish! *I* certainly don't find it plausible, but they're pleased with their story **[225]**!

[MYSIS *opens the door of* GLYCERIUM*'s house and starts to come out.*] But Mysis is coming out from her house. I'll be off to the main square to meet Pamphilus, so that his dad doesn't catch him unawares over this. [*Exit left.*]

MYSIS Aúdiui, Árchylís, iamdúdum: Lésbiam ádducí iubés. **[I.iv]** *tro.7*
    sáne pól ílla témuléntast múlier ét temeráriá,
néc satĭs dígna quoí commíttas prímo pártu múlierém. 230
Támen eam ádducam? Ínportúnitátem spéctate ániculaé
quía compótrix éius ést. Di, dáte facúltatem, óbsecró, [5]
huíc pariúndi atque ílli in áliis pótius péccandí locúm.
Sed quídnam Pámphilum éxanimátum uídeo? Véreor quíd siét. *ia.8*
Oppériar, út sciám num quíd nam haec túrbae trístitia ádferát. 235
PAMPHILUS Hoccínĕst humánum fáctu aut ínceptu?
    Hóccin ófficiúm patrís? **[I.v]**
MY. Quíd íllud ést? **PA.** Pro dĕūm fidém, quid ĕst si haéc non
    cóntuméliást? *tro.7(?)*
Uxórem décrerát dare sése mi hódie: nónne opórtuít *ia.8*
praescísse me ánte? Nónne príŭs commúnicátum opórtuít?
MY. Miserám me, quód uerbum aúdió? 240 [5] *ia.4*
PA. Quíd? Chremés, qui dénegárat sé commíssurúm mihí *tro.7*
gnátam sŭam úxorem, íd mutáuit quía me inmútatúm uidét?
Itane óbstináte operám dat út me a Glýcerió miserum ábstrahát? *ia.8*
Quod sí fit péreo fúnditús. *ia.4*
Ádeone hóminem esse ínuenústum aut ínfelícem quémquam
    ut égo sum! 245 [10] *tro.8*
Pró deum átque hominúm fidém! *tro.4^*
Núllon égo Chremétis pácto adfínitátem effúgere pótero? *tro.8*
Quót modís contémptus, sprétus! Fácta, tránsacta ómnia! Ém, *tro.7*
répudiátus répetor! Quam ób rem? Nísi si id ést quod súspicór:
áliquid mónstri alúnt; ea quóniam némini óbtrudí potést, 250 [15]
ítur ád me! **MY.** Orátio haéc me míseram exánimauít metú!
PA. Nam quíd ego dícam dé patre? Áh, *ia.4*
tantámne rém tam néglegénter ágere! Praéteriéns modó *ia.8*
mi ápŭd forum "Úxor tíbi ducéndast, Pámphile, hódie"
    inquít: "pará, *tro.7(?)*
ábĭ domum!" Íd mihi uísust dícere: "ábĭ cito ác suspénde té!" 255 [20]

MYSIS   [*shouting back over her shoulder into the house as the door closes behind her*] I heard you long ago, Archylis: you want me to fetch Lesbia! [*to the audience*] She's a real boozer, that woman, and careless; it's just not right to put her in charge of a woman for her first delivery **[230]**! Have I got to fetch her all the same? Look what the silly old woman's inflicting on her – just because they drink together! [*looking up to the sky*] Gods, I beg you, give the girl an easy birth, and let that woman's incompetence be kept for others instead!

      [*Sees* PAMPHILUS *entering in a hurry from the left.*] But I can see Pamphilus! Why on earth is he in such a state? I dread to think what's up; I'll wait, to find out if his unhappiness is going to bring any trouble **[235]**. [*Stands back by the doorway.*]

PAMPHILUS   [*to himself, not seeing* MYSIS] Is this what a human being would do or start on? Is this the way for a father to behave?

MYSIS   [*aside*] What's he talking about?

PAMPH.   Ye gods in heaven, what's this if it isn't an outrage? He'd decided to make me marry today: shouldn't I have known about it in advance? Shouldn't I have been told about it beforehand?

MYSIS   [*aside*] Oh dear, what's this I hear him saying **[240]**?

PAMPH.   I mean to say, Chremes had refused to let his daughter marry me; has he changed his mind because he can see that I haven't changed mine?! Is he so determined to tear me away from Glycerium and wreck my happiness? If that happens, I've utterly had it! To think that any lover could be as unlucky or as unfortunate as I am **[245]**! Gods in heaven and men on earth! Is there no way for me to avoid having Chremes as my father-in-law? How can they treat me with such scorn and contempt? It's all signed and sealed! Look, I'm a reject recalled! Why? – unless what I suspect is true, and they're keeping some kind of monster who can't be forced on to anyone else; that's why **[250]** they're moving against me!

MYSIS   [*aside*] Oh dear, I'm dead with fright on hearing him speak like this!

PAMPH.   And what can I say about my dad? How *could* he be so casual in dealing with something so important? He was just passing by me in the main square when he said 'You're to marry today, Pamphilus; get ready, off you go home!' From my perspective, what he was saying was 'Off you go quickly and hang yourself

Óbstipuí. Censén me uérbum pótuisse úllum próloqui? Aút   *tro.7*
úllam caúsam, inéptam sáltem, fálsam, iníquam? Obmútuí.
Quód si ego réscissem íd priŭs, quíd facerém siquís nunc mé rogét,
áliquid fácerem ut hóc ne fácerem! Séd nunc quíd primum éxsequár?
Tót me inpédiunt cúrae quaé meum ánimum díuorsaé trahúnt: 260 [25]
amŏr, mísericórdia húius, núptiárum sóllicitátió,   *ia.8*
tum pátrĭs pudór, qui mé tam léni pássus ést animo úsque adhúc
quae meō quomque ánimo lúbitumst fácere. E͞ine égo ut aduórser? E͞i mihí!
Incértumst quíd agam! **MY.** Mísera tímeo "incértum" hoc quórsus áccidát!
Sed núnc peropúst aut húnc cum ipsa aút de illa áliquid
     me áduorsum húnc loquí: 265 [30]
dum in dúbiost ánimus, paúllo mómento húc uel ĭllúc inpéllitúr.
PA. Quis hĭc lóquitur? Mýsis, sálue! **MY.** O sálue, Pámphilé!
     PA. Quid agít? **MY.** Rogás?
Labórat é dolóre atque éx hoc mísera sóllicitást, diém
quia ólim in húnc sunt cónstitútae núptiaé; tum autem hóc timét,
ne déserás se. **PA.** Hem, egone ístuc cónarí queám?   270 [35]   *ia.6*
Egŏn própter me íllam décipí miserám sinám,
quae míhi suom ánimum atque ómnem uítam crédidít,
quam ego ánimo egrégie cáram pro úxore hábuerím?
Bene ét pudíce eius dóctum atque éductúm sinám
coáctum egéstate íngenium ínmutáriér?   275 [40]
Non fáciam! **MY.** Haud uérear si ín te sólo sít sitúm;
sed uim út queás ferre. **PA.** Ádeon me ígnauóm putás,
adeón porro íngratum aút inhúmanum aút ferúm,
ut néque me cónsuetúdo néque amor néque pudór
commóueat néque commóneat út seruém fidém?   280 [45]
MY. Unum hóc scio, hánc meritam ésse ut mémor essés suí.
PA. Memor éssem? O Mýsis, Mýsis, étiam núnc mihí
scripta ílla dícta súnt in ánimo Chrýsidís

[255]!' I was stunned. Do you think I could utter a single word? Or a single excuse, even one that was silly or untrue or unreasonable? I was struck dumb. If I'd found out about it sooner, if someone now asked me what I'd be doing – I'd be doing *something* so as not to do this! But *now* what's my first plan of action to be? There are so many worries in my way, pulling my mind in different directions **[260]**: I love her, I feel sorry for her, I'm upset about the wedding – but then there's my respect for my dad; up till now he's been really lenient with me and let me do whatever I felt like. Can I disobey him? Help! I can't decide what to do!

MYSIS [*aside*] Oh dear, I'm afraid of what this 'can't decide' may lead to! But now it's essential either for him to talk to her or for me to say something about her to him **[265]**: while a mind's wavering, it only takes a small weight to tip the scales one way or the other.

PAMPH. [*hearing her voice and turning towards her*] Who's speaking here? Mysis, hello!

MYSIS Hello, Pamphilus!

PAMPH. How is she?

MYSIS As you'd expect, she's in pain from the contractions; and she's also upset, poor thing, because this is the day that was previously agreed for your wedding. What's more, she's afraid you'll abandon her.

PAMPH. What! Could I begin to do that **[270]**? Could I allow my poor darling to be caught in a trap on my account, when she's entrusted her heart and her whole life to me, when she's been especially dear to my heart and I've treated her as if she were my wife? She's been taught and brought up well and decently; could I allow her character to be changed by the force of poverty **[275]**? I won't do it!

MYSIS I wouldn't have any fears if it depended on you alone; but I'm afraid you won't be able to stand the pressure.

PAMPH. Do you think I'm so feeble, or so ungrateful or unfeeling or savage, that neither our relationship nor my love and respect could move or motivate me to stay true to her **[280]**?

MYSIS All I know is that she's earned the right to be remembered by you.

PAMPH. Remembered by me? O Mysis, Mysis, even now I've got written in my heart what Chrysis said about Glycerium. She was almost

de Glýcerió. Iam férme móriens mé uocát;
accéssi; uós semótae; nós soli; íncipít: 285   [50]
"Mi Pámphile, húius fórmam atque aétatém uidés,
nec clám te est quam ílli núnc utraéque inútilés
et ád pudīcítiam et ád rem tútandám siént.
Quod égo per hánc te déxtram oro ét geniúm tuóm,
per tuām fidém perque húius sólitúdiném,   290   [55]
te obtéstor ne ábs te hanc ségregés neu déserás.
Si te ín germáni frátris dílexí locó,
siue haéc te sólum sémper fécit máxumí,
seu tíbi morígera fúit in rébus ómnibús,
te istí uirúm do, amícum, tútorém, patrém;   295   [60]
bona nóstra haec tíbi permítto et tuaé mandó fideī."
Hanc mi ín manúm dat; mórs contínuo ipsam óccupát.
Accépi; accéptam séruabo. **MY.** Íta speró quidém.
PA. Sed quór tu abís ab īlla? **MY.** Óbstetrícem accérso.
    PA. Própera! Atque aúdin?   *ia.7*
Verbum únum cáuĕ de núptiís, ne ad mórbum hoc étiam –
    MY. Téneo.   300   [65]
CHARINUS Quíd ais, Býrriá? Daturne ílla Pámphilo hódie núptum?
    BYRRIA Síc est.   **[II.i]**   *tro.8*
CHA. Quí scis? **BY.** Ápŭd forúm modo ĕ Dáuo audíui.
    CHA. Vaé miseró mihí!   *tro.7*
Ut ánimus ín spe atque ín timóre usque ántehac ádtentús fuít,   *ia.8*
ita, póstquam adémpta spés est, lássus cúra cónfectús stupét!
BY. Quaéso edepól, Charíne, quóniam nón potést
    id fíeri quód uis,   305   [5]   *tro.8*
íd uelís quod póssit. **CHA.** Níl uolo áliud nísi Philúmenam!
    BY. Áh,   *tro.7*

on the point of death when she called my name; I came close to her; the rest of you moved away; we were on our own; she began [285]: 'Dearest Pamphilus, you can see how young and beautiful she is, and you know very well how little those two things will help her to keep either her chastity or her property now. So I beg you by this right hand of yours and by the god who watches over you, by your honour and her defencelessness [290], I beseech you not to cast her aside or abandon her. I've loved you as if you were my own brother; she has always worshipped you alone and tried to please you in everything; so I give you to her as her husband, friend, guardian, and father [295]. I hand over these belongings of ours to you and entrust them to your safekeeping.' She handed her over to my care, and death instantly took her. I accepted Glycerium; having done that, I'll keep her safe!

MYSIS   I certainly hope so.

PAMPH. But why are you leaving her?

MYSIS   I'm going to fetch the midwife.

PAMPH. Hurry! [MYSIS *starts off to the right, but* PAMPHILUS *delays her with a final instruction.*] And listen! Not a single word about the wedding – not on top of everything else, in her delicate condition!

MYSIS   I'm with you [300].

[*Exit right, leaving* PAMPHILUS *absorbed in his own thoughts on stage. Enter* CHARINUS *and* BYRRIA *from the left; they do not notice* PAMPHILUS.]

CHARINUS   What's that, Byrria? She's getting married to Pamphilus today?

BYRRIA That's right.

CHAR.   How do you know?

BYR.   I heard it from Davos just now in the main square.

CHAR.   Oh no! This is terrible! Up till now my mind has been all on edge with hope and fear; now there's no hope left it's exhausted and worn out with worry, and all in a daze!

BYR.   I do beg you, Charinus, since what you want can't come about [305], to want what can!

CHAR.   I don't want anything but Philumena!

quánto sátiust te íd dare óperam qui ístum amórem ex
    ánimo amóueas   *tro.8*
quam íd loquí quo mágĭs lubído frústra incéndatúr tuá!   *tro.7*
CHA. Facile ómnes quóm ualémus récta cónsilia aégrotís damús;   *ia.8*
tu si híc sis áliter séntiás! **BY.** Age age, út lubét. **CHA.** Sed
    Pámphilúm   310   [10]
uideo: ómnia éxperíri cértumst príŭs quam péreo. **BY.** Quíd hic agít?
CHA. Ipsum húnc orábo, huic súpplicábo, amórem huic nárrabó meúm:
credo ímpetrábo ut áliquot sáltem núptiís prodát diés;
intérea fíet áliquid, spéro. **BY.** Id "áliquid" níl est. **CHA.** Býrriá,
quid tíbi uidétur? Ádeon ád eum? **BY.** Quídni? Sí nil ímpetrés, 315   [15]
ut te árbitrétur síbi parátum moéchum si íllam dúxerít.
CHA. Ábĭn hinc ín malám rem cúm suspícióne istác, scelús?   *tro.7*
PA. Charínum uídeo: sálue! **CHA.** O sálue, Pámphilé!   *ia.6*
Ád te aduénio spém, salútem, auxílium, cónsilium éxpeténs!   *tro.7*
PA. Néque pol cónsilí locum hábeo néque ad auxílium cópiám. 320   [20]
Séd ĭstuc quídnamst? **CHA.** Hódie uxórem dúcis? **PA.** Áiunt.
    CHA. Pámphilé,
si íd facís, hodié postrémum mé uidés! **PA.** Quid ita? **CHA.** Eî mihí,
uéreor dícere: huíc dic, quaéso, Býrria! **BY.** Égo dicám. **PA.** Quid ést?
BY. Spónsam hic túam amat. **PA.** Ne íste haud mécum séntit!
    Ého dum, díc mihí:
núm quid nam ámpliús tibi cum ílla fuît, Charíne?
    CHA. Aha, Pámphilé,   325   [25]

BYR. You know, it's so much better for you to work on getting rid of that love from your mind, rather than saying things to fan the flames of your futile desire!

CHAR. When we're not sick ourselves, we all find it easy to give good advice to those who are; if you were in my place, you'd feel differently!

BYR. All right then, whatever you like!

CHAR. [*catching sight of* PAMPHILUS] But I can see Pamphilus [310]; I'm determined to try everything before I give up the ghost.

BYR. [*aside*] What's he up to?

CHAR. I'll beg him himself, I'll go down on my knees to him, I'll tell him about my love. I think I'll get him to agree at least to put off the wedding for a few days; in the meantime something will happen, I'm sure!

BYR. [*aside*] For 'something', read 'nothing'!

CHAR. Byrria, what do you think? Should I go up to him?

BYR. Why not? If you don't get him to agree [315], you'll make him think he's got you lined up as an adulterer if he marries her!

CHAR. Will you go to hell for suspecting that, you villain?

PAMPH. [*his attention finally caught by* CHARINUS' *shouting*] I can see Charinus. Hello!

CHAR. Oh, hello, Pamphilus! I come to you in search of hope, salvation, help, and advice!

PAMPH. I'm certainly not in a position to give advice, and I don't have the means to help you [320]. But what is it you want?

CHAR. Are you marrying today?

PAMPH. So they say.

CHAR. Pamphilus, if you do, this is the last day you see me!

PAMPH. Why do you say that?

CHAR. Oh dear, I'm ashamed to tell you. Tell him, please, Byrria!

BYR. [*to* PAMPHILUS] I'll tell you.

PAMPH. What is it?

BYR. This man is in love with your fiancée.

PAMPH. Well, I certainly don't share his feelings! [*to* CHARINUS] I say, tell me: there hasn't been anything more between the two of you, has there, Charinus?

CHAR. Certainly not, Pamphilus [325]!

níl! **PA.** Quam uéllem! **CHA.** Núnc te pér amicítiam
    et pér amorem óbsecró,
príncipio út ne dúcas. **PA.** Dábo equidem óperam!
    CHA. Séd si id nón potést,
aút tibi núptiae haé sunt córdi, – **PA.** Córdi! **CHA.** – sáltem aliquót diés
prófer, dúm proficíscor áliquo né uideam! **PA.** Aúdi núnciám:
égo, Charíne, ne útiquam offícium líberi ésse hominís putó,   330   [30]
quom ís nil méreat, póstuláre id grátiae ádponí sibí.
Núptiás effúgere ego ístas málo quám tu adipísciér!
CHA. Réddidísti animúm! **PA.** Nunc síquid pótĕs aut tu aút hic Býrriá,
fácite, fíngite, ínueníte, effícite quí detúr tibí;
égo id agám mihi quí ne détur! **CHA.** Sát habeó.
    PA. Dauom óptumé   335   [35]
uídeo, quoiŭs consílio frétus sum. **CHA.** Át tu hercle haúd quicquám mihí,
nísi ea quaé nil ópŭs sunt scíre! Fúgĭn hinc? **BY.** Égo uero, ác lubéns!
DAVOS Dí boní, boní quid pórto! Séd ubi inuéniam Pámphilúm,   **[II.ii]**
út metum ín quo núnc est ádimam atque éxpleam ánimum gaúdió?
CHA. Laétus ést nescíoquid. **PA.** Níl est: nóndum haec résciuít malá! 340
DA. Quem égo nunc crédo, sí iam audíerit síbi parátas núptiás, –
CHA. Aúdin tu íllum? **DA.** – tóto me óppido éxanimátum quaérere.   [5]
Séd ubi quaéram? Quó nunc prímum inténdam? **CHA.** Céssas ádloquí?
DA. Hábeo. **PA.** Dáue, adés, resíste! **DA.** Quís homost, quí me – ?
    O Pámphilé,

PAMPH. What a pity!

CHAR. Now I beg you by our friendship and by my love, first of all not to marry her; –

PAMPH. [*interrupting*] I'll certainly work on it!

CHAR. – but if that's not possible, or if you're keen on this wedding, –

PAMPH. Keen on it!

CHAR. – at least put it off for a few days while I set off somewhere so that I don't have to see it!

PAMPH. Now listen to me, Charinus: I don't think it's at all appropriate for a man of free birth **[330]** to expect to be given credit when he doesn't deserve it; I want to avoid marriage with that girl more than you want to achieve it!

CHAR. You've brought me back to life!

PAMPH. Now if either you or Byrria here can manage it, do something, make something up, think of something, achieve something to make her marry you; *I'll* work on making her *not* marry *me*!

CHAR. I'm satisfied with that. [DAVOS *comes into view, hurrying in from the right.*]

PAMPH. Good! I can see Davos **[335]**; I depend on his advice.

CHAR. [*to* BYRRIA] But *you've* never got anything to say to *me*, except unnecessary bits of information! Go away!

BYR. I certainly shall, and gladly! [*Exit left.*]

DAVOS [*not noticing the others in his hurry*] Ye gods, what good news I bring! But where can I find Pamphilus, so that I can remove the fear he's feeling now and fill his heart with joy?

CHAR. [*to* PAMPHILUS, *aside*] He's happy about something.

PAMPH. [*to* CHARINUS] It's nothing: he hasn't heard about this problem yet **[340]**!

DAVOS [*still not noticing them*] I should think, if he's heard by now that there's a wedding lined up for him, –

CHAR. [*to* PAMPHILUS, *aside*] Do you hear him?

DAVOS – that he's looking for me all over the town, in quite a state! But where can I look for him now? Where should I turn first? [*Stops to think.*]

CHAR. [*to* PAMPHILUS] Why don't you talk to him?

DAVOS I know! [*Starts off left.*]

PAMPH. [*shouting to him*] Davos! Come here! Stop!

DAVOS [*stopping and turning round*] Who's that who's ...? Oh, Pamphilus,

te ípsum quaéro! Eugé, Charíne! Ambo ópportúne: uós uoló!   345
PA. Dáue, périi! **DA.** Quín tu hoc aúdi! **PA.** Intérii! **DA.** Quíd timeás sció.
CHA. Méa quidem hércle cérte in dúbio uítast!
      DA. Ét quid tú, sció.   [10]
PA. Núptiaé mi – **DA.** Etsí scio? **PA.** – hódie –
      DA. Obtúndis, tam étsi intéllegó!
Íd paués, ne dúcas tu íllam; tu aútem ut dúcas. **CHA.** Rém tenés.
PA. Ístuc ípsum. **DA.** Atque ístuc ípsum níl períclist: mé uidé!   350
PA. Óbsecró te, quám primum hóc me líberá miserúm metu! **DA.** Ém,
líbero: úxorém tibi nón dat iám Chremés! **PA.** Qui scís? **DA.** Sció.   [15]
Tuōs patér modo mé prehéndit; aīt tibi úxorém daré
hódie, item ália múlta quaé nunc nón est nárrandí locús.
Cóntinuo ád te próperans pércurro ád forum út dicam haéc tibí. 355
Úbi te nón inuénio, ibi éscendo ín quendam éxcelsúm locúm,
círcumspício: núsquam. Fórte ibi húius uídeo Býrriám;   [20]
rógǒ; negát uidísse. Míhi moléstum: quíd agam cógitó.
Rédeunti ínterea éx ipsá re mi íncidít suspício: "Hém,
paúllulum ópsoni; ípsus trístis; de ínprouíso núptiaé: 360
nón cohaérent." **PA.** Quórsum nam ístuc?
      DA. Égo me cóntinuo ád Chremém.
Quom íllo aduénio, sólitúdo ante óstiúm. Iam id gaúdeó.   [25]

you're the very man I'm looking for! And Charinus! Good, good, good! Well met, both of you! You're the ones I want [345]!

PAMPH. Davos, I've had it!

DAVOS No, listen to this!

PAMPH. I'm done for!

DAVOS I know what you're afraid of.

CHAR. Well, my life's certainly in danger, that's for sure!

DAVOS [*to* CHARINUS] And I know what *you're* afraid of, too!

PAMPH. My wedding –

DAVOS [*interrupting*] But I know!

PAMPH. – today –

DAVOS You're banging on about it, but I *know*! [*to* PAMPHILUS] What *you're* afraid of is that you'll marry her; [*to* CHARINUS] what *you're* afraid of is that you won't!

CHAR. You've got it!

PAMPH. That's exactly it!

DAVOS But that's exactly what there's no danger of! Trust me [350]!

PAMPH. I beg you, free me from my fear as quickly as you can! I'm so unhappy!

DAVOS [*with a gesture*] There! I free you! Chremes isn't marrying his daughter to you any longer!

PAMPH. How do you know?

DAVOS I just do. Your dad got hold of me not long ago and said he was making you marry today, together with a lot of other stuff that there's no time to tell you now. At once I hurried off to you and ran over to the main square to tell you about it [355]. When I didn't find you, I climbed up to a spot where the ground's higher and looked around; you weren't anywhere. Then I happened to see this man's slave Byrria; I asked him; he said he hadn't seen you. I didn't like it; I was wondering what to do; and then, on my way back, I started to grow suspicious about the details of the thing: 'What's this? A tiny amount of food? The master in a bad mood? No warning about the wedding [360]? It doesn't add up!'

PAMPH. What's this leading to?

DAVOS I went straight off to Chremes' house. When I got there, not a soul in front of the door. That cheered me up, for a start.

CHA. Récte dícis. **PA.** Pérge! **DA.** Máneo. Intérea intro íre néminém
uídeo, exíre néminém; matrónam núllam in aédibús,
níl ornáti, níl tumúlti: accéssi, intro áspexí. **PA.** Sció: 365
mágnum sígnum. **DA.** Núm uidéntur cónueníre haec núptiís?
PA. Nón opínor, Dáue. **DA.** "Opínor" nárras? Nón recte áccipís: [30]
cérta rés est. Étiam púerum inde ábiens cónuení Chremí:
hólera et písciculós minútos férre obolo ín cenám sení.
CHA. Líberátus sum hódie, Dáue, túa opera! **DA.** Ác nullús quidém! 370
CHA. Quíd ita? Némpe huic prórsus íllam nón dat. **DA.** Rídiculúm capút!
Quási necésse sít, si huic nón dat, te íllam uxórem dúceré,   [35]
nísi uidés, nisi sénis amícos óras, ámbis! **CHA.** Béne monés.
Íbo, etsi hércle saépe iám me spés haec frústratást. Valé!
PA. Quíd igitúr sibi uólt patér? Quor símulat?
         DA. Égo dicám tibí.   375 **[II.iii]**
Si íd suscénseát nunc quía non dét tibi úxorém Chremés,
príǔs quam tūom út sese hábeat ánimum ad núptiás perspéxerít, 378   [4]
ípsǔs sibi ésse iniúriús uideátur, néque id iniúriá.   377 [3]
Séd si tú negáris dúcere, íbi culpam ín te tránsferét.   [5]
Tum íllae túrbae fíent. **PA.** Quíduis pátiar! **DA.** Páter est, Pámphilé: 380
dífficilést. Tum haec sólast múlier: díctum fáctum inuénerít
áliquam caúsam quam ób rem eíciat óppido. **PA.** Éiciát? **DA.** Citó.
PA. Cédo igitúr quid fáciam, Dáue? **DA.** Díc te dúcturum! **PA.** Hém?

CHAR. You're right.

PAMPH. Go on!

DAVOS I hung around; while I was there I didn't see anyone going in or coming out, no married woman in the house, no preparations, no commotion. – I went up and looked in.

PAMPH. I get it [365]; that's a great clue.

DAVOS Does that really seem to fit with a wedding?

PAMPH. I don't think so, Davos.

DAVOS 'Think so', do you say? You're not taking it right; it's a certainty. I even bumped into one of Chremes' slave-boys as I was coming away from there; he was bringing an obol's worth of vegetables and teeny little fish for the old man's dinner.

CHAR. That's a great weight off my mind, Davos, thanks to you!

DAVOS Well, not really [370].

CHAR. Why do you say that? It's absolutely clear that he's not giving her to *him*!

DAVOS You nincompoop! As if it followed, if he doesn't give her to *him*, that *you'll* marry her! You've got to see to it, ask the old man's friends, canvass their support!

CHAR. That's good advice; I'll be off – although my hope of this has failed me often enough before now! Goodbye! [*Exit left, leaving* PAMPHILUS *and* DAVOS *on stage.*]

PAMPH. So what's my dad up to? Why's he pretending?

DAVOS I'll tell you [375]: if he was angry with you now because Chremes won't let you marry his daughter, before discovering for certain what *your* attitude is to the marriage, even he would think he was in the wrong – and quite rightly too. But if you refuse to marry her, then he'll shift the blame on to you: that's when the trouble will start.

PAMPH. I'll put up with anything!

DAVOS He's your father, Pamphilus [380]; it's difficult. And this woman's on her own: in no time at all he'll have thought up some reason to throw her out of town.

PAMPH. Throw her out?!

DAVOS And quickly!

PAMPH. So what can I do, Davos? Tell me!

DAVOS Say you'll marry her!

PAMPH. What?!

DA. Quid ést?
PA. Egŏn dícam? **DA.** Quór non? **PA.** Númquam fáciam!
    DA. Né negá! [10]   *ia.*6
PA. Suadére nóli! **DA.** Ex eá re quíd fiát uidé! 385
PA. Ut ab ílla exclúdar, hóc conclúdar! **DA.** Nón itást!
Nempe hóc sic ésse opínor: dícturúm patrém
"Ducás uolo hódie uxórem;" tú "Ducam" ínquiés.
Cedo quíd iurgábit técum? Hic réddes ómniá, [15]
quae núnc sunt cérta eí cónsilia, íncerta út siént, 390
sine ŏmní períclo. Nam hóc haud dúbiumst quín Chremés
tibi nón det gnátam; néc tu ea caúsa mínuerís
haec quaé facís, ne is mútet suám senténtiám.
Patrí dic uélle, ut, quóm uelít, tibi iúre irásci nón queát. [20]   *ia.*8
Nam quód tu spéres "Própulsábo fácile uxórem his móribús: 395
dabĭt némo," inuéniet ínopem pótius quám te córrumpí sinát.
Sed sí te aequo ánimo férre accípiet, néglegéntem fécerís:
aliam ótiósus quaéret; ínterea áliquid ácciderít boní.
PA. Ităn crédis? **DA.** Haúd dubium íd quidémst.
    PA. Vidĕ quó me indúcas! **DA.** Quín tacés? [25]
PA. Dicám. Puerum aútem né rescíscat mi ésse ex ílla caútióst: 400
nam póllicitús sum súsceptúrum. **DA.** O fácinus aúdax! **PA.** Hánc fidém
sibi me óbsecráuit, quí se scíret nón desérturum, út darém.
DA. Curábitúr. Sed páter adést: cauĕ te ésse trístem séntiát!
SIMO Reuíso quíd agant aút quid cáptent cónsilí.   **[II.iv]**   *ia.*6

DAVOS   What's the matter?

PAMPH.   Me say that?

DAVOS   Why not?

PAMPH.   I'll never do it!

DAVOS   Stop! Don't refuse!

PAMPH.   Don't try to persuade me!

DAVOS   Think what the result will be [385]!

PAMPH.   That I'll be shut out from her house and shut up in here [*gesturing towards his father's house*]!

DAVOS   No! I think it's bound to be like this: your dad will say 'I want you to marry today'; you'll reply 'All right'. – Tell me, how will he be able to quarrel with you? This way, you'll take all his plans, which he's sure of now, and make them unsure [390] – and without any danger, because it's quite certain that Chremes won't give you his daughter, and you don't need to hold back in doing it just in case he changes his mind. Tell your dad you're prepared to marry her; then he can't reasonably be angry with you even if he wants to be! Because if you're hoping 'I'll easily drive any wife away with my behaviour [395]; no one will give me his daughter' – he'll find you one with no money rather than let you be corrupted. But if he believes you're not bothered, you'll have made him less careful about it; he'll take his time finding another girl, and in the meantime something lucky will have turned up.

PAMPH.   Is that what you think?

DAVOS   There's really no doubt about it!

PAMPH.   Watch what you're leading me into!

DAVOS   Do shut up!

PAMPH.   [*finally agreeing*] I'll say it. But we must take care he doesn't find out she's having my baby [400]; I've promised to let it live.

DAVOS   What a nerve!

PAMPH.   She begged me to give her my word about that, so that she could know I wasn't going to abandon her.

DAVOS   It'll be seen to. [*Sees* SIMO *returning from the left.*] But here's your dad; don't let him realize you're upset! [*They stay close to* GLYCERIUM'*s door, on the right of the stage.*]

SIMO   [*to the audience*] I've come back to see what they're up to and what plans they're hatching. [*Takes centre stage, looking round but not seeing* PAMPHILUS *and* DAVOS.]

DA. Hic núnc non dúbitat quín te dúcturúm negés.   405
Venít meditátus álicunde éx soló locó.
Orátiónem spérat ínuenísse sé
qui dífferát te: proín tu fác apud te út siés.   [5]
PA. Modo ŭt póssim, Dáue! **DA.** Créde inquam hóc mihi, Pámphilé,
numquam hódie técum cómmutáturúm patrém   410
unum ésse uérbum sí te díces dúceré!
BYRRIA Erŭs mé relíctis rébus iússit Pámphilúm   **[II.v]**
hodie óbseruáre, ut quíd agerét de núptiís
scirem: íd proptérea núnc hunc uénientém sequór.
Ipsum ádeo praésto uídeo cúm Dauo: hóc agám.   415
SI. Utrúmque adésse uídeo. **DA.** Em, sérua! **SI.** Pámphilé!   [5]
DA. Quasi de ínprouíso réspice ád eum! **PA.** Ehém, patér!
DA. Probe! **SI.** Hódie uxórem dúcas, út dixí, uoló.
BY. Nunc nóstrae tímeo párti quíd hĭc respóndeát.
PA. Neque ĭstíc neque álibi tíbi erit úsquam in mé mora. **BY.** Hém?   420
DA. Obmútuít. **BY.** Quid díxit? **SI.** Fácis ut té decét,   [10]
quom istúc quod póstulo ímpetró cum grátiá.
DA. Sum uérus? **BY.** Erŭs, quantum aúdio, úxore éxcidít!
SI. I núnciam íntro, ne ín morá, quom opŭs sít, siés.

DAVOS [*to* PAMPHILUS, *aside*] So far he's no doubt that you'll refuse to marry [405]. He's come from some lonely spot where he's been practising; he's sure he's thought up a speech to tear you apart. So make sure you keep your wits about you!

PAMPH. If only I can, Davos!

DAVOS Listen, Pamphilus, believe me! Your dad just won't have [410] a single word to say in reply to you if you agree to marry!

[BYRRIA *enters from the left.*]

BYR. [*to the audience*] My master's ordered me to drop everything and keep an eye on Pamphilus for today, so that I can find out what he's doing about the wedding; that's the reason why I've been following Simo as he came along. [*Sees* PAMPHILUS *and* DAVOS.] And he's right here, I see, together with Davos; I'll watch this [415]. [BYRRIA *stays on the left of the stage;* SIMO *at last catches sight of the other two.*]

SIMO They're both here, I see.

DAVOS [*to* PAMPHILUS, *aside*] Watch out now!

SIMO [*calling to* PAMPHILUS] Pamphilus!

DAVOS [*to* PAMPHILUS, *aside*] Pretend to be surprised! Turn to look at him!

PAMPH. [*obeying* DAVOS] Oh! Dad!

DAVOS [*aside*] Perfect!

SIMO I want you to marry today, as I told you.

BYR. [*aside*] Now I'm anxious for our side: how will he answer?

PAMPH. [*to* SIMO] I won't hold things up for you at all, either in this or in anything else.

BYR. [*aside*] *What* [420]*?!*

DAVOS [*aside, commenting on* SIMO's *reaction*] He's struck dumb!

BYR. [*aside*] What did he say?!

SIMO [*to* PAMPHILUS, *recovering from his surprise*] That's the right way to behave, agreeing to what I ask you with good grace!

DAVOS [*aside*] Wasn't I right?

BYR. [*aside*] From what I hear, my master's lost his wife!

SIMO [*to* PAMPHILUS] Go inside now, so that you don't keep us waiting when you're needed.

PA. Eó. **BY.** Nulláne in re ésse quoíquam hominí fidém!   425
Verum íllud uérbumst, uólgo quód dicí solét,   [15]
omnís sibi málle mélius ésse quam álterí.
Ego íllam uídi: uírginém formá boná
meminí uidéri. Quo aéquiór sum Pámphiló,
si se íllam in sómnis quam íllum amplécti máluít.   430
Renúntiábo, ut pro hóc maló mihi dét malúm!   [20]
DA. Hic núnc me crédit áliquam síbi falláciám   **[II.vi]**
portáre et eá me hic réstitísse grátiá.
SI. Quid Dáuos nárrat? **DA.** Aégre quícquam núnc quidém.
SI. Nilne? Hém? **DA.** Nil prórsus. **SI.** Átqui exspéctabám quidém.   435
DA. Praetér spem euénit, séntio: hóc male habét uirúm.   [5]
SI. Potin és mihi uérum díceré? **DA.** Nil fáciliús.
SI. Num illí moléstae quídpiam haé sunt núptiaé
proptér hŭiusce hóspitái cónsuetúdiném?
DA. Nil hércle – aut, si ádeo, bíduíst aut tríduí   440
haec sóllicitúdo: nósti? Deínde désinét.   [10]
Etenim ípsus sécum eám rem réputauít uiá.
SI. Laudó. **DA.** Dum lícitumst éi dúmque aetás tulít,
amáuit; tum íd clam; cáuit ne úmquam infámiaé
ea rés sibi ésset, út uirúm fortém decét.   445
Nunc úxore ópus est: ánimum ad úxorem ádpulít.   [15]
SI. Subtrístis uísus ést esse áliquantúm mihí.
DA. Nil própter hánc rem, séd ĕst quod súscensét tibí.
SI. Quidnámst? **DA.** Puerílest. **SI.** Quíd id est? **DA.** Níl.

PAMPH. OK. [*Goes into his house.*]

BYR. [*aside*] Can't anyone be trusted in anything [**425**]? It's true what they're always saying: everyone prefers to feather his own nest rather than someone else's. I've seen her; she was a good-looking girl, as I remember. So I can't really blame Pamphilus if he's decided he should be the one who sleeps with his arms round her, rather than Charinus [**430**]. I'll report back to him; it's bad news for him, but he'll make it bad news for me! [*Exit left, leaving* DAVOS *and* SIMO *alone on stage.*]

DAVOS [*to the audience*] He thinks I'm bringing some trick against him now; he thinks that's why I've stayed behind here.

SIMO [*addressing him*] What's Davos got to say?

DAVOS [*to* SIMO] Nothing much, just at the moment.

SIMO Nothing? Really?

DAVOS Nothing at all!

SIMO But I did think you would [**435**]!

DAVOS [*aside*] Things haven't turned out as he expected, I can tell; this has got the man worried!

SIMO Can you tell me the truth?

DAVOS [*to* SIMO] Nothing easier!

SIMO This wedding doesn't worry him at all, does it, because of his relationship with this foreign girl here?

DAVOS Absolutely not – or if it does he'll be upset about it for two or three days [**440**], you know, and then he'll stop. In fact he's been thinking the thing over logically for himself.

SIMO Good!

DAVOS While he was allowed to, and while he was the right age, he had an affair – but he did it discreetly; he made sure it would never bring any disgrace on him, as a good chap should [**445**]. Now it's time for a wife, so he's turned his mind to a wife.

SIMO [*still suspicious*] He seemed to me to be ever so slightly upset.

DAVOS Not for that reason – but there is something he's angry with you about.

SIMO What's that?

DAVOS [*feigning reluctance*] It's childish!

SIMO What is it?

DAVOS Nothing!

SI. Quin díc quid ést!
DA. A͡it nímium párce fácere súmptum. **SI.** Méne? **DA.** Té.   450
"Vix" ínquit "dráchumis ést opsónatús decém: [20]
non fílió uidétur úxorém daré.
Quem" inquít "uocábo ad cénam me͡órum aequáliúm
potíssumúm nunc?" Ét, quod dícendum híc siét,
tu quóque perpárce nímium: nón laudó **SI.** Tacé!   455
DA. Commóui! **SI.** Ego ístaec récte ut fíant uíderó.   [25]
Quidnam hóc est réi? Quíd h͡ic uolt uéteratór sibí?
Nam si híc malíst quicquam, ém, ĭllic ést huic re͡i capút!
MYSIS Ita pól quidém res ést ut díxti, Lésbiá: [III.i]
fidélem haud férme múlieri ínueniás uirúm.   460
SI. Ab Ándriást ancílla haec? Quíd narrás? **DA.** Itást.
MY. Sed h͡ic Pámphilús – **SI.** Quid dícit? **MY.** – fírmauít fidem. **SI.** Hém?
DA. Utinam aút hic súrdus aút haec múta fácta sít!   [5]
MY. Nam quód peperísset iússit tólli. **SI.** O Iúppitér,
quid ego aúdio? Áctumst, sĭquidem haec uéra praédicát!   465
LESBIA Bonum ĭngénium nárras ádulescéntis. **MY.** Óptumúm.
Sed séquere me íntro, ne ín mora ílli sís. **LE.** Sequór.
DA. Quod rémediúm nunc huíc malo ínueniám? **SI.** Quid hóc?   [10]
Adeón est démens? Éx peregrína? Iám scio: áh,

SIMO   But tell me what it is!

DAVOS   He says you're being too mean with the expenses.

SIMO   Who, me?

DAVOS   Yes, you **[450]**. 'He's scarcely spent ten drachmas on the food', he says; 'you wouldn't think he was arranging his son's marriage. Now I'll have to choose which of my friends to invite to the dinner', he says. And if I must tell you so to your face, even you are being much too stingy; it's not good!

SIMO   Quiet **[455]**!

DAVOS   [*aside*] I've shaken him up!

SIMO   I'll see that things are done properly! [*aside*] What's going on here? What's this old rogue up to? If there's any monkey-business here, look, there's the brains behind it!

[MYSIS *reappears from the right, together with* LESBIA; *they do not notice* SIMO *and* DAVOS.]

MYSIS   Yes, it's just as you've said, Lesbia: you'll hardly ever find a man who stays faithful to a woman **[460]**!

SIMO   [*to* DAVOS, *aside*] Is this a slave of the Andrian girl's? What do you say?

DAVOS   [*thrown into some confusion by the women's arrival*] Yes, she is.

MYSIS   [*continuing to* LESBIA] But this Pamphilus –

SIMO   [*aside*] What's she saying?

MYSIS   – has really backed up his promise.

SIMO   [*aside*] *What?!*

DAVOS   [*aside*] I wish either he'd lost his hearing or she'd lost her voice!

MYSIS   [*continuing*] I mean, he's given orders for the baby to be allowed to live.

SIMO   [*aside*] Great God, what's this I hear? It's all over, if she's telling the truth **[465]**!

LESBIA [*to* MYSIS] He's a good boy, by your account.

MYSIS   One of the best. – But follow me indoors; you mustn't keep her waiting.

LESBIA After you! [MYSIS *goes into* GLYCERIUM's *house, followed by* LESBIA.]

DAVOS   [*aside*] What cure can I find for this trouble now?

SIMO   [*to himself, but loud enough for* DAVOS *to hear*] What's this? Is he so mad? By a foreign woman? [*struck by a sudden thought*]

uix tándem sénsi stólidus! **DA.** Quíd hĭc sensísse aít?   470
SI. Haec prímum adfértur iám mi ab hóc falláciá:
hanc símulant párere, quó Chremétem abstérreánt.
(**GLYCERIUM** Iunó Lucína, fér opem, sérua me, óbsecró!)   [15]
SI. Hui, tám citó? Ridículum! Póstquam ante óstiúm
me audíuit stáre, adpróperat. Nón sat cómmodé   475
diuísa súnt tempóribus tíbi, Daue, haéc. **DA.** Mihín?
SI. Num inmémores díscipuli? **DA.** Égo quid nárres nésció.
SI. Hicín me si ínparátum in uéris núptiís   [20]
adórtus ésset, quós mihi lúdos rédderét!
Nunc huiús períclo fít, ego in pórtu náuigó.   480
LESBIA Adhúc, Árchylís, quae ádsolént quaéque opórtént   **[III.ii]** *ba.4*
signa ésse ád salútem ómnia huíc ésse uídeó.
Nunc prímúm fac ístaéc lauét; póst deíndé
quod iússí darí bíbere et quántum ímperáuí
date: móx ego húc reuórtar.   485   [5] *ia.4^*
Per ecástor scítus púer est nátus Pámphiló.   *ia.6*
Deōs quaéso ut sít supérstes, quándŏquidem ípsest íngenió bonó,   *ia.8*
quomque huíc est uéritus óptumae ádulescénti fácere iniúriám.
SI. Vel hŏc quís non crédat, quí te nórit, ábs te esse órtum?
            DA. Quídnam id ést?
SI. Non ímperábat córam quíd opus fácto essét puérperaé,   490   [10]
sed póstquam egréssast íllis quaé sunt íntus clámat dé uiá!
O Dáue, itán contémnor ábs te? Aut ítane tándem idóneús
tibi uídeor ésse quém tam apérte fállere íncipiás dolís?

Now I see! Yes, I've finally got it! I am an idiot!

DAVOS [*aside*] What's he claiming to have got [**470**]?

SIMO [*as before*] This is the first trick he's bringing against me now: they're pretending that she's giving birth, so as to scare Chremes off! [GLYCERIUM *is heard crying from inside the house*: Juno, Goddess of childbirth, help me, save me, please!] What? So soon? Ridiculous! Once she's heard that I'm standing in front of the door, she gets on with it! [*turns to* DAVOS] You didn't plan [**475**] the timing of this very well, Davos!

DAVOS [*nonplussed*] *Me?*

SIMO Could your pupils have forgotten their instructions, by any chance?

DAVOS I don't know what you're talking about!

SIMO [*to the audience*] If I'd really been planning a wedding, and he'd come up against me unprepared, just think what fun he'd be having at my expense! But as it is he's the one at risk, while my boat's safe in harbour [**480**]!

[LESBIA *reappears from* GLYCERIUM'*s house, talking back over her shoulder.*]

LESBIA So far, Archylis, everything points to her complete recovery: I can see all the usual symptoms; it's all as it should be. Now, first of all, make sure she washes; next, after that, give her the drink I told you to – the amount I prescribed. I'll be back shortly [**485**]. [*The door closes behind her; she addresses the world at large.*] I must say, that's an exceptionally fine boy that's been born to Pamphilus; please, gods, let him live! Pamphilus is a good man, and he hasn't wanted to do any wrong to that nice girl! [*Exit right.*]

SIMO [*to* DAVOS] And now this! Anyone who knows you must suppose that you're behind it!

DAVOS What's that?

SIMO She didn't give her instructions on the spot for how to treat the mother after giving birth [**490**], but first she comes out of the house, and then she shouts at the women indoors from the street! Oh Davos, do you have such a low opinion of me? Damn it, do you think I'm the sort of person you can set about fooling and tricking in such an obvious way? At least you might take a bit of

Saltem áccuráte, ut métui uídear cérte sí rescíuerím!
DA. Certe hércle núnc hic se ípsus fállit, haúd ego!
    SI. Édixín tibí,   495   [15]
intérminátus súm ne fáceres? Núm ueritú's? Quid ré tulít?
Credón tibi hóc nunc, péperisse hánc e Pámphiló?   *ia.6*
DA. Teneó quid érret, ét quid agam hábeo. **SI.** Quíd tacés?
DA. Quid crédas? Quási non tíbi renúntiáta sínt haec síc foré!   *ia.8*
SI. Mihĭn quísquam? **DA.** Eho, án tute íntelléxti hoc ádsimulári?
    SI. Inrídeór!   500   [20]
DA. Renúntiátumst; nám qui istaéc tibi íncidít suspíció?
SI. Qui? Quía te nóram! **DA.** Quási tu dícas fáctum id cónsilió meó!
SI. Certe énĭm sció. **DA.** Non sátĭs me pérnosti étiam quális sím, Simó.
SI. Egŏn té? **DA.** Sed síquid tíbi narráre occépi, cóntinuó darí
tibi uérba cénses. **SI.** Fálso! **DA.** Itaque hércle níl iam
    múttire aúdeó!   505   [25]
SI. Hoc égo scio únum, néminém peperísse hic. **DA.** Íntelléxerís;
sed nílo sétiús referétur móx huc púer ante óstiúm.
Id égo iam núnc tibi, ére, renúntió futúrum, ut sís sciéns,
ne tu hóc postérius dícas Dáui fáctum cónsilio aút dolís.
Prórsus á me opíniónem hanc tŭam ésse ego ámotám uoló. 510 [30] *tro.7*
SI. Únde id scís? **DA.** Audíui et crédo: múlta cóncurrúnt simúl
quí coniécturam hánc nunc fácio. Iám prius haéc se e Pámphiló
gráuidam díxit ésse; inuéntumst fálsum. Núnc, postquám uidét
núptiás domi ádparári, míssast áncilla ílicó
óbstetrícem accérsitum ád eam et púerum ut ádferrét simúl. 515 [35]

care and make it look as if you really were afraid of what I'd do if
I found out!

DAVOS   [*aside*] He really is fooling himself here – I'm not!

SIMO   Didn't I give you due notice [**495**]? Didn't I warn you not to do it?
Did that frighten you? What difference did it make? Is this what
you expect me to believe now, that this woman's had a baby by
Pamphilus?

DAVOS   [*aside*] I see where he's going wrong – and I know what to do!

SIMO   Why don't you answer?

DAVOS   [*to* SIMO] What do you mean, 'believe'? As if someone hadn't
told you it would be done like this!

SIMO   Me? Who?

DAVOS   What? Did you really see for yourself that this was a pretence?

SIMO   He's laughing at me [**500**]!

DAVOS   Someone told you! Why else did you grow suspicious about it?

SIMO   Why? Because I knew you!

DAVOS   You might almost be saying I was the one who planned it!

SIMO   Yes, I know it for a fact!

DAVOS   You don't yet really and truly know what I'm like, Simo.

SIMO   *I* don't know *you*?!

DAVOS   No: if I've begun to tell you something, you immediately think a
trick's being played on you.

SIMO   [*sarcastically*] How wrong of me!

DAVOS   All right, then! I won't risk uttering a single further sound [**505**]!

SIMO   The one thing I do know is this: no one has given birth here!

DAVOS   You've realized that, I grant you; but all the same before long a
baby will be brought back out here in front of the door. I tell you
about that now in advance, sir, to keep you fully informed, so you
won't say later that Davos was the one who planned the trick. I
want these thoughts of yours to be steered right away from me
[**510**].

SIMO   How do you know that?

DAVOS   I've heard it, and I believe it. Lots of things combine to make me
reach this particular conclusion. She said earlier on that she was
pregnant by Pamphilus; that's been found to be a lie. But now that
she can see wedding preparations going on in your house, at once
a girl's been sent to fetch a midwife for her, and to bring along a

Hóc nisi fít, puerum út tu uídeas, níl mouéntur núptiaé.
SI. Quíd ais? Quom íntelléxerás   *tro.4^*
íd consílium cápere, quór non díxti extémplo Pámphiló?   *tro.7*
DA. Quís igitúr eum ab ílla abstráxit nísi ego? Nam ómnes nós quidém
scimus quám misere hánc amárit; núnc sibi úxorem éxpetít.   520   [40]
Póstremo íd mihi dá negóti; tú taméndem has núptiás
pérge fácere ita út facís, et id spéro adiúturós deós.
SI. Ímmo abi íntro; ibi me ópperíre et quód paráto opus ést pará.
Non ínpulít me haec núnc omníno ut créderém;   *ia.6*
atque haúd scio án quae díxit sínt uera ómniá.   525   [45]
Sed párui péndo: illúd mihi múlto máxumúmst
quod míhi pollícitust ípsus gnátus. Núnc Chremém
conuéniam; orábo gnáto uxórem. Si ímpetró,
quid álias málim quam hódie has fíeri núptiás?
Nam gnátus quód pollícitust, haúd dubiúmst mihi, íd   530   [50]
si nólit, quín eum mérito póssim cógeré.
Atque ádeo in ípso témpore éccum ipsum óbuiám!
Iubeó Chremétem – **CHREMES** O, te ípsum quaérebam!
         SI. Ét ego te: óptato áduenís.   **[III.iii]**   *ia.8*
CHR Aliquót me adiérunt, éx te audítum qui aíbant hódie fíliám
meám núberé tuo gnáto: id uíso, túne an ílli insániánt!   535
SI. Auscúlta paúca: et quíd ego té uelim ét tu quód quaerís sciés.
CHR. Auscúlto: lóquere quíd uelís.   [5]   *ia.4*
SI. Per té deós óro et nóstram amícitiám, Chremé,   *ia.6*
quae incépta a páruis cum aétate ádcreuít simúl,
perque únicám gnatám tuam ét gnatúm meúm,   540
quoius tíbi potéstas súmma séruandí datúr,
ut me ádiuués in hác re atque íta uti núptiaé   [10]
fueránt futúrae fíant! **CHR.** Áh, ne me óbsecrá!
Quasi hóc te orándo a me ímpetráre opórteát!
Alium ésse cénses núnc me atque ólim quóm dabám?   545

baby as well **[515]**: if they can't get you to see a baby, the wedding won't be put off!

SIMO   Tell me, when you realized that was her plan, why didn't you tell Pamphilus at once?

DAVOS   And who tore him away from her but me? *We* all know how desperately he loved her; but now he's keen to marry **[520]**. In short, give me that job; you, on the other hand, carry on arranging this wedding as you're doing – and I hope the gods help it along!

SIMO   No, go inside! Wait for me there, and make the necessary preparations. [DAVOS *obeys;* SIMO *turns to the audience.*] He didn't altogether get me to believe him there; and yet perhaps what he said is all true **[525]**. – But I don't much care: much the most important thing for me is that my son promised me himself. Now I'll go to find Chremes and beg him to let my son marry his daughter. If I get him to agree, I can't think of a better day than the present for the wedding to take place: now that my son's promised, there's no doubt in my mind **[530]** that I'd be justified in forcing him to do it even if he refuses!

[CHREMES *enters from the right, in some agitation.*] But here's the man himself, in fact, coming this way at just the right time! [*Turns to greet him.*] Chremes, welc – !

CHREMES   [*interrupting*] Ah! You're the very man I wanted to see!

SIMO   And you likewise! I'm glad you've turned up.

CHR.   Some people have come to me and told me they'd heard from you that my daughter was marrying your son today! I've come to see whether it's you or them that are mad **[535]**!

SIMO   [*trying to placate him*] Listen a bit, and you'll find out what I want from you, as well as learning the answer to your question.

CHR.   I'm listening: tell me what you want.

SIMO   I beg you by the gods and by our friendship, Chremes, which began when we were small and grew stronger as we grew up, by your only daughter and my son **[540]**, whose salvation lies in your hands above all: help me in this matter; let the wedding take place just as it had been going to!

CHR.   [*somewhat mollified, though not yet convinced*] Please stop praying to me! As if you had to beg to get me to agree to that! Do you think I'm a different man now from when I offered her

Si in rémst utríque ut fíant, áccersí iubé;
sed si éx eá re plús malíst quam cómmodí [15]
utríque, id óro te ín commúne ut cónsulás,
quasi si ílla túa sit Pámphilíque ego sím patér.
SI. Immo íta uolo ítaque póstulo út fiát, Chremé, 550
neque póstulem ábs te ni ípsa rés moneát. **CHR.** Quid ést?
SI. Iraé sunt ínter Glýcerium ét gnatum. **CHR.** Aúdió. [20]
SI. Ita mágnae ut spérem pósse auélli. **CHR.** Fábulaé!
SI. Profécto síc est! **CHR.** Síc hercle út dicám tibí:
amántium írae amóris íntegrátióst! 555
SI. Em, id te óro ut ánte eámus, dúm tempús datúr,
dumque eiús lubído occlúsast cóntuméliís. [25]
Priŭs quam hárum scélera et lácrumae cónfictaé dolís
reddúcunt ánimum aegrótum ad mísericórdiám,
uxórem démus: spéro cónsuetúdine ét 560
coniúgio líberáli déuinctúm, Chremé,
dehinc fácile ex íllis sése emérsurúm malís. [30]
CHR. Tibi ita hóc uidétur; át ego nón posse árbitrór
neque íllum hánc perpétuo habére néque me pérpetí.
SI. Qui scís ergo ístuc, nísi perículum fécerís? 565
CHR. At ístúc perículum in fíliá fierí grauést.
SI. Nempe íncommóditas dénique húc omnís redít, [35]
si euéniat, quód di próhibeánt, discéssió.
At sí corrígitur, quót commóditatés uidé:
princípio amíco fíliúm restítuerís, 570
tibi génerum fírmum et fíliae ínueniés uirúm.
CHR. Quid ístíc? Si ita ístuc ánimum indúxti esse útilé, [40]
noló tibi úllum cómmodum ín me claúdiér.

then **[545]**? If it's to their mutual benefit for the wedding to take place, give the order for her to be fetched! But if there's more trouble than advantage for the pair of them in the arrangement, then I beg you to have a thought for both of them together, just as if she were your daughter and I were Pamphilus' father!

SIMO But that's what I want! That's the reason I'm asking, Chremes **[550]**! And I wouldn't ask you if the facts themselves didn't tell me to.

CHR. What do you mean?

SIMO There's a tiff between Glycerium and my son.

CHR. [*with irony*] I hear what you say!

SIMO Such a big one that I'm sure he can be torn away from her.

CHR. Rubbish!

SIMO That's certainly how it is!

CHR. I'll tell you how it jolly well is: when lovers feud, their love's renewed **[555]**!

SIMO Exactly! That's what I'm asking you to help me forestall while we have the chance, while his desire's stopped up by their bickering! Before these women can bring tender feelings back into his sick mind with their wicked behaviour and their fake crocodile tears, let's give him a wife! I'm sure he'll become bound to her when they're in a relationship **[560]**, and when he's made a good marriage, Chremes, and then he'll easily find a way out of his troubles!

CHR. That's how it seems to you, but I don't think it's possible either for him to stand by her for life or for me to stand by and watch!

SIMO And how do you know that, if you won't put it to the test **[565]**?

CHR. But 'putting it to the test' when my daughter's involved is a serious matter!

SIMO What all the disadvantage clearly comes down to, in the last resort, is that there may be a separation – which heaven forbid! But if he does mend his ways, look how many advantages there are: first you'll have restored a son to your friend **[570]**, and you'll find him to be a faithful son-in-law for yourself and husband for your daughter.

CHR. [*finally agreeing*] All right then: if you're convinced that it's in everyone's interest to do it this way, I don't want you to find any advantage blocked off on my side.

SI. Meritó te sémper máxumí fecí, Chremé!
CHR. Sed quíd ais? **SI.** Quíd? **CHR.** Qui scís eós nunc
    díscordáre intér se? 575 *ia.7*
SI. Ipsús mihi Dáuos, qui íntumúst e͡órúm consíliis, díxit,
et ís mihi suádet núptiás quantúm queam út matúrem. [45]
Num cénses fáceret, fíliúm nisi scíret éadem haec uélle?
Tute ádeo iam e͡iús uerba aúdiés. Heus, éuocáte huc Dáuom!
Atque éccum uídeo ipsúm forás exíre! **DAVOS** Ad te íbam.
    SI. Quídnamst? 580 **[III.iv]**
DA. Quor úxor nón accérsitúr? Iam aduésperáscit. **SI.** Aúdin?
Ego dúdum nón nil uéritu' súm, Daue, ábs te né facerés idém *ia.8*
quod uólgus séruorúm solét, dolís ut mé delúderés
proptérea quód amat fíliús. **DA.** Egon ístuc fácerem? **SI.** Crédidí, [5]
idque ádeo métuens uós celáui quód nunc dícam. **DA.** Quíd?
    SI. Sciés; 585
nam própemodum hábeo iám fidém. **DA.** Tandém cognósti quí siém!
SI. Non fúerant núptiaé futúrae! **DA.** Quíd? Non? **SI.** Séd ea grátiá
simuláui, uós ut pértemptárem. **DA.** Quíd ais? **SI.** Síc res ést. **DA.** Vidé:
numquam ístuc quíui ego íntellégere! Váh, consílium cállidúm! [10]
SI. Hoc aúdi: ut hínc te intro íre iússi, oppórtune híc fit mi óbuiam.
    DA. Hém, 590
numnám perímus? **SI.** Nárro huic quaé tu dúdum nárrastí mihí.

SIMO   You deserve the high regard I've always had for you, Chremes!

CHR.   But tell me –

SIMO   What?

CHR.   How do you know they're on bad terms at the moment **[575]**?

SIMO   Davos told me himself; he's in close touch with their thoughts, and he's urging me to hurry the wedding along as fast as I can. You don't think he'd do that, do you, if he didn't know it was exactly what my son wanted? – In fact, you'll now hear it from his lips for yourself! [*Calls into his house.*] Hey! Call Davos to come out here! [*The door opens sooner than he had expected.* DAVOS *was already about to come out and now appears.*] But here he is coming out of the house himself, I see!

DAVOS   [*to* SIMO] I was on my way to you!

SIMO   What's up **[580]**?

DAVOS   Why isn't the bride being fetched? Evening's coming on already!

SIMO   [*to* CHREMES] Do you hear that? [*to* DAVOS] I used to be quite afraid of you, Davos: I thought you'd do what the common run of slaves normally do, cheating and tricking me because my son's having an affair. –

DAVOS   Would *I* do *that*?!

SIMO   So I believed; and in fact because I was afraid of that I concealed from the pair of you what I'm now going to say.

DAVOS   What?

SIMO   I'll tell you **[585]**, because I pretty well trust you now.

DAVOS   You've finally discovered what I'm like!

SIMO   The wedding hadn't been going to take place!

DAVOS   [*feigning astonishment*] What? Not take place?!

SIMO   But I pretended because I wanted to put you both to the test.

DAVOS   Really?!

SIMO   Yes, it's true.

DAVOS   [*as before*] Well, well! I'd never have managed to work that out! Wow! What a clever plan!

SIMO   Now listen: just as I'd told you to go off inside, with perfect timing this man here bumped into me [*indicating* CHREMES]!

DAVOS   [*aside, alarmed*] What **[590]**?! Does this mean we've had it?

SIMO   I told him what you'd just told me.

DA. Quidnam aúdiám? **SI.** Gnatam út det óro, uíxque id éxoro.

  DA. Óccidi! **SI.** Hém,

quid díxtī? **DA.** Óptume ínquam fáctum! **SI.** Núnc per húnc nullást morá.

CHR. Domúm modo íbo: ut ádparétur dícam, atque húc renúntió. [15]

SI. Nunc te óro, Dáue, quóniam sólus mi éffecísti has núptiás, – 595

DA. Ego uéro sólus! **SI.** – gnátum míhi corrígere pórro eníteré.

DA. Faciam hércle séduló! **SI.** Potés nunc, dum ánimus ínritátus ést.

DA. Quiéscas! **SI.** Áge igitúr, ubi núnc est ípsus? **DA.** Mírum ní domíst.

SI. Ibo ád eum atque éadem haec quaé tibi díxi dícam itidem ílli.

  DA. Núllu' súm! [20]

Quid caúsaest quín hinc ín pistrínum récta próficiscár uiá? 600

Nil ést precí locí relíctum. Iám pertúrbaui ómniá:

erúm fefélli; in núptiás coniéci erílem fíliúm;

feci hódie ut fíerent, ínsperánte hoc átque inuíto Pámphiló.

Em astútiás! Quod sí quiéssem, níl euénissét malí! [25]

Séd ĕccum ipsúm uideo: óccidí! 605 *tro.4^*

Útinam mi ésset áliquid híc quo núnc me praécipitém darém! *tro.7*

PAMPHILUS Úbi īllest scélŭs qui pérdidít me? **DA.** Périi!

  PA. Atque hóc confíteor iúre **[III.v]** *tro.8*

mi óbtigísse, quándŏquidém tam inérs, tam núlli cónsilí sum!

Séruon fórtunás meás me cómmisísse fúttilí! *tro.7*

Érgo prétium ob stúltitiám ferŏ! Séd inultum íd numquam aúferét! 610

DA. Posthác incólumem sát sciŏ fóre me, núnc si déuito

  hóc malúm! [5] *ia.8*

DAVOS [*aside*] What ever am I going to hear?

SIMO I begged him to give his daughter; with some difficulty, I persuaded him.

DAVOS I'm done for!

SIMO [*half hearing him*] What? What did you say?

DAVOS [*recovering*] Won–derful news, I said!

SIMO Now there's no delay on his side.

CHR. I'll go home now and tell them to get things ready; then I'll report back here. [*Exit right.*]

SIMO Now, Davos, I beg you, now that you've brought about this wedding for me unaided **[595]**, –

DAVOS [*aside, bitterly*] Yes indeed, quite unaided!

SIMO – carry on striving to mend my son's ways!

DAVOS I'll certainly work hard at it!

SIMO You can do it now, while he's angry!

DAVOS Don't worry!

SIMO Well now, where is he himself at the moment?

DAVOS He's at home, of course.

SIMO I'll go to him and tell him exactly what I've told you. [*Goes indoors, leaving* DAVOS *alone on stage.*]

DAVOS I'm a dead man! Is there any reason I shouldn't go straight off to the mill **[600]**? There's no room left to beg for mercy: I've messed everything up now – I've deceived my master; I've trapped my master's son into a wedding; I've made it happen today, beyond this man's hopes and against Pamphilus' wishes! Look how clever I am! If I'd just kept quiet, no trouble would have resulted!

 [PAMPHILUS *starts to come out of his house.*] But here he is himself, I see. I'm done for **[605]**! I wish there was something here for me to throw myself off! [*Stays out of* PAMPHILUS' *sight.*]

PAMPH. Where's that villain who's ruined me?

DAVOS [*aside*] I've had it!

PAMPH. But I admit I deserve what's happened to me: I'm so feeble, so clueless! Fancy entrusting my fortunes to a worthless slave! So I'm paying the price for my own stupidity! But he'll never get off unpunished **[610]**!

DAVOS [*aside*] I'm quite sure I'll be safe in future if I escape this punishment now!

PA. Nam quíd ego núnc dicám patrí? Negábon uélle mé, modó
qui súm pollícitus ípse? Quá fidúcia íd facere aúdeám?
Nec quíd nunc mé faciám sció! **DA.** Nec mḗquidem, atque íd ago séduló!
Dicam áliquid me ínuentúrum, ut huíc malo áliquam
  próducám morám.   615
PA. Oh! **DA.** Vísus sum! **PA.** Ého dum, bóne uir, quíd ais?
 Vídĕn me cónsiliís tuís   [10]
miserum ínpedítum esse? **DA.** Át iam expédiam! **PA.** Expédies?
  DA. Cérte, Pámphilé!
PA. Nempe út modo! **DA.** Ímmo mélius, spéro. **PA.** Oh, tíbi ego
 ut crédam, fúrcifér?
Tu rem ínpedítam et pérditám restítuas? Ém quo frétu' sím,
qui me hódie ex tránquillíssumá re cóniecísti in núptiás!   620
Án non díxi esse hóc futúrum? **DA.** Díxti. **PA.** Quíd meritú's?
  DA. Crucém.   [15] *tro.7*
Séd sine paúllulum ád me rédeam: iam áliquid díspiciam. **PA.** Éī mihí,
quóm non hábeo spátium ut dé te súmam súpplicium út uoló!
Námque hoc témpus praécauére míhi me, haud te úlciscí sinít!
CHARINUS Hóccinĕst crédibile aút memorábile,   625 **[IV.i]** *da.4*
tánta uécórdia ínnáta quoíquam út siét   *cre.4*
út malís gaúdeánt átque ex íncómmodís
álteríús sua út cómparént cómmoda? Áh,
ídnest uérum? Ímmo id ést génus hominúm péssumum, ín   [5]
dénegándó modó quís pudór paúllum adést;   630
póst ubí témpus prómíssa iám pérficí,
túm coáctí necéssárió se áperiúnt.
[Ét timént ét tamén rés premít dénegáre.]
Íbi tum eórum ínpudéntíssima órátióst: [10]
"Quís tu es? Quís mihi és? Quór meám tibi? Heús,   635 *cre.co. x 2*
próxumús sum egomét mihí!"   *tro.4^*

PAMPH. What can I say to my dad now? Can I refuse, when I've only just promised him myself? How can I dare to do it? How can I have the nerve? I don't know what to do with myself now!

DAVOS [*aside*] Neither do I – but I'm working hard on it! I'll promise to think of something, so as to put off this trouble for a bit **[615]**.

PAMPH. [*seeing him*] Oh!

DAVOS [*aside*] He's seen me!

PAMPH. I say, my good fellow, look here! Do you see what a frightful tangle your advice has got me into?

DAVOS But I'll soon get you out again!

PAMPH. Get me out again?

DAVOS Certainly, Pamphilus!

PAMPH. The way you did just now, I suppose!

DAVOS No, better, I hope.

PAMPH. Oh, how can I trust *you*, you crook? Are *you* going to sort out this disastrous tangle? *There's* the man for me to rely on! I had no problems at all earlier, and then you trapped me into a wedding **[620]**! Didn't I say this would happen?

DAVOS You did.

PAMPH. What do you deserve?

DAVOS Crucifixion. – But let me recover a bit; I'll soon see something!

PAMPH. I only wish I had the time to give you the punishment I'd like to! All I've got time for now is watching out for myself, not punishing you!

[*Enter* CHARINUS *from the left, not seeing the others.*]

CHAR. Can I believe this? Can it be true **[625]**? Can anyone be so perverse that another person's troubles give them pleasure, and they secure their own advantage at the cost of someone else's disadvantage? Is that really right? No, that's the worst sort of men, the ones who are too embarrassed to refuse a request in the short run **[630]**, but later, when it's time to carry out what they've promised, then they're inevitably forced to reveal themselves. [They're afraid to refuse, but the situation forces them to.] Then they're quite shameless in what they say: 'Who are you? What have you got to do with me? Why should I let you have my girl? Look here, charity begins at home **[635]**!' But if you ask them 'Where's your

Át tamén "Ubí fidés?" sí rogés,　　　　　　　　　　　　　　*cre.3*
níl pudét híc, ubi opúst; ílli ubí
níl opúst, ibí ueréntur!　　　　　　　　　　　　638a　*tro.4*
Séd quid agam? Ádeon ád eum et cŭm eo iniúriam hánc
　　expóstulém?　　　　　　　　　　　　　　　　[15]　*tro.7*
Íngerám mala múlta? Atque áliquis dícat "Níl promóuerís".　　640
Multúm: moléstus cérte eī fúero atque ánimo mórem gésseró!　　*ia.8*
PA. Charíne, et me ét te inprúdens, nísi quid dí respíciunt, pérdidí!
CHA. Ítane? "Inprúdens"? Tándem inuéntast caúsa! Sóluistí fidém!　*tro.7*
PA. Quíd "Tandem"? **CHA.** Étiamnúnc me dúcere ístis
　　díctis póstulás?　　　　　　　　　　　　　　　　[20]
PA. Quíd ĭstuc ést? **CHA.** Postquám me amáre díxi,
　　cómplacitást tibí!　　　　　　　　　　　　645
Heú me míserum, quí tuom ánimum ex ánimo spéctauí meó!
PA. Fálsus és! **CHA.** Non tíbi sat ésse hoc sólidum uísumst gaúdiúm,
nísi me láctassés amántem et fálsa spé prodúcerés?
Hábeas! **PA.** Hábeam? Ah, néscis quántis ín malís uorsér misér,　　[25]
quantásque hic suīs consíliis míhi confláuit sóllicitúdinés　　650　*ia.8*
meŭs cárnuféx! **CHA.** Quid ĭstúc tam mírumst dé te si éxemplúm capít?
PA. Haud ístuc dícas sí cognóris uél me uél amorém meúm!
CHA. Sciŏ: cúm patre áltercásti dúdum, et ís nunc próptereá tibí
suscénset, néc te quíuit hódie cógere íllam ut dúcerés!　　　　[30]
PA. Immo étiam, quó tu mínŭs scis aérumnás meás,　　655　*ia.6*
hae núptiaé non ádparábantúr mihí,
nec póstulábat núnc quisquam úxorém daré!
CHA. Sciŏ: tú coáctus tuā uolúntate és! **PA.** Mané:
nondúm scis! **CHA.** Scío equidem íllam dúcturum ésse té!　　　[35]
PA. Quor me énicás? Hoc aúdi: númquam déstitít　　660
instáre ut dícerém me dúcturúm patrí,
suadére, oráre, usque ádeo dónec pérpulít!

word?', they don't feel any embarrassment then, when it's called for; the only time they do feel shame is when it isn't called for!

But what should I do? Should I go to him and complain to him about the wrong he's done me? Should I heap insults on him? Someone may say 'You won't make any headway **[640]**' – but I will, lots: I'll certainly be a nuisance to him, and I'll get it off my chest!

PAMPH. [*attracting his attention*] Charinus, I've ruined both myself and you without meaning to, unless the gods show some care for us!

CHAR. Oh yes? 'Without meaning to'? You've finally found an excuse! [*sarcastically*] You've kept your word!

PAMPH. Why do you say 'finally'?

CHAR. Do you *still* expect to lead me on by talking like that?

PAMPH. What do you mean?

CHAR. After I'd told you I loved her, she took your fancy **[645]**! Look what I suffer for judging your character according to my own!

PAMPH. You're wrong!

CHAR. Did you think it wouldn't give you really lasting joy if you didn't encourage my love and seduce me with false hopes? Keep her!

PAMPH. Keep her?! No, you don't realize what trouble I'm in, damn it, or what worries this man has sparked off for me with his advice **[650]** – this murdering villain!

CHAR. What's so surprising about that, if he takes *you* as his example?

PAMPH. You wouldn't say that if you knew me, or how much in love I am!

CHAR. [*sarcastically*] I *do* know: you've just had a row with your father, and now he's angry with you because of it, and he hasn't been able to make you marry her today!

PAMPH. Quite the opposite! Just to show how little you know my troubles **[655]**, they weren't planning this wedding for me, and no one was expecting to give me a wife just now!

CHAR. Yes, I know: you've been forced into it by your own free will!

PAMPH. Hang on! You *don't* know yet!

CHAR. What I do know is that you're going to marry her!

PAMPH. Why are you driving me to death? Listen to this: he never stopped **[660]** insisting that I had to tell my dad I'd marry her; he carried on urging and begging me until he drove me into it!

CHA. Quis homo ístuc? **PA.** Dáuos! **CHA.** Dáuos? **PA.** Íntertúrbat!
    CHA. Quam ób rem? **PA.** Néscio –   *ia.8*
nisi míhi deós satĭs scíŏ fuísse irátos qui aúscultáuerím!   [40]
CHA. Factum hóc est, Dáue? **DA.** Fáctŭm.
    CHA. Hém, quid aís, scelús?   665 *ia.6*
At tíbi di dígnum fáctis éxitiúm duínt!
Eho, díc mi: si ómnes húnc coniéctum in núptiás
inimíci uéllent, quód nisi hŏc cónsiliúm darént?
DA. Decéptus sum, át non défetígatús. **CHA.** Sció!   [45]
DA. Hac nón succéssit, ália adóriemúr uiá –   670
nisi si íd putás, quia prímo prócessít parúm,
non pósse iam ád salútem cónuorti hóc malúm.
PA. Immo étiam; nám satĭs crédo, si áduigiláuerís,
ex únis géminas míhi confícies núptiás!   [50]
DA. Ego, Pámphile, hóc tibi pró seruítio débeó,   675
conári mánibus pédibus nóctesque ét diés,
capitís períclum adíre, dúm prosím tibí;
tuōmst, síquid praéter spem éuenít, mi ignósceré.
Parúm succédit quód ago; at fácio séduló.   [55]
Vel mélius túte réperi, mé missúm facé!   680
PA. Cupió: restítue in quém me accépistí locúm!
DA. Faciam. **PA.** Át iam hoc ópŭst! **DA.** Em! Séd manĕ:
    cóncrepuĭt a Glýcerio óstiúm.   *ia.8*
PA. Nil ád te! **DA.** Quaéro! **PA.** Hem, núncin démum?
    DA. At iam hóc tibi ínuentúm dabó!

CHAR.   Who did that?

PAMPH. Davos!

CHAR.   *Davos?!*

PAMPH. He's messing things up!

CHAR.   Why?

PAMPH. I don't know – but I do know that the gods must have been angry with me: that's why they made me listen to him!

CHAR.   [*turning to* DAVOS] Did you do that, Davos?

DAVOS   I did.

CHAR.   What?! What's that you say, you villain [**665**]? I hope the gods grant you the disaster you deserve for what you've done! Look here, tell me: if all his enemies wanted him trapped into a wedding, what other advice would they have given than that?

DAVOS   I'm disappointed, but I haven't given up.

CHAR.   [*sarcastically*] Of course not!

DAVOS   That way didn't work; we'll try another line of attack [**670**]. – Or do you think that just because it hasn't gone too well to start with our problem can't now be steered towards a happy outcome?

PAMPH. No, it definitely can! Stay alert, and I've no doubt you'll fix up two weddings for me, not just one!

DAVOS   Pamphilus, my duty to you as your slave [**675**] is to strain every nerve, night and day, and put my own life at risk, as long as I help you; yours is to pardon me if things don't turn out as we expected. My plan isn't going too well, but I'm working hard at it. Or if you prefer, think of something better yourself, and leave me out of it [**680**]!

PAMPH. I'd like to do that! Just take me back to square one!

DAVOS   I'll do so.

PAMPH. But you must do it *now*!

DAVOS   [*striking the pose of a man rapt in thought*] Here you are! – But hang on! There's a noise from Glycerium's door. [*The noise is made by* MYSIS, *who starts to come out.*]

PAMPH. [*to* DAVOS] That's nothing to do with you!

DAVOS   [*resuming his pose*] I'm trying to think!

PAMPH. Oh yes? Are you, at last?

DAVOS   And I'll soon find the answer for you!

MYSIS Iam ubiúbi erit, ínuentúm tibí curábo et
    mécum addúctum   **[IV.ii]**   *ia.7*
tūom Pámphilúm: modo tu, ánime mí, nolí te máceráre!   685
PA. Mysís! **MY.** Quis ést? Ehĕm, Pámphile, óptumé mihi te óffers!
    PA. Quíd id est?
MY. Oráre iússit, sí se amés, era, iăm ut ad sése uénias:
uidére aít te cúpere. **PA.** Váh, perii! Hóc malum íntegráscit!   [5]
Sicín me atque íllam operá tuá nunc míseros sóllicitári!
Nam idcírco accérsor, núptiás quod mi ádparári sénsit!   690
CHA. Quibŭs quídĕm quam fácile pótuerát quiésci, si híc quiésset!
DA. Age, si híc non ínsanít satís sūa spónte, instíga! **MY.** Atque édepol
ea rés est, próptereáque núnc misera ín maerórest. **PA.** Mýsis,   [10]
per ŏmnís tibi ádiuró deós numquam eām me désertúrum,
non sí capiúndos míhi sciam ésse inimícos ómnis hómines!   695
Hanc mi éxpetíui; cóntigít; conuéniunt móres: uáleant
qui intér nos díscidiúm uolúnt! Hanc nísi mors mi ádimet némo!
MY. Resipísco! **PA.** Nón Apóllinís magĭs uérum atque
    hóc respónsumst.   [15]
Si póterit fíeri ut né patér per mé stetísse crédat
quo mínus hae fíerent núptiaé, uoló; sed si íd non póterit,   700
id fáciam in prócliuí quod ést, per mé stetísse ut crédat.
Quis uídeor? **CHA.** Míser, aeque átque egó! **DA.** Consílium quaéro.
    PA. Fórti's!
DA. Sciŏ quíd conér; hoc égo tibí profécto efféctum réddam.   [20]

MYSIS   [*talking back through the doorway to* GLYCERIUM] Wherever he is, I'll make sure I find your Pamphilus for you soon and bring him along with me; just don't torture yourself, my darling [685]. [*She closes the door behind her.*]

PAMPH.   Mysis!

MYSIS   [*looking round*] Who's that? Ah, Pamphilus, good! I wanted to meet you.

PAMPH.   What's the matter?

MYSIS   My mistress told me to ask you to come to her at once, if you love her; she says she's longing to see you.

PAMPH.   Oh no! I've had it! This trouble's starting up again! [*to* DAVOS] Look how upset and worried we both are now, thanks to you! The reason she's sending for me is because she's heard about the preparations for my wedding [690]!

CHAR.   And how easily she could have kept calm about that, if *he'd* kept quiet!

DAVOS   [*to* CHARINUS] Go on, then! If he isn't mad enough on his own, provoke him! [*Continues trying to think of a plan.*]

MYSIS   [*to* PAMPHILUS] Yes, that's just what it is; that's why the poor girl's grieving now.

PAMPH.   Mysis, I swear to you by all the gods that I'll never abandon her, not if I knew that it meant making all men my enemies [695]! She's the one I was keen to have; it's happened; we get on well together. – To hell with those who want us to split up! No one but Death will take her from me!

MYSIS   I breathe again!

PAMPH.   Apollo's oracle doesn't answer more truthfully than this! If it's possible for my father not to think it's my fault if this wedding doesn't take place, that's what I'd like; but if it's not possible [700], I'll take the easy course and let him think it *is* my fault! [PAMPHILUS' *brave speech is received in silence; he turns to* CHARINUS.] How do I strike you?

CHAR.   Miserable, the same as me!

DAVOS   I'm trying to think of a plan!

PAMPH.   Good for you!

DAVOS   I know what I'm aiming for; I'll certainly sort *this* one out for you.

PA. Iam hoc ópus est! **DA.** Quín iam habeó! **CHA.** Quid ést?
    DA. Huic, nón tibi hábeo, ne érres!
CHA. Sat hábeo. **PA.** Quíd faciés, cedó? **DA.** Diĕs híc mi
    ut sátĭs sit uéreor   705
ad agéndum: né uacuom ésse mé nunc ád narrándum crédas!
Proínde hínc uos ámolíminí; nam mi ínpedímento éstis!
PA. Ego hănc uísam. **DA.** Quíd tu? Quo hínc te agís?
    CHA. Verúm uis dícam? **DA.** Immo étiam!   [25]
(Narrátiónis íncipít mi inítium!) **CHA.** Quíd me fíet?
DA. Eho tu, ínpudéns, non sátis habés quod tíbi diéculam áddo,   710
quantum huíc promóueo núptiás? **CHA.** Daue, át tamén ... **DA.** Quid érgo?
CHA. Ut dúcam! **DA.** Rídiculum! **CHA.** Húc face ád me ut uénias,
    síquid póteris!
DA. Quid uéniam? Níl habeo. **CHA.** Át tamén, siquíd! **DA.** Age, uéniam.
    CHA. Síquid,   [30]
domi eró. **DA.** Tu, Mýsis, dum éxeó, parúmper me ópperíre hic.
MY. Quaprópter? **DA.** Íta factóst opús. **MY.** Matúra!
    DA. Iam, ínquam, hic ádero!   715

PAMPH. You must do it *now*!

DAVOS [*finally struck by an idea*] Yes, I've got it now!

CHAR. What is it?

DAVOS [*to* CHARINUS] It's him I've got it for, not you; don't get me wrong!

CHAR. That's good enough for me.

PAMPH. [*to* DAVOS] What will you do? Tell me!

DAVOS I'm afraid there may not be enough hours in the day for me **[705]** to *act*; don't imagine I've got time to *talk* about it now. So push off, you two! You're in my way!

PAMPH. I'll go to see her. [*Goes into* GLYCERIUM's *house.*]

DAVOS [*to* CHARINUS] What about you? Where are you off to?

CHAR. Do you want me to tell you the truth?

DAVOS No, just go! [*aside*] He's starting to tell me his story from the beginning!

CHAR. What will become of me?

DAVOS Look here, you shameless man, aren't you satisfied that I'm gaining a few hours for you **[710]** by putting off his wedding?

CHAR. Yes, but, Davos ...

DAVOS What is it, then?

CHAR. I want to marry her!

DAVOS Ridiculous!

CHAR. [*pointing towards his house*] Be sure to come to me here, if there's anything you can do!

DAVOS Why should I come? I haven't got a thing for you!

CHAR. Yes, but if there's anything!

DAVOS All right, I'll come!

CHAR. If there's anything, I'll be at home! [*Goes into his house.*]

DAVOS As for you, Mysis, wait for me here a moment, till I come out.

[*Starts towards* GLYCERIUM's *house, but is delayed by* MYSIS' *question.*]

MYSIS Why?

DAVOS That's what you've got to do!

MYSIS Hurry up!

DAVOS I'll be back at once, I tell you **[715]**!

[*Goes into* GLYCERIUM's *house, leaving* MYSIS *alone on stage.*]

MY. Nilne ésse próprium quoíquam! Dí uostrám fidém!　　**[IV.iii]**　　*ia.6*
Summúm bonum ésse eraé putábam hunc Pámphilúm,
amícum, amátorém, uirum, ín quouís locó
parátum; uérum ex eṓ nunc mísera quém capít
labórem! Fácile hic plús malíst quam illíc boní!　　　　　720　[5]
Sed Dáuos éxit. Mi hómo, quid ístuc óbsecróst?
Quo pórtas púerum? **DA.** Mýsis, núnc opus ést tuá
mihi ad hánc rem exprómpta málitia átque astútiá!
MY. Quidnam ínceptúru's? **DA.** Áccipe á me hunc óciús
atque ánte nóstram iánuam ádpone! **MY.** Óbsecró,　　　725　[10]
humíne? **DA.** Ex ára hinc súme uérbenás tibí
atque eā́s substérne. **MY.** Quam ób rem id túte nón facís?
DA. Quia, sí forte ópŭs sit ád erum iúrató mihí
non ádposísse, ut líquido póssim. **MY.** Intéllegó:
noua núnc relígio in te ístaec íncessít! Cedó!　　　　　730　[15]
DA. Moue óciús te, ut quíd agam pórro intéllegás.
Pro Iúppitér! **MY.** Quid ĕst? **DA.** Spónsae páter intéruenít:
repúdio quód consílium prímum inténderám.
MY. Nescíṓ quid nárres! **DA.** Égo quoque hínc ab déxterá
ueníre me ádsimulábo: tu út subséruiás　　　　　　　735　[20]
orátióni, ut quómque opŭs sít, uerbís uidé.
MY. Ego quíd agas níl intéllegó; sed síquid ést
quod méa opera ópŭs sit uóbis, út tu plús uidés,
manébo, néquod uóstrum rémorer cómmodúm.

MYSIS   Look how nothing lasts for anyone! Ye gods! I used to think Pamphilus here was the best possible thing for my mistress – her friend, her lover, her husband, ready to help in any situation. But now look how much misery he's causing her, poor thing! There's easily more trouble in it now than there was benefit then **[720]**!

[DAVOS *comes out of* GLYCERIUM'*s house, holding the baby that has just been born.* MYSIS *first sees him, then notices what he is carrying.*]

But Davos is coming out. – My dear chap, what on earth are you doing? Where are you taking the baby?

DAVOS   Mysis, for this scheme of mine now I need you to display your wickedness and cunning!

MYSIS   What ever are you planning to do?

DAVOS   Take this baby from me quickly, and put it down in front of our door.

MYSIS   What **[725]**, on the ground?!

DAVOS   Take some foliage from the altar here and spread it down first.

MYSIS   Why don't *you* do it?

DAVOS   Because, just in case I have to swear to my master that I didn't put it there – so that I can do it with a good conscience.

MYSIS   I see! That's a new kind of scruple that's just got into you. Give it here **[730]**!

[*Takes the baby and puts it down gently in front of* SIMO'*s door, first spreading some foliage from the altar, as* DAVOS *had instructed.*]

DAVOS   Get a move on! I want you to understand what I'm going to do next. [*Sees* CHREMES *approaching from the right.*] Great god!

MYSIS   What is it?

DAVOS   Here's the girl's father coming along. I must reject the first plan I was laying.

MYSIS   I don't know what you're talking about!

DAVOS   I'll pretend I'm arriving too, from the right here. You make sure **[735]** that you back up my story with what you say – whatever's appropriate! [*Exit left (= stage right).*]

MYSIS   [*addressing* DAVOS *as if he were still present*] I've no idea what you're up to, but if there's anything you need my help for, since you see things better than I do, I'll stay; I don't want to hold up anything that's in the interests of you people.

CHREMES Reuórtor, póstquam quae ópŭs fuére ad núptiás 740 **[IV.iv]**
gnataé paráui, ut iúbeam accérsi. Séd quid hóc?
Puer hérclest! Múlier, tún posísti hunc? **MY.** Úbi ĭllic ést?
CHR. Non míhi respóndes? **MY.** Núsquamst. Vaé miseraé mihí!
Relíquit mḗ homo atque ábiit! **DAVOS** Dí uostrám fidém, [5]
quid túrbaest ápŭd forúm! Quid ĭlli hóminum lítigánt! 745
Tum annóna cárast! (Quíd dicam áliud nésció.)
MY. Quor tu, óbsecro, híc me sólam? **DA.** Hem, quae haéc est fábulá?
Eho, Mýsis, púer hic úndest? Quísue huc áttulít?
MY. Satĭn sánu's quí me id rógites? **DA.** Quem égo igitúr rogém [10]
qui hic néminem álium uídeam? **CHR.** Míror únde sít. 750
DA. Dictúra es quód rogo? **MY.** Aú! **DA.** (Concéde ad déxterám.)
MY. Delíras! Nón tute ípse –? **DA.** (Vérbum sí mihí
unúm praetérquam quód te rógŏ faxís, caué!)
Male dícis? Úndest? Díc clare! **MY.** Á nobís! **DA.** Hahaé! [15]
Mirúm uero ínpudénter múlier sí facít 755
meretríx! **CHR.** Ab Ándriást haec, quántum intéllegó.
DA. Adeón uidémur uóbis ésse idóneí
in quíbŭs sic ínludátis? **CHR.** Véni in témporé!

CHR.   [*to the audience*] Now that I've made the necessary preparations for my daughter's wedding, I've come back **[740]** to give the order for her to be fetched. [*Sees the baby lying on the ground, and* MYSIS *standing next to it.*] But what's this? Good heavens, it's a baby! Woman, did you put this here?

MYSIS   [*to herself, looking round for* DAVOS] Where is that man?

CHR.   Aren't you going to answer me?

MYSIS   [*as before*] He isn't anywhere. Oh no! This is terrible! He's abandoned me and gone away! [DAVOS *returns from the left, as if from the centre of town.*]

DAVOS   [*as if to the world at large, intending to be heard by* CHREMES] Ye gods, what a crowd there is in the main square! What a lot of men are quarrelling there **[745]**! *And* the food prices are high! [*aside*] I don't know what else to say!

MYSIS   [*to* DAVOS] Why on earth did you leave me here on my own?

DAVOS   [*ignoring her question, pretending to see the baby for the first time*] Hey, what's this performance? Look here, Mysis, where does this baby come from? Who brought it here?

MYSIS   Are you in your right mind, asking me that?

DAVOS   Who *can* I ask, then? I can't see anyone else here!

CHR.   [*aside*] I wonder where it comes from **[750]**.

DAVOS   [*to* MYSIS, *pretending not to notice that* CHREMES *is there*] Are you going to answer my question?

MYSIS   Really!

DAVOS   [*whispering to* MYSIS, *so that* CHREMES *cannot hear*] Move over to the right!

MYSIS   [*obeying him, i.e. moving to the audience's left, away from* CHREMES] You're crazy! Didn't you yourself – ?

DAVOS   [*interrupting her, whispering*] If you utter a single word over and above what I ask you, watch out! [*aloud*] Are you insulting me? Where does it come from? Speak up!

MYSIS   From our house!

DAVOS   Ha ha! Very surprising, of course, if a woman behaves shamelessly **[755]** who's a tart!

CHR.   [*aside*] She's from the Andrian girl's, as far as I understand.

DAVOS   Do you women really think we're the sort of people you can play tricks on like this?

CHR.   [*aside*] I've come at the right time!

DA. Propera ádeo púerum tóllere hínc ab iánuá! [20]
(Mané: cauĕ quóquam ex ístoc éxcessís locó!) 760
MY. Di te éradícent! Íta me míseram térritás!
DA. Tibi égo dico án non? **MY.** Quíd uis? **DA.** Át etiám rogás?
Cedo, quóium púerum hic ádposísti? Díc mihí!
MY. Tu néscis? **DA.** Mítte id quód sció; dic quód rogó! [25]
MY. Vostrí. **DA.** Quóius nóstri? **MY.** Pámphili.
       DA. Hém, quid? Pámphilí? 765
MY. Eho, ăn nón est? **CHR.** Récte ego hăs sémper fúgi núptiás!
DA. O fácinus ánimaduórtendúm! **MY.** Quid clámitás?
DA. Quemne égo heri uídi ad uós adférri uésperí?
MY. Ŏ hóminem audácem! **DA.** Vérum: uídi Cántharám [30]
suffárcinátam! **MY.** Dís pol hábeo grátiám 770
quom in páriundo áliquot ádfuérunt líberaé!
DA. Ne illa íllum haud nóuit quóius caúsa haec íncipít:
"Chremés si pósitum púerum ante aédis uíderít,
súam gnátam nón dabít." Tanto hércle mágĭs dabít! [35]
CHR. Non hércle fáciet! **DA.** Núnc adeo, út tu sís sciéns, 775
nisi púerum tóllis iám ego hunc ín mediám uiám
prouóluam téque ibídem péruoluam ín lutó!
MY. Tu pól homo nón es sóbriús! **DA.** Falláciá
alia áliam trúdit: iám susúrrari aúdió [40]
ciuem Átticam ésse hanc! **CHR.** Hém? **DA.** "Coáctus légibús 780
eam uxórem dúcet." **MY.** Au óbsecro, án non cíuis ést?

DAVOS   Hurry up, now: pick the baby up from this doorway! [*whispering*] Stay there! Don't move an inch away from where you are **[760]**!

MYSIS   Damn and blast you! You've got me all upset! I'm frightened!

DAVOS   [*aloud*] Are you listening to me or not?

MYSIS   What do you want?

DAVOS   Are you still asking? Tell me, whose is this baby you've put down here? Answer, please!

MYSIS   Don't you know?

DAVOS   Never mind what I know; answer my question!

MYSIS   It's yours.

DAVOS   Ours? Whose?

MYSIS   Pamphilus's.

DAVOS   What did you say? *Pamphilus's* **[765]**?

MYSIS   Well, isn't it?

CHR.   [*aside*] I was right all along to try to avoid this wedding!

DAVOS   What outrageous behaviour!

MYSIS   What are you shouting about?

DAVOS   Didn't I see it being brought to your house yesterday evening?

MYSIS   You shameless man!

DAVOS   It's true! I saw Canthara with a bundle stuffed under her cloak!

MYSIS   Well, thank heaven **[770]** there were some respectable women present at its birth!

DAVOS   She obviously doesn't know the man she's started on this for! [*imitates* GLYCERIUM*'s voice*] 'If Chremes sees a baby put in front of the house, he won't give his daughter.' – Oh yes he will, all the more so!

CHR.   [*aside*] Oh no he won't!

DAVOS   And now, just to keep you fully informed **[775]**, if you don't pick the baby up, I'm going to roll it straight into the middle of the street, and I'm going to roll you around in the mud there too!

MYSIS   You're obviously drunk, mate! [*Picks the baby up.*]

DAVOS   One trick follows another! Now I hear the story's being whispered abroad that she's a citizen of Attica!

CHR.   [*aside*] *What?!*

DAVOS   [*imitating an imaginary voice*] 'He'll be forced by the laws **[780]** to marry her.'

MYSIS   Really! Are you saying she's *not* a citizen?

CHR. Ioculárium ín malum ínsciéns paene íncidí!
DA. Quis hĭc lóquitur? Ó Chremé, per témpus áduenís:
auscúlta. – **CHR.** Audíui iam ómnia. **DA.** Ánne haec tu ómniá? [45]
CHR. Audíui, inquam, á princípio. **DA.** Audístin, óbsecro? Ém 785
scelera! Hánc iam opórtet ín cruciátum hinc ábripí!
Hic ĕst ílle: nón te crédas Dáuom lúderé!
MY. Me míseram! Níl pol fálsi díxi, mí senéx!
CHR. Noui ómnem rem. Ést Simo íntus? **DA.** Ést.
    MY. Ne me áttigás, [50]
sceléste! Sí pol Glýcerió non ómnia haéc – 790
DA. Eho, inépta, néscis quíd sit áctum? **MY.** Quí sciám?
DA. Hic sócer est. Álio pácto haud póterat fíerí
ut scíret haéc quae uóluimús. **MY.** Praedícerés!
DA. Paullum ínterésse cénses éx animo ómniá, [55]
ut fért natúra, fácias án de indústriá? 795
CRITO In hác habitásse plátea díctumst Chrýsidém, **[IV.v]**
quae sése inhonéste optáuit párere hic dítiás
potiús quam in pátria honéste paúper uíuerét.
Éius mórte ea ád me lége rédierúnt boná.
Sed quós percónter uídeo: sáluete! **MY.** Óbsecró, 800 [5]
quem uídeo? Estne híc Critó, sobrínus Chrýsidís?
Is ést! **CR.** O Mýsis, sálue! **MY.** Sáluos sís, Critó!
CR. Itắn Chrýsis? Hém! **MY.** Nos quídĕm pol míseras pérdidít.

CHR.   [*aside*] A hilarious mess I'd almost stumbled into without realizing it!

DAVOS   [*pretending to notice* CHREMES *for the first time*] Who's speaking here? Oh, Chremes! You've come at the right time: listen. –

CHR.   I've heard everything already.

DAVOS   Have you? All of it?

CHR.   I heard it from the start, I tell you.

DAVOS   Did you really hear it? Look [785] what criminals they are! This one should be taken straight off to be tortured! [*to* MYSIS] This is the man; don't imagine you're fooling *Davos*!

MYSIS   Oh dear! [*to* CHREMES] I swear everything I said was true, sir!

CHR.   I know the whole story! [*to* DAVOS] Is Simo indoors?

DAVOS   He is. [CHREMES *goes straight into* SIMO's *house;* DAVOS *moves towards* MYSIS.]

MYSIS   Don't touch me, damn you! I swear, if I don't tell Glycerium about all of this [790], –

DAVOS   [*interrupting*] Look here, you silly woman, don't you know what we've done?

MYSIS   How could I know?

DAVOS   He's his father-in-law. There was no other way to get him to know what we wanted him to.

MYSIS   You should have warned me!

DAVOS   Do you think it makes a small difference whether you do everything instinctively and naturally or according to a careful plan [795]?

[*Enter* CRITO *from the right, coming from the harbour.*]

CRITO   [*to the audience*] This is the street where they told me Chrysis used to live. She chose to acquire wealth here by less respectable means rather than living poor but respectably in her own country. Now that she's died, her property's reverted to me by law. [*Catches sight of* DAVOS *and* MYSIS.] But I can see some people to ask. [*addressing them*] Hello!

MYSIS   Good heavens [800], who's this I see? Is it Crito, Chrysis' cousin? Yes, it is!

CRITO   Oh, Mysis! Hello!

MYSIS   Hello, Crito!

CRITO   So Chrysis has – ? Awful!

MYSIS   Yes, we're really upset; it's shattered our lives.

CR. Quid uós? Quo pácto hic? Sátine récte? **MY.** Nósne? Síc;
ut químus, áiunt, quándo ut uólumus nón licét.   805   [10]
CR. Quid Glýceriúm? Iam hic suŏs paréntis répperít?
MY. Utinam! **CR.** Án nondum étiam? Haud aúspicáto huc me ádpulí.
Nam pól, si id scíssem, númquam huc tétulissém pedém:
sempér eius díctast ésse haec átque habitást sorór;
quae illĩûs fuére póssidét; nunc me hóspitém   810   [15]
litís sequí quam id míhi sit fácile atque útilé
aliórum exémpla cómmonént. Simul árbitrór
iam aliquem ésse amícum et défensórem eī; nám feré
grandícula iám proféctast íllinc: clámitént
me sýcophántam, heréditátem pérsequí,   815   [20]
mendícum. Tum ípsam déspoliáre nón lubét.
DA. Ŏ óptume hóspes! **MY.** Pól, Crito, ántiquom óbtinés!
CR. Duc me ád eam, quándo huc uéni, ut uídeam. **MY.** Máxumé.
DA. Sequar hós: noló me in témpore hóc uideát senéx!

CHREMES Sátĭs iam, sátĭs, Simó, spectáta ergá te
      amícitiást meá;   820   **[V.i]**   *tro.7*
sátĭs perícli incépi adíre: orándi iám finém facé.
Dúm studeo óbsequí tibi, paéne inlúsi uítam fíliaé!
SIMO Ímmo enĭm núnc quom máxume ábs te póstulo átque oró, Chremé,
út benefícium uérbis ínitum dúdum núnc re cómprobés!   [5]
CHR. Vídĕ quam iníquos sís prae stúdio: dŭm id effícias
      quód lubés,   825
néque modúm benígnitátis néque quid me óres cógitás.
Nám si cógités remíttas iám me oneráre iniúriís.

CRITO   What about you? How are you getting on here? Everything OK?

MYSIS   Us? So-so: as well as we can, as they say, since we can't live as we'd like to **[805]**.

CRITO   What about Glycerium? Has she found her parents here yet?

MYSIS   If only she had!

CRITO   Still not? [*to himself*] That's an unlucky landfall for me. If I'd known that, I'd certainly never have brought myself here. She was always said and believed to be her sister; she's in possession of everything that used to belong to her. I'm a stranger here **[810]**, and I've got the example of others to remind me how easy and profitable it's going to be for me to take the matter to court! Besides, I expect she's got someone as her friend and protector by now; she was already pretty well grown up when she left home. People would denounce me as a swindler, a legacy-hunter **[815]**, a beggar! [*louder, so that* DAVOS *and* MYSIS *can hear*] Anyway, I don't want to impoverish the girl herself!

DAVOS   What an excellent stranger you are!

MYSIS   Yes, you're the same as ever, Crito!

CRITO   Now that I've come here, take me to see her.

MYSIS   Certainly. [*Takes him into* GLYCERIUM's *house, still carrying the baby.*]

DAVOS   [*to the audience*] I'll follow them; I don't want the old man to see me just at the moment! [*Goes into* GLYCERIUM's *house. After a short pause,* CHREMES *and* SIMO *enter from* SIMO's *house.*]

CHR.   That's enough now, Simo! You've made enough of a test of my friendship towards you **[820]**. It's enough, the risk that I embarked on; don't ask any more of me now. While I've devoted myself to doing what you wanted, I've almost gambled away my daughter's life!

SIMO   But it's now more than ever that I beg and beseech you, Chremes: you undertook earlier to do me a favour; now's the time for you to confirm your words in practice.

CHR.   Look how unreasonable your eagerness makes you! As long as you can bring about what you want **[825]**, you don't think about how far I can take my goodwill, or what you're asking of me! If you did think about it, you'd finally stop heaping unfair demands on me!

SI. Quíbus? **CHR.** At rógitas? Pérpulísti me út homini ádulescéntuló
ín alio óccupáto amóre, abhórrenti áb re uxóriá,   [10]
fíliam út darem ín sedítionem átque in ĩncértas núptiás,   830
eiús labóre atque eiús dolóre gnáto ut médicarér tuó.
Ímpetrásti: incépi, dúm res tétulit. Núnc non fért: ferás.
Íllam hinc cíuem esse áiunt; púer est nátus; nós missós facé.
SI. Pér ego té deõs óro ut ne íllis ánimum indúcas créderé,   [15]
quíbus id máxume útilést illum ésse quám detérrumúm.   835
Núptiárum grátia haéc sunt fícta atque íncepta ómniá;
úbi ea caúsa quam ób rem haec fáciunt érit adémpta his, désinént.
CHR. Érras: cúm Dauo égomet uídi iúrgantem áncillám. **SI.** Scio.
                         CHR. Át
uéro uóltu, quom íbi me adésse neúter túm praesénseránt.   [20]
SI. Crédo, et íd factúras Dáuos dúdum praédixít mihi; ét   840
nésció qui id tíbi sum oblítus hódie, ac uólui, díceré.
DAVOS Ánimo núnciam ótióso esse ímpero –
                   CHR. Ém Dauóm tibí!   [V.ii]
SI. Únde egréditur? **DA.** – meõ praesídio atque hóspitís.
                   SI. Quid ĩllúd malíst?
DA. Égo commódiorem hóminem, aduéntum, témpus nón uidí. **SI.** Scelús,
quémnam hic laúdat? **DA.** Ómnis rés est iam ín uadó.
                   SI. Cesso ádloquí?   845
DA. Érus est! Quíd agam? **SI.** O sálue, bóne uir! **DA.** Éhĕm Simo!
                   Ó nostér Chremé!   [5]

SIMO   Which ones?

CHR.   What a question! You prevailed on me to give my daughter to a young lad who was engrossed in an affair with another woman and had no desire to marry, to hand her over to a quarrelsome and insecure marriage [830], so that I could cure *your* son with *her* pain and *her* distress! You got your way: I embarked on your plan while circumstances allowed. Now they don't allow: you must make allowances. They say she's a citizen from here; a boy's been born. – Leave us out of it!

SIMO   I beg you by the gods not to let yourself believe them; it's particularly in their interest to make him out to be as bad as possible [835]! It's because of the wedding that they've made all this up and set it in train. Once they've been deprived of that motive for their behaviour, they'll stop!

CHR.   You're wrong! I saw her girl arguing with Davos myself!

SIMO   I know!

CHR.   But they weren't acting: neither of them had realized I was present before they began.

SIMO   I believe you: Davos told me earlier that the women would do this [840]. I meant to tell you about it, but somehow I just forgot.

[Enter DAVOS from GLYCERIUM's house, talking back to those indoors and not seeing CHREMES and SIMO.]

DAVOS   Set your minds at rest now, I tell you, –

CHR.   [*to* SIMO] There's Davos for you!

SIMO   [*astonished*] Where's he coming out from?

DAVOS   – and put your trust in me and the stranger. [*Closes the door behind him.*]

SIMO   What the hell's going on?

DAVOS   [*to himself, still not seeing the others*] I haven't seen a man, arrival or timing that were more convenient.

SIMO   The scoundrel! Who's he praising?

DAVOS   The whole affair has reached shallow waters.

SIMO   Why don't I speak to him [845]?

DAVOS   [*catching sight of* SIMO, *aside*] It's the master! What am I to do?

SIMO   Good day to you, my good fellow!

DAVOS   [*struggling to recover his composure*] Ah, Simo! – Chremes, sir! – Everything's ready now indoors.

Ómnia ádparáta iám sunt íntus. **SI.** Cúrastí probé!
DA. Úbi uolés, accérse. **SI.** Béne sane! Íd enimuéro hinc núnc abést!
Étiam tu hóc respóndes: quíd ĭstic tíbi negótist? **DA.** Míhin? **SI.** Itá.
DA. Míhĭn? **SI.** Tibi érgo! **DA.** Módo ĭntroíui –
  SI. Quási ego quám dudúm rogém!   850
DA. – cúm tŭo gnáto una. **SI.** Ánne est íntus Pámphilús?
  Cruciór misér!   [10]
Ého, non tú dixti ésse intér eos ínimicítias, cárnuféx?
DA. Súnt. **SI.** Quor ígitur híc est? **CHR.** Quíd ĭllum cénses?
  Cum ílla lítigát!
DA. Ĭmmŏ uero índignúm, Chremé, iam fácinus fáxo ex me aúdiés.
Néscioquís senéx modo uénit – éllum! –, cónfidéns, catús. 855
Quóm faciém uideás, uidétur ésse quántiuís pretí: [15]
trístis uéritás inést in uóltu atque ín uerbís fidés.
SI. Quídnam adpórtas? **DA.** Níl equidém nisi quód ĭllum audíui díceré.
SI. Quíd ait tándem? **DA.** Glýceriúm se scíre cíuem esse Átticam.
  SI. Hém?
Drómŏ, Dromó! **DA.** Quid ést? **SI.** Dromo! **DA.** Aúdi!
  SI. Vérbum si áddiderís –! Dromó!   860
DA. Audi, óbsecró! **DROMO** Quid uís? **SI.** Sublímem intró
  rape húnc quantúm potést!   [20] *ia.8*
DR. Quem? **SI.** Dáuom. **DA.** Quam ób rem? **SI.** Quía lubét!
  Rape, ínquam! **DA.** Quíd fecí? **SI.** Rapé!

SIMO   [*sarcastically*] You've seen to things very well!

DAVOS   Fetch the bride whenever you want.

SIMO   Very good indeed! That is of course the one thing that's missing from our present situation! Will you answer this: what business do you have in that house?

DAVOS   Me?

SIMO   Yes.

DAVOS   Me?

SIMO   Yes, you!

DAVOS   I went in just now –

SIMO   As if I were asking how long ago [850]!

DAVOS   – together with your son.

SIMO   [*astonished*] Is Pamphilus in there? I can't stand it! Look here, didn't you say they'd broken up, you villain?

DAVOS   They have.

SIMO   So why is he here?

CHR.   [*breaking in, sarcastically*] Why do you think? He's having a row with her!

DAVOS   No, Chremes, listen to me; I'll tell you something scandalous. Some old man turned up just now – there he is indoors! – , bold and sharp [855]. To look at, he seems to be as worthy as they come: his face looks stern and sincere, and his words sound honest.

SIMO   What's this you're bringing up?

DAVOS   Nothing at all, except what I heard him say.

SIMO   Well, what *does* he say?

DAVOS   That he knows Glycerium is a citizen of Attica.

SIMO   What?! [*shouting indoors*] Dromo! Dromo!

DAVOS   What's the matter?

SIMO   Dromo!

DAVOS   Listen!

SIMO   If you add a word – ! Dromo [860]!

DAVOS   Listen, I beg you!

DROMO   [*appearing from* SIMO*'s house*] What do you want?

SIMO   Lift him up and take him indoors, as quickly as possible!

DROMO   Who?

SIMO   Davos.

DAVOS   Why?

SIMO   Because I want him to! [*to* DROMO] Take him in, I say!

DA. Si quícquam inuénies mé mentítum, occíditó! **SI.** Nil aúdió!
Égo iam té commótum réddam! **DA.** Támen etsi
   hóc uerúmst? **SI.** Tamén! *tro.7*
Cura ádseruándum uínctum! Atque aúdin? Quádrupedém
   constríngitó! 865 *ia.8*
Age núnciam: égo pol hódie, sí uiuó, tibí [25] *ia.6*
osténdam erúm quid sít perícli fálleré,
et íllí patrem! **CHR.** Áh, ne saéui tánto opere! **SI.** Ó Chremé,
pietátem gnáti! Nónne té miserét meí?
Tantúm labórem cápere ob tálem fíliúm! 870
Age, Pámphile! Éxi, Pámphile! Écquid té pudét? [30]
PAMPHILUS Quis mé uolt? Périi, páter est! **SI.** Quíd ais, ómnium –?
   CHR. Áh, [V.iii]
rem pótius ípsam díc, ac mítte mále loquí!
SI. Quasi quícquam in húnc iam gráuius díci póssiét!
Aín tándem: cíuis Glýceriúmst? **PA.** Ita praédicánt. 875
SI. "Ita praédicánt"? O ingéntem cónfidéntiám! [5]
Num cógitát quid dícat? Núm factí pigét?
Vidĕ num eiús colór pudóris sígnum usquam índicát!
Adeo ínpoténti esse ánimo ut praéter cíuiúm
morem átque légem et suí uolúntatém patrís 880
tamen hánc habére stúdeat cúm summó probró! [10]
PA. Me míserum! **SI.** Hem, módone id démum sénsti, Pámphilé?
Olim ístuc, ólim, quom íta animum índuxtí tuóm,
quod cúperes áliquo pácto effíciundúm tibí,
eodém die ístuc uérbum uére in te áccidít! 885
Sed quíd ego? Quór me excrúcio? Quór me máceró? [15]

DAVOS   What have I done?

SIMO   Take him!

DAVOS   If you find I've made anything up, you can kill me!

SIMO   I won't hear a word! I'll stir you up now!

DAVOS   [*to* SIMO] Even though this is true?

SIMO   Even so! [*to* DROMO] Make sure you keep him tied up! [DROMO *starts to carry* DAVOS *indoors;* SIMO *stops him with a further instruction.*] – And listen: tie his hands and feet together [**865**]! [*Shouts at* DAVOS *as* DROMO *carries him into his house.*] All right, then! My god, as sure as I'm alive, I'll show you how dangerous it is to deceive your master – and him to deceive his father!

CHR.   Please stop being so brutal!

SIMO   Oh Chremes, what a devoted son I have! Don't you pity me? That I should have so much trouble for such a son [**870**]! [*Shouts to* PAMPHILUS *in* GLYCERIUM's *house.*] Pamphilus! Pamphilus! Come on, come out here! Have you any shame? [PAMPHILUS *comes out of* GLYCERIUM's *house.*]

PAMPH.   Who wants me? – I've had it! It's my dad!

SIMO   Look here, you utter – [SIMO *cannot find a word strong enough for his anger.*]

CHR.   Please just say what the facts of the matter are, and cut out the abuse!

SIMO   As if it would be possible in the circumstances to say anything too harsh against him! [*to* PAMPHILUS] Tell me, then: Glycerium's a citizen, is she?

PAMPH.   So they say [**875**].

SIMO   'So they say'! How utterly brazen! Does he think what he's saying? Is he sorry for what he's done? Look at his face: does it show any sign of shame? How can he be so wilful? In spite of the traditions and laws of his city, and the wishes of his own father [**880**], he aims to live with her in the utmost disgrace!

PAMPH.   I'm in a mess!

SIMO   What? Have you only just realized it, Pamphilus? It was then, then when you convinced yourself that one way or another you had to satisfy your desires – that was the day when those words really applied to you [**885**]! – But what am I doing? Why am I torturing

Quor meám senéctutem huiús sollícito améntiá?
An ŭt pro huiús peccátis égo supplícium súfferám?
Immo hábeat, uáleat, uíuat cum ílla! **PA.** Mí patér!
SI. Quid "Mí patér"? Quasi tu húius índigeás patrís!   890
Domus, úxor, líberi ínuenti ínuitó patré;   [20]
addúcti qui íllam hinc cíuem dícant: uícerís!
PA. Patér, licétne paúca? **SI.** Quíd dicés mihi? **CHR.** Át
tamén, Simo, aúdi. **SI.** Ego aúdiám? Quid aúdiám,
Chremé? **CHR.** At tándem dícat! **SI.** Áge, dicát: sinó.   895
PA. Égo me amáre hanc fáteor; si íd peccárest,
                 fáteor íd quoqué.   [25]   *tro.7*
Tíbi, patér, me dédo: quíduis óneris ínpone, ímperá.
Vís me uxórem dúcere? Hánc uis míttere? Út poteró ferám.
Hóc modo te óbsecro, út ne crédas á me adlégatum húnc seném:
síne me expúrgem atque íllum huc córam addúcam. **SI.** Addúcas?
                 PA. Síne, patér!   900
CHR. Áequom póstulát: da uéniam. **PA.** Síne te hoc éxorém!
                 SI. Sinó.   [30]
Quíduis cúpio dúm ne ab hóc me fálli cómperiár, Chremé!
CHR. Pró peccáto mágno paúllum súpplicí satis ést patrí.
CRITO Mítte oráre: una hárum quaéuis caúsa me út faciám monét, **[V.iv]**
uél tu uél quod uérumst uél quod ípsi cúpio Glýcerió.   905
CHR. Ándrium égo Critónem uídeo? Cérte is ĕst! **CR.** Sáluos sís, Chremé!
CHR. Quíd tu Athénas ínsoléns? **CR.** Euénit. Séd hicinést Simó?

myself? Why do I torment myself? Why am I troubling *my* old age with *his* folly? So that *I* pay the penalty for *his* sins? No! Let him keep her! To hell with him! Let him live with her!

PAMPH. Dad, please!

SIMO   What do you mean, 'Dad, please'? As if you felt any need for this dad here **[890]**! You've found a home, a wife and children against your dad's wishes; you've brought in people to say she's a citizen from here: you've won!

PAMPH. Dad, may I say something?

SIMO   What can you say to me?

CHR.   All the same, Simo, listen to him.

SIMO   Me listen? What am I to listen to, Chremes?

CHR.   Do just let him speak!

SIMO   All right, let him speak; I agree **[895]**.

PAMPH. I admit that I love her; if that's a sin, I admit that too. I give myself up to you, dad: lay on me whatever burden you will, give me any command. Do you want me to marry? Do you want me to abandon her? I'll bear it as best I can. My one request is this: please do not think that this old man was put up to it by me. Let me clear myself and bring him here to meet you.

SIMO   Bring him here?!

PAMPH. Please, dad **[900]**!

CHR.   It's a reasonable request; give your consent.

PAMPH. Please agree to it!

SIMO   All right. [*Exit* PAMPHILUS *to* GLYCERIUM's *house.*] I'm happy to agree to anything, as long as I don't find that I'm being deceived by him, Chremes!

CHR.   From a father, a small punishment is enough for a big crime.

[PAMPHILUS *reappears, with* CRITO.]

CRITO   [*to* PAMPHILUS] You can cut out the pleading. Any one of these reasons prompts me to do it, whether it's you, or the fact that it's true, or the fact that I wish well to Glycerium herself **[905]**.

CHR.   [*astonished*] Is it Crito of Andros that I see? Yes, it surely is!

CRITO   Hello, Chremes!

CHR.   What brings you to Athens? You don't often come.

CRITO   It turned out that way. But is this Simo?

CHR. Híc. **CR.** Simó, – **SI.** Men quaéris? Ého tu, Glýcerium
hínc ciuem ésse aís? [5]
CR. Tú negás? **SI.** Itane húc parátus áduenís? **CR.** Qua ré? **SI.** Rogás?
Túne inpúne haec fácias? Túne hic hómines ádulescéntulós 910
ínperitos rérum, edúctos líbere, ín fraudem ínlicís?
Sóllicitándo et póllicitándo ēorum ánimos láctas? **CR.** Sánun és?
SI. Ác meretríciós amóres núptiís conglútinás? [10]
PA. Périi! Métuo ut súbstet hóspes. **CHR.** Sí, Simo, húnc norís satís,
nón ita árbitrére. Bónus est híc uir. **SI.** Híc uir sít bonús? 915
Ítane adtémperáte euénit, hódie in ípsis núptiís
út ueníret, ántehac númquam? Est uéro huic crédundúm, Chremé!
PA. Ní metuám patrem, hábeo pro ílla re íllum quód moneám probé. [15]
SI. Sýcophánta! **CR.** Hem? **CHR.** Síc, Crito, ést hic: mítte.
          CR. Vídeat quí siét.
Sí mihi pérget quaé uolt dícere, éa quae nón uolt aúdiét. 920
Égo ístaec móueo aut cúro? Nón tu tuōm malum aéquo animó ferás?
Nam égo quae díco uéra an fálsa audíerim iám scirí potést.
Átticús quidam ólim náui frácta ad Ándrum eiéctus ést [20]
ét ístaec úna párua uírgo. Tum ílle egéns forte ádplicát
prímum ad Chrýsidís patrém se. **SI.** Fábulam ínceptát! **CHR.** Siné! 925

CHR.   Yes.

CRITO   Simo, –

SIMO   [*interrupting*] Are you looking for me? Look here, you! Are you saying Glycerium's a citizen from here?

CRITO   Are you saying she isn't?

SIMO   Is that what you've been primed to come here and say?

CRITO   Why?

SIMO   What a question! Do you expect to get away with this? Do you entice and ensnare the young men of this city **[910]** – lads with no experience of the world, with a respectable upbringing? Do you seduce their minds by pressurizing and promising? –

CRITO   Are you in your right mind?

SIMO   – And do you fix up marriages to cement their affairs with prostitutes?

PAMPH.   [*aside*] Help! I'm afraid the stranger won't hold up!

CHR.   If you knew him properly, Simo, you wouldn't think that: this is an honest man.

SIMO   This man? Honest **[915]**? Has it just '*turned out*' so conveniently that he *turned up* today – on the very day of the wedding – and never before this? Oh yes, he's a man we should believe, Chremes!

PAMPH.   [*aside*] If I wasn't afraid of my dad, I've got something good I could suggest to him to meet that point.

SIMO   Swindler!

CRITO   What?

CHR.   That's how he is, Crito; take no notice.

CRITO   It's up to him how he is. If he carries on saying what he likes to me, he'll hear things he doesn't like **[920]**. [*to* SIMO] Do I interfere in your affairs? Do I care about them? Can't you bear your own troubles calmly? As for what *I* tell you, you can now find out whether the story I've heard is true or false. There was once a man from Attica who was shipwrecked off the coast of Andros and cast ashore – and she was with him; she was a little girl. Well, being destitute, he happened to turn first for help to the father of Chrysis.

SIMO   He's making it up!

CHR.   [*to* SIMO] Quiet **[925]**!

CR. Ítane uéro obtúrbat? **CHR.** Pérge. **CR.** Tum ís mihi cógnatús fuít
qui eûm recépit. Íbi ego audíui ex íllo sése esse Átticúm.
Ís ibi mórtuóst. **CHR.** Eîus nómen? **CR.** Nómen tám cito?
   Phánia? Hém,   [25]
perií! Verum hércle opínor fuîsse Phániam. Hóc certó sció: *ia.8*
Rhamnúsiúm se aiébat ésse. **CHR.** O Iúppitér!
   CR. Eadem haéc, Chremé,   930
multi álii in Ándro audíuere. **CHR.** Útinam id sít quod spéro! Eho, díc mihí,
quid eám tum? Suâmne esse aîbat? **CR.** Nón. **CHR.** Quoiam ígitur?
   CR. Frátris fíliám.
CHR. Certé meást! **CR.** Quid aís? **SI.** Quid tû ais?
   PA. Árrige aúris, Pámphilé!   [30]
SI. Qui crédis? **CHR.** Phánia íllic fráter meûs fuít. **SI.** Noram ét sció.
CHR. Is béllum hinc fúgiens méque in Ásiam pérsequéns
   proficíscitúr;   935
tum illám relínquere híc est uéritus. Póstilla hínc primum aúdió
quid ílló sit fáctum. **PA.** Víx sum apúd me: ita ánimus cómmotúst metú,
spe, gaúdió, mirándo tánto tám repéntino hóc bonó!   [35]
SI. Ne istám multímodis tûam ínueníri gaúdeó! **PA.** Credó, patér!
CHR. At scrúpulús mi etiam únus réstat quí me mále habet.
   PA. Dígnus és   940
cum tûá relígione, ódium! Nódum in scírpo quaéris! **CR.** Quíd ístud ést?
CHR. Nomén non cónuenít. **CR.** Fuit hércle huic áliud páruae.

CRITO That's how he interrupts, is it?

CHR. [*to* CRITO] Carry on.

CRITO Well, the man who took him in was a relative of mine. It was there that I heard from him that he was from Attica. He died there.

CHR. His name?

CRITO His name, so quickly? [*struggling to remember*] Was it Phania? Oh damn it! Well, I certainly think it was Phania. This much I know for sure: he said he came from Rhamnus.

CHR. My god!

CRITO Many others on Andros [930] heard the same story, Chremes.

CHR. I pray that what I hope is true! Here, tell me, what about her at that time? Did he say she was his?

CRITO No.

CHR. Whose, then?

CRITO His brother's daughter.

CHR. She's mine, for certain!

CRITO What?

SIMO What's that you say?

PAMPH. [*aside*] Prick up your ears, Pamphilus!

SIMO What makes you think that?

CHR. That Phania was my brother!

SIMO I know: I knew him.

CHR. He set out from here to avoid the war and follow my tracks to Asia [935], and he was afraid to leave the girl here. Since that time, this is the first person I've heard from about what became of him.

PAMPH. I can hardly control myself! My mind is in such a turmoil of fear, hope, joy, and amazement at this good fortune: it's so great, so sudden!

SIMO [*to* CHREMES] I really am delighted for a number of reasons that we've discovered that girl to be your daughter!

PAMPH. I'm sure you are, dad!

CHR. But there's one detail left that still worries me.

PAMPH. [*aside*] You *deserve* to be worried [940], you and your scruples, you boring man! You're looking for a knot in a bulrush!

CRITO [*to* CHREMES] What's that?

CHR. Her name doesn't fit.

CRITO No, she had a different one when she was little.

CHR. Quód, Critó?
Numquíd meminísti? **CR.** Id quaéro. **PA.** Egon húius
mémoriám patiár meaé [40]
uolŭptáti obstáre, quom égomet póssim in hác re médicarí mihí?
Heus, Chrémĕ! Quod quaéris Pásibúlast. **CHR.** Pásibúla? Ipsást.
CR. Eást. 945
PA. Ex ípsa míliéns audíui. **SI.** Omnís nos gaúdere hóc, Chremé,
te crédo crédere. **CHR.** Íta me dī ament, crédo! **PA.** Quód restát, patér, –
SI. Iamdúdum rés reddúxit me ípsa in grátiam.
PA. Ó lepidúm patrém! [45]
De uxóre, ita út possédi, níl mutát Chremés? **CHR.** Causa óptumást,
nisi quíd patér ait áliud. **PA.** Némpe id. **SI.** Scílicét.
CHR. Dos, Pámphile, ést 950
decém talénta. **PA.** Accípio. **CHR.** Própero ad fíliam. Ého mecúm, Critó!
Nam illám me crédo haud nósse. **SI.** Quór non íllam huc tránsferrí iubés?
PA. Recte ádmonés: Dauo égo ïstuc dédam iám negóti.
SI. Nón potést. [50]
PA. Qui? **SI.** Quía habet áliud mágis ex sése et máius. **PA.** Quídnam?
SI. Vínctus ést.
PA. Patér, non récte uínctust! **SI.** Haúd ita iússi!
PA. Iúbĕ solui, óbsecró! 955

CHR.   What was it, Crito? You can't remember, can you?

CRITO   I'm trying to.

PAMPH.   [*aside*] Am I going to let his memory get in the way of my happiness, when I hold the cure for this in my own hands? [*to* CHREMES] Hey, Chremes, the name you're looking for is Pasibula!

CHR.   Pasibula? That's the one!

CRITO   That's it [945]!

PAMPH.   She's told me herself a thousand times!

SIMO   I'm sure you realize that we're all delighted about this, Chremes!

CHR.   I most certainly do!

PAMPH.   [*hesitantly*] As for the remaining matter, dad ...

SIMO   Circumstances have long since reconciled me to it!

PAMPH.   Oh you darling dad! And Chremes doesn't want to change the situation of my wife, given that I've taken possession of her?

CHR.   Your case is very strong – unless your father says otherwise.

PAMPH.   Naturally he agrees!

SIMO   Of course!

CHR.   Her dowry is [950] ten talents, Pamphilus.

PAMPH.   I accept it!

CHR.   I'm impatient to see my daughter! Here, come with me, Crito: I don't think she knows me! [*Exeunt* CHREMES *and* CRITO *to* GLYCERIUM*'s house, leaving* SIMO *and* PAMPHILUS *on stage.*]

SIMO   Why don't you give orders for her to be moved over to our house?

PAMPH.   A good suggestion! I'll give the job to Davos at once. [*Starts to move towards their house, but is detained by* SIMO*'s next words.*]

SIMO   That's impossible.

PAMPH.   Why?

SIMO   Because he's involved in something else that suits him better and matters more to him.

PAMPH.   What's that?

SIMO   He's tied up.

PAMPH.   Dad, it was wrong to tie him up!

SIMO   I didn't *tell* them to do it wrong!

PAMPH.   Tell them to untie him, please [955]!

SI. Age, fíat. **PA.** Át matúra! **SI.** Eo íntro. **PA.** O faústum et félicém diém!
CHARINUS Prouíso quíd agat Pámphilús. Atque éccum!

    PA. Aliquís me fórsitán   **[V.v]**
putĕt nón putáre hoc uérum; at míhi nunc síc esse hóc uerúm lubét.
Égo deōrúm uitám proptérea sémpitérnam esse árbitrór   *tro.7*
quód uolŭptátes eōrum própriae súnt. Nam mi ínmortálitás   960
pártast, sí nulla aégritúdo huic gaúdio íntercésserít.   **[5]**
Séd quem ego míhi potíssimum óptem, quoí nunc haéc narrém, darí?
CHA. Quíd íllud gaúdist? **PA.** Dáuom uídeo; némost quém mallem ómniúm.
Nam húnc sció mea sólide sólum gáuisúrum gaúdiá.
DAVOS Pámphilús ubinam híc est? **PA.** Dáue! **DA.** Quís homost?

    PA. Égo sum. **DA.** O Pámphilé!   965 **[V.vi]**
PA. Néscis quíd mi obtígerit. **DA.** Cérte; séd quid mi óbtigerít sció!
PA. Ét quidem égo. **DA.** More hóminum euénit út quod sím nanctús malí
priŭs rescíscerés tu quam égo íllud quód tibi éuenít boní.
PA. Glýceriúm mea suōs paréntis répperít! **DA.** Factúm bene! **CHA.**
    Hém?   **[5]**
PA. Páter amícus súmmus nóbis. **DA.** Quís? **PA.** Chremés!

    DA. Narrás probé !   970
PA. Néc mora úllast quín eām uxórem dúcam! **CHA.** Num ílle sómniát

SIMO   All right, OK!

PAMPH. But hurry!

SIMO   I'm going in. [*Goes into his house.*]

PAMPH. What a lucky day! What a happy outcome!

[*Enter* CHARINUS *from his house. He stays on the left of the stage, and* PAMPHILUS *does not notice him.*]

CHAR. I've come out to see what Pamphilus is up to – and there he is!

PAMPH. Someone might perhaps think I don't think this is true; but I *want* this to be true, just as it is now! The reason why I believe that the life of the gods is everlasting is because pleasure is permanently theirs; I've won immortality **[960]** if no sorrow intervenes in my joy! But who would I most like to meet now to tell about this?

CHAR. [*aside*] What's he happy about?

[DAVOS *comes slowly out of* PAMPHILUS*'house, having just been untied.*]

PAMPH. I can see Davos. There's no one at all I'd rather see: I know he's the only one who'll genuinely share my joy!

DAVOS [*looking round*] Where's Pamphilus out here?

PAMPH. [*calling to him*] Davos!

DAVOS Who's that?

PAMPH. It's me!

DAVOS [*finally seeing him*] Oh, Pamphilus **[965]**!

PAMPH. You don't know what's happened to me!

DAVOS No – but I know what's happened to *me*!

PAMPH. And so do I.

DAVOS It's happened the usual way: you've found out about the bad luck that I've had, quicker than I have about the good luck that's happened to you.

PAMPH. My Glycerium's found her parents!

DAVOS That's good news!

CHAR. [*aside, astonished*] What?!

PAMPH. Her father's a great friend of ours.

DAVOS Who?

PAMPH. Chremes!

DAVOS I'm glad to hear it **[970]**!

PAMPH. And there's nothing to stop me marrying her at once!

CHAR. [*aside*] Is he having wish-fulfilment daydreams?

éa quae uóluit uígilans? **PA.** Túm de púero, Dáue, – **DA.** Ah, désiné!
Sólus és quem díligánt di? **CHA.** Sáluos súm si haec uéra súnt!
Cónloquár. **PA.** Quis homóst? Charíne, in témpore ípso mi áduenís! [10]
CHA. Béne factum! **PA.** Aúdisti? **CHA.** Ómnia. Áge, me in tūís
     secúndis réspicé.   975
Túos est núnc Chremés; factúrum quaé uolés scio ĕsse ómniá.
PA. Mémini. Atque ádeo lóngumst íllum me éxspectáre dum éxeát.
Séquere hac me; íntus ápŭd Glycérium núnc est. Tú, Daue, ábī domúm,
própera, accérse hinc qui aúferánt eām! Quíd stas? Quíd cessás?
     DA. Eó!   [15]
PA. Ne éxspectétis dum éxeánt huc: íntus déspondébitúr;   980
íntus tránsigétur síquid ést quod réstet. Plaúdité!

PAMPH. And as for the baby, Davos, –

DAVOS [*interrupting*] Oh, stop it! Are you the only one the gods love?

CHAR. [*aside*] I'm saved, if this is true! I'll speak to him. [*Moves towards the others.*]

PAMPH. Who's that? Charinus! You've turned up just at the right time!

CHAR. Congratulations!

PAMPH. Did you hear?

CHAR. Everything! And now spare a thought for me in your good fortune [975]: Chremes is on your side now; I know he'll do everything you want.

PAMPH. I won't forget. And in fact it'll take a long time if I wait for him to come out: follow me in here; he's inside with Glycerium now. [*Ushers* CHARINUS *into* GLYCERIUM's *house, turning at the doorway to address* DAVOS.] As for you, Davos, go off home, quickly, fetch people to move her from here! [DAVOS *is still slow in his movements.*] Get a move on! What are you hanging about for?

DAVOS I'm going! [*Goes into* PAMPHILUS' *house.*]

PAMPH. [*to the audience*] Don't wait for them to come out here: the betrothal will take place inside – if there's anything left over, it'll be settled inside [980]. Please give us your applause! [*Goes into* GLYCERIUM's *house.*]

ALTER EXITUS

PA. Mémini. Atque <ádeo ut uólui cómmodum húc senéx
    exít forás>.   977a *tro.*7
CHA. M..[.]o[
CHA. [
PA. Te éxpectábam: est dé tūa ré quod ágere egó tecúm uoló.   980a
Óperam dédĭ ne me ésse oblítum dícas tuaé gnatae álteraé:
tíbi me opínor ínuenísse dígnum te átque illá uirum. **CHA**. Áh,
périi, Dáue! Dé meo amóre ac uíta núnc sors tóllitúr.
CHR. Nón noua ístaec míhi condício est, sí uoluíssem, Pámphilé.   [5]
CHA. Óccidí, Daué! **DA**. Manĕ! **CHA**. Périi! **CHR**. Id quam ób rem
    nón uolui éloquár: 985a
nón idcírco quód eum omníno adfínem míhi nollem, – **CHA**. Hém?
    DA. Tacé!
CHR. – séd amicítia nóstra quae ést a pátribus nóstris tráditá
nóbis áliquam pártem stúdui adaúctam trádi líberís.
Núnc cum cópiam hánc fortúna utríque ut óbsequerér dedít,   [10]
détur. **PA**. Béne factum! **DA**. Ádi ătque age hómini grátiás.
    CHA. Salué, Chremés,   990a
amícorúm meōrum ómniúm †mihi agíssimé†!   *ia.*6
Quod míhi non mínus est gaúdió quam †id quod abs te expecto†,
me répperísse ut hábitus ántehac fuí tibí.
CHR. Animúm, Charíne, quód ăd cumque ádplicáuerís,   [15]
studium éxinde út erit túte exístimáberís.   995a
Id ita ésse fácere cóniectúram ex mé licét:
aliénus ábs te támĕn quis tu ésses nóuerám.
CHA. Ita rés est. **CHR**. Gnátam tíbi meám Philúmenám
uxórem et dótis séx talénta spóndeó.   [20]

ALTERNATIVE ENDING (to replace 977–81), not by Terence

PAMPH. I won't forget. [*Sees* CHREMES *coming out of* GLYCERIUM's *house.*] And in fact <here's the old man coming out of doors just as I wanted>! [...] [*to* CHREMES, *as* CHARINUS *and* DAVOS *withdraw to one side of the stage*] I was hoping to see you: there's something that concerns you that I want to discuss with you **[980a]**. I've taken steps so that you can't say I've forgotten your other daughter: I think I've found you a husband who's good enough for you and for her.

CHAR. [*to* DAVOS, *aside*] Help! I can't stand it, Davos! They're on the point of drawing the lot that my love and my life depend on!

CHR. What you propose is nothing new to me, Pamphilus – if it was what I'd wanted.

CHAR. [*as before*] I've had it, Davos!

DAVOS [*to* CHARINUS, *aside*] Hang on!

CHAR. I can't stand it!

CHR. [*still to* PAMPHILUS] I'll tell you why I didn't want it **[985a]**. It wasn't because I didn't want him to be related to me at all, –

CHAR. [*to* DAVOS, *aside*] What's he saying?

DAVOS [*to* CHARINUS] Quiet!

CHR. – but because of the friendship between us, which was handed down to us by our fathers: I was keen for it to be handed on to our children with something added to it. But now that fortune has given me the chance to help both of you, let him have her!

PAMPH. Good!

DAVOS [*to* CHARINUS, *aside*] Go up to the man and say 'Thank you' to him!

CHAR. [*obeying*] Hullo, Chremes **[990a]**! You're the dearest of all my friends to me! And that gives me no less pleasure than †what I hope for from you† – that I've discovered what you thought of me previously.

CHR. Charinus, whatever you turn your mind to, you'll be judged according to how you apply yourself to it **[995a]**. You can conclude that from my case: although I was against you, I knew what you were like.

CHAR. That's true.

CHR. I promise you my daughter Philumena in marriage, with a dowry of six talents.

COMMENTARY

Characters

The manuscripts of Terence do not include a cast-list, but it is customary to include one in modern editions, using mainly the Latin labels attached to the names of the characters in the scene-headings in the manuscripts (see Introduction, section 9). The names of the characters are Greek (Latinized as appropriate) and nearly all found in Greek comedy, but not necessarily reproduced from Menander's *Andria* or *Perinthia* (since we know that Terence changed the names of some characters, at least in the case of *The Eunuch*). We do not know the names of any of the characters in Menander's *Andria*, though his *Perinthia* included a slave called Daos and characters called Sosias and (probably) Pyrrhias; Daos' master was called Laches, a name not used by Terence in this play.

One striking feature of Greek New Comedy, reproduced in Latin comedy, is that some names (most notably the slave-name Daos) recur in several plays. It does not follow that the same *character* was seen as reappearing in play after play, but rather that the names had become so conventional for comic characters that they could be given to different characters in different plays. There is a strict distinction between names appropriate for male slaves and those appropriate for male citizens (sometimes stricter than was observed in real life at Athens); and some names were clearly felt to be appropriate for fathers while others were appropriate for sons, though some others (such as Chremes in Latin comedy) are found to cross the generations. (On the general question see P. G. McC. Brown, 'Masks, Names and Characters in New Comedy', *Hermes* 115.2 (1987), 181–202; on slave-names see K. Vlassopoulos, 'Athenian Slave Names and Athenian Social History', *ZPE* 175 (2010), 113–44, esp. 121–25.) Some (e.g. Austin) have tried to show that the etymology of a name made it particularly appropriate for the character in question, but in most cases in Terence the appropriateness is rather limited. Plautus often used more elaborate and exotic names which were entertaining in themselves (Duckworth, 346–50); Terence reverted to the more restrained practice of Menander.

Pamphilus and Philumena are the names of the young couple whose marriage is at risk in Terence's next play, *The Mother-in-Law*. For this reason Penwill, 130 claims that 'In effect, what the *Hecyra* presents is a 'Pamphilus and Philumena Part II'", in which Pamphilus has after all 'bowed to parental pressure, deserted Glycerium and married Philumena'. However, Penwill himself well brings out the considerable differences between the characters called Pamphilus in the two plays, and if Terence had really wanted us to see him as the same character in a different situation he could surely have kept the names of Simo and Chremes instead of changing them to Laches and Phidippus respectively. Pamphilus and Philumena are simply conventional names for a boy and a girl in comedy, and, while it is interesting to compare and contrast the presentation of the two Pamphiluses, that does not make the later play a sequel to the earlier one.

Simo: the name of an older-generation Athenian citizen also in Pl. *Most.* and *Ps.*, and cited as the name of a victim of comic trickery by Horace, *Ars* 238. The Greek equivalent (*Simōn*) was the name of the father in Menander's *Eunouchos*. The name has been thought to be derived from Greek *simos* ('snub-nosed'), though that has a long first vowel, whereas in the name it is short. It has been suggested (Austin, 66) that a Latin audience might think of *simia*, 'ape' (though that too has a long first vowel), and also of *simulo* ('I pretend'), which is twice used of Simo's behaviour (48, 588) and twice of the plot he comes to suspect (472, 500).

Sosia: the name of a slave in Pl. *Amph.* and Ter. *Hec.* The Greek equivalent (*Sōsias*) is the name of a slave in Ar. *Wasps* and of what are generally thought to be slaves in Men. *Kolax*, *Perik.*, and *Perinthia*; cf. GS 465–66 on Sosias as a typical slave-name in Greek comedy, though W. Furley, *Menander, Perikeiromene or* The Shorn Head (London, 2015), 98 argues that Sosias in *Perik.* is a free man (or perhaps a freedman). The name derives from Greek *sōizō* ('I save'), perhaps suggesting 'the man who keeps things safe'.

Davos: the name of a slave also in *Phormio*, and the title of a comedy by Caecilius. The Greek equivalent (*Daos*) is the name of a slave in at least eight plays by Menander, including *Perinthia*, and came to be associated particularly with comic trickery (Men. *test.* 115 K-A; see also below on Chremes). Probably derived from the ethnic name of a Phrygian or Thracian people.

Mysis: a name found only here in Greek or Latin literature, meaning 'woman from Mysia'. *Ancilla* is the regular term in comedy for a female slave, as at 461, 514, 838.

Pamphilus: the name of a young married man in *The Mother-in-Law* (see above), apparently reproduced from the Greek original (cf. Apollodorus

Carystius fr. 13 K-A). The Greek equivalent (*Pamphilos*) was the title of a comedy by Eubulus; see R. L. Hunter, *Eubulus, The Fragments* (Cambridge, 1983), 172 on further evidence for the name, which comes in several Greek comic fragments. It means 'All loving' or 'Loved by all' in Greek and was regarded by Donatus on *Ad.* 26 as an appropriate name for a boy in comedy.

Charinus: the name of a young man also in Pl. *Merc.* and *Ps.* The Greek equivalent (*Charinos*) was the name of a character in Men. *Messenia*, shown as young on the Mytilene mosaic illustrating that play. From Greek *charis* ('charm').

Byrria: the Greek equivalent *Pyrrhias* ('red-haired', suggesting Thracian origin) is the name of slaves in Men. *Dysk.* and *Sik.* and has been plausibly restored at *Perinthia* 8 as the name of a fellow-slave of Daos. At Rome a gladiator called Birria is said to have been in Milo's entourage and to have struck the first blow against Clodius (Ascon. *in Mil.* 28.1–5).

Lesbia: a name not otherwise found in comedy, and very rare outside it, though made famous by Catullus as the pseudonym of his beloved. It means 'woman from Lesbos'; Donatus on 226 suggests that it evokes the wine for which that island was famed (cf. below, 228–33n.).

Chremes: the name of an older-generation Athenian citizen also in *The Self-Tormentor* and *Phormio*, but of a younger one in *The Eunuch*. In Greek it is the name of an old man in Ar. *Ekkl.*, and it is cited by Antiphanes fr. 189.22 K-A as one of the typical names of characters in comedy. It is possibly related to Greek verbs meaning 'roar', 'neigh', or 'clear one's throat'. When Horace at *Sat.* I.10.40–41 writes of 'Davos fooling the old man Chremes' he probably chooses the names as representative of the genre rather than having in mind specifically *An.* 740–89; he treats Chremes as the typical name of a comic old man also at *Ars* 94.

Crito: the name of an old man also in *Phormio*. The addressee of Diodorus fr. 1 K-A has the equivalent Greek name *Kritōn*. Derived from Greek *kritēs*, 'judge'.

Dromo: the name of slaves also in *The Self-Tormentor* and *The Brothers*. The Greek equivalent *Dromōn* ('Runner') is the name of a slave in Men. *Sik.*; GS 633 discuss the evidence for it elsewhere in Greek comedy. The name could evoke the stock motif of the 'running slave' (cf. on 338–74), though we do not see Dromo running in this play, where he makes only a brief appearance at 860–65.

Glycerium: not otherwise found as a name in comedy. Greek *Glykerion* is a diminutive form of *Glykera*, the name of the heroine of Men. *Perik.*, derived from *glykys*, 'sweet'. It was not unusual for female Greek names to have diminutive neuter endings. This was not this character's original name; cf. on 942.

Philumena: named at 306; also the name of Pamphilus' wife in *The Mother-in-Law* (see above), and the title of a play by Caecilius. The equivalent Greek name *Philoumenē* ('Beloved') is found in Men. *Sik.*

Archylis: the name of a slave at Pl. *Truc.* 130, 479. Not found in Greek, though Archilla is known from Athens. From *archō*, 'I rule': she seems to be in charge of the slaves in Glycerium's house. [The manuscripts have Archilis or Archillis; Bentley preferred the spelling Archylis, as being a more accurate transliteration of what the Greek name would be if it existed, and most editors have followed him.]

Plot summary Each of Terence's plays is preceded in the manuscripts by a twelve-line summary of the plot in iambic senarii, written in the second century CE by Gaius Sulpicius Apollinaris, who became tutor to the future emperor Pertinax and to the writer Aulus Gellius. Although they add nothing to our understanding of the plays, it is customary to include these summaries in modern editions.

1. *meretriculae*: this diminutive form is found at Pl. *Rud.* 63, *Truc.* 309.
3. *dat fidem*: cf. 401–402 for this idiom.
4. *Nam*: either this is similar to the use at 51 to introduce a new element in the story or (if it means 'for') the implied logic is that Pamphilus had to promise to marry Glycerium because his father had another girl in mind for him.
    desponderat: cf. on 102 *despondi*.
5. *gnatam*: cf. on 49, and contrast *natum* four lines below.
7. **quid haberet animi**: *haberet* rather than *habeat*, since the author treats *simulat* in line 6 as a 'historic' present. *animi* is partitive genitive; cf. on Prologue 2 *id ... negoti*, and 600n.
8. *suasu*: a rare noun, found at *Ph.* 730. OLD takes it to be dative here ('Pamphilus does not resist Davos' advice'), but that is unnecessary. The trisyllabic scansion is unexpected, though Lucr. IV.1157 has *suadent* as three syllables.
11. **adgnitam** = *agnitam*, from *agnosco*.

[**12.   *aliam dat***: the manuscripts have *dat aliam*, which does not scan. We might have expected *alteram* rather than *aliam*, since Chremes has only one other daughter; cf. 100 'his only daughter', 540 'your only daughter'.]

1–27 Prologue

The author has been criticized for combining two plays by Menander in composing his play, thus allegedly 'contaminating' Menander's plays. But the same charge could be brought against Naevius, Plautus, and Ennius, whose relaxed approach to their Greek models this author prefers to follow. His critics are advised to keep quiet in future, and the audience are requested to give the play a favourable hearing.

See section 6.7 on 'The Prologue' in the Introduction.

Metre: iambic senarii. Note how the lack of resolutions in 9–10 and 13–14 slows down the pace of the lines to add clarity to the exposition. Similarly in 16 the slogan of Terence's critics is made to sound more emphatic by the lack of resolutions, as is Terence's declaration of allegiance to his predecessors at 18–20.

1.   the author: *poeta* (Greek ποιητής, lit. 'maker'), a word used by Terence only in his prologues, usually with reference either to himself or (as in line 7) to his rival. It is found several times in Plautus and had clearly become a standard term for an author in Latin. Unlike those of Plautus, Terence's prologues never refer to the author by name, taking for granted that the audience know who he is. The Greek word is sometimes used by the chorus in Aristophanes' parabases with reference to the playwright (*Acharnians* 633, *Knights* 509, *Wasps* 1016).

quom: the pre-classical form of the conjunction *cum* (distinguishing it from the preposition), here used temporally.

animum ... adpulit: the same idiom at 446. Donatus claims that the metaphor in *adpellere* in both places is from putting ships in to shore (this nautical sense is perhaps literal at 807). In fact the verb is used of various kinds of moving or driving, but Fantham, 42–43 notes that '*Andria* is rich in sea metaphors (cf. 480, 562, 845), and the plot is preoccupied with voyage and shipwreck'. See also on 193 *adplicat*.

to writing: some have seen significance in the fact that Terence (here and at *HT* 7, *Hec.* 6, *Ad.* 25) uses of his own activity the verb (*scribere*) which some Plautine prologues (*Asinaria* 11, *Casina* 33, *Trinummus* 19) use of the activity of the authors of the original Greek plays being adapted into Latin, suggesting that Terence thus puts himself on a level with those authors (though he himself never uses the verb of them); similarly, the fact that he uses the verb *facere* both of his own plays in lines 3 and 26 and of Menander's in lines 9 and 12 has been seen as significant. See S. McElduff, 'More than Menander's Acolyte: Terence on Translation', *Ramus* 33 (2004), 120–29, at p. 123 (following Cicu there referred to), Germany, 225–26. However, it is not clear what other verb Terence might be expected to have used in this line, and he elsewhere uses *scribere* of Latin authors other than himself (*HT* 43, *Hec.* 27, *Ad.* 16).

2. *negoti*: partitive genitive, dependent on *id* (GL 369, Pinkster, 1019–22); cf. 521.

3. should please the public: some modern scholars have seen Terence as having an educational purpose and as writing with an élite audience in mind (so, for instance, E. Fantham, 'Terence and the Familiarisation of Comedy' *Ramus* 33 [2004], 20–34, repr. in *Roman Readings* [Berlin, 2011], 195–214). Neither strand of this approach is supported by the way the prologue presents him here.

ut placerent: explanatory, giving the content of *id* ... *negoti* (GL 557). The words *populo ut placerent* could hint at a technical formula *populo placere* in the sense 'to be agreed on as a formal decision by the people in assembly' (cf. OLD *placeo* 5.b), as suggested by G. Focardi, 'Lo stile oratorio nei prologhi terenziani', *SIFC* 50 (1978), 70–89, at p. 72 with n. 1. If so, Terence plays on the formula by using *placere* in a different sense and by using *populus* to refer to his audience.

quas fecisset fabulas: for *fabulae quas fecisset*, with attraction of the antecedent into the case of the relative pronoun (GL 617 n. 2). For the verb, cf. on 'to writing' at 1 above; it is used already in Plautus of the writing of plays (*Capt.* 55, 1029), and at *Cas.* 860–61 *nec fallaciam astutiorem ullus fecit / poeta* it is found together with the noun *poeta*, the first word of this prologue, derived from the verb which is the Greek equivalent of *facere*. So too in the prologue to *Phormio* Terence is referred to as *poeta* in line 1, his writing as *facere* in line 4.

4. *multo*: ablative of difference with *aliter*, as more commonly with comparatives (GL 403).

5. prologues: probably a rhetorical plural (see Introduction p. 33). It is presumably also for rhetorical effect that Terence's critic, the 'malicious old author' of lines 6–7, becomes plural in the rest of the prologue.

prologis: the word is first attested here and at *HT* 11, *Ph.* 14, *Hec.* 9 in surviving Latin. Here and at *Ph.* 14 it denotes the text of the prologue, in the other two cases the prologue-speaker. It clearly derives from the Greek πρόλογος, with the first syllable long as if using the Latin *prō-* (as in *proloquī*).

scribundis: contrast 1 *scribendum*. This variation in the spelling of gerunds and gerundives of the third and fourth conjugations found in the manuscripts of Terence has been studied by A. Traina, *Forma e suono* (ed. 2, Bologna, 1999), 129–43. It is not always clear why one form rather than the other has been chosen (nor to what extent we can accept the variation as reflecting Terence's original intentions), though it has been guessed that here *scribundis* may echo the language of some legal formula.

operam abutitur: verbs which take the ablative in classical Latin often take the accusative in Early Latin, though Plautus frequently and Terence overwhelmingly use the ablative with the simple *utor*. Both authors use only the accusative with *abutor*.

6. not to tell the plot: we need not suppose that Terence ever did intend to write prologues that told the plot. On the implication that that was what prologues were expected to do see the second paragraph of section 6.7 of the Introduction.

qui: an old ablative or instrumental form from *quis* or *qui*, here and at 307, 334, 402 used as a final adverb meaning the same as *ut* (see OLD *quī²* 4); at 53 and elsewhere it is used as an interrogative adverb meaning 'how' or 'why' (OLD 1). Different uses again at 148 and 512.

7 malicious old author: Donatus (on line 1) identifies Terence's critic, to whom he replies in other prologues as well, as Luscius of Lanuvium, a rival playwright of whose plays two lines and two titles survive; see C. Garton, *Personal Aspects of the Roman Theatre* (Toronto, 1972), 41–139. Terence refers to him as a 'malicious old author' again at *HT* 22 and as 'old' at *Ph.* 1 and 13; on the other side, according to *HT* 23–24, Luscius accused Terence of lacking experience.

8. uitio dent: OLD *uitium* 1.b 'to reckon as a fault'; GL 356 ('Dative of the Object for which'); Pinkster, 793 ('functioning as object complement').

quaeso: 'please', here used parenthetically (OLD 3).

animum adtendite: OLD *attendo* 1.b 'to learn by listening, observe'. [Donatus knew of this reading, and Nonius p. 57 L quotes the line with *animo adtendite*, though all surviving manuscripts have the commoner *animum aduortite* or *aduertite*, for which see OLD *animaduerto* 2 'to pay attention to, attend to, heed'. Either reading is possible, but the manuscripts are unanimous in reading *adtendite* at *Ph.* 24, and that is the accepted reading at *Eun.* 44, both in prologues.]

9. Menander ... Perinthos: see the Introduction, section 6.2. Andros is the most northerly of the Cyclades, in the southern Aegean; Perinthos was a Greek city on the northern coast of the Sea of Marmora, half way between Byzantium and the Hellespont.

10. *utramuis*: understand *fabulam*.

norit ... nouerit: future perfect in both cases. The shorter forms of the perfect, future perfect and pluperfect are common in comedy, the longer forms sometimes being found at the end of the line for metrical convenience.

11–12. *dissimili argumento, dissimili oratione ... ac stilo*: ablative of quality (GL 400, Pinkster, 782–83). [In line 11 all manuscripts except one have the order *dissimili sunt*, which gives the line one syllable too many; Guyet's transposition of these words restores the metre, and the order *sunt dissimili* is also found in three manuscripts mentioned by Bentley (though he prefers to keep *dissimili sunt* and read *et tamen*, as at 59, at the end of the line), as well as in a manuscript more recently collated: see the discussion by Perutelli, 100–101.]

sed tamen: for the combination, see OLD *tamen* 2.c.

words and style: *oratio* ('words') presumably, as Donatus says, refers to the content of what the characters say (cf. 251, 736, and elsewhere in Terence), *stilus* (apparently for the first time in this sense in surviving Latin) to the style in which it is couched, both being contrasted with the 'plot' of the play. We know nothing about the relative dating of Menander's *Girl from Andros* and *Girl from Perinthos*, but Plutarch, *Mor.* 853F appears to imply that the playwright's style matured in the course of his career, which might help to account for the stylistic differences between them if one was significantly later than the other. For Donatus' comments on other differences between the two plays see the Introduction, section 6.2. If they had as little overlapping material as Donatus tells us about, we may wonder how similar their plots really were: does Terence exaggerate their similarity in order to make his combination of the two plays seem more reasonable? His language at 13–14 makes clear that he regards *The Girl from Andros* as his main source, not that he views both plays as having contributed equally to his play; this too may suggest that there were clear differences between them in content as well as style. On the other hand, it is not unlikely that both plays concerned the fortunes of a foreign girl at Athens and included broadly similar plot developments.

13–14 He: Terence.

what was suitable: this gives us no clue to the details of what has been transferred.

conuenere: Terence (unlike Plautus) shows a slight preference for the older form *-ēre* over *-ērunt* as the third person plural ending of the perfect indicative active. Cf. 81 *perduxere*, 740 and 810 *fuere*, 931 *audiuere*; but *-erunt* at 219, 534, 771, 799. (C. F. Bauer, *The Latin Perfect Endings -ere and -erunt* [Philadelphia, 1933, repr. New York, 1966] has a full discussion of the practice of Plautus and Terence. See also D. W. Pye, 'Latin 3rd Plural Perfect Indicative Active – its Endings in Verse Usage', *Transactions of the Philological Society* 62.1 [1963], 1–27, including pp. 8–15 on *-ĕrunt*, a scansion required six times in Plautus and at *Eun.* 20, possible but not required at a number of places in both authors, including *An.* 534 and 799.)

into *The Girl from Andros*: the prologue-speaker takes for granted that we know this is the name of the play we are about to watch.

transtulisse: understand *se* as the subject of this infinitive; cf. 145 *comperisse*, 358 *uidisse*, 394 *uelle*, 470 *sensisse*, etc.

usum: understand *esse*.

15 *isti*: OLD *iste* B.5.b 'often w. contemptuous or derogatory connotation; esp. applied by a prosecutor to the defendant' (though Terence here casts himself as the defendant); cf. 21 *istorum*. For the lightening of the first syllable cf. on 237 *illud*.

16 **'contaminated'**: or 'spoiled'. Terence's use of this verb (presumably the term used by his critics, though Goldberg 1986, 50 suggests it was chosen by Terence as part of his rhetorical strategy) has led modern scholars to use the noun *contaminatio* ('spoiling') as a term of art in discussing Terence's procedure of incorporating material from another Greek play into the primary play which he was adapting. (*HT* 17 shows that it was the Greek plays that Terence was accused of spoiling, not his Latin versions.) He followed the same procedure in *The Eunuch* and *The Brothers* but was there accused of 'theft' (plagiarism from earlier Latin comedies), not 'contamination'. If he has correctly represented their view, Terence's critics may have objected to his procedure on aesthetic grounds, showing such reverence for Greek comedies that they regarded it as a sin to tamper with them in this way; or they may have feared that the procedure would reduce the number of plays available for other Latin playwrights to adapt, if a play was felt to have been 'spoilt' for further use once any part of it had been adapted. For a summary of the issue see Duckworth, 202–208 or G. Guastella, *La contaminazione e il parassita* (Pisa, 1988), 11–80.

18 Naevius, Plautus, and Ennius: three of Terence's greatest predecessors. Naevius (who produced plays from 235 to 204) and Ennius (239–169) were better known for other types of composition, but Plautus (active between about 205 and 184) wrote only comedies; plays by Plautus are the earliest Latin works to have survived complete. On the basis of this passage, scholars for some time (particularly in the late nineteenth and early twentieth centuries) devoted much effort to trying to establish which of Plautus' surviving plays were 'contaminated' in the sense defined in the previous note. It is now generally accepted that Plautus is more likely to have added material of his own invention than to have taken it from a supplementary Greek source (for a summary of the history of the debates see L. Schaaf, *Der Miles Gloriosus des Plautus und sein griechisches Original* (Munich, 1977), 11–14). It is thus possible that Terence means simply that these authors had adapted Greek plays with some freedom, not necessarily by combining material from more than one Greek model; if so, he perhaps redefines the accusation of his critics to make it easier to answer. It certainly seems to be true that Plautus was very free in his adaptations; indeed, he is generally held to have been far freer than Terence. Too little survives of the comedies of Naevius and Ennius for us to judge their degree of freedom. Terence does not include his most immediate predecessor, Caecilius (see Introduction, the opening paragraph of section 6.1), in his list. It does not follow that Caecilius was significantly different from the others in his approach to adaptation, and the surviving fragments of his work show him to have composed very much in the style of Plautus: see Wright, 87–126, including pp. 99–101 on our passage here. Rather, Caecilius' name did not command the same authority as those of the other three.

    Naeuium, Plautum, Ennium: similar asyndetic lists at 54 *aetas, metus, magister*, 257 *ineptam..., falsam, iniquam*, 261 *amor, misericordia..., sollicitatio*, 295 *uirum..., amicum, tutorem, patrem*, 319 *spem, salutem, auxilium, consilium*, 334, 718, 844, 889 *habeat, ualeat, uiuat*, 891 *Domus, uxor, liberi*, 937–38 *metu, / spe, gaudio*. Many of these passages convey strong emotion, and here we may feel that the list of names is given added

emphasis by the punchy asyndeton. (F. Leo, *Ausgewählte Kleine Schriften*
[Rome, 1960], I.163–84 discusses lists with three members in Plautus, with
or without asyndeton, and gives some examples from Menander, Terence,
and other Greek and Latin authors.)

19   takes as his authorities: Terence claims to be following in the footsteps
of his great predecessors, whereas modern scholarship has tended to see him
as striking out on a new path of his own, particularly with regard to his Latin
style (see Wright) but also in terms of fidelity to his Greek originals (see
Haffter 1953 and Ludwig).

20–21   carelessness ... undistinguished carefulness: 'he reverses the
expected value of each term' (Goldberg 1986, 51); one would normally expect
neglegentia to be a critical term, *diligentia* to have positive connotations.

   try to match: *aemulari* perhaps implies that Terence sets himself up as
a rival to his predecessors (as suggested by G. Williams, 'Roman Poets as
Literary Historians: some aspects of *imitatio*', *Illinois Classical Studies* 8.2
[1983], 211–37, at p. 217), though in this context that implication may not
be strongly felt.

   carelessness: i.e. they did not care about 'spoiling' the Greek plays that
they adapted, as in the first meaning given by OLD for the verb *neglego*: 'To
regard as of no consequence, be indifferent to, disregard, ignore'. Terence
does not mean to imply that his great predecessors had been sloppy writers,
and *neglegentia* conveys a carefree attitude that is not best caught by the
translation 'carelessness'; but I have retained that traditional translation for
the sake of the contrast with *diligentia* in these two lines. (Goldberg 1986,
51 takes *neglegentia* here to refer to 'the studied ease of the careful writer',
contrasted with 'the labored fidelity of a pedantic copyist'.)

   istorum: see on 15 *isti*.

   obscuram: probably 'undistinguished' (OLD 5), or 'unremarkable',
rather than 'incomprehensible' (OLD 8).

22   *Dehinc*: 'so', 'therefore' (OLD 1.a), as at 190. At 79 and 562, however,
it means 'after that' (OLD 1.b). This word scans as a monosyllable (by
synizesis) in Plautus and Terence; cf. 79, 190, 562.

23   their own abuses: i.e. their shortcomings (*malefacta*, things they
have 'done badly') in their own plays, if all these critics are playwrights –
though perhaps the only playwright Terence has in mind is Luscius, whose
shortcomings he does indeed criticize in the prologues to *HT* (30–34) and
Eun. (7–19), in both cases also uttering vague general threats of further

criticism in the future. At *HT* 33–34 Luscius' *maledicta* are contrasted with his *peccata* ('faults'); here there is more obvious word-play with *maledicere*, giving *malefacta* an unusual sense.

24　Give us a favourable hearing: for this sense of *faueo* Shipp compares Quint. IV.1.73 *iudices ... ut attendant et ut faueant rogamus* ('we beg the judges to pay attention and to give us a favourable hearing'). Some have followed Donatus' suggestion that it here means 'be silent' (OLD 5), and it is true that prologues do sometimes ask for silence: see next note, and *Eun.* 44 *cum silentio animum adtendite*. But that meaning of *faueo* is religious in origin, and here a forensic nuance is more likely.

pay attention: OLD *adsum* 19; cf. Pl. *Trin.* 22 (the end of the prologue) *adeste cum silentio* ('pay attention in silence') and Pl. *Amph.* 151 (also the end of the prologue) quoted on 217 below. *Adeste aequo animo* is also found in prologues at *HT* 35 and (with the addition of *per silentium*) *Ph.* 30.

be fair: OLD *aequus* 6.

examine the evidence: OLD *cognosco* 4 'To investigate judicially'. In this context 'examining the evidence' means watching the play.

25　find out for certain: cf. Martin 1976 on *Ad.* 12 *pernoscite*: 'the prefix *per*- ('thoroughly') emphasises the earnestness of T.'s appeal.'

spei: partitive genitive with *ecquid*, as 2 *negoti*; cf. also 600n. OLD *spes* 3 'A prospect, hope; promise (of future achievements)'. The word here scans as a monosyllable by synizesis.

relicuom: = classical *reliquum*, scanned as four syllables; probably OLD 5 'Remaining yet to be, future, further' rather than 3 'Remaining, available, that is left to one'.

26　fresh plays: at *HT* 4 Terence stresses that that play is 'a fresh comedy' (*integra comoedia*), and he proclaims the newness of his play in other prologues as well (*Ph.* 24, *Ad.* 12, and cf. *Hec.* 5). He does not here specify what the 'freshness' of his future plays will consist in; at *HT* 4 he claims that that play is both new (not previously performed) and based on a Greek original that has not previously been adapted into Latin.

comoedias: for the case, cf. on 3 *quas fecisset fabulas. comoedia* and *fabula* are used interchangeably in Latin, though R. Hunter, 'Some Dramatic Terminology', in S. Frangoulidis, S. J. Harrison, G. Manuwald (eds), *Roman Drama and its Contexts* (Berlin and Boston, 2016), 13–24, at p. 16 suggests tentatively that Terence proclaims his commitment to Hellenism by using the Greek term here.

27 drive them off the stage: *exigere* is found in this theatrical use only here, at *Hec.* 12 and 15, and in ancient commentaries on Terence's prologues (TLL V.2.1541, 21–33) but was clearly a current term in Terence's time.

in advance: the implication seems to be that if the spectators do not think well of this play they will be unwilling even to start sitting through any future ones. (Some scholars prefer to take *prius* to mean 'rather' [OLD 2], not 'in advance'.)

Setting

The stage setting and movements of the characters have to be deduced from indications in the text, since stage directions are not included in the manuscripts. In working them out, I have assumed that Terence normally made characters reappear from the direction in which they had been seen going off and also that he normally tried to avoid the awkwardness of having an exit in one direction immediately followed by the entry of another character from the same direction, which might lead the audience to wonder why the two parties had not bumped into each other in the wings. I have made Davos exit left to the main square at 227 and reappear from the right (from the direction of Chremes' house) at 338: his account at 359–61 leaves us free to suppose any amount of off-stage movement. If Chremes' house lay in the same direction as the main square, the staging of 731–46 would be very awkward. (Some scholars, such as Germany, 237–38, suppose Davos to exit in one direction at that point in order to run round the back of the stage building and reappear from the other direction, because they believe Chremes to come from the direction of the main square; mine is a simpler solution.)

I have placed Lesbia's house off to the right for the sake of the staging at 300/301. The text itself offers no clues to its location.

I do not accept the general modern belief that there was a fixed convention by which the main square was regularly imagined to be off to the audience's right, the harbour to their left. I see no point in such a convention, and I do not believe there is adequate evidence for it. It is more likely that each play conjured up its own off-stage locations and that the choice of left or right was quite arbitrary. (For the same approach to the setting of Menander's comedies see A. H. Sommerstein's edition of *Samia* (Cambridge, 2013), 95–96. Beare, 248–55 discusses the evidence that has been adduced for fixed conventions at both Athens and Rome.) In the case of this play, lines

734–45 suggest that the main square lies to the audience's left: at 734–35 Davos says that he will pretend to be arriving 'from the right', and at 744–45 he pretends to be coming from the main square; since actors generally face the audience as much as possible, we should expect Davos' right to be the audience's left as he speaks at 734–35. (Those who think otherwise suppose him to have his back to the audience at that point.)

That the setting is Athens is explicit at 907 but was probably assumed from the start by the spectators as the obvious location in the absence of any other indications.

Some editors place Charinus' house off-stage, leaving only two houses visible to the spectators. But 957 'I've come out' suggests very strongly that Charinus' house too is visible, and nothing tells against this. 712 'Be sure to come to me here' also most naturally suggests a visible on-stage house.

The altar was a regular feature of the Greek and Roman comic stage, corresponding to the representation of Apollo of the Streets (Apollo Agyieus) in the form of a pillar with a conical top that stood outside Athenian houses in real life. Its exact position on the stage is not clearly indicated. Altars were decorated with foliage as a preliminary to the performance of a sacrifice; we may speculate that Simo has so decorated it as part of his pretence that a wedding is to take place. The foliage plays a part in the play at 726–30.

28–171   Simo expounds the situation to his ex-slave (freedman) Sosia, whom he has put in charge of the wedding preparations in his house: the preparations are in fact a ruse to put pressure on his son Pamphilus to marry the daughter of Chremes or else to put himself in the wrong if he refuses to do so. Such a strange plan requires explanation, and Simo duly gives an account of the background in some detail to show why he thinks it necessary. As usual in drama, we have been thrown into the middle of a story and need the help of an introductory scene to get our bearings. Sosia's main function is to receive and react to Simo's narrative, and (although he is given some instructions at 168–70 which might lead us to expect that he will contribute something to the play as it develops) he never reappears; he is thus what is called a 'protatic' character, one who appears only in the first part of a play to help the exposition. The bulk of the scene is essentially a narrative monologue by Simo, but it is enlivened by Sosia's comments, and Terence has gone to some trouble in the opening lines to make Sosia a character of interest in his own right.

On this opening scene, and Terence's addition of Sosia to be the recipient of Simo's confidences and instructions, see the Introduction, pp. 17–18. It is not clear why Terence chose to make Simo's addressee his freedman (not a traditional figure of ancient comedy) rather than his wife (as in *The Girl from Perinthos*), but it may be worth noting that Sosia, the slave so loyal that he has been rewarded with his freedom, is the polar opposite of Davos, who is to be Simo's main antagonist in the play and will be sent off for cruel punishment at 861–65; the opening scene starts with the focus on Simo's treatment of Sosia and ends at 159–70 with the focus on his suspicions of 'that rascal Davos' (159), immediately followed by a confrontation between Simo and Davos himself at 175–205. It has also been suggested that making Sosia a freedman enabled Terence to use him to fill out his portrayal of Simo: 'his role as eager client helps to define Simo's role as an autocratic patron and father' (Anderson 2003–2004, 5). Other, more technical, factors may have played a part in Terence's decision as well. As noted in the Introduction, it is likely that in Menander's *Girl from Andros* and *Girl from Perinthos* some details of the background narrative were given by a divine prologue rather than by the father. If so, Terence has put more of it into the mouth of the father, and he may have felt (even if a degree of artificiality was almost inevitable in expository scenes of this kind) that a wife was not suitable to be the recipient of such a lengthy narrative, since it might seem strange that she did not already know at least some of it; he may also have felt that an uninterrupted monologue of such length without any interlocutor at all would not be acceptable to his audience. We cannot tell from Terence's play whether Simo even has a wife still, nor do we know whether the wife of *The Girl from Perinthos* appeared again in that play. Lines 50 and 168–70 at least convey that Simo has some purpose in confiding his secret plan to Sosia, even if nothing seems to come of his instructions, as noted above. The overall effect would perhaps not have been very different if Terence had made Sosia a slave still in Simo's household rather than a freedman, and Aristophanes' *Wealth* opens with a scene in which a master expounds the initial situation to a slave ('because I regard you as the most faithful and thievish of all my slaves', 26–27). On the other hand, if Sosia no longer lives in Simo's house, it is not implausible that he needs to be told something of the background (as noted by Rawson cited in the note on line 31).

F. Jacoby, 'Ein Selbstzeugnis des Terenz', *Hermes* 44.3 (1909), 362–69 suggested that Terence, being himself a freedman, wished to start his first play by expressing his own gratitude to his former master for the humane treatment he had received from him and invented Sosia to represent himself (even though the gesture would be lost on most of the audience, as Jacoby acknowledged). This seems a rather simplistic approach (even if we accept that Terence really was an ex-slave), and it fails to take into account that it is Simo himself, not Sosia, who proclaims at 35–39 how well he had treated him. Altogether it does not seem likely that Terence would have wanted to imply that the devious Simo represented his former master (see Introduction, section 6.3, and Anderson 2003–2004, 7 on how Simo's lengthy narrative 'reveals more about his behavior as a father than about Pamphilus as a son'). We may note here that, even when talking to his devoted ex-slave, Simo has some difficulty in coming to the point: he is so much in need of Sosia's loyalty and discretion in furtherance of his devious plan that he starts in a roundabout way by reminding him how well he had treated him and what a model slave Sosia had been. Even Sosia almost loses patience with him at 40–45.

Simo's narrative of past events (51–149) was admired by Cicero, who cites it four times in his rhetorical works to illustrate points about oratory that he or a speaker in one of his dialogues wants to make: see *Inv.* I.27 (quoting line 51 as an example of a fictional narration) and 33 (praising Simo for doing in his speech exactly what he said he would at 49–50), *de Orat.* II.172 (citing lines 110–12 as an 'argument from the smaller to the greater') and 326–28 (cited on 117 below). In addition, Cicero and Horace both quote the expression *hinc illae lacrumae* (see on 126); and see the notes on 67–68, 185, 189 (the latter two from Simo's confrontation with Davos) for further quotations from the opening scenes in Cicero's writings. This play was clearly a familiar reference point a century or so after Terence's death; Cicero does not always name either the author or the play, so confident is he that his quotation will be recognized. (See Anderson 2003–2004 on Cicero's use of the play in his rhetorical works.)

The provisions being carried by the accompanying slaves at the very beginning are clearly not lavish by the standards of a wealthy household, to judge from what Davos says at 360 ('A tiny amount of food?') and from his discussion with Simo at 450–56. The illustrated manuscripts show two slaves, one holding a dead bird by its feet and also carrying a round pot, the other bringing five fish suspended from a ring and holding what may be a palm branch; Sosia is shown holding a long ladle (see D. Wright, *The Lost*

Late Antique Illustrated Terence [Vatican City, 2006], 12 and plate 4). These precise details are not indicated by the text, and the pot and ladle are the sort of thing we might expect Simo to have in his house anyway; the purpose of the palm branch (if that is what it is) is unclear. Anderson 2004, 11 believes the slaves to belong to Sosia, the whole visual element of their arrival to have been added by Terence together with Sosia, and the manuscripts to preserve a memory of how the scene was regularly staged. But the first part of this is bound up with his belief that Sosia is a professional cook, on which see below on line 31. Anderson may be right that neither Menander's *Girl from Andros* nor his *Girl from Perinthos* began with a procession of slaves carrying provisions, but we cannot be sure: Menander, *Samia* 283–97 shows the arrival of a similar group, and *Aspis* opens with a procession of silent characters, though of a different kind. For the arrival of a number of people carrying provisions for a party, see also Pl. *Aul.* 280–362, *Ba.* 109–69, *Cas.* 719–50, *Merc.* 741–82, *Ps.* 790–892, *Truc.* 551–630, Ter. *Ad.* 361–81. Such an entry here provides scope for comic business even before a word has been spoken, though the suggestion of O. Knorr, 'Theatralisches Spektakel und Metatheater in der Andria und der Hecyra des Terenz', *Gymnasium* 115 (2008), 435–51, at pp. 437–43 that the slaves danced to musical accompaniment is entirely fanciful. J. Wright, 144–45 discusses similar processions of baggage-carriers in a number of Plautus' plays.

Metre: iambic senarii, as in all Terence's opening scenes. A. S. Gratwick, in *The Cambridge History of Classical Literature*, *II*, *Latin Literature* (Cambridge, 1982), 77–137, at pp. 124–26 discusses the style and rhythm of lines 101–29.

28 *istaec*: the common form of the neuter plural in Terence (formed like *haec*), though *ista* is also found. The final *-c* was in origin a deictic particle *-ce*. The ablative feminine singular *istac* at 32 and 317 is similarly formed, as is the feminine singular *istaec* at 483 and 730. OLD has a separate entry for these forms under *istic* rather than *iste*.

29 *dum*: often added as an adverb to imperatives or to exclamations such as *Eho* at 184, 324, 616.

paucis: understand *uerbis*, and also an infinitive such as *adloqui*.

30 *ut curentur*: understand *uis* from *uolo* in 29 as the main verb to which this is subordinate. See OLD *uolo*[1] 6.c for *uolo* followed by *ut*.

31 **skill**: this has been taken to refer specifically to Sosia's skill as a cook, but E. Rawson 'Freedmen in Roman Comedy', in R. Scodel (ed.), *Theater* *and Society in the Classical World* (Ann Arbor, 1993), 215–33, at pp. 218–20 is surely right to argue that what Sosia thinks Simo has made him responsible for is 'the general organization of the feast'. In either case, Sosia evidently continues to perform services for his former master, as was not unusual in both Athens and Rome: see Treggiari 1969, 75–78, Mouritsen, 146–51, Kamen, 36–42, and cf. Anderson 2004, 18: Simo 'insists on holding the freedman to his *officium* and obliging him to humble himself as a spy in the household again' (see 168–70). At 69ff. Simo tells him what has been happening next door for the last three years, and what Pamphilus has been up to; this suggests that Sosia has not continued to live in his household but has been called in from outside for a special purpose.

   hoc: ablative of comparison.

32   *Nil*: OLD *nihil* 11 '(used w. advl. force) In no respect, not at all'; cf. 160, 187, etc.

   the skill I need: OLD *opus*[1] 12; cf. 99 *Quid uerbis opus est?*, 446 *uxore opus est.*

34   loyalty: *fides* 'was the basis of the right relationship between freedman and patron' (Treggiari 1969, 80–81; cf. Mouritsen, 61–63).

35–39 Simo no doubt represents himself in the best possible light, and Sosia is hardly going to disagree. But there is no reason to doubt that slaves were sometimes treated humanely by their masters: see Zelnick-Abramovitz, 54–57. As noted by K. Dover (Aristophanes, *Frogs*, Oxford, 1993, 48), at Athens 'a speaker in court considered that he would make a favourable impression on the jury if he professed to have rewarded loyalty and long service (e.g. Dem. xlvii. 55f.)'.

35   Ever since I bought you, from your childhood onwards: slaves of all ages could be bought and sold at markets in both Greece and Italy. There is no way of telling in what circumstances Sosia had come to be on the market. These words show that he is significantly younger than Simo, perhaps now about thirty years old while Simo is about sixty. He thus cannot be a great deal older than Simo's son Pamphilus. He must have been freed several years ago (cf. on 31), i.e. not long after reaching adulthood. If we can believe the opening sentence of Suetonius' *Life*, Terence himself was freed at a comparably early age, and it seems from scattered remarks in Treggiari 1969, 11–20 that early manumission was not unusual at Rome; see also her account of Cicero's freedman Tiro, pp. 259–63, and cf. Fabre, 197–98, Mouritsen, 150–51. We need not doubt that it was also possible in Greece (see Zelnick-Abramovitz, 155–64), so Terence's addition of Sosia to the play does not create any implausibility in the Greek setting.

37   my freedman: both at Athens and at Rome an ex-master could retain some rights over his former slave (cf. on 31). There has been some debate about how free an ex-slave was in these circumstances (see Fabre, 127, Mouritsen, 146–47, Kamen, 42). At Rome a former slave automatically became a citizen, whereas at Athens he was not entitled to citizenship except by special decree; the question of Sosia's civic status is not raised.

38   *propterea quod*: a long-winded expression which Simo uses again at 584, its only other occurrence in Terence; see Maltby 1979, 145–46 on how this contributes to the presentation of Simo.

seruibas: this form of the fourth conjugation imperfect (for *-iebas*) is common in Early Latin and found later too: see Palmer, 270–71. [The manuscripts all have the classical form *seruiebas*, which does not scan correctly. At 90, on the other hand, *comperiebam* (again, the reading of the manuscripts) is metrically possible, and I have accepted it, though K-L and some others do not; *seruiebat* is required by the metre at *Ph.* 83.]

you behaved like a free man: for freedom as a reward for upright behaviour cf. Pl. *Cas.* 283–85, Mouritsen, 163–64.

40   *Haud muto factum*: literally, 'I'm not changing what has been done'. But Donatus is surely right to suggest that it must be an idiomatic way of saying 'I don't regret doing it'. There should probably be an uncomfortable pause here, as indicated in the translation: Simo finds it hard to come to the point, and Sosia is somewhat perplexed and anxious about what Simo is leading up to.

42   I'm pleased that it's given you pleasure: the translation tries to convey the word play in *gratum ... gratiam. habeo gratiam* more strictly means 'I'm grateful'.

aduorsum te: see OLD *aduersus*[4] 11 '(w. ref. to feelings or behaviour) In relation to, with regard to, towards'. Quintilian I.7.25 tells us that the first person to spell *-uor-* as *-uer-* was said to have been Scipio Africanus (probably the younger holder of that name, Terence's contemporary). Similarly *aduorto* (156, 767) and *uoster* (716, 739, 744) probably began to be spelt *aduerto* and *uester* at about this time.

43   *hoc*: the following sentence (starting with *nam*) explains what it is that troubles Sosia.

molestumst: the contraction of *est* is normal; cf. 44 *exprobratiost* 77 *ingeniumst*, etc. The phenomenon is fully discussed by Pezzini.

43–44 *commemoratio ... exprobratio*: the use of two abstract nouns with identical endings brings the concepts into sharper relief: see H. J. Molsberger, *Abstrakter Ausdruck im Altlatein* (Frankfurt on Main, 1989), 111.

44 *inmemoris benefici*: the second genitive is dependent on the first, with which the pronoun *mei* is to be understood. There is no need to suppose that *inmemoris* means 'forgotten' and agrees with *benefici*, as some supposed in antiquity according to Donatus, nor to change *inmemoris* to the dative *inmemori* (giving to *exprobratio* the construction of the verb *exprobro*) as most editors have done.

45   Why don't you tell me: for this use of *quin* with an imperative, an extension of its use with the indicative in questions that are 'equivalent to commands or exhortations' (as at 399), see OLD *quin* A.1.b, Barrios-Lech, 138–39.

dic quid est: the indicative is often used in Early Latin in indirect questions, e.g. after an imperative which could be taken as a self-contained instruction. See Pinkster, 629–32.

quod me uelis: for the double accusative see OLD *uolo*[1] 3 'to want (a person for something)', Bennett, II.251, Pinkster, 169 ('almost confined to Plautus and Terence').

The lack of metrical resolutions in this line perhaps betrays a certain exasperation on Sosia's part, whereas in 47 it helps to ram Simo's point home.

47   this wedding: this is the first hint for the audience of the (apparent) purpose for which provisions have been taken into the house, and it makes clear that there is a background calling for explanation.

has: cf. on 3 *quas fecisset fabulas* for the attraction of this word into the relative clause.

48   *Quor*: the pre-classical form of *cur*; cf. Introduction, section 7, and 63 *quomque* below.

49   *gnati*: 'Early Latin probably distinguished between the noun *gnatus/a* and the participle *natus/a*' (Goldberg 2013 on *Hecyra* 124).

51   Well then: for this use of *nam* to introduce a narrative after a preliminary announcement see OLD *nam* 6.

finished his military service: literally, 'left the ephebes', the term applied to Athenian male citizens during their two years of compulsory military service between the ages of eighteen and twenty. The same expression is found at Pl. *Merc.* 61 and a very similar one at *Merc.* 40; it may be a close translation of a

Greek idiom, since ἐξέρχονται ('they come out') is found in a similar context at Xen. *Cyrop.* I.2.12. There was no precise equivalent to the ephebes at Rome, and Plautus and Terence evidently relied on their audience's knowledge of the Athenian institution. Similarly, Caecilius preserved the title *Synephebi* ('Ephebes Together') for one of his comedies, and *ephebus* continued to be used in Latin, normally with reference to Greeks. Maltby 1985, 121 notes that four of the eleven occurrences of Greek words in this play 'are concentrated in Simo's opening speech (51 *ephebus,* 57 *philosophus,* 88 *symbola,* 125 *attat*) and suggests that Terence's intention 'may be to reinforce the Greek setting of the play'. As Maltby shows, Terence uses Greek words less frequently in his first three than in his last three plays and less frequently than Plautus altogether. (Cf. also on 316 *moechum.*)

[*et* was added at the end of the line by Umpfenbach for the sake of the sense (Guyet suggested *ac*); it is not in the manuscripts.]

[**52 erat**: J. B. Loman's restoration of this form in place of the manuscript reading *fuit* is the simplest way to make the line scan correctly (*Specimen Critico-Litterarium in Plautum et Terentium* [Amsterdam, 1845], 79–80). *erat* was also read by Kauer in his edition.]

53 qui: 'how'; cf. on 6.

54 his age, and fear, and his teacher: for the asyndetic list of three nouns in the Latin see on 18; sometimes, as here, the list is simply a list, without any particular rhetorical effect. Donatus is doubtless right to say that *magister* represents the Greek παιδαγωγός, the slave who was put in charge of a boy in childhood and escorted him to and from school; so OLD *magister* 8.c.

55 what pretty well all young lads do: the hobbies specified were in fact the preserve of the wealthiest families both at Athens (cf. e.g. Isocrates, *Areopagiticus* 45) and at Rome, where it seems that hunting with dogs was a very recent import (see M. Dickie, 'The speech of Numanus Remulus (*Aeneid* 9, 598–620)', *PLLS* 5 [1985], 165–221, at pp. 188–94). Greek philosophers were a sufficiently familiar element of Roman life for them to be expelled from the city in 161, five years after this play was put on (Suet. *Rhet.* 1, Gell. XV.11.1; cf. G. Garbarino, *Roma e la filosofia greca dalle origini alla fine del II secolo a.C.* [Turin, 1973], II.370–72 on evidence for the presence of Greek philosophers in Rome at about this time. See also P. R. Coleman-Norton, 'Philosophical Aspects of Early Roman Drama', *CP* 31.4 [1936], 320–37, including at 337 a list of passages in Plautus and Terence where the noun *philosophus* or the verb *philosophor* is used.)

56   ut ... adiungant: explanatory of 55 *quod*; cf. on 3 *ut placerent*. For *animum adiungere* see OLD *adiungo* 6.b 'to apply (the mind)'.

57   ad philosophos: governed by *animum adiungant*. The construction would be clearer if Terence had written *ad equos alendos* instead of *equos alere* in explanatory apposition to *ad aliquod studium*.

58   horum: picking up the singular *quod* in 55, but plural because influenced by the fact that three hobbies have been listed in 56–57. See also J. T. Allardice, *Syntax of Terence* (Oxford, 1929), 5: 'A change from singular to plural sometimes takes place, especially if the preceding Noun or Pronoun be indefinite or generic'; cf. on 627 *gaudeant*, 628 *comparent*.

praeter: OLD 2.b 'to a greater degree than'; again in Simo's mouth at 121, 122. Karakasis, 116 sees this as a peculiarity of Simo's language.

nil: verbs which normally take the dative (such as *studeo*) are often found with a neuter pronoun in the accusative; cf. 157 *id operam do*.

61   nothing in excess: one of the most famous Greek proverbial maxims (see Otto, 243); Sosia's moralizing does not sparkle. With *ut* understand something like *agas*, as Donatus suggests: the *ut*-clause is explanatory, as in 56.

62–66   'Simo, as a rather tyrannical parent, praises in his son qualities which would seem to others weakness and lack of independence' (Shipp on 63).

62   tolerate ... and put up with: Simo is characteristically long-winded. The verbs in this and the next two lines are in the 'historic infinitive', a feature of Latin narrative style (see Pinskter, 527–30), unless the infinitives are to be taken as explaining *Sic*.

63   quomque: the pre-classical form of *cumque* (cf. Introduction, section 7), to be taken closely with *quibus*, together meaning 'whoever'; cf. 263 *quae ... quomque*.

65   ita ut: OLD *ut* 4 ''In the same way as (...so), in the manner that'; cf. Bennett, I.106–13.

66   inuenias ... pares: the generalizing second singular is regularly found in the subjunctive; see Bennett, I.319–21 for Early Latin; Pinkster, 483–84.

67–68   Sosia continues to moralize, though this time with a bit of a bite, probably not noticed by Simo; it is even possible that he speaks aside here. Cicero at *De amicitia* 89 makes Laelius criticize Sosia's sentiment on the grounds that obsequiousness is harmful to your friends if it shows tolerance of their faults; and Donatus says that wise men disapprove of it. Line 68 became proverbial, and the second half has precedents in Greek: see Otto, 368.

It may seem mildly paradoxical that *obsequium* (here translated 'being obsequious') is regarded by many modern scholars as one of the fundamental obligations (in the sense 'dutiful respect' or 'devoted service') of a freedman to his former owner (Mouritsen, 53, 58). But perhaps scholars have made too much of the word in that context: see J. F. Gardner, *Being a Roman Citizen* (London, 1993), 23–25.

these days: we need not look for any particular feature of the 160s BCE to justify this remark which perhaps makes Sosia sound unexpectedly old (cf. on 35).

69 Well: *interea* often introduces a new point in a narrative (see OLD *interea* c), though a temporal sense ('meanwhile') is not wholly excluded either here or at 117 or 129.

70 moved into our neighbourhood here: in fact into the house next door; it is a convention of these comedies that rich and poor live next door to one another. Athens was a natural place to move to in search of a better life; but Chrysis (who is first named at 85) perhaps had another motive for moving there of which Simo knows nothing, namely to help Glycerium find her family; see Crito's question at 806: 'Has she found her parents here yet?'. However, we cannot be sure that Glycerium came to Athens at the same time; all we know is that she arrived at least nine months ago, long enough to have met Pamphilus and to be now on the point of giving birth to his child (a detail of which Simo at this stage is quite unaware).

[If the text is correct, *uiciniae* is either a partitive genitive, as in *ubi gentium* ('where on earth?') or locative; there is the same uncertainty at *Ph.* 95 *hic uiciniae*. Donatus knew of a reading *uiciniam* (apparently also written by the first hand of C), which would be accusative of goal of motion as at *Ph.* 878 *huc ... foras*.]

71 her relatives had failed to look after her: at Athens (and doubtless also on Andros) a woman's closest male relative was expected to make proper provision for her. It turns out at 796–99 that Chrysis' cousin Crito was her closest male relative; not surprisingly, his account there gives no hint that he had failed to look after her. Here and at 74ff. Simo seems remarkably well informed about her; but she was his next-door neighbour, and, as we learn at 84–91, he was not above making enquiries about her activities.

72 young and extremely beautiful: this sort of detail might lead the audience to expect that Chrysis will turn out to be the main female love interest of the play; Glycerium is described in similar terms at 118–20. The title *Andria* means 'the female from Andros', and it would be natural at this stage to assume that it refers to Chrysis. Sosia's reaction at 73 shows that he expects to learn that Simo's son has become entangled with this woman: why else has Simo started to tell her story? The Latin text has *Andria* with reference to Chrysis at 73 and 85, with reference to Glycerium at 215 and (probably) 461 and 756. I have chosen to call her a 'girl' at those points in the translation and to translate the play's title as 'The Girl from Andros' because I believe it more probably refers to Glycerium than to Chrysis. But others (including Thornton Wilder) have thought otherwise: see Introduction, p. 15.

integra: OLD *integer* 11'Unimpaired by age, youthful'.

74 [*Primo*: this is the reading in ancient grammarians quoting the line; the manuscripts have *Primum*. *Primo* is the correct form for the sense 'At first, originally, to begin with' (OLD 1).]

parce ac duriter: the combination recurs at *Ad.* 45, and cf. Pl. *Most.* 154 *parsimonia et duritia*, *Truc.* 310–11 *parsimonia duritiaque*, Cato fr. 93 Sblendorio Cugusi (from a speech delivered in 183 BC) *in parsimonia atque in duritia*. M. Lentano, 'Parce ac duriter. Catone, Plauto e una formula felice', *Maia* 45 (1993) 11–16 examines the ideological overtones of the contrast between hard work and pleasure in the Roman context; see the summary in Leigh, 161 n. 12.

75 **by weaving wool**: the respectable alternative to prostitution for a woman trying to make her way in the world; so at *HT* 285 it is reassuring for the young lover that his girl friend weaves wool. As noted by Donatus here and on 274, the ultimate purpose of the inclusion of this detail is to reassure the audience that *Glycerium* has been well brought up by Chrysis' family.

77–78 **It's human nature to prefer pleasure to work**: more literally, 'just as the nature of all people is liable to turn from work to pleasure'. At 74 Simo has described her life as 'frugal and hard', but it evidently does not occur to him that it might have been economic necessity that forced her into prostitution. Chremes at *HT* 446–47 shows a more sympathetic understanding of how the world works: *Ea coacta ingratiis / postilla coepit uictum uolgo quaerere* ('She, forced to do so against her will, began after that to earn her living as a prostitute').

79 *dehinc*: cf. on 22.

began in the trade: for *quaestus* as the trade of a prostitute see *Hec.* 735, 756, *HT* 640, Ovid, *Ex Ponto* II.3.20. *occipit* is the first of several examples of the 'historic present' in Simo's narrative; cf. 105 *moritur*, 115 *prodeo*, etc.

Commentary 175

See Pinkster, 401–409 on this, 'the narrative tense *par excellence* in Latin stories' (405). Cf. also on 128–29.

80   her lovers: cf. 87. It was an accepted fact of Athenian life that a woman in Chrysis' position might be kept by a number of men at the same time; see U. E. Paoli, *Comici latini e diritto attico* (Milan, 1962), 22–25; E. Fantham, 'Sex, Status, and Survival in Hellenistic Athens: A Study of Women in New Comedy', *Phoenix* 29.1 (1975), 44–74, at 51 n. 22, 63 with n. 44 [= *Roman Readings* (Berlin, 2011), 87–88 n. 22, 101–102 with n. 44].

80–81   *filium ... meum*: the separation of the two words ('hyperbaton'), and their position at the end of the lines, gives them some emphasis: this is where Chrysis becomes relevant to Simo's son, who is the major focus of his narration.

81   to keep them company: *esset* could mean 'to eat' (from *edo*), and some editors prefer this interpretation, citing 88–89 in its support.

82   immediately I said to myself: in the Latin the verb is omitted, a common ellipse in narrative passages; cf. Virgil, *Aen.* I.37 *haec secum*. For the use of *mecum* in this sort of expression cf. 442 *secum ... reputauit*, OLD *se*[1] 7.b.

83   he's had it: *habet* was the term applied to a gladiator who had been mortally wounded; see OLD *habeo* 16.d.

83–84   I'd watch their slave-boys entering or leaving; cf. *Ad.* 26–27 for the duty of slave-boys to escort their young masters home after a night out. At this point Simo starts to spy rather obviously on his son, though the fact that Chrysis lives next door makes his behaviour seem not wholly improbable.

84   *Heus, puer*: See Barrios-Lech, 162–66 on the use of *Heus* as an 'attention-getter'. *puer*, like its Greek equivalent παῖς, is a normal term for a male slave; see OLD *puer* 5.

85   *sodes*: a colloquial contraction of *si audes*, with *audes* meaning 'you're willing to, prepared to', as at Pl. *Ps.* 78, 1322, *Rud.* 870, 1030. Adams, 68 notes that in Terence (unlike Plautus) *sodes* is found only in the mouth of men, a point also made by T. F. Carney, 'The Words *sodes* and *quaeso* in Terentian Usage', *Acta Classica* 7 (1964), 57–63. Carney additionally notes that the word is most frequently addressed to slaves or social inferiors.

Chrysis: the name of a prostitute or ex-prostitute in Men. *Eunouchos*, *Kolax* (fr. 4 Arnott = 4 S) and *Samia*, from Greek *chrysos* ('gold'). It was also the title of a Greek comedy by Antiphanes.

86   *Teneo*: OLD 23 'To grasp mentally, understand'.

86–87   Phaedrus, or Clinia, or Niceratus: Athenian names, the latter two found in comedy. Clinia is the name of a young man in *HT* and in Men. *Misoumenos* and *Theophoroumene*, the friend of an older man at Pl. *Asin.* 866, Niceratus the name of an older man in Men. *Samia*, a young man in PCG *adesp.* 1017, both of uncertain age in some other Greek or Latin passages.

[**87**   Unless we suppose Terence to have been unaware that the second vowel in *Niceratum* is long, there is one syllable too many in the line as transmitted. The lack of an object for *amabant* is also strange, and I have tentatively printed *eam* for the manuscripts' *simul* (which I take to have originated in a marginal comment) to meet both points. Otherwise the neatest solution is to follow Ritschl, III.324f. in either deleting *tum* or moving it to the start of the next line, unelided before *amabant*. Some editors make the line scan by changing *Niceratum* to *Nicaretum*, an Athenian name listed twice in J. S. Traill, *Persons of Ancient Athens* XIII, Toronto, 2004 (the female name *Nicarete* is commoner).]

88   *Eho*: this word, scanning as two light syllables and found almost exclusively in Plautus and Terence, is commonly followed by a question (as at 500, 710 etc.) or an imperative (as at 667, 931; at 184 and 951 the imperative is to be understood). Its use as an 'attention-getter' is discussed by Barrios-Lech, 166–68.

   Pamphilus: first named here.

88–89   He paid his share: a *symbola* was 'a sum contributed towards the expenses of a common meal by each participant' (OLD). The noun is Greek (see on 51), and such dinners were a feature of Athenian life. The Greek noun is regularly used in Latin comedy, e.g. at *Eun.* 540, very little thereafter; Cicero's Latin equivalent *collecta* at *de Orat.* II.233 caught on only in Christian Latin.

89   I was pleased: the same expression at 60.

90–91   *nil ... quicquam*: 'nothing at all'; the addition of *quicquam* adds emphasis, as at *Ad.* 366 *nil quicquam uidi laetius.* It was doubtless naïve of Simo to suppose that the slaves were telling him the whole truth; admittedly, it seems from 96ff. that Pamphilus' self-restraint had become the talk of the town, but perhaps Simo himself had made it so by boasting of it.

93   tangles with: as in a wrestling match or struggle of some kind.

   eiusmodi: 'of that kind' (OLD *modus* 12.c). This word fills the last three metrical elements of the line, so *eius* must fill one element, scanning either as one heavy or as two light syllables. At 115 and 232 *eius* scans as two syllables of which the first is heavy but at 809 as two of which the first is light. This suggests that either of the proposed scansions is possible here and also for *eius* at 210, 274, etc. Similarly *huius* at 210, 480, etc. (*huiusce* has a light first syllable at 439). See Questa, 69–70.

94   still isn't tempted by the opportunity: literally, 'his mind none the less isn't influenced in that matter'. Simo's verbosity matches his pomposity.

95   *scias*: for the subjunctive, see on 66.

   unaided: OLD *ipse* 7.

   modum: OLD *modus* 5.b 'to impose a limit or check, set bounds' (with a variety of verbs); so at Pl. *Curc.* 300, Prop. III.19.4. Cf. the verb *moderor*.

96   Quom ... tum: see OLD *cum*² 14 'introducing one of two co-existing or co-ordinate circumstances or actions, usually followed by *tum* which indicates the more particular or noteworthy circumstance'.

97   *dicere ... laudare*: 'historic' infinitives; see on 62.

99   To cut the story short: cf. 114 'But I needn't go on about it', 165 'but I needn't waste words on that'. As Anderson 2003–2004, 4 says, 'these rhetorical fillers, whose real meaning Simo ignores, do serve the dramatist's purpose of emphasizing the long-winded egotism of the father'. However, he can sometimes be brief: see on 117.

100–101   to seek me out ... with a very large dowry: the normal expectation in New Comedy is that a girl will be given in marriage with a dowry, unless her family is very poor, and also that parents will try to arrange the marriages of their offspring. *ultro* has been taken to suggest that it was more normal for the boy's family to take the initiative, as at Pl. *Trin.* 449–50, 499, and Donatus' comment *dat contra officium soceri* ('he gives, contrary to what is expected of a father-in-law') suggests that he feels there is something irregular about Chremes' behaviour here. Treggiari 1991, 126 quotes only this passage as 'an example of initial approach by the woman's father', but she sees nothing unusual in it, and it was the clear duty of a girl's father to see that she found a husband both at Athens and at Rome. Some scholars have assumed that the dowry is what really matters to Simo, but he himself would presumably not benefit from it; it is Pamphilus who accepts the dowry offered by Chremes at 951 (where see note on the size of the dowry).

102   I agreed, and engaged her to marry him: there is no suggestion that Simo consulted Pamphilus. Cf. 151–53, where Simo portrays Pamphilus hypothetically as accepting that his father will arrange a marriage for him, and 238–39, where Pamphilus' complaint is not that he has not been consulted but that he has not been given advance notice. The strict legal situation, both at Athens and at Rome, was that a son could ignore his father's wishes in making his own plans to marry or not to marry, but in both societies 'this was rather a question of domestic practicalities than of law' (MacDowell, 86 on Athens; for Rome see Treggiari 1991, 176–80). It cannot have been unthinkable for a son to be bullied or cajoled into taking a bride of his father's choice or too much in awe of his father to think of resisting. At 263 Pamphilus is reduced to a jelly at the thought of disobeying Simo, though this is because Simo has treated him so leniently up till now. In Menander's *Samia* the fathers of the boy and girl have agreed on their marriage without consulting them (113–18), but lines 145–62 show the boy and his father discussing the matter. Unfortunately the text is too fragmentary for us to know in what spirit the father introduced the subject, though he would probably not have forced the marriage on his son against his will; in fact the boy himself is wildly enthusiastic about the proposal. *Phormio* is another play in which a father has planned a marriage for his son without consulting him. At *HT* 1054–66 we see a son being required to marry by his father but allowed to select his bride for himself.

despondi: both the girl's father and the boy's father can be said to *despondere* a girl to a boy; for the boy's father cf. *Hec.* 124, *Ad.* 735.

dictust = *dictus est*, with contraction of *est* accompanied by loss of one *s* from the resulting *dictusst*. The phenomenon is fully discussed by Pezzini; as his chart on p. 53 shows, this is one of a number of places where the contracted form is not found in the manuscripts but has been restored for metrical reasons.

104 [*Ferme*: the manuscripts have *Fere*, which means exactly the same; OLD has one entry to cover both forms. Charisius 259.4B attests to *Ferme* as an alternative reading, and since in general *fere* is far commoner than *ferme* (see TLL VI.1.492.11–64) it is perhaps more likely that *Ferme* was miswritten as *Fere* than the other way round. But the evidence is not conclusive, and Terence used both forms (*ferme* at 284 and 460, *fere* at 813).]

quibus: for this use of the ablative cf. e.g. Caes. *Gal.* III.23.2 *paucis diebus quibus eo uentum erat.*

105 That's good news!: Sosia distorts the form of words that one would normally use on hearing of a death: see *Ph.* 751 *male factum*; Catullus 3.16, Cic. *Att.* XV.1.1 *o factum male.* See 969 for a more conventional use of Sosia's words here.

106   Beasti = *beauisti* (cf. 586 *cognosti* = *cognouisti*, 591 *narrasti*, 653 *altercasti*, 832 *Impetrasti*, 847 *Curasti*). On this verb, which almost disappears after Plautus and Terence except in the past participle *beatus*, see Nisbet and Hubbard on Horace, *Odes* II.3.7.

ei: more likely to be the exclamation (as at 73) than the dative of *is*: see Martin 1964, 3.

metui a Chryside: for the construction see OLD *metuo* 3.c 'to fear danger (from)'.

Ibi tum: a colloquial pleonasm; cf. 131, 223, 634.

107   [amabant: M. A. Muretus in his 1555 Venice edition of Terence conjectured *amarant* (= *amauerant*) and has been followed by several editors. But it is perhaps over-logical to insist on the pluperfect here.]

frequens: OLD 5 'Assiduous, constant, regular'. Donatus claims that it is a military term, *ut miles apud signa* ('like a soldier in camp'), and such a usage is found e.g. at Cic. *Verr.* V.33, Livy III.24.5; but that does not seem appropriate here, and there is no reason to think it was the primary use of the word. *frequens* is here used predicatively, like *lubens* at 337.

108   tristis interim: understand *erat*, as often.

112   amasset = *amauisset*.

What will he do for me: 'Simo gets egotistic pleasure from Chrysis' death and Pamphilus' grief because he applies it hypothetically to his own eventual death' (Anderson 2003–2004, 8).

114   officia: *officium* in Early Latin can mean 'expected or appropriate behaviour', as at 236 and 330 (see OLD 4), as well as 'duty', as at 168.

Quid: cf. on 322.

multis: understand *uerbis*, as with 29 *paucis*. For the ablative with *moror* see OLD *moror* 7.b 'to waste time (on), delay (over)', quoting Ovid, *Rem.* 461 *Quid moror exemplis?*

116   Hem: a common expression of surprise or alarm in Early Latin, also found later, e.g. in Cicero's *Letters*. Müller, 121–23 discusses the various nuances with which Terence uses this interjection in this play, where it is particularly frequent.

117   The corpse was carried out: the funeral starts with the carrying of the corpse from the house where it has been laid out. For *Ecfertur*, see OLD *effero*[1] 3 'To carry out for burial'. Note the brevity of the narrative style here and at 127–29. However, Antonius at Cic. *de Orat.* II.326–28 maintains that Terence in this passage was aiming at charm rather than brevity for its own sake; he also praises Terence for not reducing the narrative to the bare essentials of *Ecfertur, imus, ad sepulcrum uenimus, / in ignem inpositast* (a combination of 117 with 128–29), or even simply *In ignem inpositast*, but making it charming and lively and easier to follow.

118   one young girl in particular: OLD *unus* 8.

120   *nil supra*: understand something like *esse posset*.

[**121   *Quae quom***: most manuscripts have *Quae tum*; *Quia tum* is also found. Both readings have been accepted by editors, but Bentley pointed out that we do not need *tum* and proposed *cum* (= *quom*) instead, comparing 18 *Qui quom hunc accusant*. Admittedly, *tum* at 839 is similarly redundant, so I follow Bentley with some hesitation.]

123   beautiful and noble: at 274 Pamphilus says she has been 'taught and brought up well and decently'; this is appropriate (or so the audience will feel) for a girl who is destined to be reunited with her Athenian citizen family. Indeed the audience may already begin to suspect this will be the outcome. cf. Men. *Heros* 40, Ter. *Eun.* 132 *forma honesta*.

In Thornton Wilder's *The Woman of Andros* Glycerium is visibly pregnant at the time of this funeral, a detail which may draw our attention to a certain chronological vagueness in Terence's account: how much time has elapsed between the day of the funeral and the day of the play's action, on which Glycerium gives birth? See Scafuro, 366–69, arguing that probably not very long has elapsed and that Simo failed to realize the clear implications of Glycerium's appearance at the time.

the accompanying slave-girls: like Bacchis in *Hec.* and *HT* and Thais in *Eun.*, Chrysis has been so successful at her trade that she has acquired a number of slaves.

125   *Attat*: a shortened form (with the second vowel lengthened) of *attatae*, an exclamation imported from Greek, here expressing a sudden realization. (An alternative scansion is to keep the second vowel short, since at this place in the iambic senarius Plautus sometimes allows a light syllable to stand instead of a heavy one; the place is known as a *locus Jacobsohnianus* [named after H. Jacobsohn]. See Questa, 279–99, though on pp. 293–94 Questa denies [perhaps too dogmatically] that Terence used this licence. Another possible case is 437 *dicere*, though *breuis in longo* before a change of speaker would be acceptable there in any case [see Introduction, the end of section 8.3 (b)].)

126   *hinc illae lacrumae*: this became a proverbial expression used to convey a sudden realization, even in contexts where tears were irrelevant; see Cic. *Cael.* 61, Hor. *Ep.* I.19.41; see Introduction pp. 36–37.

128–29 Simo alternates the 'historic' present with the perfect tense (required by the metre for *uenimus*), apparently for metrical convenience alone.

129 she was put on the pyre: cremation was practised both at Athens and at Rome, though at the time of Menander it seems to have been on the decline at Athens: see I. Morris, *Death-Ritual and Social Structure in Classical Antiquity* (Cambridge, 1992), 140 fig. 32; J. Toynbee, *Death and Burial in the Roman World* (London, 1971; repr. Baltimore, 1996), 32–40.

fletur: impersonal passive, used to indicate an action in which everyone takes part; cf. Wackernagel, 187–88. On the use of the impersonal passive in general see Bennett, I.7–9, Pinkster, 267–72.

Interea: see on 69.

134 Why are you going to kill yourself?: this suggests that Pamphilus believed Glycerium planned to throw herself on to the pyre, like Evadne on her husband's pyre at Eur. *Suppl.* 1012–71; so too the remark imagined for Pamphilus by Simo at 140.

is perditum: for the construction, see OLD *eo*[1] 12.

138 *satis ... causae*: understand *mihi erat*.

139 *commerui*: essentially synonymous with *peccaui*; see OLD *commereo* 2 'To commit, be guilty of (an offence)'.

145 *indignum facinus*: a self-contained exclamation in the accusative, here quoting Chremes' words: '(he said that it was) a disgrace [cf. OLD *indignus* 6] (and that) he had discovered'; with *comperisse* understand *se* as subject. The exclamation occurs several times in Terence, e.g. at *Eun.* 70. On the accusative of exclamation see GL 343.1, Pinkster, 363–68.

146 treating this foreign girl as if she were his wife: officially, an Athenian citizen could not marry a non-citizen. Such couples could cohabit, but presumably Pamphilus and Glycerium have not in fact openly set up house together. They have, however, entered into a relationship with each other, and Pamphilus himself claims at 273 to have treated Glycerium as if she were his wife. Rome may have taken a more relaxed attitude than Athens, particularly if Plautus' *Cistellaria* can be accepted as evidence for it; see W. Stockert, *T. Maccius Plautus* Cistellaria, *Einleitung, Text und Kommentar* (Munich, 2012), 25 n. 122, 30 n. 159.

146–47 I denied it hotly: 'treating her as if she were his wife' goes beyond what Simo has evidence for, but even so his hot denial suggests that he has not been very straight in his dealings with his old friend; at 135 he said 'it became obvious that they were established lovers', which is not so very different.

illud: for the lightening of the first syllable cf. on 237 *illud*.

negare: 'historic' infinitive; see on 62.

instat factum: understand *esse*, and see OLD *insto* 7.d (*factum instare*), 'to maintain that a thing has been done or is as stated', citing Pl. *Merc.* 242 and this passage.

148   *qui*: this is generally agreed here to be the indefinite adverb (cf. on 6), used several times by Plautus to reinforce *ut*; see Lindsay on Pl. *Capt.* 553, OLD *qui²* 6.b. It means 'in some way', but it is not natural to include it at all in translating into English.

149   *daturum*: understand *esse*, as often with the future infinitive.

[As noted by Victor 2007, 5, there is some attraction in the reading *hic* (for *haec*) of one late manuscript, with *hic* meaning 'in this circumstance', as at 638.]

150   *causa*: understand *erat*.

uehemens: OLD 5.6 '(of arguments, etc.) forcible, powerful'.

Why ever not?: literally, 'How? Tell me.' See on 6 *qui*, and OLD *cedo²* 2 'Tell me, describe to me, explain to me', often with a question (again at 383, 389, 705, 763).

151–53   **You've laid down … in the meantime**: Simo quotes what he imagines Pamphilus would say, as at 139–41, though this time without an introductory 'He'd say'; similarly Davos at 773–74 quotes without preamble the alleged thoughts of those in Glycerium's household, and cf. 221–23 where he quotes the story he believes Pamphilus and Glycerium to have concocted. Simo portrays Pamphilus as accepting that his father will arrange a marriage for him in the near future ('You've laid down' presumably referring to the fact that Simo has already accepted a marriage proposal, even if that has come to nothing). Note the implication that marriage was expected to restrain a man's behaviour, something one might not expect from reading some modern accounts of ancient marriage.

151   *Tute*: for this emphatic form of *tu* see OLD *tu* 2.b; again at 500, 579, etc.

praescripsti = *praescripsisti*.

152   **to please someone else**: i.e. a wife. *Mos* is used in the same way at

HT 203 *ex illius more uiuere*; see OLD *mos* 5.d and the idiom *morem gerere* (below, 641) at OLD 6.

[**153 *meo me***: the manuscripts have the unmetrical *me meo*; *meo me* is the reading of the lemma in Donatus and is accepted by all editors.]

154 *locus*: OLD 14 'Room for action, scope, opportunity, opening'; cf. 206, 233, 601, 718.

[**155** The manuscripts have *nolit*; *nolet* is attested by Donatus as an alternative reading. Shipp is doubtless right that the future indicative 'makes his refusal less improbable than the subjunctive', in contrast with 165 *Sin eueniat*, but either would be entirely acceptable here. The present indicatives in 154 and 156 perhaps make the future indicative more likely, but the case is not clear cut.]

156 punish: OLD *animaduerto* 8; a transitive verb, written either as one word (as at 767) or two (as here), retaining the last two letters of *animum*, though they are elided for scansion purposes.

157 that's what I'm working on: OLD *opera* 2. For the construction of *id*, see on 58 *nil*.

159 that rascal Davos: Davos is introduced to the audience as a scheming slave of the type that had become traditional on the Roman stage and is found particularly in the comedies of Plautus, one who delights in trickery as much for its own sake as for the sake of its ultimate purpose. See Fraenkel, ch. 8; Duckworth, 249–53.

consili: on *consilium* as a programmatic word for a slave's scheming in Plautus and Terence see Sharrock, 11–15. The word is used repeatedly in this play of the plots both of Davos and of Simo.

161 *manibus pedibusque*: the same idiom (without -*que*) at 676; see Otto, 210, and add [Quint.] *Decl.* 12.6 *pedibus manibus*. [Bentley deleted -*que* here to make the expression conform with 676, but perhaps we should accept that some variety was possible.]

162 *adeo*: OLD *adeo*² 6.b 'yes and, what is more, or rather'.

163 *Rogas?*: a formulaic response to a question, often conveying surprise or indignation that the question has been asked: 'How can you ask?' cf. 184, 267, 909; a stronger version at 762 *At etiam rogas?*

164 An evil mind, an evil heart: *malus* ('evil', 'wicked') can refer to the roguishness characteristic of a traditional comic slave: at *Amph.* 268 Mercury says *Itaque me malum esse oportet, callidum, astutum admodum* ('So I must be very wicked, cunning, and clever'); at *Ps.* 581–82 Pseudolus praises his own *malitia fraudulenta* ('fraudulent wickedness'), and at 724–26 he says he needs someone *malum, callidum, doctum* ('wicked, cunning, smart') to assist him in his trickery; cf also *Ps*. 705a *per malitiam, per dolum et fallacias* ('through wickedness, through trickery and deception'). Simo here hints at a view of Davos as a traditional comic trickster which becomes more explicit at 582–84.

If I catch him – : threats are often left incomplete, a sign of the speaker's anger; see 860 'If you add a word – ', and R. G. Austin on Virgil, *Aen*. I.135.

165   *opust*: see on 102 *dictust*.

167   [**I'll have to get him to forgive Pamphilus**: the manuscripts all read *qui mi exorandus est* ('whom I'll have to persuade'), and most editors follow them. But Donatus attests that there was an alternative reading *cui* (= *quoi*: see next note) *mi expurgandus est*, and that is perhaps more likely to have been banalized into the reading of the manuscripts than to have arisen from miswriting. *Expurgo* comes again at 900 *sine me expurgem* and at *Hec*. 277 and 742, *exoro* at 592, 901 and in other plays; either reading is entirely possible.]

   quoi = *cui*; cf. 211, 230, 962. I follow K-L in using this old form throughout, though the manuscripts generally have *cui*; similarly 336, 765, 772 *quoius* for *cuius*, 178 etc. *quoiquam* for *cuiquam*; see Introduction p. 38.

   I'm sure: this is sometimes the nuance of *spero*, similar to English 'I trust'; cf. 314, 407, 553, 560, *Eun*. 203 (with Donatus' comment), 872.

   confore: future infinitive of *confio* ('To be done, be accomplished; to come about, happen', OLD 1).

   Simo's confidence in his ability to persuade Chremes is largely justified: see 533–74.

168   **your job**: Moodie, 149 says 'Simo's use of *officium* ['job'] here hints at his awareness of Roman comedy's conventions, since the preparation and execution of deceptions usually is the purview of a lower-status character'. The clearest case of *officium* meaning 'the behaviour appropriate to a theatrical role' is Pl. *Asin*. 173–75. Since a freedman is not a traditional comic role, it is not clear that such conventions are here evoked, but Simo could certainly be said to be assigning a role to Sosia at this point.

169–70   *obserues filium quid agat*: *filius*, the subject of the subordinate clause *quid agat*, is made the object of the main clause, like *tuom ... animum* at 378, and often elsewhere, particularly in comedy: see Pinkster, 759–63.

171   **I'll see to it**: these words echo Sosia's first (30 'you want these preparations to be properly seen to', with the same verb, *curare*); cf.

Anderson 2004, 16, suggesting that the repetition underlines the fact that Sosia still has to perform services for his former master. In fact nothing more is heard of Sosia; he was a convenient device for introducing the story. According to Posani, 42, he turns out to be so incompetent at making a good pretence of the wedding that Davos has no difficulty in seeing through it (see 359–61); but it is not clear that Sosia should be held responsible for the shortcomings spotted by Davos.

[**Let's go inside now**: the manuscripts give these words to Sosia, but it is more appropriate for Simo to remain in control. On the other hand, it would not be appropriate for him politely to allow Sosia to go in first, so 'You go ahead; I'll follow' should be spoken by Sosia, obsequiously making way for his former master. The situation is different at Pl. *Cist.* 773 *I prae; iam ego te sequar* ('You go ahead; I'll follow you at once', a citizen woman to a slave), where the characters are not about to enter the house of the speaker, though it is also similar in that both characters go indoors immediately.]

nunciam: three syllables, of which the last is here elided. This is the usual scansion when the word reinforces a command, instruction, or exhortation; cf. 329, 424, 842, 866. In other contexts *nunc iam* should be regarded as two words rather than one.

[**I'll follow**: the manuscripts are divided between *sequar* and *sequor*. The present tense is often used to refer to the imminent future, particularly with verbs of motion, and *I prae: sequor* is found again in the mouth of someone leaving the stage at *Eun.* 908.]

The stage is empty, and we have to imagine what is happening indoors before Simo reappears at 172. It is tempting to suppose that Menander's *Girl from Andros* had a divine prologue at this point to reassure the spectators about Glycerium's future (see Introduction, p. 18). This is one of a number of cases in Plautus and Terence where there is no text between a character's exit and re-entry; see *HT* 171–72, 873–74 for two further examples. The cases are discussed by M. Johnston, *Exits and Entrances in Roman Comedy* (Diss. Columbia, 1933), 114–19. Some scholars suppose that the gap was covered by a musical performance of some kind, as it explicitly is at *Ps.* 573a (but only there); others are happy to believe that off-stage time was very elastic in ancient drama and that the audience accepted even a very short pause as sufficient to cover whatever action they had to imagine as taking place while the stage was empty.

Some editors have supposed that Simo does not leave the stage at all at this point but stays to round the scene off with a brief monologue, cut short by the entry of Davos at 174 (in which case it should be Simo, not Sosia, who says 'You go ahead; I'll follow' at 171). On this view, Simo must have observed Davos' reaction on learning of the wedding before the play began, and *modo* at 173 should be translated 'earlier' rather than 'just now'; either meaning is possible. However, Davos at 175 appears to be reacting to a fresh piece of news, rather than something he had learnt of some time earlier. Also, if he had heard earlier about the revived wedding plans, it is not explained why he had stayed at home while Simo went shopping, instead of going immediately to warn Pamphilus (as he does at 227). In addition, it has been claimed (e.g. by Shipp p. 135 top, Denzler, 9 n. 29, Perutelli, 106–107) that Simo is significantly better informed about his son's reaction at 172–74 than he had been at 155–71 and must therefore have learnt something in the meantime; we need not suppose that he has himself discussed the matter with Davos indoors but merely that he has witnessed Davos' reaction to the news that a wedding is imminent, no doubt as a result of Sosia's faithfully carrying out his instructions – so Glücklich, 35 with n. 73, 41. I am not convinced that Simo is better informed at 172–74, since we could see his thoughts as fluctuating as he reflects on the situation and on the likely outcome. But overall I accept the conclusion that Simo most probably went indoors at 171 and that this and 819 are the two places in the play where the stage is empty.

172–205 Simo reappears from his house. Although he gives no motive for his entry, either at the beginning of the scene (where Davos' entry interrupts his monologue) or at the end (where he storms off uttering dire warnings against Davos), we learn from Pamphilus' words at 254 that he has by then met Pamphilus in the main square and told him to prepare to get married today. Similarly Davos does not say why he has come out of the house until 226–27, where he explains that *he* will head for the main square to find Pamphilus. Characters do not always give a reason for their entry, and it is unlikely that the audience would be troubled by the lack of one, as long as their attention was held by the action on stage.

At 175–205 we witness the first encounter between Simo and Davos, culminating in Simo's threat of dire punishment if Davos does anything to hinder the wedding. This fits with Simo's plan to make it look as if he really is preparing to hold the wedding today; he has urged Sosia at 169 to 'terrify Davos', and now he tries to do the same himself. But he also hopes that it really will be possible for the wedding to go ahead if no obstacles are thrown in its way: see 165–67.

Simo's asides at 179 and 183 show that he is overhearing Davos' monologue, and Davos' remark at the end of 183 suggests that he has heard Simo's aside. This sort of artificiality is common in scenes of this kind.

Metre: 172–74 are in iambic senarii. Davos' entry introduces the first lines in the play with musical accompaniment, almost entirely in iambics: 175 iambic octonarius, 176 iambic dimeter, 177 iambic octonarius, 178–79 trochaic septenarii, 180–95 iambic octonarii. The switch to trochees at 178 serves to emphasize Davos' point, which is further reinforced by the fact that the line starts with five spondaic words, with repeated *qu-* in the first two; Simo counters with an aside in the same metre before the iambic octonarii resume. At 196–98 Simo interrupts the sequence of octonarii (which continue thereafter from 199 to 214) with three senarii for the start of his threat to Davos, returning to octonarii for the threat itself. It is likely that the effect was emphasized by having the musical accompaniment stop for these three lines: T. J. Moore, 'When did the *tibicen* play? Meter and musical accompaniment in Roman comedy', *TAPA* 138 (2008), 3–46, at pp. 18–19 argues that this was normal even for isolated senarii such as 226. For further discussion of the metre of this section see Moore 2013, 90–93, pointing out (among other things) the symmetrical structure of 16 iambic octonarii (180–95), three iambic senarii (196–98), 16 iambic octonarii (199–214); this assumes that 208 is not interpolated. He also observes on p. 90 that this is the only Roman comedy in which the first character to sing is the scheming slave.

174   *ipse*: for the lightening of the first syllable cf. on 237 *illud*.

175   **to come off like that**: see OLD *abeo* 7.c '(of incidents, actions, etc.) to be allowed to pass, escape criticism, go by'; cf. e.g. Catul. 14.16 *Non, non hoc tibi, false, sic abibit*.

175–76   **I was afraid all along**: this translation assumes that *semper* qualifies *uerebar*. Donatus appears to favour taking it with *lenitas*, as if it were an adjective ('a use of which there are sporadic, and generally uncertain, examples elsewhere', Shipp, 135), 'my master's constant mildness'; in favour of this see Scafuro, 374–77, Karakasis, 86 (and cf. on 345 *euge*). At 262 Pamphilus acknowledges that Simo has always shown leniency towards him (and Simo himself also proclaims at 36 'how fair and mild' his treatment of Sosia had always been), but that does not require us to take *semper* as qualifying *lenitas* here.

178   any of us: as at 180–82, Davos identifies himself wholeheartedly with Pamphilus' cause.

quoiquam = *cuiquam*; again at 425, 626, 716. Cf. on 167 *quoi*.

179   a heavy punishment for you: *malum* is the regular word for the punishment of slaves in Comedy (e.g. at 431 and 611 below, *Eun*. 714, *Ph.* 644, 851). References to slave-punishments are common in these plays; cf. 199 'I'll flog you with the whips and send you to work at the mill', 600 'straight off to the mill', 621 'crucifixion'. At 860–65 Davos is taken indoors to have his hands and feet tied together.

180   *Id*: like *hoc* at 409 and 497, this is explained by the following accusative and infinitive.

duci: OLD *duco* 17 'To lead on (into a false or undesirable position)'; cf. 644.

181   half-asleep: *interoscito* (from *oscito*, 'I yawn') is found only here and in a scholiast on Lucan VI.126.

[**182   *ne esset***: on the scansion see the note attached to the end of Introduction, section 8.8 (d).]

183   What's the villain saying?: Simo could hear Davos perfectly well at 179; perhaps Davos has moved further away from him since then.

villain: literally, *carnufex* means 'executioner', but it is used as a general term of abuse. The word is used of Davos again at 651, 852.

184 is remarkable for having six changes of speaker in one line, perhaps a way of showing how flustered Davos is.

Hem: cf. 116.

Eho dum: cf. on 88 *Eho*, 29 *dum*.

Quid ais?: often used to introduce a question, essentially to attract the interlocutor's attention and not in itself expecting an answer; cf. 301, 517, 575, 616, 872. Here Davos cheekily pretends to take it literally as a question. For a discussion of the various uses of the idiom see Barrios-Lech, 172–76.

Rogas?: as at 163.

185   *Id populus curat scilicet*: quoted by Cic. *Att*. XIII.34.1.

186   Are you concentrating: OLD *ago* 22 'to turn one's attention to'.

Hoccin = *Hocne*; the full form *hocce* has its final vowel weakened to *i* when the interrogative *-ne* is added to it, and *ne* is not infrequently abbreviated to *-n*.

istuc: understand *ago*. For the form (from *istud-ce*) see on 28 *istaec*.

Note the contrast of the first-person pronoun *hoc* ('what I'm saying') and the second-person pronoun *istuc* ('what you're saying').

186–87 for me to look into that now is to behave like an unreasonable father: 'The verses are dense with hypocrisy… Simo, as we know from his own *narratio* in I 1, made diligent and persistent inquiries before his son's wedding…' (Scafuro, 376–77).

187 *antehac*: two syllables as a result of synizesis; cf. on 22 *Dehinc.* Again at 303, 917.

188 *Dum tempus ad eam rem tulit*: for the use of *tulit* here cf. 443 *dumque aetas tulit*; *HT* 215 *rerum quas fert adulescentia*, 573 *multa fert lubido*; *Ad.* 730 *quod res ipsa fert*; Cic. *Verr.* II.73 *quae tempus illud tulit et causa*. This belongs either under OLD *fero* 30.d '(of time) to bring with it (situations, etc.)' or 31 '(of circumstances, etc.) To prompt, suggest'. But the addition of *ad eam rem* seems to have no parallel.

189 But today's the day that ushers in a different lifestyle and requires different behaviour: Cicero quotes this line with reference to the political situation when writing to Cornificius a year after Caesar's assassination at *Fam.* XII.25.5. He quotes it with *defert*, but there is no reason not to accept the *adfert* of Terence's manuscripts: see Martin 1964, 3–4.

190 *Dehinc*: cf. on 22.

191 *Hoc quid sit?*: the subjunctive is used as if Simo were repeating a question asked by Davos and implying 'Do you ask what I mean?' (i.e. as if 'what I mean' were an indirect question).

193 a mind that's sick: cf. 559, and Maltby 2012 on *Ph.* 822 on the imagery of love as a disease in Terence. On medical imagery more generally in Greek and Roman comedy (as at 468 *remedium*, 831 *medicarer*, 944 *medicari*) see Fantham, 14–18.

adplicat: this passage is cited at OLD *applico* 6.b 'to apply (one's mind to)'. As with *animum … adpulit* at 1 and 446, a nautical metaphor may be felt: cf. OLD *applico* 4.

194 *hercle*: 'by Hercules', used to add emphasis and found almost exclusively in the mouth of male speakers; see Adams, 47–49, Maltby 1985, 115–17, with references to earlier discussions.

Really?: as at 435, *Hem* here expresses (perhaps feigned) surprise; an interrogative intonation seems appropriate. cf. Luck, 10, Müller, 44–45.

not Oedipus: Oedipus as a young man had saved the city of Thebes from a plague by solving the riddle of the Sphinx. The same part of his story is referred to at Pl. *Poen*. 443–44. Terence's characters do not often refer to Greek mythology, but it is clear from Plautus that Roman audiences were familiar with it (see Fraenkel, ch. 3). For Donatus there is additional rudeness in the implication that Simo is like the Sphinx, a cruel and monstrous creature.

196–200   Simo spells out the threat that he had left incomplete at 164. Sherberg, 101–102 (cited with approval by Lefèvre, 72) sees an inconsistency between his words to Davos here and the strategy he announced at 159ff. of allowing Davos a free rein. That, if true, would show that Simo is unable to restrain himself when actually in the presence of Davos, not necessarily (as Sherberg suggests) that 159ff. reproduce Menander while 196ff. were added by Terence. In fact, however, Simo does not say in 159ff. that he will give Davos a free rein but only that Davos' schemes will be rendered harmless by the fact that the wedding preparations are a pretence; and the suppressed threat at 164 is entirely consistent with what Simo says here.

196   *hodie*: frequently found in threats; cf. 866. It is often impossible to tell whether it means 'today' (which would be entirely appropriate here and could remind us that the action of an ancient comedy normally takes place on one day) or is being used as a particle to add emphasis (OLD *hodie* 3, a usage not confined to threats: see 410 below).

199   **work at the mill**: see on 179. For a slave, to be sent to work at the mill on his master's country property was to be condemned to hard labour, since the mills in question were hand-driven; see the entry on 'mills' in the Oxford Classical Dictionary. For such punishments in Greece, see Lysias I.18, Men. *Heros* 1–3.

200   **your terms and prospects**: *omen* is difficult to translate here (and cannot be paralleled in this idiom) but conveys a weighty assurance that things will turn out as the speaker threatens, that his words are ominous.

201   *intellextin* = *intellexistine*; cf. 151 *praescripsti* and for -*n* 186 *hoccin*.

   nondum ... ne hoc quidem: the double negative reinforces the point, as at 205 *neque ... haud*.

202   *locutu's* = *locutus es*; cf. on 102 *dictust*. Pezzini, 90–97 discusses contraction of *es*, which recurs in this play at 621, 702, 724, 749 (in all cases restored by editors, not found in the manuscripts).

203   *deludier*: Terence uses this form of the passive infinitive at the end of the line, where it is convenient for the metre; it was almost certainly obsolete, or well on the way to becoming obsolete, at the time he was writing. M. del Castillo Herrera, 'Los infinitivos passivos en -*ier* en la literatura latina: de

Plauto a Juvenal', *Latomus* 70.1 (2011), 51–66 discusses the range of uses of this form in Latin literature, suggesting on pp. 54–55 that Terence tends to make his speakers use it when saying something emphatic or determined (i.e. not simply for metrical convenience). That fits well enough here and at 275 and 332, less well at 573 and (as she herself admits in n. 10) at a number of points in other plays.

204 *Bona uerba*: see OLD *bonus* 17.b 'of good omen, auspicious'; Davos is saying (ironically) 'May your words turn out to be auspicious'. His precise form of words is found elsewhere only at Macr. *Sat.* I.5.4, II.1.4 in this idiom, but see K. F. Smith on Tib. II.2.1 *dicamus bona uerba*.

I can tell: Donatus quotes Menander's Greek νῦν δ' οὐ λέληθας †μεναμ† (Men. fr. 35 K-A: 'As it is, you haven't escaped my notice'). *Nil fallis* is a close equivalent of οὐ λέληθας, but 'As it is' suggests a slightly different development of the dialogue in Menander.

[***Sed dico*:** Donatus on 495 quotes this with *Edico*, which some editors print here (with or without *sed*). But Donatus' scribes may have been influenced by the fact that that is the verb used by Terence at that point.]

[**205** Donatus preserves a comment on *haud*, which was clearly in his text; the manuscripts have *hoc*, which is perfectly acceptable but perhaps more likely to have been introduced by someone who did not see that the two negatives reinforce one another (as in 201).

dices: the manuscripts are divided between this and *dicas*; P. J. H. Mueller, *De veterum grammaticorum in Terentio studiis criticis* (Aachen, 1926), 41 argues that the future indicative is more appropriate and was replaced (here and elsewhere) by a corrector who thought that a potential subjunctive was needed.]

206–27 Davos, left on his own, reflects on the situation before leaving to warn Pamphilus about it. His monologue falls into two halves, the division being reinforced by a change of metre at 215. The iambic octonarii continue until 214, while he lays bare his predicament, but at 215–24 the music stops and Davos gives the audience in iambic senarii the sort of information that might have been included in an expository prologue (and perhaps was included in such a prologue in Menander's play: see Introduction, p. 18). He reverts to an octonarius at 225 in which he dwells on his own reaction to what he has just told us, then a senarius at 226, and a final octonarius at 227. The iambic senarius at 226 marks the appearance of Mysis from Chrysis' house; if Moore is right (see on 172–205), the music stopped for this one line and resumed for the following line. A change of metre for such an entry announcement (regularly introduced with *sed*) is common in Terence: see Bruder, 6–7. It happens again at 234 and 605; and 682 has an entry announcement half way through the line in the new metre. We might have expected Terence to allow Davos to continue with a second senarius at 227, but he must have wanted to round Davos' appearance off with a line in the metre with which it began at 175.

A monologue in which a slave reflects on the challenge facing him is common in ancient comedy: see PCG *adesp.* 1006, 1007.29–42, 1063.2–23, 1096.13–16 and perhaps 83–90, Pl. *Epid.* 81–103, *Ps.* 394–414, *Trin.* 717–28, Ter. *HT* 668–78a.

J. Barsby, 'Native Roman Rhetoric: Plautus and Terence', in W. J. Dominik and J. Hall (eds), *A Companion to Roman Rhetoric* (Malden, MA and Oxford, 2007), 38–53, at pp. 44–45 gives a stylistic analysis of Davos' monologue, pointing out a number of unobtrusive rhetorical effects in the first part (alliteration and various types of verbal balance, 'playing with the sounds of similar words', as well as antithetically balanced clauses at 209 and 210). There is a similar rhetorical flourish at 218, but 215–24 mainly display a simpler narrative style and even what could be seen as a parody of the naive style of early Latin prose narrative at 221–23.

206 Self-address in monologues is frequent in ancient comedy.

segnitiae ... socordiae: the two nouns and their related adverbs are also linked at Pl. *Asin.* 254 *quin tu aps te socordiam omnem reice et segnitiem amoue*, Livy XL.27.2 *segnius socordiusque oppugnabant*.

[**208 my master**: this must here refer to Pamphilus, which is possible since Davos is a slave in the service of the son as well as the father. But the ambiguity is awkward, given that Davos has just been on stage with Simo, to whom he has referred as his 'master' at 175 and 183. Admittedly, at Pl. *Ps.* 493 *erus* refers to both father and son in the same line; but the content there makes it clear which is which, and there is no possible ambiguity. As it happens, Davos uses *erus* elsewhere only of Simo (at 508, 602, 728, 846) and regularly addresses or refers to Pamphilus by name. Line 208 is repeated in the manuscripts either before or after line 181 of *Phormio*, where it has been suspected of being interpolated from this passage. In fact the awkwardness is greater here, and I have deleted the line accordingly; the addition of a line to amplify or heighten a point is a common type of interpolation in ancient texts.

astu: the ablative of *astus*, used adverbially, meaning the same as *astute* at 183.]

209 I can't decide: for the use of *certumst* here see OLD *certus* 2.b '(my) mind is made up, (I am) determined'.

211 uerba dare: OLD *uerbum* 6 'To deceive, hoodwink, impose on'.

213–14 [if he feels like it: the manuscripts have *aut si lubitum fuerit*, which is awkward since *aut* ('or') leads us to expect that the consequences 'if he feels like it' will be different from the consequences 'if he catches me out'; in fact being sent to the mill is simply an amplification of 'I've had it' (which is what *perii* idiomatically means), not an alternative. The simplest solution is to delete *aut*, with C. Conradt, *Die metrische Composition der Comödien des Terenz* (Berlin, 1876, repr. Delhi, 2017), 72 n. Barsby translates *aut* as 'in any case' (cf. Posani: 'del resto'), but can the word mean this? Victor 1999b, 269–70 finds further fault with the logic of 'if he feels like it' and proposes *aut si ei dubium fuerit*, translating 'why, even if he but suspects'; but it is not clear that *aut si* can be used like *uel si* to mean 'even if', and *ei dubium fuerit* seems a weak way to say 'he suspects' (his alternative suggestion *dubitum fuerit* would be better, if we could believe that Terence used the verb *dubare*, from which he derives *dubitum*). Victor objects particularly to 'right or wrong', but see below on this.]

fuerit: we might have expected *erit*, but it is idiomatic for Plautus and Terence to use the future perfect form of *esse* in the future perfect of deponent or semi-deponent verbs: cf. *Ph.* 516 *promeritus fueris*, *Ad.* 603 *fueris functus*, de Melo, 41 n. 31.

ceperit: future perfect. There has been much debate about the use of this tense in Early Latin, particularly in main clauses; in subordinate clauses it regularly conveys the expected notion of one future event preceding another, as with *senserit* and *lubitum fuerit* in this line. The best explanation for its use here (and at 381 *inuenerit*) is probably that offered for some other passages by R. Risselada ('The End of Time: A Perfect Future in Latin', in C. Kroon and D. den Hengst [eds], *Ultima Aetas: Time, Tense and Transience in the Ancient World* [Amsterdam, 2000], 25–39), that it conveys a 'retrospective evaluation' (p. 37): someone in the future looking back will judge that Simo had been seizing the excuse. It is not always immediately obvious in main clauses why the future perfect has been used rather than the simple future, but Risselada argues that closer scrutiny of the wider context often shows it to be appropriate; so too de Melo, 21–50, Pinkster, 462–72. De Melo argues that the future perfect is often used idiomatically 'when the future perfect in the main clause describes an automatic result of the subordinate clause […], what unavoidably happens at the same time as the event in the subordinate clause comes true' (p. 40). That does not fit here, but it works for 397 *feceris*, 570 *restitueris*.

right or wrong: *quo iure quaque iniuria* (literally 'by which right and by which wrong'), a 'polar' expression conveying the absolute inevitability of the punishment; see Jebb on Soph. *Ant.* 40, Wilamowitz on Eur. *HF* 1106. Simo will in fact be perfectly justified in punishing Davos if he catches him out, but it would be missing the point of the expression to object to the inclusion of *quaque iniuria* ('or wrong'), just as it would be to find fault with the practicality of Creon's issuing an instruction to 'those who are present and those who are not' at Soph. *Ant.* 1109. Understand something like *poterit* for the completion of the sense. We might have expected *causam ceperit qua dabit* ('he'll seize an excuse by which he will send me'), but the relative pronoun becomes absorbed in an expression which Donatus tells us was proverbial (Otto, 180 offers no further examples of it, but *iure an iniuria* is found e.g. at Cic. *Verr.* II.150, *Mil.* 57): as Kauer puts it in his commentary, it is as if Terence had written *ius uel iniuriam inuenerit* rather than *causam ceperit*.

praecipitem … dabit: cf. 606, *Ph.* 625 *ut praecipitem hanc daret*, *Ad.* 318 *praecipitem darem*, Pl. *Ps.* 494 *iuberes hunc praecipitem in pistrinum trahi*; OLD *do*[1] 19.b 'to cause to go, etc.'. [The manuscripts have *me* after *praecipitem*; this has been deleted on metrical grounds, but we must understand *me* as the object of *dabit*.]

215 that's not the end of my troubles: Davos takes for granted that he will be blamed for the consequences of Pamphilus' reckless behaviour. In a similar context at Pl. *Aul.* 74–78 the slave Staphyla reveals to the audience that her master's daughter is due to give birth any day and concludes that the best solution for herself is to commit suicide.

216 his wife or his mistress: of course she could not literally be his wife at this stage; see on 146. Davos' indifference to the terminology perhaps shows his awareness that Pamphilus does in some sense treat or regard her as his wife and that word has got around that he does so. [The manuscripts have *siue ista* at the start of the line, which is metrically impossible: editors agree on reading *si* for *siue*.]

217 just listen: lit. 'it's worth listening' (OLD *pretium* 2.b). Davos comes close to acknowledging the presence of the audience, a very rare phenomenon in Terence's plays (apart from the prologues and the brief audience address at the end of each play), though commoner in Menander and Plautus. The closest parallel in Terence is *Hec.* 361–62: 'I can't find any suitable starting point to begin telling you what's happened to me.' Cf. also the end of Mercury's prologue at Pl. *Amph.* 151–52: *Adeste: est operae pretium spectatoribus / Iouem et Mercurium facere hic histrioniam* ('Pay attention: it will be worth your while to see Jupiter and Mercury performing as actors here').

218 *amentium, haud amantium*: note the word-play.

219 **let the baby live, whatever it turns out to be**: literally, 'to take up the baby, whatever she gives birth to'. *tollere* refers to the father's picking the baby up from the hearth as a symbolic sign that he wishes it to be reared (see OLD 2). The normal thing to do with unwanted babies was to leave them somewhere out in the open to die (to 'expose' them); at 464–69 Simo is astonished to hear that Pamphilus proposes not to expose his child by a foreign woman (i.e. a woman he cannot marry: see on 146). The point of 'whatever it turns out to be' is that girls were normally more likely than boys to be exposed at birth; cf. *HT* 626–27.

220 **some bogus story**: this story is a strong hint for the spectators that Glycerium will be reunited with her family by the end of the play. In dismissing it here as a 'bogus story' that Pamphilus and Glycerium 'are making up' and in 224–25 as implausible rubbish, Davos remains in character and does not seem to speak as the all-knowing prologue figure found in some comedies by Menander and Plautus. But as members of the audience we shall take his scepticism with a pinch of salt and shall not be surprised to learn towards the end of the play that the story has not been made up at all. We may also smile at the suggestion that a standard story-pattern of New Comedy is implausible rubbish; Sharrock, 145 notes that *Fabulae* at 224, as well as meaning 'rubbish', could remind us that the story is familiar from *fabulae* in the sense of 'plays' (as noted too by Compagno, 51 and Knorr, 169).

221–24 There are two small differences between Davos' account here and the slightly fuller account at 923–25 and 935–36: (1) Davos' summary might give the impression that only Glycerium survived the shipwreck, whereas we learn at 923–25 that the old man did so as well; (2) by specifying that the old man was a businessman (*mercator*) Davos might seem to be implying that trade was the motive for his journey, whereas we are told at 935–36 that his

Commentary

motive was 'to avoid the war'. For Mazzarino, 23–34, these differences are a sign that Davos' narrative here derives from Menander's *Perinthia* (with Perinthos changed to Andros as the site of the shipwreck), while the later account comes from his *Andria*. But it is simpler to conclude that in the later scene we learn further details that are not relevant to Davos' exposition here; the later account amplifies but does not seriously contradict this one. (So A. Klotz in his review of Mazzarino, *DLZ* 71.12 (1950), 534–35, and Lefèvre, 56 n. 57.) Glycerium (who must be Davos' ultimate source for the story) is unlikely to have known all the relevant details, and it is not implausible that we learn more later from people in a better position to know them.

221–23 *fuit olim quidam ... is ... is ... ibi tum*: the style is that of the simplest form of story-telling; see E. Fraenkel, *Kleine Beiträge zur klassischen Philologie* (Rome, 1964), I.237, II.56–57, who notes that at 923–28 we have *Atticus quidam olim ... tum ille ... tum is ... ibi ego ... is ibi mortuost*. For Fraenkel, *Fabulae* at 224 (and *Fabulam* at 925) suggests 'fairy-tales'. Davos quotes the story in direct speech (cf. the start of the note on 151–53), rounding it off in indirect speech at 223–24.

221 **citizen of Attica**: Attica was the Greek region of which Athens was the capital; to be an Athenian citizen was to be a citizen of Attica. On the use of the terms 'Attic' and 'Athenian' in Greek see C. Patterson, '*Hai Attikai*: the other Athenians', in M. Skinner (ed.), *Rescuing Creusa: New Methodological Approaches to Women in Antiquity* (Lubbock, Texas, 1987), 49–67, at pp. 50–53. Plautus and Terence both use the adjective *Atticus*, but Plautus also three times uses *Atheniensis*.

[I have with some hesitation followed Bentley in adding *hinc* (cf. 833, 892, 908) after *olim* to avoid breaking Meyer's law (see Introduction, section 8.4). I am not convinced that it is required for the sense, since Davos surely does not need to spell out that the old man came from Attica, but Bentley's instinct that there was something wrong with the rhythm of *olim quidam senex* seems to have been confirmed by Meyer's researches.]

223 *ibi tum*: cf. on 106.

225 *Miquidem*: the first syllable is light, as often happens (by 'enclisis') when a personal pronoun is followed by *quidem*; so too the second syllable of *quandoquidem* at 487, 608, and the first syllable of *siquidem* at 465 (and in Augustan poetry). See Questa, 153–71.

atque: used adversatively (OLD 9), in the sense of *atqui*; so too at 350, 525, 607, 614, 640.

226 *ab ea*: 'from her house'; cf. 682 *a Glycerio*, 754 *a nobis*.

226–27 I'll be off to the main square to meet Pamphilus: in fact Simo meets Pamphilus before Davos can do so.

hinc me ad forum: understand *amouebo* (cf. *Ph*. 566 *modo te hinc amoue*). *Forum* is the word regularly used by Plautus and Terence where a Greek playwright would presumably have referred to the *agora*, the main market-place. They never use the word *agora*, and *forum* was perhaps accepted as the nearest Latin equivalent without seeming intrusively Roman in a play set at Athens (if anyone cared about that).

ut: Terence is fond of starting a new clause with a monosyllable at the end of a line, often, as here, preceded by elision; cf. 248, 252, 256, etc.

228–33 Mysis has six lines of trochaic septenarii, from which we learn that she is a slave who has been sent to fetch the midwife Lesbia. We have just been told at 215–16 that Glycerium is pregnant; now it becomes clear that the birth is imminent. Mysis' first words are addressed back through the doorway to her fellow-slave Archylis, a common device when a character enters from indoors and a means for the playwright to conjure up a world behind the scenes that the spectators cannot see. Mysis then comments on Lesbia's drinking habits and incompetence as a midwife.

It has often been noted that when Lesbia appears later in the play at 459–67 and 481–88 there is no obvious sign that she is drunk or incompetent, and it has been suggested that this is because Mysis' remarks here derive from Menander's *Perinthia* whereas Lesbia's later appearance derives from his *Andria*. The reason for the former belief is that *Perinthia* fr. 4 Arnott (= 4 S) says 'The old woman didn't miss a single cup but drank from the bowl every time it came round' (οὐδεμίαν ἡ γραῦς ὅλως / κύλικα παρῆκεν, ἀλλ᾽ ἔπιε τὴν ἐν κύκλῳ); if Terence's play follows *Perinthia* closely, it is hard to see who this could be about except the midwife. On the other hand, nothing in Mysis' speech quite corresponds with this description of an old woman at a party, and the fragment may be a sign that Terence did not follow Menander so very closely after all: fondness for alcohol is part of Greek Comedy's stereotypical portrayal of women of all kinds, and it is not inevitable that the old woman in the fragment is a midwife. (Could the fragment come from a description of a celebratory party at the end of the play, as at Men. *Dysk*. 946–49?) For Menander's *Andria*, see on 483–85: there is good evidence that in that play the midwife gave instructions similar to those given by Lesbia at that point; whether she showed signs of bibulousness, we cannot tell. Given the stress on Lesbia's bibulousness and incompetence at 229–33, it is striking that nothing is made of this when she appears later, but the reason is not necessarily that the different passages derive from different Menandrian plays: an alternative possibility is that either Menander or Terence exploited the stereotypical portrayal of such a woman for comic effect in these lines but did not wish to labour the point later in the play, or else that we are to realize later on that Mysis has here been unfair to Lesbia. For Germany, 241 the 'surprisingly sober midwife' of the later scenes is a deliberate effect: we are to notice that she is 'generically anomalous' (like other characters in this play, according to Germany). J. Welsh, 'Singing the *Sermo Comicus* with Terence', in Papaioannou 2014, 59–74, at 64–65, on the other hand, sees signs of traditional comic style in her lyric passage at 481–85 (though the few details he adduces are very slight); and Shipp p. 161 suggests that the metre there could be a hint that Lesbia has after all been drinking.

228 Archylis: addressed again at 481 by a character emerging from Glycerium's house, but never seen on stage.

229 *pol*: 'by Pollux', used (like *hercle* at 194) to add emphasis and found more frequently in the mouth of female than of male characters in Comedy, very significantly so in Terence, who clearly uses it as a marker of female speech. See Adams, 50–54. Shipp points out that *temulenta* 'seems to be used in Early Latin only of women'; see Adams, 75 for the possibility that it too was a marker of female speech, though the evidence base is very small.

231 Look: addressed to the spectators, or perhaps to the world at large. See D. Bain, 'Audience Address in Greek Tragedy', *CQ* 25 (1975), 13–25, at pp. 20–21, with references to earlier discussions.

inportunitatem: 'persistent lack of consideration for others, unreasonableness in one's demands, relentlessness, oppressiveness, disobligingness, etc.' (OLD). (Barsby translates 'See how the old woman nags me', perhaps rightly.)

silly old woman: the diminutive form *aniculae* is contemptuous.

232–33 Mysis ends with a prayer that Lesbia's incompetence should damage others rather than her mistress, the kind of apotropaic prayer noted by Nisbet and Hubbard on Horace, *Odes* I.21.13. This example is discussed at length by O. Weinreich, *Religionsgeschichtliche Studien* (Darmstadt, 1968), 7–37, who notes that it is rare for the proposed alternative victim not to be an enemy of some kind and concludes that this is Roman rather than Greek and therefore added by Terence, not reproduced from Menander. Accepting that Mysis' speech otherwise derives from *Perinthia* and that Lesbia's later appearances derive from *Andria* (see above on 228–33), he argues that Terence added this prayer in order to prepare us to see a sober and competent Lesbia, since we are to realize that the prayer is answered by the gods; he further argues that Terence added Lesbia's prayer at 487–88 to balance Mysis' prayer here and bind the two passages yet more closely together. Unfortunately, Weinreich offers little positive evidence that Mysis' prayer is peculiarly Roman in form, and he perhaps makes too much on pp. 24–25 of the fact that she hopes Lesbia will harm anyone in the vicinity (rather than her mistress) without specifying any enemies.

obsecro: on parenthetic *obsecro* as a marker of female speech cf. on 721.

for others: Donatus asks whether *in aliis* means *in aliis mulieribus* ('for other women') or *in aliis rebus* ('for other matters'). Weinreich p.8 says it must obviously mean the first, and it is hard to see in what sphere other than midwifery Mysis might expect Lesbia to be a danger.

234–300 At 234 Mysis sees Pamphilus coming into view, visibly overwrought: he has met his father in the main square (we never learn what Pamphilus was doing there in the first place, nor how he has failed to bump into Davos, who set off towards the main square in search of him at 227), and his father has told him that he is to marry today. His complaints about this treatment alternate with speculation about Chremes' motives in agreeing to allow his daughter to marry Pamphilus after all, combined with laments about the predicament he finds himself in, torn between his duties to Glycerium and to his father. He becomes aware of Mysis' presence at 267 and assures her at some length that he has no intention of abandoning Glycerium. At 300 Mysis continues on her way to fetch the midwife, leaving Pamphilus alone on stage.

This is our first view of Pamphilus, and we see immediately that he is very energetic in expressing his feelings: he has nearly thirty lines of highly emotional monologue, followed by nearly thirty lines more in which he assures Mysis that he will not abandon Glycerium, at many points again expressing his emotions in very strong terms. The style of his monologue at 236–64 makes clear his mental turmoil: his very first line has anaphora of *Hoccin*, and at 237 he exclaims *Pro deum fidem!*; at 238–39 *nonne oportuit* is repeated, with a chiastic arrangement of *oportuit praescisse me ante* and *prius communicatum oportuit*; *inuenustum* and *infelicem* at 245 are near synonyms, as are *contemptus* and *spretus*, *facta* and *transacta*, both pairs placed in asyndeton at 248. There are many examples of expressive alliteration and assonance (e.g. 244 *fit ... funditus*, 249 *repudiatus repetor*); rhetorical questions and exclamations abound. Pamphilus' dialogue with Mysis at 270–98 starts with the interjection *Hem*, immediately followed by two questions, with anaphora of *egone*. Similarly at 277–78 there is anaphora of *Adeon* in a rhetorical question, with the list of abstract nouns linked by *neque* in 279 and the wordplay in *commoueat neque commoneat* at 280. At 282 the question *Memor essem?* is followed by the passionate *O Mysis, Mysis*. Even Chrysis' dying words, as reported by Pamphilus at 286–96, contain e.g. anaphora of *per* in 289–90 and of *Si ... siue ... seu* in 292–94, the near-synonyms *abs te ... segreges* and *deseras* in 291, and the list of nouns in 295. Pamphilus' excited state is also shown by a constant shift in the metres that he uses, with a variety of iambic and trochaic lines (see below).

At 254–55 Pamphilus quotes his father's all-too-brief instructions in the main square, at 286–96 he quotes Chrysis' fuller instructions on her deathbed (both, as it happens, committing Pamphilus to a long-term relationship with a woman). Such verbatim quotation is a common feature of monologues in ancient drama (for Menander see R. Nünlist, 'Speech within Speech in Menander', in A. Willi (ed.), *The Language of Greek Comedy* (Oxford, 2002), 219–57), and it provides an obvious opportunity for the actor to show off his powers of impersonation, though at 286–96 it is to be hoped that he would not go over the top in imitating a female voice.

Mysis utters three short asides at 237, 240, and 251; at 264–66 (still speaking aside) she decides she had better intervene. She does then participate in dialogue with Pamphilus, though it is still he who dominates the conversation. Although she says little, she makes an important contribution by intervening when Pamphilus is at his most indecisive and by saying just the right things to strengthen his resolve to stand by Glycerium. This was noted by Donatus in his comments at several points (discussed by Brown 2012, 23–30), and it is argued for by Rambelli, 132–37 and by N. Zorzetti, 'Ruoli minori e struttura "etica" nell'*Andria* terenziana', in *Interpretazioni latine* (Padua, 1978) 1–41, at 1–13. Donatus makes similar comments at 684, the beginning of the next scene in which Pamphilus and Mysis are on stage together. Interestingly, it is thus the slave-girl who strengthens the resolve of the young citizen.

Some scholars have suggested that in Menander's *Andria* Mysis left on her errand before Pamphilus entered and that by keeping her on stage Terence has converted a simple monologue into an overheard monologue followed by dialogue. Terence can be seen to have done similar things elsewhere (cf. J. C. B. Lowe, ''The *Eunuchus*: Terence and Menander', *CQ* 33.2 (1983), 428–44, at pp. 428–31), and if he has kept Mysis on here he has added a significant element to the scene. The case for Mysis' being an addition to this scene was argued by Rambelli, 131–46, alleging awkwardness at various points, and by Denzler, 45–51, mainly on the grounds that it would be characteristic of Menander to introduce his young lover in a monologue on an otherwise empty stage. The main awkwardnesses detected by Rambelli were the fact that Glycerium at 690–93 is said to know about the new wedding plans in spite of Pamphilus' instruction to Mysis at 299–300 to say nothing to her about them, and that Pamphilus at 693–701 repeats the promise never to abandon Glycerium that he had already given at greater length in 270–98; Rambelli also believed that Pamphilus ought to have asked Mysis at 267 the question he asks her at 299. I am not convinced that any of these is seriously awkward (see the notes on 267 'How is she?', 690, 694–701), and (against Denzler) I cannot believe that Menander had a firm rule never to introduce his young lover in a monologue that was overheard. (Denzler, 49–50 also strangely claims that Mysis' remarks have very little effect on Pamphilus. For further arguments against his views see W. Steidle, 'Menander bei Terenz', *Rh. Mus.* 116 (1973), 303–47, at pp. 322–25.) It may be true that Terence has added Mysis to this scene, but the case has not yet been made.

The surviving fragments of Menander's *Georgos* open with a monologue (not overheard) by a boy who has returned from a business trip to find preparations on foot for his own wedding – a problem for him as the girl next door is on the point of giving birth to his child. His dilemma is thus very similar to that of Pamphilus here, though that play otherwise has little in common with *The Girl from Andros*.

Metre: Mysis changes to iambic octonarii on seeing Pamphilus come into view, just as Davos changed metre at 226 on seeing Mysis appear (Moore 2013, 93–94 suggests that the audience might well have been expecting the trochaic septenarii to continue for an extended passage, in line with the normal metrical structures of Plautus' plays). It is possible that Pamphilus starts with four iambic octonarii at 236–39, but the sequence may well be broken by a trochaic septenarius at 237 (see on 237 *illud* for the metrical ambiguity of the line); after that, only at 248 does he settle down to successive trochaic septenarii, and even then the run from 248 to 260 is interrupted by iambic lines at 252–53 (and perhaps also 254). At 261–69 the metre changes to iambic octonarii, changing again to unaccompanied iambic senarii at 270–98 when Pamphilus and Mysis have made contact; characteristically, however, the metre does not change immediately on their greeting one another but only three lines later and in mid-sentence: Terence does not always compose in neat metrical blocks. In this case Mysis' *ne deseras se* at the beginning of 270 are the words that put an end to the musical accompaniment (Moore 2013, 96). The scene is rounded off at 299–300 with two lines of iambic septenarii; the new metre is introduced with *sed*, as at 226, 234 and elsewhere (see Bruder, 7 n. 1). Detailed examination of Pamphilus' monologue shows some link between changes of metre and variations in content, though the relationship between the two is fluid. For Moore 2013, 94 the metre in 235–55 'becomes unusually erratic, reflecting Pamphilus' confusion and anger, as well as Mysis' anxiety'.

234   *quidnam,* **235** *num quid nam*: *nam* is frequently added to interrogative words; cf. 321 *quidnamst,* 325 *num quid nam,* etc. (OLD has a separate entry for *quisnam.*)

 siet = *sit*: the archaic form (obsolete already in Plautus' day) is used for metrical convenience at the end of the line, as with the passive infinitive *deludier* at 203.

235   **if his unhappiness is going to bring any trouble**: reading *turbae tristitia,* with Bentley, for the manuscripts' *turba tristitiae*; see Victor 1996, 371.

[**236**   *Hoccinest*: if this is the correct text, it represents *hoccine* (cf. on 186) combined with contracted *est,* with the final syllable lightened by iambic shortening. This breaks Hermann-Lachmann's law (see Introduction, section 8.4), which is allowable at the beginning of the line. The manuscripts also have *Hoccinest* later in the line, where the law should not be broken; I have followed K-L in reading *Hoccin* at that point.]

 factu aut inceptu: ablative of the supine as ablative of respect (GL 436). [The manuscripts all have *factum aut inceptum,* but Donatus knew of some with the supines, which were perhaps more likely to be changed in copying to the nouns in -*um* than the other way round. All editors since Bentley have accepted the reading printed.]

 officium: cf. on 114.

237 *illud*: if the first syllable of this word is lightened, this line is a trochaic septenarius; if not, it is an iambic octonarius. Iambic shortening of the first syllable of *ille, ipse, iste* after a light monosyllable (or elided disyllable) is common: see Questa, 108–16. Cf. 15 *isti*, 146 *illud*, 174 *ipse*, 229 *illa*, etc. In such cases we must suppose that the accent on the first syllable of the pronoun was sufficiently weakened to allow that syllable to be lightened. An isolated trochaic septenarius would perhaps bring out Mysis' alarm on hearing Pamphilus' first words.

Pro: see OLD *pro²* for this interjection.

deum: genitive plural.

fidem: OLD *fides¹* 1.c. Understand *obsecro* or *inploro*; cf. on 716 *Di uostram fidem.*

238 *decrerat* = *decreuerat*; cf. 241 *denegarat* = *denegauerat*.

239 *communicatum*: understand *esse*.

240 *Miseram me*: accusative of exclamation (Pinkster, 365); cf. 788 *Me miseram*, 646 and 882 *Me miserum*. This exclamation in the mouth of women is commoner in Terence overall than *Me miserum* in the mouth of men; see Adams, 73. Mysis shows a particular fondness for the adjective *misera*, applying it to herself or Glycerium (or both) also at 251, 264 (where see n.), 268 (echoed by Pamphilus at 271), 693, 719, 743, 761, and 803.

uerbum: OLD *uerbum* 10 'A phrase, formula'.

242 *suam*: scans as one syllable by synizesis, elided before *uxorem*; so too 510 *tuam*. See the note attached to the end of Introduction, section 8.8 (c). (Some editors, however, prefer to scan this line as an iambic octonarius, with *suam* as two syllables of which only the second is elided.)

inmutatum: this could be the past participle of *inmuto*, which means much the same as *muto* (cf. 275 *inmutarier*, Pl. *Amph.* 456 *ubi inmutatus sum?*), but it is more pointed if it means 'unchanged', formed with OLD *in-²* (negative) rather than *in-¹* (intensive), as it does at Cic. *Inv.* II.162, *Tim.* 28, Vitr. VI.4.2. Spengel favours the alternative view that Chremes is imagined to have changed his mind because he can see that Pamphilus has changed from misery to happiness on learning (previously) that he will not have to marry, but it is easier to understand *inmutatum* as referring to his unchanging constancy.

245 **To think that any lover could be…**: a typical lover's complaint, as at (e.g.) Men. *Aspis* 286–87, Ter. *Hec.* 281–82, 293. The construction is the accusative and infinitive of exclamation (GL 534, Pinkster, 365–67), found again at 253 (with the accusative understood), 425, 609, 716, 870, 879 (these last two with the accusative understood).

Adeon = *Adeone*; cf. on 186 *hoccin*. Here *-ne* is combined, as often, with an exclamatory accusative and infinitive; see OLD *-ne* 1.c. It is debated whether *-ne* in such contexts should be regarded as affirmative or interrogative: see Pinkster, 366.

inuenustum: this must here mean 'unlucky in love', though elsewhere in surviving Latin it means 'unlovely'. The noun *uenustas* means 'luck in love' at *Hec.* 848.

246   Pro deum atque hominum fidem: cf. 237 *Pro deum fidem*, with the notes there.

247   Is there no way for me to avoid having Chremes as my father-in-law?: as Büchner, 54 notes, there is a double irony here for those who know how the play will end: not only is the renewed danger of having to marry Philumena the result of a pretence of which Chremes himself is at this point quite unaware, but when Glycerium turns out to be Chremes' daughter Pamphilus will be only too happy to have him as his father-in-law. Terence's audience of first-time viewers cannot be aware of this second irony; Büchner believes that Menander's audience was not aware of it either, i.e. that it had not been spelt out in an expository prologue omitted by Terence. See Introduction, p. 16.

Chremetis: forms of the oblique cases of this name differ. The genitive is here *Chremetis*, at 368 *Chremi*; the accusative is *Chremem* at 361 and 527 (*Chremen* is also found in the γ manuscripts at these points), *Chremetem* at 533. For the vocative I have followed K-L in using *Chreme* throughout, though at many points there is manuscript evidence for *Chremes*.

248   contemptus, spretus = *contemptus et spretus sum*.

Facta, transacta = *Facta et transacta sunt*. Donatus says the combination is proverbial; it is found also at Cic. *Cat.* III.15 *factum atque transactum est*.

Em: OLD *em²* 'Here (there) you are! Look at this (that)!'. For its position at the end of the line, cf. on 226–27 *ut*. Terence is particularly fond of an exclamation in this position; cf. 252, 306, 469 *Ah*, 351, 785 *Em*, 420, 462, 590, 592, 928 *Hem*.

249   unless what I suspect is true: Pamphilus has evidently never yet seen Chremes' daughter, although they had earlier been engaged and a date fixed for their wedding. As we shall shortly learn, however, Charinus has fallen in love with her, and his slave Byrria has seen her and judges her to be beautiful (428–29). A citizen boy at Athens would not normally have had an opportunity to get to know a respectable citizen girl at all intimately, but we can imagine, if we like, that Charinus and Byrria had seen the girl taking part in a religious procession of some kind (so GS 535). We need not see Charinus' love as 'foreign to what we know of New Comedy' (Beare, 98), even if Terence has added Charinus to the play out of his own head.

Nisi si: for the pleonastic expression see OLD *nisi* 7, Barsby 1999 on *Eun*. 160.

250 *aliquid monstri*: for the genitive Donatus compares *Hec*. 643–44 *Sed quid mulieris uxorem habes?* ('But what sort of woman do you have as a wife?') and says that *aliquod monstrum* would have sounded milder. *Quid hominis* is used similarly, e.g. at *Eun* 546 and Caecilius 280 W.

251 *itur ad me*: military language, as Donatus notes.

252 *Ah*: see on 248 *Em*.

253 *tantamne*: see on 245 *Adeon*.

agere: understand *eum* as the subject of this infinitive, and cf. on 245 for the construction.

[**254** *apud*: if this line is a trochaic septenarius, the second syllable is lightened by iambic shortening. Questa, 93–94, however, takes it as an iambic octonarius, leaving open the question of whether to start the line *mihi apud* with iambic shortening or *mi apud* without. He notes on p. 92 that the second syllable of *apud* often is lightened before a consonant; cf. 302 below. Similarly some editors take **255** as an iambic octonarius with the first foot filled by *abi* as an iambic word, i.e. with no iambic shortening at that point.

255 *uisust* = *uisus est*; cf. on 102 *dictust*.

256 **Do you think**: addressed to an imaginary hearer: cf. on 231.

Censen = *Censesne*; cf. 299 *audin*, 317 *Abin*, 337 *Fugin*, 616 *Viden*, 749 *Satin*, and for *-n* = *-ne* cf. on 186 *Hoccin*.

Aut: for the new clause starting at the end of the line cf. on 226–27 *ut*. [Some manuscripts have *Aut* at the start of 257, making that line an iambic octonarius.]

257 *ineptam saltem, falsam, iniquam,* **261** *amor, misericordia, ... sollicitatio*: for the asyndetic lists cf. on 18 *Naeuium, Plautum, Ennium*. For *saltem* = 'even' see OLD 2 '(in negative or quasi-negative sentences)'.

258 *rescissem* = *resciuissem*; cf. 808 *scissem*.

259 *ut hoc ne facerem*: see GL 545 n. 1 '*ut nē* is found for *nē* with apparently no difference in signification'; also 546 n. 3. Cf. lines 327, 699, 834, 899. Further examples in Pinkster, 695.

261 *sollicitatio*: only here, according to OLD, does this mean 'vexation, worry' (like *sollicitudo*); elsewhere it is used of incitement to disloyalty or infidelity or the like. But it is not found very often.

263 *quae ... quomque* = *quaecumque*: cf. on 63 *quomque*.

Eine ego ut aduorser?: for this use of *ut* see OLD *ut* 44 'in indignant qus., with or without *-ne*, rejecting an idea as outrageous, preposterous, etc.' *Ei* scans as a monosyllable by synizesis.

Ei mihi: here *Ei* is the exclamation, always a monosyllable.

264 **I can't decide**: cf. on 209.

Misera: Adams, 73 discusses the possibility that this use of *misera* in apposition to the subject of a first-person verb represents an artificial stereotyping of female speech by Terence. But in this play *miser* is otherwise used thus by Pamphilus at 649 and Simo at 851.

[*quorsus*: an alternative form to *quorsum* (127, 176), restored here by Bentley in place of the manuscripts' *quorsum* for the sake of the metre. An alternative approach is to read *incertumst* for *incertum* and keep *quorsum* (i.e. to make Mysis quote the whole of Pamphilus' *incertumst*, not just the adjective), as suggested by A. Klette, 'Beiträge zur Kritik des Terenz', *RM* 14 (1859), 461–70, at p. 467.]

accidat: OLD *accido*[1] 5.c '(w. advs.) to turn out, result'; much the same as *euadas, euaderet* at 127, 176.

265 *peropust*: the prefix *per-* intensifies (cf. 455 *perparce*, 486 *per* ... *scitus*). *Peropus* comes only here.

ipsa: perhaps here meaning 'my mistress'; cf. on 360 *ipsus*.

[*de illa aliquid*: the manuscripts have *aliquid de illa*, which does not scan; Fleckeisen's transposition of *aliquid* restores the metre.]

aduorsum: cf. 42.

266 *momento*: OLD includes this passage under *momentum* 1 'A movement, impulse, push', but it belongs equally well under 7.b 'that which exerts a decisive influence or turns the scale'.

267 *Quis hic loquitur?*: a standard formula in Roman Comedy when a newly arrived character realizes that there is another character on stage who has said something; cf. 783, Bain, 158–60. (As usual in this expression *hic* is lightened by iambic shortening; the line starts with a proceleusmatic.) F. H. Sandbach, 'Donatus' Use of the Name Terentius and the End of Terence's *Adelphoe*',

BICS 25 (1978), 123–45, at p. 125 presents the case for seeing this formula and the succeeding exchange of greetings (with which cf. 318 and 802) as typically Terentian. The artificiality of the staging (with Pamphilus giving vent to his feelings in a lengthy monologue while Mysis comments aside) is compounded by the fact that Pamphilus hears one of Mysis' asides (cf. on 172–205); but she has decided that the time has come to speak to him, so it is not implausible that she speaks a little louder at this point.

O salue, Pamphile; the addition of *O* in the reply (found again at 318, *HT* 406, *Hec.* 82) probably conveys Mysis' attempt to make Pamphilus think she is glad to see him, though Shipp says 'Mysis pretends to be taken by surprise'. Donatus offers both possibilities: '*o' interiectio est optantis aduentum aut repente percussi.* (For the scansion of *Pamphile*, see Introduction, the end of section 8.3 (b).)

How is she?: Pamphilus' first thought is for Glycerium, whom he does not need to name.

Rogas?: cf. on 163.

**271   *Egon* = *Egone*; cf. 384, 504, 584.

273   as if she were my wife: cf. on 146. The repetition of the point here helps to keep alive in the audience's mind the likelihood that she will in fact end up as his wife (cf. 220n.).

274   She's been taught and brought up well and decently: cf. on 123 'beautiful and noble'. For the stress on the upbringing of a girl who will turn out to be of citizen birth, cf. *HT* 226 *habet bene et pudice eductam, ignaram artis meretriciae* ('his girl's been well and decently brought up and knows nothing of the ways of tarts'), *Eun.* 748 *Educta ita uti teque illaque dignumst* ('She's been brought up the right way both for you and for her').

275   changed by the force of poverty: this was what happened to Chrysis, as reported at 71ff.; Pamphilus is determined that Glycerium should not like her be driven to prostitution.

inmutarier: for this form of the passive infinitive cf. on 203 *deludier*.

**277   *ut queas*: understand *uereor* from *uerear* in 276. For *ut* = *ne non* cf. on 349.

**277–80   cf. 234–300n. on the stylistic features that show the strength of Pamphilus' feelings. At Men. *Sam.* 624–25 Moschion says he is enslaved to his beloved by a similar list of factors: 'my oath, my desire, the length and closeness of our relationship'.

**277, 278   *Adeon* = *Adeone*: cf. on 186 *Hoccin*.

282   O Mysis, Mysis: the repetition shows that Pamphilus is continuing to express strong feelings.

284–98   Pamphilus describes how Chrysis on her deathbed entrusted Glycerium to his care. He sets the scene in 284–85 with brief asyndetic and elliptical utterances (with *uos semotae* understand *estis*, with *nos soli* understand *fuimus*) before quoting Chrysis' last words in full. It is remarkable to have a deathbed scene described in such detail in a comedy; Pamphilus needs to remind himself of what Chrysis had said, to strengthen his determination to resist his father. His account confirms that Chrysis' words are indeed 'written in his heart' (283). (For a fuller discussion see Brown 2012, 30–44, referring to other places in comedy where death is mentioned.)

286   Dearest Pamphilus: *Mi* with a name in the vocative is a marker of female speech in Terence, though not exclusively so (at 134 Pamphilus is said to have exclaimed *Mea Glycerium*) and generally in contexts where the speaker has reasons to wish to win the addressee round; see Adams, 69–73.

287   *clam te est*: see OLD *clam* 2.c on *clam esse* 'to be unknown to, escape the knowledge or notice of'. *clam* as a preposition regularly takes the accusative in Early Latin.

utraeque: the use of the plural is unusual; Shipp compares Pl. *Amph.* 223 *utrique imperatores*. Cf. also Pl. *Most.* 1137.

288   sient: cf . 234 *siet*.

289   *Quod*: OLD 1.b 'As to which, wherefore, now, etc.'; cf. Horace, *Ep.* I.7.94–95 *Quod te per genium dextramque deosque Penatis / obsecro et obtestor*, Virgil, *Aen.* II.141–43 *Quod te per superos et conscia numina ueri ... oro*.

per hanc te dextram: this position of *te*, between the preposition and the noun it governs, is common in prayers and requests; see 538 and 834 below; Lindsay on Pl. *Capt.* 977 *per tuom te genium opsecro*; Nisbet and Hubbard on Horace, *Odes* I.8.2 (1–2 *per omnes / te deos oro*).

by this right hand of yours and by the god who watches over you: see the passages from *Captiui* and Horace's *Epistles* quoted above. Chrysis evidently takes Pamphilus by the right hand to add formal binding force to her request; cf. Pl. *Amph.* 923 *Per dexteram tuam te, Alcumena, oro, opsecro*. *Genius* is defined thus by OLD: 'The male spirit of a *gens*, existing during his lifetime in the head of the family, and subsequently in the divine or spiritual part of each individual'; see also the entry on *genius* in the Oxford Classical Dictionary.

[The manuscripts offer the unmetrical text *quod ego te per hanc dexteram oro et ingenium tuom*. Donatus attests the reading *genium* for *ingenium*, and this is accepted by all editors; in addition to the passages quoted above, cf. [Tib.] III.11 [= IV. 5]. *7–8 per te dulcissima furta / perque tuos oculos per geniumque rogo*.

Since Terence elsewhere uses the full form *dexteram/dexterum* only at the end of a line (734, 751, *Eun.* 775), we should probably read *dextram* here (cf. *HT* 493, 732, *Ad.* 583), though the statistical basis is not large; cf. A. G. Engelbrecht, *Studia Terentiana* (Vienna, 1883), 25–26. The simplest way to cure the metre is to move *te* to follow *hanc*, as most editors do. *oro* is not strictly necessary with *obtestor* following at 291, and indeed appeals of this kind are sometimes in later writers found without any first-person verb of appeal at all (see TLL X.1.1158.14–32); but the occurrence of *te* with *obtestor* at 291 (after its occurrence in this line) shows that Chrysis there makes a fresh start, so it is not inappropriate to keep *oro* here. (Some editors have kept *dexteram* and deleted *oro*: so K-L, Posani, Barsby.)

Since the sequence *per ego* is very common in such contexts (cf. R. G. Austin on V. *Aen.* IV. 314 *Per ego has lacrimas dextramque tuam te*), some editors have chosen to move *per* to precede *ego* here, making further adjustments to the line to make it scan. However, this word order was not invariable: e.g. *Capt.* 727 has *Per deos atque homines ego te optestor*.]

290 by her defencelessness: as (apparently) a non-citizen resident at Athens, Glycerium is in an insecure position; at 382 Davos takes it for granted that Simo will be able to 'throw her out of town' if he wishes to.

291 abs: this form of *ab* is found particularly before *te* in Plautus and Terence; see 489, 492, 551, 582, 823.

292–94 Si … siue … seu: appealing to past benefits in support of a request is common in prayers; see Nisbet and Hubbard on Horace, *Odes* I.32.1 *si quid*.

292 I've loved you as if you were my own brother: the bond between brother and sister was probably particularly strong in the ancient world; cf. P. Walcot, 'Romantic Love and True Love: Greek Attitudes to Marriage', *Ancient Society* 18 (1987), 5–33, at pp. 32–33.

295 husband, … guardian, and father: these terms are not to be understood literally; the effect is similar to that of Andromache's address to Hector at Homer, *Iliad* VI.429–30 (cited by Donatus on 718) as her 'father, mother, brother, and husband'. At Athens, for as long as Glycerium is believed to be a foreign resident, she requires a προστάτης to act as her guardian, but we need not suppose that Chrysis envisages formal registration of Pamphilus in that capacity. At Rome, a fatherless citizen woman (which Chrysis believes Glycerium to be) required a 'guardian' (*tutor*), but he could not be appointed in this way at the behest of another woman; nor could a woman be given in marriage by a woman either at Athens or at Rome. *uirum* is probably used with similar technical imprecision at 718, though the meaning 'a real man' would not be inappropriate there; *pace* Lefèvre, 57, it would be less appropriate here.

296   I hand over these belongings of ours: as we shall learn at 799, Chrysis does not have the power to dispose of her property in this way. But, having become her own mistress at Athens, it is not surprising that she gives no thought to her relatives on Andros.

[*fidei*: scans as two syllables in Early Latin, and many editors prefer to print *fide*, a form of the dative for which there is some ancient evidence; see Gellius IX.14.21–24; Lindsay on Pl. *Capt.* 464 *die*, TLL VI.1.662.18–26.]

297   She handed her over to my care: cf. Cic. *Fam.* VII.5.3 (in a letter of recommendation) *hominem tibi ita trado de manu, ut aiunt, in manum istam* ('I thus hand the man over to you from my hand, as they say, into yours'); we need not suppose that Glycerium was physically present to be handed over to Pamphilus (cf. 285 'we were on our own'). Donatus sees a reference to the wedding ceremony, in which a woman was said to 'come into the power' (*in manum conuenire*) of her husband, but *in manum dare* is not a formula found in that context; see E. Fraenkel, *Gnomon* 36 (1964), 781. (G. Williams, *Tradition and Originality in Roman Poetry* [Oxford, 1968], 402 nonetheless thinks 'Terence is playing with the concept of marriage'.)

299   audin = *audisne*: cf. on 256 *Censen*.

300   Not a single word about the wedding: Pamphilus probably assumes that Mysis has overheard his expostulations at 236–57 (as indeed she has) and will know that he refers to the fact that he is now once again threatened with having to marry Chremes' daughter this very day. Alternatively, since he has not told Mysis anything about that, he urges her not to remind Glycerium that this was the day originally fixed for the wedding (cf. 268–69).

caue: understand *dicas* or *ne dicas* (cf. on 403), 'watch out that you don't say a single word'.

ne ad morbum hoc etiam: understand something like *accedat*, as suggested by Donatus: 'so that this doesn't get added to the pain of childbirth' (which Mysis told Pamphilus about at 268); Mysis understands his point without waiting for him to complete the sentence. For *morbus* of childbirth or its immediate after-effects cf. Pl. *Truc.* 520, *Hec.* 366, also the use of *aeger* and *aegrotus* at *Truc.* 464 *puerperio ... aegram, Ad.* 921–22 *puerperam ... aegrotam.*

Teneo: cf. 86.

301–37 Pamphilus remains on stage, absorbed in his own thoughts, while two new characters enter from the direction of the main square in the middle of a lively conversation. We quickly learn that they are Charinus and his slave Byrria and that Charinus is in love with the girl Pamphilus is apparently being obliged to marry. Donatus tells us that Terence has added these characters to the play: see the Introduction, pp. 18–19, 21 on this and on the comic effects thereby created. Charinus and Pamphilus make contact at 318, and Pamphilus assures Charinus that he has no desire to marry Philumena. At 335 Davos is seen approaching, and Charinus sends Byrria away.

Metre: as at 236ff., the liveliness of the text is enhanced by constant changes of metre, though somewhat more clearly structured, particularly at 305–308 (Moore 2013, 97–99): 301 trochaic octonarius, 302 trochaic septenarius, 303–304 iambic octonarii, 305 trochaic octonarius, 306 trochaic septenarius, 307 trochaic octonarius, 308 trochaic septenarius. The following eight lines (309–16) are all iambic octonarii, as Charinus catches sight of Pamphilus and considers approaching him; this phase of the scene is rounded off with a trochaic septenarius at 317 as Charinus curses Byrria. At this point Pamphilus notices Charinus, and the two greet one another in a solitary iambic senarius at 318, before the metre finally settles down to trochaic septenarii, which in fact continue from 319 to 383.

301 *Quid ais?*: cf. on 184, though here it shows that the two characters are in mid-conversation as they enter and that Charinus cannot bring himself to believe what Byrria has told him.

Byrria: it is now accepted that the final vowel in such names is short and that Ritschl's law is broken in the fifth element: see A. Minarini, *Studi Terenziani* (Bologna, 1987), 134–35.

Datur ... nuptum: see OLD *nubo* 1.b for the supine of *nubo* after *dare* and similar verbs; cf. *Ph.* 720, *Ad.* 346.

302 *Qui*: 'how'; cf. on 6.

e: cf. 854 *ex me audies*, OLD *ex* 14.c 'indicating source of knowledge, information, etc.'.

Vae misero mihi: a strong expression of distress, as at 743.

303   all on edge: OLD *attentus* 2 'intent, concentrated'.

304   cura confectus: OLD *conficio* 14 '(esp. of grief, worry, etc.) To overwhelm, prostrate'. These words go together, reinforced by alliteration; there is a caesura after *lassus*, which helps us not to take *cura* with that word.

305–308   The slave acts as wise adviser to his master, as at *Eun.* 57–78, where Donatus (on 57) comments that 'comic poets are allowed to make slaves wiser than their masters in the *palliata*, though this is generally not allowed in the *togata*'. However, Byrria's worldly wisdom does not translate into effective scheming on his master's behalf.

305   edepol: a variant form of *pol* (cf. on 229), used proportionately more by men than by women in Plautus but more by women in Terence; see Adams, 51–52. Its only other occurrence in this play is at 692, in the mouth of a woman, but there does not seem to be any significance in the fact that it here comes in a man's mouth.

   fieri: the first syllable is light, as at 529; cf. Questa, 185 top.

305–306   since ... to want what can: Donatus says this is a proverbial expression; see on the similar words of Mysis at 805.

307   satiust = *satius est*; cf. on 102 *dictust*, and OLD *satis* A.7 '(compar.) Better, preferable'.

   id dare operam: cf. on 157, and on 58 *nil*.

   qui: cf. on 6.

[The manuscripts add *tuo* at the end of the line. This must be deleted for metrical reasons; perhaps a scribe's eye wandered to *tua* at the end of the next line.]

308   quo: effectively the same as *qui* in 307; OLD *quo*² 3 'In order that by these means, so that thereby', citing 472 below. As can be seen from OLD, this use of *quo* is standard in Classical Latin with *magis* and other comparatives.

   to fan the flames: Fantham, 7–11 discusses fire imagery in Greek and Roman comedy.

309   recta: OLD *rectus* 8 'Right in the circumstances, proper'.

310   in my place: *hic* is probably the adverb of place ('here') rather than the pronoun ('this person', i.e. 'me'), though Donatus takes it to be the pronoun.

   All right then: the imperative of *ago* is used colloquially to mark a concession; cf. 713, 895, 956. Here the repetition of the word probably indicates impatience, as at *HT* 722, *Ph.* 559, 662. The idiom is discussed by Müller, 114.

311 *certumst*: cf. on 209.

hic: the nominative singular masculine of the pronoun scans light in Plautus and Terence, as sometimes later.

312 A strikingly high-flown line, consisting overwhelmingly of long syllables, with no resolutions, and repeated *-abo* endings.

313 *prodat*: OLD *prodo* 4 'To extend, prolong (a period); also, to put off, defer'.

The idea that Pamphilus might be in a position to postpone his wedding (or that he would be willing to do so if he really wanted to marry) is, of course, absurd.

314 I'm sure: cf. on 167.

315 *Adeon* = *Adeone* (the verb *Adeo* plus the interrogative suffix *-ne*, abbreviated to *-n* as at 186 *Hoccin*). On this use of the present tense to refer to a future event see Pinkster, 400 on 'the use of the present indicative in requests for advice addressed to one or more persons present. This use is different from the so-called 'deliberative' use of the present subjunctive.'

316 *moechum*: this Greek word (μοιχός) is found several times in Plautus, at *Eun.* 957, 960, 992, and in a number of later authors. It appears to have become embedded in Latin as a colloquial word. The Latin term *adulter*, which became common later, is found only at *Amph.* 1049 in Plautus and not at all in Terence; *adulterium* is found at *M. G.* 90 and 802 and combined with a verb derived from *moechus* at *Cas.* 976 *In adulterio, dum moechissat*. In general, the use of Greek loan-words is typical of slaves in comedy (though not restricted to them; cf. on 51), but Maltby 1985, 121 notes that this is the first of only four Greek words spoken by slaves in this play, the others being *euge* at 345, *opsonium* at 360, and *opsonor* at 451, all in the mouth of Davos. (On Terence's use of Greek words see also on 51 'finished his military service', 345 *Euge*.)

Byrria here moves from wise advice to cheekiness towards his young master. That is characteristic of slaves in comedy.

317 *Abin hinc in malam rem*: an imprecation found in various forms several times in Plautus and Terence, e.g. *Capt.* 877 *Abi in malam rem*, *Eun.* 536 *Malam rem hinc ibis?*, *Ph.* 930 *In* (= *Isne*) *hinc malam rem?* For *Abin* (= *Abisne*) cf. on 256 *Censen*.

for suspecting that: lit. 'with that suspicion of yours' (cf. on 186 *istuc* for *istac* as the second person pronoun, and on 28 for the form of the ablative).

you villain: OLD *scelus* 3 '(esp. as a colloq. term of abuse) One whose very existence is a crime'; cf. 607, 665, 844.

318 Pamphilus has been standing wrapped in his own thoughts for seventeen lines while the audience focused on the other two characters; he finally has his attention caught by Charinus' shouting.

O salue, Pamphile: cf. on 267.

319   hope, salvation, help, and advice: cf. the run of four imperatives at 334. This stylistic feature here marks the urgency of Charinus' entreaty. In the Latin the words form two phonically linked pairs.

320   *pol*: cf. on 229; here in the mouth of a man, as at 808, 866, whereas it comes eight times in Mysis' mouth. The use of the word by a man here seems not to be significant, unless it is somehow a sign of the hopelessness of Pamphilus' perceived position. (Cf. on 305 *edepol*.)

321   *quidnamst*: cf. on 234.

322   *postremum*: OLD *postremum* 2 'For the last time'.

Quid ita: OLD *quis*¹ 16 [on *quid* as an adverb] 'For what reason? why?; *quid ita?* how so?'. Again at 371.

Ei mihi: cf. 263.

323   *uereor*: used of feeling reluctance or shame; cf. 488, 638a, and OLD 4 '(w. inf.) To be afraid, scruple (to do something)'.

324   *Ne*: OLD *ne*² (affirmative particle) 'Truly, indeed, assuredly (nearly always foll. by a personal pron., *ille* or *iste*)'.

mecum sentit: OLD *sentio* 6.b '*sentire cum*, to agree with'.

Eho dum: cf. 184.

325   *amplius*: the same euphemism at *Eun*. 143 *Etiamne amplius?*

Aha: this exclamation, which scans as two light syllables (like *Eho*), is found elsewhere in strong denials or refusals (e.g. at Pl. *Ba*. 87 *Aha minime*, *Capt*. 148–49 *Aha, Hegio, / numquam istuc dixis*). It is not otherwise found in Terence, but there is no need to change it to *Ah*, as some editors do, although *Ah* is found in similar contexts (as shown by Müller, 126–30).

326   What a pity: lit. 'How I wish (there had been)!' cf. OLD *uolo*¹ 11 '*uellem* (indicating an unfulfilled wish) Would that'.

327   *ut ne*: cf. on 259.

Dabo equidem operam: cf. 157.

potest: OLD *possum* 6.b '*potest* (impers.), it can be done or happen, it is possible'.

328   cordi: OLD *cor* 5.b '*cordi esse alicui*, to be dear or pleasing to someone, to be his delight' (the dative as at 8 *uitio*).

Charinus takes no notice of Pamphilus' interjection; cf. on 341 *Quem*.

329   profer: either this has the same construction as *prodat* in 313, with *dies* as the object of the verb (OLD *profero* 10.b 'to extend in duration, prolong (a period)', or *aliquot dies* is in the 'Accusative of Extent in Time' (GL 336, Pinkster, 844–45) and we understand *nuptias* as the object of *profer* (OLD 10 'To put off to another time, postpone, defer').

330   ne utiquam: 'In no way, by no means' (OLD *neutiquam*).

officium: see on 114.

a man of free birth: *liber*, like *liberalis* at 123 and *libere* at 911, conveys something more than simply not being a slave: a free man is expected to observe certain standards of behaviour.

331   to be given credit: lit. 'to have it credited to himself as a favour'; cf. OLD *appono* 8 'To set down in accounting, reckon, attribute (to)'. *gratiae* is 'Dative of the Object for Which' (cf. 8 *uitio*), *sibi* 'Dative of Personal Interest' (cf. Pinkster, 892–96). *id* seems to refer rather vaguely to the action performed by the man who does not deserve to be given credit for it.

332   quam: since *malo* = *magis uolo* it is naturally followed by *quam*.

adipiscier: for this form of the passive infinitive cf. on 203 *deludier*.

334   do something, make something up, think of something, achieve something: Pamphilus rounds off this stretch of dialogue with a stylistic echo of Charinus' urgent entreaty at the start of it at 319. Charinus and Byrria will not in fact come up with a scheme of any kind.

qui: cf. on 6. In 335 *qui ne* is the equivalent of *ut ne* at 259, 327.

335   Sat habeo: OLD *satis* 4 '*satis habere*, To consider sufficient, be content (with or that)'.

336   quoius: the older form of *cuius*; cf. on 167 *quoi*. It here scans as one syllable, as at 541, 765, and regularly in Terence; the only place where he scans it as two syllables is 772 (Questa, 77–78).

haud quicquam: understand a verb like *mones*.

337   nil opus sunt scire: OLD *opus*[1] 13 '*opus esse*, (in quasi-personal const.) To be needed or requisite'; cf. 740 *quae opus fuere ad nuptias*. *nil* as at 32 *Nil istac opus est arte*. The construction here with the infinitive is sometimes found with impersonal *opus est*, as with *peropust* at 265.

Fugin = *Fugisne*: cf. 256 *Censen*, 317 *Abin*, where, as here, the apparent question is an impatient form of command.

Ego uero: understand *fugio*. Byrria's departure enables Terence to make the following scene a display of Davos' control over the two boys without the distraction of the presence of a second slave (Glücklich, 117).

338–74 Davos enters from the direction of Chremes' house, talking to himself and failing to notice that Pamphilus, the man for whom he is looking, is on stage; when they finally establish contact, Davos tells Pamphilus about his exciting discovery: he has worked out from good evidence that neither Simo nor Chremes is actually planning to hold a wedding today, so Pamphilus and Charinus have nothing to fear for the time being. At 370–74 he sends Charinus off to canvass support for his own marriage plans.

The arrival of a slave with a piece of news (good or bad) is a stock scene of Roman comedy. It is known as a 'running slave' scene (*seruus currens*, the term used by Terence in the prologues to *The Self-Tormentor*, lines 31 and 37, and *The Eunuch*, line 36), since the speed of the slave's arrival is often remarked on, and Plautus sometimes makes the slave utter a lengthy monologue commenting on the urgency of his business before he gets down to delivering his news. Terence is here much more restrained; he preserves more of the traditional flavour of such scenes at *Ph.* 177ff. and *Ad.* 299ff. One traditional element that he retains at 344–45 is that the slave has to be recalled by the very person he is trying to find; but this too is here reduced to a minimum. J. C. B. Lowe, 'Terence and the Running-Slave Routine', *Rh. Mus.* 152.3–4 (2009), 225–34, at pp. 31–32 argues that in all these three cases (and also at *Ph.* 841ff.) Terence has added the elements which remind us of the traditional stock scene, though in this case the addition amounts to rather little, and there is nothing (other than the presence of Charinus) that could not have come much like this in Menander's *Girl from Andros*.

At 339 and 347–49 Davos seems to take for granted that Pamphilus has now learnt that the wedding is on again, though at 226–27 he assumed that Pamphilus did not yet know. The audience is unlikely to ask itself how Davos can be sure that Pamphilus now knows.

Metre: trochaic septenarii, continuing from 319–37. We might have expected Davos' arrival to be marked by a change of metre, but it is not.

338 Di boni: an exclamation found also at *HT* 254, *Eun.* 225, *Ad.* 440; in the first two examples, as here, it is followed by exclamatory *quid* with a partitive genitive: *quid turbaest* and *quid hoc morbist* respectively. Note the word-play in *boni, boni*.

But where can I find Pamphilus: in a similar context at *Ph.* 192, with Antipho and another character looking on, the 'running slave' Geta says 'But where can I find Antipho?'.

340   *nescioquid*: OLD *nescio* 5.b '*nescio quid*, something or other', amounting to a pronoun and often written as one word; here in the accusative as an 'inner object' (GL 333.1: 'Neuter Pronouns and Adjectives are often used to define or modify the substantive notion that lies in the verb', and n. 1: 'With verbs of Emotion this Acc. gives the grounds of the emotion'). The third syllable is light: see Questa, 163 n. 4.

he hasn't heard about this problem yet: the 'problem' is the fact that Pamphilus will have to marry Philumena. In fact Davos heard of it before Pamphilus did: see on 172–205.

341   *Quem*: the antecedent is *Pamphilum* in 338. Davos' syntax takes no account of the asides in 340, which he has not heard. Similarly in 341–42 his sentence continues over the aside, as did Charinus' at 328; cf. *HT* 343–47, *Eun.* 754–55, *Ph.* 736–37, *Ad.* 304–306 for sentences continued over the remarks of other characters (in the first two of those cases independent conversations, not asides).

342   Do you hear him?: Davos' last words have shown that he does after all know about Pamphilus' problem.

343   *intendam*: OLD 10 '(intr.) To direct one's steps, set out (for)'.

Cessas adloqui: cf. 845 *Cesso adloqui*, and Maltby 2012 on *Ph.* 285: '*cesso* + inf. is used commonly in Terence to denote an action that is overdue'. [K-L and Thierfelder read *conloqui* with p and the first hand of D.]

344   *Habeo*: as at 498 *quid agam habeo*, OLD *habeo* 11.b; here understand 'where to look for him'. Davos must have stood briefly reflecting before making his decision and starting to set off (so Donatus). [*Habeo* is attested as a reading by Donatus; the MSS all have *Abeo* ('I'm off', a reading also attested by Donatus), which is rather abrupt. The manuscripts of Donatus also give *Adeo* as a lemma, and Victor 1996, 371–72 suggests that that might be spoken by Pamphilus ('I'll go up to him'). But Terence always has the future *Adibo* in such a context (e.g. at *HT* 179), and there is nothing wrong with *Habeo* in Davos' mouth here.]

Quis homost qui me: Davos catches sight of Pamphilus before he can complete his sentence.

345 *Euge*: Greek εὖγε, found also at *HT* 677, *Ad*. 911, and over thirty times in Plautus. The final vowel must scan long here and at Pl. *Ba*. 1105, *Most*. 260; in all its other occurrences it could be either long or short. It is short in Greek, and it is not clear how it came to be lengthened in Latin. Some editors print *Eugae*, a form found six times in Plautus in manuscript A and once in B. On Greek loan-words in the mouth of slaves see on 316 *moechum*; Karakasis, 89 sees significance in the fact that in this play three are spoken by Davos, whom he also believes to combine *semper lenitas* at 175 in imitation of Greek idiom.

Ambo opportune: understand *adestis* (Donatus).
346 *Quin*: cf. 45.
347 *in dubio*: OLD *dubius* 9 '(neut. as sb.) an unpromising or dangerous situation'; different at 266.

And I know what *you're* afraid of too: Davos has recently told Byrria about Pamphilus' impending wedding (cf. 302, 357); perhaps that was when Byrria told him of Charinus' love for Philumena. Otherwise it is strange that Pamphilus appears to have been unaware of it before 322–24.
348 *Obtundis*: OLD 2 'To assail (the ears) with repeated demands, assertions, etc.', though probably here understand *me* as the object, as at OLD 2.b.

Note the liveliness of the dialogue here, with Davos twice interrupting Pamphilus and preventing him from completing his sentence.
349 *Id paues*: as at 180, *Id* is explained by the following clause, in this case a clause of fearing.

ut: as usual with verbs of fearing, particularly in Early Latin, this is used instead of *ne non* (GL 550, Pinkster, 702–703).
350 *Istuc ipsum*: understand *paueo*.

Atque: adversative, as at 225.

that's exactly what there's no danger of: lit. 'that very thing is no danger'; *pericli* is partitive genitive (cf. 600n.).

Trust me: OLD *uideo* 4.a.
351 **free me**: a mildly paradoxical request from a free man to a slave; the same paradox at 370.

Em: as at 248.
[**352** *scio*: Bentley was perhaps right to prefer *scies*, as at 116. That was found as a variant in one of his manuscripts and is also the reading of p.]
353 *prehendit*: OLD 2 'To catch hold of (a person in order to converse with him), accost, buttonhole'. This could be present or perfect tense, but

it is notable that Davos continues with the 'historic' present (cf. 79n.) right
down to 364. That adds vividness to his narrative, which is further enlivened
by a succession of elliptical sentences or clauses: 357 *nusquam*, 358 *rogo*,
negat uidisse, Mihi molestum, the whole of 360 (three sentences in tricolon),
361 *Ego me continuo ad Chremem*, 362 *solitudo ante ostium*. The brevity of
his narrative style is also notable in 363–65.

ait tibi uxorem dare: understand *se* as the subject of *dare*. [Most
manuscripts include *sese* in the text, but that creates difficulties for the
metre.]

354 item: OLD 4 'In addition, as well, likewise'. Davos refers to his
conversation with Simo at 184–205.

356 ibi: picks up *ubi* (OLD *ibi* 2.b, of time).

359 Hem: cf. on 116; not to be confused with *Em* at 351, though similarly
placed at the end of the line and preceded by an elision.

360 paullulum opsoni: the diminutive form *paullulum* emphasizes the
smallness of the provisions. *opsonium* (here in the partitive genitive) is the
Latinization of the Greek ὀψώνιον; Shipp p. 53 points out that in Greek
the word hardly ever has the meaning it acquired in Latin but usually
means 'salary, wages'. On the other hand, the verb ὀψωνεῖν, like the Latin
opsonare or *opsonari*, means 'to buy food', and several related words such
as the noun ὀψωνία have the same frame of reference (related to ὄψον,
relish or expensive fish); clearly those words infuenced the Latin usage of
this noun. *Opsonium* comes several times in Plautus, in Terence only here
and at *Ad.* 286. On the use of Greek words, cf. on 316, 345.

ipsus: an early form of *ipse*. For the meaning, see OLD *ipse* 12 'The
master, esp. the master of the house, 'himself''.

361 Quorsum: OLD 2.b 'to what end? with what in view?; (often w.
ellipsis of vb. of saying or sim.)'.

nam: see on 234 *quidnam*.

Ego me continuo ad Chremem: as at 226, understand a verb of motion.

362–69 If a wedding were really about to take place, one would expect a
great deal of bustle in the bride's house as she was prepared for the ceremony.
Also, it was the custom at Athens for an animal to be sacrificed in the
houses of both bride and groom (see Menander, *Samia* 190, 211, 399–404,
Vérilhac-Vial, 291–93). The wedding feast might be held in either house, or
in a religious sanctuary, but was probably normally organized by the father
of the bride (Vérilhac-Vial, 299–304). For Roman weddings the evidence

for the location of sacrifices and feasts is unclear (see Hersch, 119–22 on sacrifices, 212–19 on feasts), but in either society the absence of activity in the bride's house on the day of her wedding would be strange.

362   *illo*: OLD has a separate entry for this adverbial form, which means the same as *illuc*.

id gaudeo: *gaudeo* normally takes the ablative, but the use of the accusative of the neuter pronoun is similar to that with *studeo* at 58 *nil*.

364   **no married woman in the house**: this perhaps implies that Chremes no longer has a wife, since one might expect her to have been in the house anyway if still alive. If a wedding were really being prepared for, the bride's mother would doubtless normally have been expected to take charge of many of the wedding preparations, though at Athens a significant part was also played by the *nympheutria*, a married woman who escorted the bride during the wedding procession and perhaps also supervised the dressing of the bride before she set off (Vérilhac-Vial, 297, 317–18, 368–69); obviously there is no sign of such a woman in the house either. For Rome there is very little evidence on who participated in the ceremonies (see Hersch, 71 n. 40, 143–44; also 191–99 on the paucity of evidence for the role of the *pronuba*), though some modern commentators speak of married women from the neighbourhood lending a hand in the house and accompanying the bride in the procession. This passage perhaps supports such a notion, if Terence referred to something that he expected to be familiar to his Roman audience and was not simply reproducing a detail from Menander.

365   *ornati, tumulti*: partitive genitives with *nil* (cf. 600n.); second-declension forms of fourth-declension nouns are common in Early Latin. I have accepted the view of OLD, *ornatus*² 2 (citing only this passage) that *ornatus* here refers to preparations in a general way. But the preparations certainly included the decoration of the house with flowers and greenery, both at Athens (Vérilhac-Vial, 302) and at Rome (Treggiari 1991, 163 n. 26), and perhaps 'decoration' (OLD 3) is the meaning here.

366   *magnum signum*: Pamphilus has caught Davos' elliptical style.

367   *narras*: *narro* often = *dico*: cf. 434, 461, 734.

accipis: OLD 20 'To interpret, construe'.

368   *puerum*: see on 84.

Chremi: for the form cf. on 247 *Chremetis*. [The manuscripts here overwhelmingly read *Chremis*, but *Chremi* is supported by a note in Donatus.]

369 *pisciculos minutos*: as with *paullulum* at 360, the diminutive form emphasizes the smallness of the fish; here it is further reinforced by the addition of *minutos*.

ferre: 'historic' infinitive (cf. on 62), or perhaps understand as 'I saw that he was bringing', or 'He said that he was bringing'.

obolo: ablative of price (GL 404, Pinkster, 881–83). Terence consistently preserves references to Athenian currency, as at 451 and 951 below; the terms were doubtless familiar to his audience. An obol was worth one sixth of a drachma, a fairly trivial sum.

Menander, *Perinthia* fr. 6 Arnott (= 2 S) may perhaps lie behind this line: see Introduction, p. 21.

370 *Liberatus*: as at 351.

Ac: adversative, like *atque* at 225, 350.

nullus: OLD 6 '(w. advl. force) = Not a bit, not at all'.

371 *Quid ita*: cf. 322.

prorsus: OLD *prorsus*[1] 2 'Thoroughly, in every respect, altogether, quite, absolutely. **b** (often strengthening a negative)'; cf. 435 *Nil prorsus*, 510 *Prorsus*.

caput: OLD 7 'A person, individual'.

373 *uides*: OLD 18 'To consider, attend to (a course of action, etc.)'.

ask the old man's friends: it is not clear why Davos does not advise Charinus to ask the old man (Chremes) himself, nor what Charinus refers to in the following line when he says that his hope has often failed him in the past: does he mean that previous requests have been rebuffed or that he has never yet plucked up the courage to ask? We might expect his father (if still alive) to have marriage plans for him, as Simo does for Pamphilus, but we learn nothing about Charinus' family situation. In general, Davos' advice to Charinus in 372–73 echoes Pamphilus' at 333–34; again, there is no sign that it leads to any action on Charinus' part (Gilula, 89).

375–403 Davos explains to Pamphilus that Simo has set up the pretence in order to put him to the test; Davos has correctly intuited what Simo is up to (cf. 154–58). He advises Pamphilus to take the wind out of Simo's sails by agreeing to marry Chremes' daughter, since he is confident that Chremes will never agree to the marriage and that Pamphilus will thus buy time in which something may turn up to enable him to cement his relationship with Glycerium.

Metrically this scene consists of three almost equal sections. The trochaic septenarii continue for nine lines until 383, the line in which Davos makes his suggestion. There follow ten lines of iambic senarii (unaccompanied) in which Pamphilus reacts with astonishment and Davos reassures him, and a further ten lines of iambic octonarir (accompanied) in which Davos repeats his instruction and amplifies the case for it. See Bruder, 53 (with n. 2) on similarities between the shifts to senarii at 384 and 270, p. 44 on 394ff.; also Moore 2013, 99–100 on this whole stretch.

375   sibi uolt: OLD *uolo*[1] 16 'To have as one's object or purpose, aim at, be after', again at 457.

376   id suscenseat: for the construction cf. on 58 *nil*; as at 180 and 349, *id* is explained by the following clause.

377–78   I accept Bothe's transposition of these two lines, which produces a more coherent sequence of thought. In 378 *tuos animus*, the subject of the subordinate clause *ut sese habeat*, is made the object of *perspexerit*; cf. on 169–70. The separation of *tuom* from *animum* adds emphasis to the notion that it is *Pamphilus'* attitude that Simo hopes to ascertain.

   ut sese habeat: 'how it is disposed'; OLD *habeo* 21. [*ut sese habeat animum* was the word order long preferred by editors, and it has now been found in several late manuscripts (see Victor 2007, 7). The δ manuscripts have *ut habeat sese animum*, which is possible if *tuom* is treated as one syllable by synizesis and elided. The γ manuscripts have *animum ut sese habeat*, which is unmetrical.]

   ipsus = *ipse*, as at 360.

   ipsus sibi esse: either the second syllable of *ipsus* is light (with ecthlipsis of the final *s*, and Ritschl's law being ignored in the second element of the line) or the first syllable of *esse* is lightened by iambic shortening; see Questa, 230.

   iniurius … iniuria: note the word-play.

379   negaris = *negaueris*; cf. on 10 *norit*.

380   illae turbae: the force of *illae* seems to be '(the trouble) that will flow from his anger', though it is sometimes taken to mean 'the usual, the well-known' (OLD *ille* 4).

   patiar! Pater est, Pamphile: note the word-play and alliteration.

381   dictum factum: an idiomatic way of saying 'no sooner said than done', also found at *HT* 904 (and cf. *HT* 760 *Dictum factum reddidi*). [The manuscripts insert *ac* between the words, probably from ignorance of the idiom.]

inuenerit: future perfect; cf. on 213–14 *ceperit*.

382 to throw her out of town: Davos doubtless exaggerates how far Simo could go, but as a foreign woman Glycerium would be in a very weak position if a citizen decided to make life difficult for her.

383 *Cedo*: cf. on 150. Again at 389, 705, 763.

384 *Ne nega*: *Ne* with the present imperative in Early Latin regularly means 'Stop doing' whatever the addressee is doing; cf. Pinkster, 516–17. It also comes at 543 *ne obsecra* and 868 *ne saeui*.

386 shut up in here: Pamphilus evidently takes it for granted that he will stay in his father's house after his marriage; see also on 952. His overall point is reinforced by the word-play in *excludar ... concludar*. OLD has a separate entry for this adverbial use of *hoc*, which means the same as *huc*. Donatus takes *concludar* to suggest the caging of an animal; cf. Fantham, 47.

388 *Ducas uolo*: see OLD *uolo*¹ 6.d for *uolo* with the subjunctive; again at 418, 708.

389 *Hic*: OLD *hic*² 5 'In the present case or circumstances, in the circumstances just indicated'.

391 *omni*: the first syllable of *omnis* is sometimes lightened by iambic shortening, in spite of normally carrying the accent. The reason is unclear: see Questa, 118–20. There is another possible case at 694. Cf. on 237 *illud* for the similar, and commoner, treatment of *ille*, *iste*, and *ipse*.

hoc: explained in the following *quin*-clause.

392–93 and you don't need to hold back in doing it just in case he changes his mind: this must be the meaning of the words (with *ne ... sententiam* explaining *ea causa*), reinforcing the point that Chremes will not let Pamphilus marry his daughter. *haec quae facis* ('what you are doing') might seem difficult when the required meaning is 'what I am telling you to do', and future *facies* might be thought easier; but the future reference is clear from the context. A number of commentators and translators have preferred a different interpretation, with *neque* adversative, *ea causa* looking backwards rather than forwards, and *haec quae facis* referring to Pamphilus' affair with Glycerium. Thus Barsby: 'But you mustn't for that reason alter your present behaviour or he may change his mind.' However, that seems a pointless digression from Davos' explanation of his suggested plan, weakening what he has just said.

minueris: OLD *minuo* 4 b 'to modify, tone down (a policy, statement, etc.)'; here perfect subjunctive (Bennett, I.171 foot).

395 *quod*: OLD 6 b '(w. pres. subj. presupposing a contingency [...])' supposing that, if'.

396 **one with no money**: a father who could not afford to give his daughter a dowry (see on 100–101) might well feel that he could not be choosy about the husband he accepted for her.

397 **you're not bothered**: for *aequo animo* see OLD *aequus* 8 'with calmness, patience, or resignation'; different at 24.

accipiet: similar to the use at 367.

397–98 *feceris, acciderit*: future perfect; cf. on 213–14 *ceperit. feceris* seems a good example of de Melo's 'resultative' use (outlined at the end of that note); *acciderit* more straightforwardly conveys that something will have turned up before Simo finds another girl.

398 **he'll take his time finding another girl**: as at 391–93, Davos is quite certain that Chremes will not agree to marry his daughter to Pamphilus. [For *aliam* all manuscripts except p have *alia*, which is read by Spengel. But 'another girl' seems more appropriate than 'other means (to put an end to your relationship with Glycerium)'.]

something lucky will turn up: Davos' longer-term strategy is no better thought out than Charinus' at 314. (Donatus takes him to be referring to Simo's death.)

399 *Itan* = *itane*.

Do shut up: see OLD *quin* A.1 for this use of *quin* 'in questions equivalent to commands or exhortations'. It is found only twice elsewhere in Terence but is far commoner in Plautus: see Barrios-Lech, 86–89.

400 **we must take care he doesn't find out**: Simo will in fact learn about the baby, and about Pamphilus' promise to let it live, at 459–64, though he will not react as Pamphilus must fear he will. Pamphilus' remark here will increase the tension of that moment for Davos and for the audience.

cautio: OLD 1.b '*cautio est ne*, one must take care that ... not', citing a number of examples from comedy.

401 **I've promised to let it live**: see on 219, with *suscipio* (OLD 4) used in the sense there given to *tollo*. *suscepturum* = *me suscepturum esse*.

What a nerve: lit. 'What a daring deed!'. Davos reacts as if he were not already well aware of Pamphilus' promise (as 219 shows him to be). Similarly at Men. *Aspis* 310 Daos reacts with apparent astonishment to a piece of news that he already knows; the effect in each case is to underline the seriousness or awkwardness of the situation. For a far more extended example see Pl. *Ps.* 340–79, with W. G. Arnott, 'Calidorus' surprise: a scene of Plautus' *Pseudolus*, with an appendix on Ballio's birthday', *Wiener Studien* NS 16 (1982), 131–48.

fidem: OLD *fides*[1] 2 'A guarantee, promise, assurance'.

402 sibi: goes with *ut darem*; the sense is *me obsecrauit ut hanc fidem sibi darem. hanc fidem* is brought to the front for emphasis, and *qui se sciret non deserturum* receives similar emphasis from its placing within the clause *hanc fidem sibi ut darem.*

qui = *ut*: cf. on 6.

non deserturum = *me non deserturum esse*; *se* is the object of *deserturum.*

403 Curabitur: cf. Sosia's *curabo* at 171. But by using the impersonal passive here Davos distances himself somewhat from Pamphilus' concern over the baby; according to Donatus, this conveys the difficulty of keeping the birth secret (cf. Wackernagel, 188).

caue ... sentiat: *caueo* can be used with or without *ne* + a verb in the subjunctive to mean 'take care that ... not', effectively a circumlocution for a negative imperative; see GL 271.2. [Nonius 409 M = 659 L quotes this passage with *ne te tristem sentiat*, a reading supported by J. E. G. Zetzel, 'Andria 403 (II 3, 29)', *Hermes* 102.2 (1974), 372–76.]

404–31 A new phase in the action is heralded with a return to unaccompanied iambic senarii, which continue to 480; cf. Moore 2013, 100: 'Characters who oppose the union of lovers, especially *senes* like Simo, often bring a stop to the music in Plautus.' Simo returns from the town centre to see what Davos and Pamphilus are up to. Hard on his heels comes Byrria, who in his turn has been sent by Charinus to keep an eye on Pamphilus. Byrria is thus present to witness Pamphilus' astonishing agreement to marry Philumena when Simo renews his request that he do so. Since he has no idea that this is part of a scheme suggested by Davos, Byrria naturally assumes that Pamphilus has betrayed Charinus. By adding Byrria to the scene (cf. Introduction, p. 21) Terence has created a splendid further complication for the entertainment of his audience. On the page, it may look a bit awkward that Simo says nothing from 404 to 416 while Davos and Pamphilus converse aside for seven lines and Byrria explains his mission for a further four, and also that, before leaving to break the news to Charinus, Byrria has a further seven lines at 425–31 while Simo and Davos (unaware of his presence) remain silent. However, competent actors will think of appropriate business to keep themselves plausibly occupied while the audience's attention is concentrated elsewhere. Ancient comedy is full of aside comments and aside conversations; they add considerably to the entertainment, and the audiences surely paid attention to the characters who were speaking without worrying about the fact that other characters were not. Similarly at 301–17 the focus was on Charinus and Byrria, and Pamphilus could safely be left to stand absorbed in his own thoughts. A comparable case in Menander is *Samia* 639–57; cf. on 642 below.

Byrria comes on only to overhear and then go off again; he makes no contact with the others on stage, and they do not see him (Denzler, 59; Kruschwitz 2004, 34 n. 37).

This is the first scene in the play that requires four speaking actors on stage, an arrangement almost certainly not found in plays by Menander (see GS 16–19, K. B. Frost, *Exits and Entrances in Menander* [Oxford, 1988], 2–3). The others are 459–67 (where Terence has perhaps added Lesbia's words), 684–708 (where Charinus has been added), 861–66 (where Terence has perhaps added Dromo's words), and 904–52 (where possibly Pamphilus was not present in Menander's play). On such scenes in Terence see Lowe; at p. 153 he draws attention to the 'extra emotional dimension' contributed by Byrria's asides and adds 'It is reasonable to speculate that an actor on the Roman stage would exaggerate this comic element with appropriate gesticulation'.

404   *Reuiso* = *Redeo ut uideam* (Donatus). Characters often explain to the audience the reason for their return to the stage; so Byrria at 412–14, Chremes at 740–41, Charinus at 957 (*Prouiso quid agat Pamphilus*). Simo does not see Davos and Pamphilus until 416.

quid agant aut quid captent consili: this is exactly what Simo told Sosia to keep an eye on at 170. He perhaps now hopes to receive a report from Sosia, though in the event he is distracted by what happens on stage,

406   **some lonely spot where he's been practising**: so Moschion at Men. *Samia* 94–95 goes off to a lonely spot to practise what he will say to his father. In fact we cannot say what Simo has been doing since he met Pamphilus in the forum (as described at 252–56); he gave no reason for his departure at 205.

Donatus quotes a line and a half from Menander at this point: 'the eyebrow-raisers [i.e. philosophers] say that a lonely spot is good for thinking up solutions' (εὑρετικὸν εἶναί φασι τὴν ἐρημίαν / οἱ τὰς ὀφρῦς αἴροντες,

Menander fr. 37 K-A). If this is from this part of Menander's *Andria*, Terence must have abbreviated Davos' remark.

408 *qui*: cf. on 6. As at 512, this could here be a true ablative (OLD *qui*² 3 'By which means, whereby, wherewith') rather than a final adverb.

to tear you apart: cf. Pl. *Ps.* 359 *iam ego te differam dictis meis*, OLD *differo* 2 'To confound, bewilder' – but it would be a pity to lose the image of pulling in different directions in translating.

keep your wits about you: OLD *apud* 11 '*apud se*, in one's senses'; cf. 937 below.

sies = *sis*: cf. on 234 *siet*. Again at 424; *siet* at 454.

409 **If only I can**: for *ut* introducing a wish (like *utinam*) see OLD *ut* 42.

Listen: for this parenthetical use of *inquam* (lit. 'I say') see OLD 2.a 'emphasizing a word, phr., or sentence'.

410 *hodie*: probably emphatic, as at 196, rather than temporal.

commutaturum: cf. *Ph.* 638–39 *tria non commutabitis / uerba hodie inter uos*, OLD 5 '*uerba commutare*, to exchange words, talk'.

412 *relictis rebus*: the same expression at *HT* 840, *relictis rebus omnibus* at *Eun.* 166; OLD *relinquo* 3 'To leave, quit, relinquish (an occupation, obligation, condition, etc.)'.

412–13 **keep an eye on Pamphilus**: it is not clear why Charinus has come to distrust Pamphilus since 370–74 (F. Leo, *Geschichte der römischen Literatur* [Berlin, 1913, repr. Darmstadt, 1967], 240–41 n. 1), nor where he has met Byrria, whom he had driven away at 337 (Büchner, 69). But such things are unlikely to worry an audience.

414 *id*: OLD *is* 13.a '*id* (internal acc.) For that reason, on that account'; here redundant with *propterea*.

415 *adeo*: cf. 162.

agam: cf. 186.

417–18 On the metatheatrical play in these lines see Introduction, p. 29.

417 *Ehem*: similar to *Hem* at 116, here expressing Pamphilus' (feigned) surprise at finding that his father is present; cf. 846. Müller, 106–108 discusses the various uses of this interjection in Terence.

418 **I want you to marry today**: Simo says exactly what Davos had supposed he would say at 388.

420 *istic*: OLD *istic*² 2 'In that matter of yours'.

423 *uerus*: OLD 6.c 'uttering or expressing the truth, truthful'.

excidit: OLD *excido*¹ 6 '(w. abl.) To be deprived or disappointed (of)'.

425 *fidem*: OLD *fides*[1] 6 'Good faith, honesty, honour' or 9.b 'trustworthiness, reliability'.

426 *uerbum*: OLD 10 'A phrase, formula; a proverb, saying'. Otto, 16 quotes Eur. *Medea* 86 and Men *sent*. 814 Jaekel-Pernigotti as Greek examples of the view that we all love ourselves most of all.

428 I've seen her: cf. on 249. As Donatus remarks, Byrria here corrects Pamphilus' supposition there that Philumena must be 'some kind of monster'.

   good-looking: Byrria uses the same expression (*forma bona*) as Sosia at 119.

429 *uideri*: cf. Pinkster, 323–24: 'the present infinitive has a past reference point in an accusative and infinitive clause that depends on a cognition verb in the present tense (especially one of remembering)'. Understand *eam* as the subject of *uideri*. [All manuscripts and ancient quotations have *uidere*, but many editors have accepted Bothe's change to *uideri*, which Donatus (in an enigmatic note) appears to offer as a possible interpretation of *uidere*.]

   ***aequior*:** OLD *aequus* 7 'Inclined towards, sympathetic or favourable (to)'.

431 he'll make it bad news for me: Byrria puns on *malum* as a personal misfortune (OLD *malum*[1] 2 'A misfortune, woe, trouble', cf. 215) and as punishment (cf. on 179).

   This is the last we see of Byrria. When Charinus next appears, at 625, he has clearly received Byrria's report.

432–58 Left on his own with Davos, Simo tries unsuccessfully to get to the bottom of Pamphilus' willingness to agree. He remains convinced that Davos must be up to no good.

   The metre continues to be iambic senarii.

433 *gratia*: OLD 7.c '*ea gratia*, for that purpose'.

434 *narrat*: cf. on 367.

   [*Aegre quicquam*: *Aegre* ('scarcely') is the conjecture of L. Schopen, *De Terentio et Donato* (Bonn 1821), 22–23 for the manuscripts' *Aeque*. Simo's next words show that the phrase must mean something like 'Nothing much', but it is not clear how *Aeque quicquam* could do so. Donatus suggests that the force of *Aeque*, together with *nunc quidem*, is 'I've just as much got something to say now as I had earlier [i.e. at 185, where Davos refused to be drawn on the question of Pamphilus' having an affair]'; but why should Davos choose to refer back to that? For a fuller discussion see Victor 2015, 301–302. Victor himself proposes *Ecqui* for *Aeque*, with Davos asking 'Is there any way I could say anything at the moment?'. *Ecqui* is an extremely rare form but is found at

Pl. *Aul.* 16 and perhaps also *Mil.* 1111. Some editors make Simo the speaker of the whole line, asking Davos a succession of questions; but *Nilne* seems a bit flat if Simo has effectively already asked this.]

435 *Hem*: cf. 194.

Nil prorsus: cf. 371.

436 *Praeter*: OLD 3 'Out of line with, contrary to'; cf. 678, 879.

437 *Potin es* = *Potisne es* = *Potesne*: the present forms of *possum* are formed from *potis* + *sum*; see OLD *potis*.

dicere: for the scansion see Introduction, the end of section 8.3 (b), and on 125 *Attat*.

438 *quidpiam*: OLD *quispiam*² 1.c '(acc. of neut. sg. used w. advl. force) in any degree, at all'.

439 *hospitai*: OLD *hospita*¹ 4 'A stranger, alien'. The archaic genitive ending *-ai* (for which see W. de Melo, 'The Language of Roman Comedy', in J. Clackson (ed.), *A Companion to the Latin Language* (Wiley-Blackwell, 2011), 321–43, at p. 323) is restored for the sake of the metre by K-L here and by several editors at *HT* 515 *Cliniai*. [Bentley had already proposed *propter hospitai huiusce consuetudinem*. An alternative approach is to keep the manuscripts' *hospitae* and change the word-order to *huiusce propter consuetudinem hospitae* (so D. Erasmus in his 1532 Basel edition, followed by almost all subsequent editors); but that is a less economical solution than K-L's.]

440 *adeo*: OLD *adeo*² 8 'as an ancillary particle giving emphasis or prominence to a word or sentence'.

442 *uia*: *consilio, ratione* (Donatus); OLD 6.d '*uia* (abl.), in the proper way, methodically'. [Several manuscripts have *recta* after *eam rem*. Bentley read *Etenim ipsus eam rem recta reputauit uia*, omitting *secum*; Fleckeisen and Barsby read *id* for *eam rem*, followed by *recta reputauit uia*, keeping *secum*.]

443 *ei*: here two heavy syllables; see Questa, 73.

tulit: see on 188; Davos here echoes what Simo said to him there.

444–45 he made sure it would never bring any disgrace on him: this does not tally with Simo's account at 144–49, but Davos is trying to present Pamphilus in the most favourable light possible.

infamiae, sibi: datives as at 331.

445 *fortem*: OLD *fortis* 4.b '(colloq., of persons, their conduct) honourable, decent, worthy'.

446   *animum ... adpulit*: cf. on 1.

447   *Subtristis*: only here in surviving Latin before St Jerome.

448   *quod suscenset*: cf. 376 *id suscenseat* for the construction.

449   [*feigning reluctance*]: an alternative canvassed by Donatus is that Davos here stalls for time because he cannot immediately think what to say.
   Quin dic quid est: cf. on 45.

451   *drachumis*: cf. on 369 *obolo*. The Greek drachma sometimes becomes *drachuma* in Latin, just as (for instance) Alcmene becomes Alcumena: see Palmer, 231, G. Meiser, *Historische Laut- und Formenlehre der lateinischen Sprache* (2nd edn, Darmstadt, 2006), paragraph 65.2.

   est opsonatus: *opsonor* is deponent at Pl. *Aul.* 295, *Sti.* 681, more commonly active in Plautus and at *Ad.* 117 and 964. Here the evidence of the manuscripts clearly favours *opsonatus* over the impersonal passive *opsonatum* (written in C and P but changed to *opsonatus* in both cases). For this Greek-derived word see on 360 *paullulum opsoni*.

454   *potissimum*: 'in preference to the others'; the meanness of the provisions implies a severely restricted number of guests.
   quod: cf. on 395.

455   *tu quoque*: this is probably best taken to mean 'even you' (OLD *quoque* 4), since 'you too' makes little sense here. Donatus suggests an implied train of thought: 'I admit that he is wrong to be so childishly angry, but you too are at fault'; however, this leans rather heavily on *puerilest* in 449 (though Haffter 1934, 138 n. 1 singles it out as a particularly fine interpretation). 'Even you' would tone down the criticism by implying that Simo is not normally at all stingy.
   perparce: understand *sumptum facis*. For the form, see on 265 *peropust*; again, the word is found only here in surviving Latin literature, except that Charisius 180B quotes *Ad.* 45 (probably wrongly) as using it.
   it's not good: Davos caps Simo's 'Good!' at 443.

456   **I've shaken him up**: as Donatus notes, Davos has shown Simo that his pretended wedding preparations have not been very convincing.
   uidero: de Melo, 47–48 discusses this idiomatic use of the future perfect rather than the simple future of *uideo* when it means 'see to', 'see that' (for which cf. on 736 *uide*).

457   *rei*: genitive singular (partitive genitive; cf. 600n.); here two heavy syllables, as sometimes elsewhere.
   uolt ... sibi: cf. 375.

458 *illic*: perhaps the pronoun (OLD *illic*[1] 4 'That person or thing (indicated by the speaker)'), as at 742, 934, rather than the adverb (OLD *illic*[2] 1 'At that place, over there').

rei: dative singular; always a monosyllable in Plautus and Terence (see Questa, 61).

caput: OLD 13 'The prime mover or leader (in any action), ring-leader, principal'. Simo does not realize that Davos has seen through his plan, but Davos has made him feel uneasy about it.

459–80 Mysis returns with the midwife, and almost as soon as they have entered her house Glycerium is heard crying out with the pain of giving birth. Simo regards this as an implausible pretence designed to discourage Chremes from letting Pamphilus marry his daughter. Simo has been expecting Davos to plot against his plans since the start of the play (cf. 159–64, 196–200, 404, 457–58); now at last he thinks he has caught him out. He is of course right to think that Davos is plotting against him, but his suspicion in this case is unfounded. In addition, the baby whose birth he doubts is in fact his own grandchild. There is much irony here for the audience to enjoy.

The metre continues to be iambic senarii.

459 *pol*: cf. on 229.

dixti = *dixisti*.

460 **you'll hardly ever find a man who stays faithful to a woman**: for this sentiment cf. *Hec.* 58–59.

haud ferme: OLD *fere, ferme* 3.b '(w. *non* or *haud*) hardly ever, seldom'.

inuenias: cf. on 66.

461 [The assignation of speakers in this line is uncertain; in particular, it is hard to decide who could plausibly say *Quid narras?*, which elsewhere in Terence expresses astonishment at what has been said and even rejection of it. The one exception is *Eun.* 671–72, where the expression follows a question in the mouth of the same speaker: *Quid huc tibi reditiost? Quid uestis mutatio? / Quid narras?* This suggests that the best solution may be Barsby's, as printed in the text, though the tone of *Quid narras?* is rather different here. Simo has been a keen observer of the household next door for some time (cf. 83–91, 115–36), so it is not surprising that Mysis looks familiar to him. But he is not quite certain about her, so he asks Davos for confirmation: hence the punctuation of *Ab Andriast ancilla haec* as a question, with *Quid narras?* functioning like *Quid ais?* after the question *nonne hoc monstri similest?* at *Eun.* 334. Simo has no particular reason to comment on Mysis' arrival, but this is Terence's way of showing that he is aware of it; we are then not surprised that he overhears her subsequent remarks. (For other possibilities see Victor 1996, 372–73; his own suggestion to assign *Quid narras? Ita est* to Lesbia as a response to Mysis' remark at 459–60 is attractive, but *Quid narras?* remains anomalous.)]

   narras = *dicis*, as at 367.

462   *fidem*: cf. 401.

463   **for the baby to be allowed to live**: cf. 219.

465   **It's all over**: OLD *ago* 21.c '*acta* (*haec*) *res est, actum est*, it is all up with me (us, etc.), I am (we are) undone'.

   siquidem: cf. on 225 *Miquidem* for the scansion.

469   **By a foreign woman**: cf. on 219.

   ah: for its position at the end of the line cf. on 248.

470   *sensisse*: understand *se* as the subject of this infinitive.

472   **they're pretending that she's giving birth**: only someone predisposed to suspect trickery (or someone acquainted with Plautus' *Truculentus*: see 507, 512–13, 515 nn.) would leap to this conclusion. On the other hand, Pamphilus' promise to let the baby live must indeed seem scarcely credible, as Davos' comment at 218 shows.

   quo = *ut*; cf. on 308.

473   **Juno, Goddess of Childbirth**: Glycerium's cries are heard from inside the house, like those of girls giving birth at Pl. *Aul.* 691–92, Ter. *Ad.* 486–87 (and also in Caecilius' *Plocium*, as reported by Gell. II.23.18). She calls on Juno Lucina, the goddess believed by the Romans to preside over childbirth. The Greeks attributed this function to Artemis, whose Latin equivalent was Diana, and Catul. 34.13–14 treats Juno Lucina as a cult-title of Diana. Donatus notes that Menander 'calls her Diana', Eugraphius that he 'calls her Artemis', both perhaps suggesting that Menander's *Andria* had a similar off-stage cry at this point (as some of his plays certainly did, according to an ancient commentator on Theocritus cited by K-A on Menander fr. 38).

   obsecro: on this as a marker of female speech see on 721.

474   *Hui*: 'exclamation of surprise or other strong emotion' (OLD).

475–76   **You didn't plan the timing of this very well**: lit. 'These things weren't distributed appropriately enough by you in terms of their timing'. This may reflect the vocabulary of theatrical production, though *discipuli* in 477 resumes the language of teacher and pupil found in *magister* at 192.

477   your pupils: Glycerium and Mysis, and perhaps also Lesbia. Simo uses the masculine plural *discipuli* as a generalizing term.

478   Hicin = *Hicne*; cf. on 186 *hoccin*, but the nominative masculine singular of this pronoun always scans short in Plautus and Terence, i.e it is always *hic*, not *hicc* (Questa, 21). For -*ne* here see OLD -*ne* 7 'in statements, app. serving to underline a personal, demonstrative, or other pron., esp. one placed outside the clause of which it is subject, object, etc.' [The manuscripts have *hicine* or (wrongly for Terence) *hiccine*. K-L print the abbreviated form *hicin* to avoid a self-contained tribrach word at the start of the senarius (on which see Questa, 232–35, 241–44); they have been followed by most subsequent editors.]

479   what fun he'd be having at my expense: *ludos reddere* for the commoner *ludos facere*; see OLD *ludus* 4.b to 'put on a show' for someone, fool or shame him', playing on *ludi* in the sense of festivals at which shows were put on (OLD 3). On the importance of *ludos facere* in Plautine comedy, and its link to the festival context, see G. Petrone, *Teatro antico e inganno: finzioni plautine* (Palermo, 1983), 202–209.

480   he's the one at risk: Simo has threatened Davos with dire punishments if he catches him scheming (196–205). In the event Davos manages to divert the blame away from himself at 502–22. Simo in any case seems more intent on showing that he is cleverer than Davos thinks him (475–77, 492–94) than on punishing him.

   my boat's safe in harbour: on nautical imagery in Greek and Latin comedy see Fantham, 19–24.

481–523   Lesbia reappears from Glycerium's house (very soon after the birth!), issuing and partly repeating instructions to Archylis indoors about the treatment of Philumena. Simo finds further implausibility in the fact that she has started to leave the house before giving her instructions, and he remains convinced that no one has really given birth in Glycerium's house. Davos decides to fall in with his mistake and assures him that before long a baby will be brought out from the house and passed off as being Glycerium's; he insists that he himself has nothing to do with the (supposed) plot and has indeed been instrumental in detaching Pamphilus from Glycerium. Simo sends him indoors to help with the wedding preparations.

   Lesbia at 481–85 sounds more authoritative than we might have expected from Mysis' account of her at 228–33 (see n. there); Donatus on 485 suggests that she sounds like a professional doctor. Handley, 19–20, on the other hand, suggests that Mysis' words have prepared us for Lesbia's doorstep loquacity at this point.

Metre: Lesbia's instructions to Archylis consist of four lines of bacchiac tetrameters, followed by what could be an anacreontic but is usually analysed as a catalectic iambic dimeter. She comments to the world at large in a solitary iambic senarius at 486 and ends with a prayer to the gods in two lines of iambic octonarii, a metre which continues for the first eight lines of the following dialogue between Simo and Davos. (Moore 2013, 101 sees these ten iambic octonarii as balancing those at 394–403, the last time this metre was used.) There follow two lines of iambic senarii (497–98, marking the point at which Davos decides on his new tactic), a further eleven lines of iambic octonarii (499–509), seven trochaic septenarii (510–16), a catalectic trochaic dimeter at 517 and six more trochaic septenarii at 518–23. Overall, Simo and Davos converse in iambic lines from 489 to 509, in trochaic lines from 510 to 523. 510 reinforces the point Davos was making in 509, but it can be seen as introducing a new section of the dialogue, in which Davos summarizes the case for supposing Lesbia to be part of a plot and insists that he himself separated Pamphilus from Glycerium. On the 'new style of polymetry' in this passage as a whole see Moore 2013, 101–102; lines 481–86 are also discussed by Questa, 439, noting that enjambment helps to subordinate the rhythmic pattern to the sense of the words.

481–86 is the first of two lyric passages in the play, the other being 625–38a. To judge from the fragments of Menander's *Andria* quoted on 483 and 484, Terence has changed the metre from what he found in his Greek original, just as Plautus can be seen to have done at *Bacchides* 494–561 (cf. Menander, *Dis Exapaton* 11–112) and Caecilius in *Plocium* (see Aulus Gellius II.23). Caecilius includes lyric metres in his adaptation; Plautus does not at that point of *Bacchides*, but overall his plays contain quite a number of lyric passages. By contrast, the only further lyric passage in all of Terence's plays is *Ad.* 610–17.

481   *oportent*: this and other normally impersonal verbs are sometimes found in a personal construction (see OLD *oportet* 4), here balancing *adsolent*. [*oportent* is preserved only in E; all other manuscripts have *oportet*.]

483   **make sure she washes**: Donatus tells us that Terence here reproduces Menander's 'wash her at once' (λούσατ' αὐτὴν αὐτίκα = Menander fr. 39 K-A, in iambic or trochaic rhythm, not bacchiac). Donatus does not specify which of Menander's plays he is quoting from, but it is reasonable to take frs 39 and 40 (see on 484) together as suggesting that it was in *Andria* that the midwife gave instructions similar to those given here by Lesbia.

istaec: feminine singular; cf. on 28. [The manuscripts are divided between the readings *istaec ut* and *ista ut*; if we read *istaec*, we must delete *ut* for the sake of the metre. *fac* ('make sure that') can be followed by the subjunctive with or without *ut* (OLD *facio* 16.a; cf. 408 and 712 with *ut*).]

deinde: trisyllabic only here, regularly in Terentianus Maurus, and in some later authors (see TLL V.1.406.72–81). To preserve the normal disyllabic scansion (with *dein* as one syllabe by synizesis, as at 441) Fleckeisen, followed by several editors, introduced the Early Latin form *poste*; but Questa, 439 and others regard the trisyllabic scansion as acceptable within the metrical constraints of a lyric passage.

484 give her the drink I told you to: Menander fr. 40 K-A (said by Photius to come from *Andria*) is generally accepted as lying behind this passage: 'and after that, my dear, the white of four eggs' (καὶ τεττάρων / ὠιῶν μετὰ τοῦτο, φιλτάτη, τὸ νεοττίον). Terence has omitted the precise detail and the address 'my dear', made Lesbia refer to a previous instruction rather than give her orders for the first time (perhaps thereby slightly weakening the implausibility detected by Simo – so Büchner, 77), and, as at 483, changed the metre (iambic trimeters) to bacchiacs.

bibere: infinitive of purpose after *dari*; see Bennett, I.418–19.

485 I'll be back shortly: in fact we never see Lesbia again. [*reuortar* is the reading of most manuscripts, though E and the first hand in D have *reuortor*, and that is the reading of Donatus' manuscripts in his commentary on this line (though he does not comment on the idiom). H. Sjögren, *Zum Gebrauch des Futurums im Altlateinischen* (Uppsala, 1906), 7–9 showed that Plautus regularly uses the future *reuortar* in this context, though the present is regular with *redeo*. This is the only comparable occurrence of *reuorti* in Terence, and Sjögren insisted that Terence must have followed the Plautine usage. It is perhaps best to accept this, though it is possible that Terence's use differed from that of Plautus.]

486 *Per*: cf. on 265 *peropust*. Here the prefix is separated from the rest of the word by the insertion of another word (tmesis), as at Cic. *De Orat.* II.271 *per mihi scitum uidetur* (the only other occurrence of this adjective in classical Latin), though *ecastor* is more emphatic than *mihi*. See OLD *per-*: 'Before adjs. and advs. it has an intensive force […]; in this situation it is used freely and tmesis is common'. For the meaning of *perscitus* see OLD *scitus*[1] 4 '(colloq., as a general term of praise) Calculated to satisfy, nice, excellent. **b** (esp.) nice-looking, attractive'.

ecastor: 'by Castor', an oath used only by women; contrast on 194 *hercle*, 229 *pol*, 305 *edepol*. Oaths by Castor are commoner in Plautus than in Terence (B. L. Ullman, 'By Castor and Pollux', *Classical Weekly* 37 (1943), 87–89, at p. 88).

487 *superstes*: there cannot be any implication here of 'remaining alive after the death of another' (OLD 3); Lesbia prays simply that the baby should survive.

quandoquidem: cf. on 225 *Miquidem* for the scansion.

ipse: Pamphilus.

488 *est ueritus*: cf. on 323 *uereor*. [*est ueritus* is the word order preferred by most editors. Bentley found it in a Cambridge manuscript, and it has now been found in some further late manuscripts (see Victor 2007, 7). The main manuscripts have *ueritus est*, which breaks Hermann-Lachmann's law (Introduction, section 8.4).]

adulescenti: *adulescens* is far more commonly used of a man (as at 466) than of a woman; it is feminine twice elsewhere in Terence (*Ph.* 794, *Hec.* 661, in both cases with *mulier* added), and at Pl. *Mil.* 966, Afranius 52 R[3], and in a fragment of Varro. The feminine diminutive *adulescentula* is found at 118, *HT* 602 and 654, and three times in Plautus.

489 *Vel*: OLD 4.b 'for instance, now'.

490–91 What Simo finds implausible is standard dramatic technique in New Comedy, a way of helping the audience to visualize what is going on behind the scenes (as at 228, 684–85, 842–43). The text thus draws attention to the artificiality of a convention that the audience normally (presumably) accepted without thinking about it. cf. Fraenkel, 97: 'It brings out forcefully the stupidity of the old man, who suspects something extraordinary behind a totally normal situation' (though that does not convey the metatheatrical humour of the passage). Menander probably used the same technique in his *Andria*: see the fragments quoted on 483 and 484. N. Zagagi, 'The Dramatic Function of 'Speaking back into the House' in Menander's *Dyskolos*', *ZPE* 148 (2004), 99–113 discusses Menander's use of the technique in *Dyskolos*.]

490 *quid opus facto esset*: cf. 523 *quod parato opus est*, 715 *Ita factost opus* (OLD *opus*[1] 12.c).

492 *tandem*: OLD 1 'Really, I ask you, after all', adding emphasis and 'expressing a strong sense of protest or impatience'.

494 *accurate*: this is probably the adverb ('carefully') used elliptically, with something like 'you ought to act' understood and contrasted with *aperte* in 493; the adverb *accurate* is used in the context of scheming at Pl. *Capt.* 226 and *Mil.* 945. Alternatively, it could be the plural imperative of *accuro* ('see to it that'), addressed to Davos and his (supposed) fellow-conspirators; but Simo otherwise addresses Davos alone in this passage.

496 *ueritu's* = *ueritus es*, like 202 *locutu's*.

  re tulit: OLD *refert*, commonly printed as one word.

497 *Credon*: cf. on 315 *Adeon*.

498 *Teneo*: cf. 86.

  habeo: as at 344.

499 *credas*: the subjunctive is similar to that at 191 *hoc quid sit?*, though here Davos is responding to Simo's *Credon* in 497: 'Why do you ask what you're to believe?'

  As if someone hadn't told you: Davos' tactic is to go along with the idea that the birth is a pretence; his suggestion that Simo must have been told about it is ultimately very flattering to Simo, since it implies that it would otherwise have required exceptional perspicacity to see through the pretence, though Simo at first feels insulted by it at 500.

500 *Mihin quisquam?*: understand *renuntiauit*.

  Eho: cf. on 88.

  an: OLD *an²* 1 'Can it really be that … ?'.

  tute: cf. on 151.

  [*adsimulari*: the manuscripts have the archaic form *adsimularier*, a form normally restricted to the end of a line, as at 203 *deludier*, 275 *immutarier*, 332 *adipiscier*, 573 *claudier*. Its retention here would require the lightening of *an* and the deletion of *hoc* to make the line scan and also acceptance of the last syllable of *adsimularier* as *breuis in longo* (not in itself impossible: see Introduction, section 8.3 (b)), as well as the unusual position of the form in the line. K-L accept this, but most do not.]

501 *qui*: 'how' or 'why'; cf. on 6.

503 *enim*: regularly an emphatic particle in Early Latin.

  me pernosti … qualis sim: for the construction see on 169–70, 377–78.

504 *Egon te?*: understand *non pernouerim*.

504–505 *dari tibi uerba*: cf. 211.

506 You've realized that: Davos explicitly goes along with Simo's mistaken conviction. [*Intellexeris* (concessive subjunctive, 'I'll grant that you figured it out') was proposed by Victor 2015, 302–303 in order to continue the run of iambic octonarii; the manuscripts have *Intellexti*, making the line an iambic septenarius. Moore 2013, 102 sees a septenarius here as an ironic echo of 299–300, the only previous iambic septenarii in the play, where Mysis told Pamphilus that she was going to fetch the midwife. But Simo's certainty that no one has given birth has been well enough established by now, and it is not clear that much would be added by the alleged echo.]

507 a baby will be brought back out: 'back' because, as Davos makes clear at 513–15, his claim is that Mysis has just smuggled this baby into the house (so Thierfelder on p. 22 of his vocabulary list). At 768–70 Davos claims that the baby had been smuggled in the previous evening by a different slave; the story grows in his mind as the play progresses.

A woman claiming falsely that she had just given birth would naturally be keen to corroborate her story by displaying a baby, even if the mere existence of such a child would not in fact be proof that it was hers (see below on 515). In the event nothing comes of this at this stage; later (at 721–22) Davos himself brings the baby out of the house, but it is not clear how much of the future action he foresees at this stage (cf. Introduction, pp. 24–25). At 840–41 Simo refers back to Davos' prediction here.

At Pl. *Truc.* 448ff. Phronesium does not display her supposititious baby on stage, but she puts on an act of having been weakened by the experience of childbirth.

[Most manuscripts have *sed nihilo setius puerum deferent huc ante ostium*; D¹Lp have *sed nihilo minus referetur mox huc puer ante ostium*. Bentley read *sed nihilo setius mox puerum huc deferent ante ostium*, and he was followed e.g. by Dziatzko. It is hard to be sure, but I find the singular passive more plausible than the plural active.]

508 *ere*: the standard way for a slave to address his master in Plautus and Terence, though only here in this play.

ut sis sciens: cf. 775, Bennett, I.459 for this use of the present participle of *scio* with *sum*. As Shipp notes, it appears to be a legal formula.

[**509** The manuscripts add *mihi* either before or after *hoc*, making the line unmetrical. The word would in any case be awkward in combination with *Daui* instead of *meo* in the same sentence.]

510   *Prorsus*: cf. 371.

tuam: for the scansion cf. on 242 *suam*.

511   *Unde*: OLD 2 'From or by what person? from whom?'.

512   *qui*: cf. on 6 and 408.

512–13   **She said earlier on that she was pregnant**: Davos has long been aware of her pregnancy (cf. 215–16), but he cannot previously have admitted to Simo that he had heard of it. At Pl. *Truc.* 389–96 Phronesium explains her motive for having pretended to be pregnant; in her case it really was a pretence.

513   **that's been found to be a lie**: nothing justifies this claim, other than Simo's suspicions in this very scene. It is, of course, completely untrue.

515   *accersitum*: supine of purpose (GL 435), with *obstetricem* as its object. Note the change of construction in *ut adferret*, also expressing purpose, in the second half of the line.

to bring along a baby as well: cf. 768–70 (a different elaboration of the same idea: cf. on 507). Suppositititious babies are listed by Terence in the prologue to *Eunuchus* (line 39) among the stock motifs of comedy – together with 'the deception of an old man by a slave'! Davos knows that Simo will be ready to suspect that he is having a traditional theatrical trick played on him, but Simo fails to realize the way in which he is really being tricked.

Suppositititious babies are also listed among the stock motifs of comedy by Satyros in his Life of Euripides (writing about Greek New Comedy, and claiming that Euripides in his tragedies also developed such motifs to perfection), and at Pl. *Capt.* 1031; at *Truc.* 401–409 Phronesium describes how a baby was found for her to pass off as her own. See also *Cist.* 133–44, 551–53, and for further cases in Greek life and drama see C. Austin and S. D. Olson on Ar. *Thesm.* 339–41.

516   *Hoc*: explained in the following *ut*-clause.

nil: here used with adverbial force; see OLD *nihil* 11 'In no respect, not at all'.

mouentur: OLD *moueo* 9 'To interfere with, disturb, violate'. Here the present tense is used with reference to the future (cf. on 171 'I'll follow').

517   *Quid ais?*: cf. 184.

518   *id consilium capere*: understand *eam* as the subject of *capere*.

why didn't you tell Pamphilus: it is not clear why Simo assumes that Davos did not do so, but his question enables Davos to strengthen the case for trusting him, now claiming that he was responsible for tearing Pamphilus away from Glycerium.

519 nos quidem: *quidem* emphasizes *nos*. Davos has claimed at 444–45 that the world at large was ignorant of Pamphilus' passion for Glycerium; here he says that those closest to him knew all about it.

520 amarit = *amauerit*; cf. 379 *negaris*.

now he's keen to marry: cf. 446 'he's turned his mind to a wife'.

521 Postremo: OLD 4 'To sum up, in short, in fact'.

id ... negoti: cf. 2. Davos probably refers to the 'job' of ensuring that Pamphilus sticks to his (alleged) desire to marry, though Donatus suggests that he means the task of dealing with the display of the baby.

[*tamendem*: if this is the true reading, it must be a strengthened form of *tamen*, perhaps also found at Pl. *Merc.* 595, *Mil.* 585. The manuscripts read *tamen*, leaving the line a syllable short, though *idem* has been added above the line in D, and Donatus clearly read *tamen idem* (taking it in one of his comments to be one word, but uncertain whether it means *tamen* or *tandem*). Lindsay restored the form *tamendem* and printed it in K-L, but most editors have read *tamen idem* (as two words), with *idem* (nom. masc. sing.) somehow reinforcing *tu*. However, it is doubtful whether *idem* can be used quite like this. The closest parallel is perhaps Caecilius 96–97 R³ *si ego obdormiuero, / tute idem ubi eris experrectus?*, but without a context for the fragment we cannot know why Caecilius wrote *idem* rather than *ipse*. Cf. also on 599 *itidem*.]

524–74 Simo remains suspicious of Davos, but, now that Pamphilus has agreed to marry Chremes' daughter, his priority is to persuade Chremes too to agree and to ensure that the wedding takes place today. Chremes appears (his first appearance in the play), and Simo succeeds in overcoming his initial reluctance.

Metre: iambic senarii, except for four lines of iambic octonarii followed by an iambic dimeter at 533–37 for the agitated arrival of Chremes. On the unusual insertion of such a brief accompanied passage see Moore 2013, 102–103: among other things, 'the music stops [at 538] to emphasize Simo's earnestness as he begs Chremes to allow the marriage to occur' (so too Bruder, 48, 75). On the other hand, it is not unusual to have a change of metre for the arrival of a new character (at 533); the insertion of two accompanied lines in mid-dialogue at 663–64 is more striking.

525 atque: adversative, as at 225.

haud scio an: OLD *scio* 4.b '(in cautious assertions) I do not know that... not..., I am inclined to think that...'.

526 *parui pendo*: OLD *pendo* 6.b '(w. *magni*, *parui*, etc.) to regard as of (great, little, etc.) importance'.

maxumumst: OLD *maximus* 5 'most important'.

527, 530 *pollicitust* = *pollicitus est*: see on 102 *dictust*.

527 *ipsus* = *ipse*, as at 360.

Chremem: at 533 the accusative form is *Chremetem*; cf. on 247 *Chremetis*.

529 *quid* = *quor*: cf. 322.

alias: the adverb, 'at another time' (OLD *alias* 1).

fieri: cf. on 305 for the scansion with a light first syllable.

530 *quod pollicitust*: OLD *quod* 10 'In view of the fact that, seeing that, inasmuch as'.

531 **even if he refuses**: i.e. 'even if he changes his mind'.

532 *adeo*: 'in fact' (OLD *adeo²* 8).

eccum: 'Here he is!' (OLD); cf. 580, 605, 957. The word is formed of *ecce* plus an accusative ending thought to be the equivalent of *hunc*; *eccillum* is also found, as are *eccam*, *eccas*, *eccos*.

obuiam: cf. 590; here understand *uenientem*.

533 *Iubeo Chremetem*: Simo would have added *saluere* (cf. *Ad.* 460–61), but Chremes is in such a state that he interrupts him; he does not return Simo's greeting either.

optato: adverb, 'In accordance with one's wishes' (OLD). [Many editors follow the manuscripts (all except p) in giving *optato aduenis* to Chremes, but *aduenis* is more appropriately addressed to him than to Simo.]

534–35 During his shopping expedition before the play began Simo evidently made public his pretence that he was laying in provisions for his son's wedding.

534 *auditum*: understand *esse*; the impersonal passive is used instead of *se audiuisse*.

aibant = *aiebant*; cf. 932 *aibat*. At both places the manuscripts have the fuller form, which does not scan correctly. At 930, on the other hand, *aiebat* is confirmed by the metre, as is *aiebas* at *HT* 924. (Cf. 38n. on *seruibas*, though *aio* is not fourth conjugation.)

535 *id*: explained by the following indirect question.

uiso = *ad uidendum uenio* (Donatus); cf. 404 *reuiso*.

[**536** *pauca*: most manuscripts read *paucis* (for which cf. 29); if that is accepted, either the first *et* has to be deleted, or *quid ego te* must be changed (with Bentley) to *quid te ego*, to make the line scan. However, p reads *pauca*, and Donatus knew of this reading (see Lindsay 1925, 32). It is preferable to read this and make no change.]

538–43   The urgency of Simo's appeal is marked by the formal balance of the first four lines: twice *per* is followed by a double object, with a relative clause attached to the second object, and each line is self-contained. At 543 the alliteration of *fuerant futurae, fiant* brings the lengthy sentence to a fine climax. Shipp also notes that the vocative *Chreme* at the end of 538 is the first of four in this scene: cf. 550, 561, 574. Overall we may compare Chrysis' deathbed appeal reported by Pamphilus at 286–96.

538   *Per te deos oro*: see on 289 *per hanc te dextram*, and cf. 834 *Per ego te deos oro* (again Simo to Chremes). [Many manuscripts have the unmetrical *Per ego te*, on the strength of which Bentley read *Per te ego*.]

541   *quoius*: cf. on 336.

summa: OLD *summus* 9 'Greatest or highest in degree, utmost, extreme'.

542   *uti*: an early form of *ut*.

543   *ne obsecra*: cf. on 384 *Ne nega*.

546   *in remst*: OLD *res* 13.b *in rem esse, uideri* 'to be, seem to be, of advantage or in one's interest'. This expression is found with *utrique* also at Pl. *Capt.* 398, where Lindsay argues that *utrique* is an early genitive form; cf. 608 *nulli* below. Lindsay is followed by Questa, 72 n. 5, but others (including OLD) accept it as the standard dative.

give the order for her to be fetched: cf. 581 'Why isn't the bride being fetched?', 741 'I've come back to give the order for her to be fetched', 848 'Fetch the bride whenever you want'. It is evidently taken for granted that the wedding ceremony will take place in the bridegroom's house and will be preceded by the formal fetching of the bride in a procession from her house; other evidence suggests that it was normal, at least at Athens, for this procession to take place only after some initial ceremonies (including the wedding feast) in the bride's house, but there were exceptions; see on 362–69. On the procession, see Vérilhac-Vial, 312–26 and J. H. Oakley and R. H. Sinos, *The Wedding in Ancient Athens* (Madison, 1993), 26–35 (for Greece), Hersch, 140–44 (for Rome).

548   *id*: explained by the following *ut*-clause.

[The main manuscripts have *id te oro*, which requires a hiatus after *oro* to make the line scan. G. Fabricius' transposition to *id oro te* in his 1548 Strasbourg edition of Terence has been accepted by most editors as the simplest solution, and Bentley said it was the reading of a Cambridge manuscript.]

549 *quasi si*: a pleonastic expression similar to 249 *Nisi si*.

552 **There's a tiff between Glycerium and my son**: Simo has no evidence for this, only Davos' claims at 440–46 and 519–20 that Pamphilus has decided it is time to marry. At 576 he asserts that Davos had told him of the tiff, which is not strictly true, but it is only a slight exaggeration of what Davos said at 519–20. It may seem surprising that Davos himself does not contradict Simo at 597 when Simo says that Pamphilus is now angry, and that at 832–33 he even confirms that there is a row between Pamphilus and Glycerium. But in the former passage he is unlikely to quibble over details, and in the latter he knows that he has something more important to communicate. We need not follow Rambelli, 146–60 in supposing that Terence has abbreviated the dialogue at 504–509 and that Menander at that point made Davos explicitly claim to have engineered hostility between the two lovers.

553 *Fabulae*: cf. 224; see on 220.

555 *amantium irae amoris integratiost*: this has a proverbial ring, and similar thoughts are found elsewhere, though not exactly in these words; see Otto, 17. This line has become a textbook example of a copulative verb agreeing in number with the complement rather than the subject (i.e. after the subject *irae* we should have expected *sunt*, not *est*); that may perhaps have been how Thackeray, Trollope, and others came to know it (see Introduction, section 6.8), as suggested by I. Hurst, *Victorian Women Writers and the Classics: The Feminine of Homer* (Oxford, 2006), 13 n. 9.

556 *id*: object of *ante eamus*.

557 *occlusast*: this metaphorical use of *occludere* seems to be unparalleled, though Fantham, 62 compares Plautus' use of the verb with *linguam* as its object, and 573 *claudier* is similar.

558 *these women*: of course Simo has Glycerium chiefly in mind, but he regards her whole household as conspiring to win Pamphilus back.

560 *consuetudine*: elsewhere in the play this noun is used of Pamphilus' friendship with Chrysis (110) or of his relationship with Glycerium (279, 439). R. D. Brown on Lucr. IV.1283–87 quotes a number of passages in ancient literature in which the continuity of a relationship is seen as helping to keep it stable.

561 *liberali*: i.e. to a citizen woman of good birth.

deuinctum: on this common metaphor see Fantham, 50.

562 *sese emersurum*: *emergo* is here (as sometimes elsewhere) a reflexive verb; understand *eum* as the subject.

his troubles: a diplomatic way for Simo to refer to his son's involvement with a woman other than his prospective bride.

563–64   *neque ... neque* reinforce the preceding *non*; see OLD *neque* 7.d on *neque ... neque* with 'negative force retained after another negative'. Various alternative possibilities of interpretation and punctuation have been canvassed (e.g. Marouzeau and Posani both take *neque me perpeti* to be the start of a new clause which is never completed, and J. T. Hooker, 'Terence, *Andria* 560–565', *RFIC* 105 (1977), 129–30 takes these words to mean 'and I don't think he [Pamphilus] can bear me'), all in my view unnecessarily complicated or otherwise implausible. H. L. Levy, 'Terence, *Andria* 560–565 again', *RFIC* 106 (1978), 177–78 refers to some earlier discussions and revives an unconvincing suggestion of his own.

I take *hanc* to be Chremes' daughter and the object of *habere*; Donatus thinks it is deliberately ambiguous which of *illum* and *hanc* is subject and which object, and among recent editors Marouzeau and Posani take *hanc* to be the subject ('that she can keep hold of him'); effectively the same point is conveyed in either case. Many commentators have taken *hanc* to refer to Glycerium, but I see no advantage in that.

perpetuo ... perpeti: note the play on words; literally *perpeti* (*per* + *pati*) means 'To put up with or tolerate to the end' (OLD). Chremes will not be able to bear seeing his daughter married to an unfaithful husband.

565   how do you know that: 'that' refers principally to Chremes' fears for the stability of the proposed marriage.

periclum: OLD *periculum* 1 '(usu. in phr. *periculum facere*) Test, trial, proof'.

566   *istuc*: 'that phrase of yours'; cf. on 186.

568   there may be a separation – which heaven forbid: Simo quotes a formula found in Greek marriage contracts, as was shown by F. Cairns, 'Terence, *Andria* 567–68', *CR* n.s. 19.3 (1969), 263–64. Cairns takes 567 *huc redit* to mean 'falls on me', referring to the fact that Simo will be obliged to return the dowry to Chremes if the marriage does not last. More probably, however, in view of Terence's use elsewhere of *huc redit* and similar expressions, the *si*-clause explains *huc*, much as a *quom*-clause explains *hoc* at *Ph.* 966–67, and *huc redit* means 'comes down to this'; Shipp suggests that *si* is used instead of the usual *ut* 'to make it sound more hypothetical'. J. Foster, 'Terence, *Andria* 567–68 Again', *CR n.s.* 21.2 (1971), 170–71 takes the construction slightly differently, with *huc redit* meaning effectively 'comes down to the following formula' and line 568 being delivered in such a way that it was recognizably a standard form of words; but that might be puzzling for Terence's audience, unless they were acquainted with the wording of Greek marriage contracts. However we take it, it is likely that Terence is following Menander's Greek here, as Cairns says.

separation: Simo perhaps hopes that this will sound less alarming than 'divorce'. Even so, his attitude to the risk he invites Chremes to submit his daughter to seems rather cavalier.

570 *restitueris*: future perfect; cf. on 213–14 *ceperit*. There might seem to be no difference between this and the simple future *inuenies* in 571, but it is possible to take this as a 'resultative' future perfect (cf. de Melo, cited on 213–14), while *inuenies* refers to a longer-term future prospect.

572 *Quid istic?*: cf. 420, OLD *istic²* 2 '*quid istic?* (sc. *dicendum* or sim.), very well then! as you like!'. As noted by Questa, 111, the first syllable of either *istic* or *istuc* must be lightened (cf. on 237 *illud*), but not both.

istuc: cf. on 186.

induxti: see OLD *induco* 12.b on *inducere animum* with accusative and infinitive 'to bring oneself to believe, convince oneself (that)'. cf. 883; slightly different with infinitive only at 834.

573 *claudier*: for the form, cf. on 203 *deludier*. The verb is here used metaphorically in the sense of *intercludo*, 'block off, cut off'; so Fantham, 44–45. OLD lists this passage under *claudo¹* 3.b 'to make inaccessible' (figuratively). 557 *occlusast* is similar.

575–604 Simo tells Chremes that Davos is the source of his knowledge that Pamphilus and Glycerium are on bad terms. Davos enters, confident that he is one step ahead of Simo and thus happy to pretend that he wants to hurry the wedding along. However, he learns that his trick has backfired, since Simo has persuaded Chremes to let the wedding go ahead after all. Chremes goes home to see to the necessary preparations, and Simo goes indoors to break the news to Pamphilus; Davos, left on his own, laments the consequences of his own excessive ingenuity.

Metre: accompanied iambic lines, septenarii from 575 to 581, octonarii thereafter, from the point at which Simo starts to explain to Davos how things now stand. According to Moore 2013, 103–104, 'Iambic octonarius was the dominant meter of Davos' opening monologue, and it has been associated with him and his plans at several points throughout the play. It is therefore especially poignant that Davos should realize in this meter that all his clever plans have led to disaster.'

575 *quid ais?*: cf. on 184.

576 **Davos told me himself**: see on 552.

intumust = *intumus est*: cf. on 102 *dictust*, and OLD *intimus* 5 'Most intimate, closest'.

577 **he's urging me to hurry the wedding along as fast as I can**: Once again (cf. on 552) this is not quite what Davos said at 521–22, but it is only a slight extension of it, and it prepares us for Davos' apparent impatience to have the wedding proceed at 580–81. For *quantum queam* meaning 'as fast as I can' see OLD *quantum*[2] 3.b.

[The manuscripts are divided between *suadet* and *persuadet*. K-L and Thierfelder read *persuadet*, but 'urging' seems more appropriate than 'persuading', if the latter implies that the urging is successful.]

578 *censes*: syntactically, this is a parenthesis, interrupting *num faceret*.

579 *Tute*: cf. on 151.

adeo: as at 532; again at 585.

[*uerba audies*: the manuscripts have *audies uerba*; editors transpose these words for the sake of the metre, following Faernus.]

579–80 At Men. *Aspis* 163–64 Smikrines is about to knock at the door to summon Daos when Daos himself comes out. That is similar to the staging here, though Daos there is not looking for Smikrines.

580 *eccum*: cf. on 532.

I was on my way to you: Davos is not content to wait for Simo indoors, as he was told to do at 523.

581 **Why isn't the bride being fetched?**: cf. on 546.

Do you hear that?: Simo takes Davos' impatience to confirm what he has just told Chremes, as he said Davos would do at 579. This was the effect Davos was hoping for, confident that he was calling Simo's bluff; but he knew nothing about Simo's conversation with Chremes, and there is a shock in store for him. [All manuscripts except p add *tu illum*, which is not required by the sense and spoils the metre. The reading of the Vienna papyrus is uncertain: see Danese, 151–52.]

582 *dudum*: 'previously'.

non nil = *multum*.

583 **the common run of slaves**: OLD *uulgus* 3 'The members as a whole of a particular class or category'.

583–84 cheating and tricking me because my son's having an affair: Simo refers to the standard behaviour of slaves in comedy. At 469–94 he was ready to suspect Davos of theatrical machinations; he was wrong there, but his view of Davos' aims in general has been more accurate than he now realizes.

584 *propterea quod*: cf. on 38.

filius: for the scansion see Introduction, the end of section 8.5.

586 You've finally discovered what I'm like: Davos builds on what he had said at 503. For *qui = qualis* see OLD *qui*¹ 2. Editors generally print this as a question, which is entirely possible.

587 *ea gratia*: 'for that purpose', anticipating the *ut*-clause; see OLD *gratia* 7.c. Karakasis, 59–60 discusses this phrase as a feature of Early Latin.

588 *Quid ais?*: similar to the use at 301.

Vide: this functions here as an interjection; it is not addressed to anyone in particular. cf. J. B. Hofmann *La lingua d'uso latina* (transl. by L. Ricottilli, 3rd edn, Bologna, 2003), 149–50.

589 I'd never have managed to work that out: Davos had in fact worked it out (cf. 375–80), but he continues to flatter Simo (as he did at 499–501), still confident that he has outwitted him. He has no idea what a bombshell he is to receive.

Vah: this exclamation can express a variety of emotions, here (feigned) admiration, at 688 distress.

591 *perimus*: this could be either present or perfect (for *periimus*).

dudum: 'just now', as at 653. Simo refers to what Davos had told him at 440–46 and 519–20 (though see 552n.).

[**592** *Quidnam audiam?*: this reading is attested by Donatus, who says the future tense is reproduced from Menander's τί ποτ' ἀκούσομαι; ('Whatever am I going to hear?', fr. 42 K-A). The manuscripts of Terence have *audio* for *audiam* ('What's this I hear?'), but there is no reason for Davos to respond like that to what Simo has just said.]

592–93 Simo half hears Davos' aside *Occidi*; Davos has to pretend that he had said *Optume*.

593 *dixti*: there is hiatus after this word, marking a pause while Davos tries to think of a way to rescue the situation (so Lindsay 1925, 35).

on his side: OLD *per* 9.

594 Chremes confirms Simo's last remark by heading for home. He has had nothing to contribute to the discussion between Simo and Davos, but

Simo referred to him at 590–93, and his presence made it clear to Davos how things stood (Kruschwitz 2004, 38 n. 48).

modo: can be used with reference to the immediate future; see OLD *modo*[1] 5.c.

tell them to get things ready: OLD *dico*[2] 2.c. *adparetur* is impersonal passive, as at *Eun.* 583 *dum adparatur*. [The manuscripts, with the possible exception of the second hand in p, have *adparentur*; Guyet's correction has been accepted by almost all editors.]

renuntio: present for future; cf. on 171 'I'll follow'.

596 [The manuscripts have *corrigere mihi gnatum*: the first two words are metrically awkward, for rather complicated reasons expounded by R. Raffaelli, *Ricerche sui versi lunghi di Plauto e di Terenzio* (Pisa, 1982), 36–37 n. 36. The neatest solution is to change them to *mihi corrigere* (so Barsby), but the position of *mihi* is then surprising: it is the sort of word that does not normally come first in its clause unless it carries some emphasis (see J. N. Adams, 'Wackernagel's law and the position of unstressed personal pronouns in Classical Latin', *Transactions of the Philological Society* 92.2 [1994], 103–78). It is thus better to read *gnatum mihi corrigere* with Fleckeisen in his first edition; in his second edition he reads *corrigi mihi gnatum*, but the passive infinitive is not quite natural.]

597   **while he's angry**: see on 552.

598   *Quiescas*: OLD *quiesco* 6.b 'to avoid becoming excited, remain calm'.

Age: OLD *ago* 24.d 'in weakened sense as a call for attention or consideration'; slightly different from the use at 310.

where is he himself: Simo sent Pamphilus indoors at 424, and he has been standing outside the house ever since. So perhaps this question is part of a reminder to himself rather than a genuine request for information. In any case, he has lived through some interesting developments since 424; if he does need to be reminded of his son's whereabouts, that is not implausible.

Mirum ni: OLD *mirus* 3.e 'I should be surprised if … not, I feel sure that'. But Davos knows that Pamphilus is at home, having been there himself from 524 to 580, so (here and elsewhere) a less tentative translation ('of course') is appropriate. Davos was also present when Simo sent Pamphilus indoors at 424.

599   **tell him exactly what I've told you**: there is no need for Simo to tell Pamphilus that Chremes has only now agreed that the wedding should go ahead, since he has no reason to think that Pamphilus ever doubted that

Chremes had already agreed to this. Simo is clearly so pleased with the success of his manoeuvre that he wishes others to know about it.

itidem: this word ('in the same way') is somewhat redundant, another sign of Simo's long-windedness (cf. on 38). [Donatus attests a reading *idem*, also found in P and in the first hand of C and accepted by some editors. That would have to be taken as nom. masc. sing., used 'in weakened sense' (OLD 7 or 9.b), but none of the examples quoted in OLD is quite the same as this. (For a possible but very uncertain use of *idem* for *ipse* see on 521 *tamendem*.)]

I'm a dead man: OLD *nullus* 4.b 'ruined, done for'; similar to *occidi* at 592, 605.

600 *causae*, 601 *loci*, 604 *mali*: partitive genitives with *quid, nil*; cf. 25 *ecquid spei*, 166 *nil ... morae*, 170 *quid ... consili*, 338 *boni quid*, 350 *nil pericli*, 365 *nil ornati, nil tumulti*, 457 *Quidnam ... rei*, 745 *quid turbae*, *Quid ... hominum*.

600 the mill: see on 179, 199. There is no reason for Davos to fear punishment from Simo in the current circumstances, nor to feel any need to beg him for mercy (601). It is rather Pamphilus' anger that he has to fear, and Pamphilus makes clear at 610 and 623 that he would like to be able to punish him. Presumably only Simo could send him to work at the mill, but Davos cites that as an extreme example of the punishment he knows he deserves.

602 I've deceived my master: Davos presumably has in mind the lies he told to Simo at 442–46 and 519–20, and perhaps also the fact that he had hoped to call Simo's bluff by getting Pamphilus to agree to the pretended marriage; all of this has now backfired on him.

in nuptias conieci: OLD lists this passage under *conicio* 8 'To make (a person) the victim of, involve in', but it probably also carries some connotations of 7 'To put (a person in prison, chains, etc.)'. The expression recurs at 620, 667. Fantham, 39 treats it as a metaphor from hunting or snaring.

erilem filium: the standard term in comedy for the master's son.

604 *Em astutias*: for *Em* followed by the accusative cf. 785–86 *Em / scelera*, 842 *Em Dauom tibi*; further examples at OLD *em*² a.

Quod: cf. on 289; for its use with *si* see OLD 1.a.

no trouble would have resulted: we cannot say how things would have turned out if Pamphilus had not agreed to marry Chremes' daughter at 420.

There would doubtless have been trouble of a different kind in store for Pamphilus and Davos, but at least they might still have hoped to put off a marriage that now seems inevitable.

605–24 Pamphilus enters from his house, having learnt from his father that Chremes has agreed to the marriage, and reproaching himself for his folly in taking Davos' advice. When he catches sight of Davos, he lets him know his feelings; he is not reassured by Davos' promise to find a solution.

Metre: 605–10 various trochaic lines, 611–20 iambic octonarii, 621–24 trochaic septenarii. The change from iambic to trochaic metre at 605 marks the appearance of a new character, and the shifts within the trochaic metres at 605–10 perhaps reflect the tenseness of the situation; after that, the changes in metre at 611 and 621 do not mark significant changes in content,

605   *Sed eccum ipsum uideo*: cf. 532, 580. *ipsum* refers to Pamphilus.
606   *praecipitem darem*: cf. on 214. Here Davos has in mind (exaggeratedly) a more literal suicidal jump.
607   **Where's that villain**: although Pamphilus comes out looking for Davos, it is only after nine lines that he catches sight of him; he is wrapped up in his own thoughts, and Davos is trying to stay out of his line of vision.

   scelus; cf. on 317 'you villain'. Since the word refers to a person, the masculine pronoun *ille* is used.

[The manuscripts have the unmetrical *Ubi illic est scelus qui me perdidit*, except that the second hand in G and L has *ille*, the Oxyrhynchus papyrus has *scelestus* (*scelus* with *est* written above it), and Bentley reports that 'many manuscripts' have *qui me hodie perdidit*; the only manuscript with that reading so far identified in an apparatus is b, reported by S. Prete in his 1954 edition of Terence's plays. If the line is to scan as a trochaic octonarius, the simplest solution is to follow Dziatzko and read *Úbi íllest scélŭs qui pérdidít me*; K-L's *íllicst* involves an unlikely contraction of *est* (see Pezzini, 35). Spengel's *Úbi íllic ést scelŭs quí me pérdit* is closer to the manuscripts, but it would perhaps be a pity to lose the perfect tense. Umpfenbach and Marouzeau accept Bentley's aposiopesis *Úbi íllic ést scelús qui me hódie –* , with *perdidit* omitted.]

   Perii: cf. 591 *numnam perimus?*, 592 *Occidi*, 599 *Nullus sum*, 605 *occidi*. Davos has been reduced to uttering stereotypical expressions of despair.

   Atque = *Atqui*: cf. on 225; again at 614.
608   *quandoquidem*: cf. on 225 *Miquidem* for the scansion.

nulli: this form of the genitive of *nullus* is found occasionally; see the beginning of the OLD entry. *nulli consili* is 'Genitive of Quality' (GL 365, Pinkster, 775–77, 1002–1003).

609 ***Seruon*** = *Seruone*; cf. on 245 *Adeon*.

610 [All the manuscripts (with the possible exception of E) read *Ergo* at the start of the line, as do the manuscripts of Servius quoting the line on *Aen*. XII.352. E perhaps had *Ego*, which is also found in some manuscripts of Servius on *Aen*. IX.230. Neither *Ergo* nor *Ego* is strictly necessary, but both make sense. With *Ergo* the line scans as a trochaic septenarius (like 609), with caesura after the bisyllabic eighth element *ferŏ*, which, though controversial, is not clearly inadmissible (cf. Questa, 361–63). Most editors have preferred to read *Ego*, in spite of its weak manuscript attestation, making the line an iambic octonarius (like the following lines). That has entailed reading *numquam id* for the manuscripts' *id numquam* in order to avoid hiatus between *inultum* and *id*. It is more economical to accept *Ergo* and leave the rest of the line unchanged.]

Sed inultum id numquam auferet: cf. *HT* 918 *At ne illud haud inultum, si uiuo, ferent*, *Ad.* 454 *haud sic auferent*. This idiomatic use of *aufero* is not noted by OLD or TLL, but cf. *Priapea* 83.39 *licebit hoc inultus auferas semel*, and also OLD *fero* 37 for *impune ferre* and similar phrases meaning 'To get away with, escape punishment, etc., for'.

611 According to Donatus, Menander at this point had fr. 43 K-A ἂν θεὸς θέλῃ, / οὐκ ἂν ἀπολοίμην ('If God so wills, I won't die'). Terence has not followed this closely.

malum: cf. on 179.

[This line as printed has its main caesura after a monosyllabic ninth element (*me*), which would be irregular in Plautus but is perhaps acceptable in Terence (Questa, 351–54 is not entirely clear but seems to end by accepting the possibility; he does not discuss this line). Some editors have sought to avoid it by deleting either *fore* or *me* or *nunc*, thus achieving caesura after the eighth element, with a heavy second syllable of *scio*. The manuscripts differ in where they place *nunc, si*, and *hoc*: the second hand in the Oxyrhynchus papyrus seems to have read *si nunc*, and the δ manuscripts have *hoc nunc si*. The text printed is that of the γ manuscripts.]

[**613** ***ipse***: I have printed this in place of the manuscripts' *ducere* (which I assume originated in a marginal gloss amplifying *sum pollicitus*), which is metrically awkward (breaking Hermann-Lachmann's law: see Introduction, section 8.4) and not required for the sense: cf. 527, 530 *pollicitust*, in the first case reinforced by *ipsus gnatus*. B. Victor, 'Terentiana', *CQ* 57.1 (2007), 117–24, at pp. 117–18 proposes *pollicitus sum accipere* or *capere* (the manuscripts offer both *sum pollicitus* and *pollicitus sum*), but neither infinitive is quite convincing. He is, however, surely right to want to retain *fiducia*, changed by editors to its near-synonym *audacia* (found in a medieval gloss) in order to cure the metrical fault while keeping *ducere*. See OLD *fiducia* 4 for the required meaning of this noun: 'Confidence in oneself, assurance, courage, boldness'. Victor cites Pl. *Epid.* 697 for the combination of *qua fiducia* with a part of *audere*.]

614   me, mequidem: ablatives (OLD *facio* 22.b, Pinkster, 877). For the scansion of *mequidem* cf. on 225 *Miquidem*.

ago: OLD 22 'To work at (without necessarily finishing), be engaged on or busy at'.

615   producam: OLD *produco* 10 'To extend in time, draw out, prolong'. [Many editors, including K-L, have read *productem* on the basis of a note in Donatus' commentary, but there is no good evidence for the existence of such a verb: see B. Victor, 'A linguistic ghost', *Latomus* 49 (1990), 161.]

616   Eho dum..., quid ais: cf. on 184.

bone uir: sarcastic; cf. OLD *bonus* 3.

Viden = *Videsne*; cf. on 256 *Censen*. Here the second syllable is lightened by iambic shortening.

[The manuscripts have *tuis consiliis*; Guyet transposed these words to make the line scan as an iambic octonarius. An alternative approach (adopted by Spengel and Marouzeau) has been to move *Oh* to the end of 615 and make 616 a trochaic octonarius ending *tuis consiliis miserum*, leaving 617 as a trochaic septenarius (starting *inpeditum*) before the iambic octonarii resume at 618.]

617   impeditum ... expediam: cf. Pl. *Epid.* 85–86 *neque ego nunc quo modo / me expeditum ex impedito faciam, consilium placet*; *Hec.* 297 *impeditum in ea expediui animum meum*.

618   ut credam: see on 263 *Eine ego ut aduorser?*.

furcifer: 'One who is punished with the 'fork' [see FVRCA 3], scoundrel, villain, gallows-bird' (OLD).

620   hodie: cf. on 196, 410, though here a temporal meaning would be entirely appropriate.

coniecisti in nuptias: cf. on 602.

621 Didn't I say: at 386.

An: introducing an indignant question; OLD *an*² 1.

meritu's = *meritus es*, like 202 *locutu's*.

crucifixion: the most extreme form of punishment imaginable; cf. on 179.

622 *sine ... redeam*: for the imperative *sine* followed by a subjunctive see OLD *sino* 6.b.

Ei mihi: cf. 263.

625–83 Charinus enters, having heard from Byrria about Pamphilus' compliance with his father's wishes at 412–31. He vents his feelings at some length, first on his own (625–41) and then to Pamphilus' face (642–49). Pamphilus has some difficulty in getting him to understand that his compliance had been part of a tactic suggested by Davos (649–64). The scene ends with Davos assuring Pamphilus and Charinus (as he had assured Pamphilus at 617 and 622) that he will be able to think up a new scheme; he adopts a thinking pose as Glycerium's door is heard to open.

If Terence has added Charinus to the play (cf. Introduction, pp. 18–19, 21), there was presumably nothing to correspond to this scene in Menander's *Andria*. The effect of its insertion is both to accentuate the tension between Charinus and Pamphilus and to magnify the unfortunate results of Davos' well-motivated meddling; as at 338–74, Davos is on stage together with the two boys, but he now seems much less securely in control of events (Glücklich, 121). By making Davos at 669 bring us back to the point the dialogue had reached before Charinus' entry, Terence uses a technique analysed by Fraenkel, 78–80, 98 in the detection of insertions by Plautus. Charinus' complaints of betrayal by a friend have something in common with PCG adesp. 1017, 51–71 K-A (English translation in D. L. Page, *Select Papyri III: Literary Papyri: Poetry* [Loeb Classical Library, London and Cambridge, Mass., 1941], 303–305, lines 35–65 in his numbering) and Pl. *Ba.* 540–51 (perhaps interpolated), though the contexts are different. Many monologues in Greek and Latin drama begin with generalizations which the speaker then applies to his own case, though that is not exactly what Charinus does at 639–41. Denzler, 55–58 argues against the view that lines 625–69 derive from Menander's *Perinthia*; I do not find all his arguments compelling, but I do not quarrel with his conclusion: there is no reason why Terence should not have composed all of this out of his own head.

Metre: 625–38a is the second lyric passage in the play (cf. the final paragraph on 481–523). 625 consists of four dactyls (the only dactylic line in Plautus or Terence), 626–34 are cretic lines, and 635–38a are a mixture of cretic cola (635), cretics (637–38) and trochaic lines (636, 638a). This is in the main the scansion proposed by Questa, 440–41. Charinus' complaints are similar to those of Pamphilus at 236–64 (in both cases starting with *hoccinest*), though unlike Pamphilus he couches them in general terms and does not specify the details of his own case until he is face to face with Pamphilus at 645–48. Both passages have musical accompaniment, but the use of lyric metres here reinforces the effect of Charinus' feelings of betrayal.

639 marks a change of metre as Charinus turns from his general complaints to wondering what he should do. 639–54 are a mixture of trochaic septenarii and iambic octonarii, 655–81 iambic senarii with the exception of 663–64 which are iambic octonarii; 682–83 round the scene off with two further lines of iambic octonarii. The senarii start at the point where Pamphilus begins to explain the situation to Charinus. The iambic octonarii at 663–64 mark the moment at which Charinus learns that Davos was responsible for Pamphilus' behaviour; they interrupt senarii just as 533–37 did earlier (see on 524–74), but the effect here is more striking in not coinciding with the entry of a new character. (However, Bentley may have been right to convert these lines into senarii: cf. on 663 *Interturbat*.)

The metre of this section is discussed by Moore 2013, 105–108; Moore sees a significant association of iambic octonarii with Davos' responsibility for Pamphilus' plight.

625   *Hoccinest*: cf. on 186 *hoccin*, 236.

***memorabile*:** classified by OLD under *memorabilis* 2 'Fit to be spoken of', together with Pl. *Curc.* 8 *Istuc quidem nec bellum est nec memorabile.* But Shipp may be right to suggest that the nuance is 'a thing that one can speak of as true'.

626   *ut siet*: explains what it is that is barely credible; cf. OLD *ut* 38. (*ut* in 627 introduces a standard consecutive clause after *tanta*: see OLD *ut* 32.)

627   *malis*: *alterius* in 628 goes both with *malis* and with *incommodis*.

627 *gaudeant*, 628 *comparent*: plural after singular *quoiquam*, a natural shift; cf. on 58 *horum*. For *comparent* see OLD *comparo*[1] 5 'To obtain by questionable means or for improper purposes, procure, get hold of'.

629   *uerum*: probably OLD *uerus*[1] 9 'Morally right or true, just, honest'.

***Immo*:** Charinus corrects himself, offering the unexpected view that the worst sort of people are not those who take pleasure in the misfortunes of others but those who lead others on with false promises out of misplaced embarrassment. When confronted with Pamphilus at 643–48, however, the overall tendency of his reproaches is to charge Pamphilus with maliciousness rather than feeble-minded embarrassment (Denzler, 58). We may compare Men. *Dis Exap.* 110, where Sostratos accuses Moschos of 'wronging' him, shortly after a monologue which had ended at 99–102 with a declaration that he does not blame Moschos at all; Sostratos and Charinus both try to think things through but are too overwrought to stick to their conclusions.

630 *quis* = *quibus*, the only occurrence of this form in Terence.

paullum: probably here temporal, 'for a short while' (OLD 2.c), though some have taken it to mean 'to a small extent' (1.a, 2.a). In any case OLD has a separate entry for this use of the neuter as an adverb.

630–31 *modo ... post*: see OLD *modo*[1] 6 on *modo ... modo*: 'At one time ... at another, now ... now, first ... then; (also w. other words replacing the one or other *modo*)'. Here *modo* is probably reinforced by *paullum*, 'for a short while' (OLD 2.c), though some have taken that to mean 'to a small extent' (1.a, 2.a).

631 *ubi tempus*: understand *est*; cf. 637 *Ubi fides?*. In both places the second syllable of *ubi* is heavy, as is the second syllable of *ibi* in 638a.

[**633** The deletion of this line was proposed by A. Klette, *Exercitationes Terentianae* (Diss. Bonn, 1855), 11–12: the line adds nothing to the sense, *res premit* is unusual Latin for 'the situation forces them' (TLL X.2.1180.7–18 perhaps suggests that *premo* in the sense of *cogo* became idiomatic in later Latin), and the hypermetric elision at the end of the line is unexpected (though Questa, 440 accepts it, and Spengel eliminates the problem by moving *denegare* to follow *timent* earlier in the line; the Oxyrhynchus papyrus apparently read *denegant* at the end of the line, a possibility also considered by Spengel.). The line looks like a marginal summary that has been incorporated into the text and adapted to fit the metre.]

634 *Ibi tum*: cf. on 106.

635 *quor meam tibi*: this is elliptical: we have to supply both a noun to agree with *meam* and a verb. This kind of ellipse is characteristic of Terence, e.g. at *Eun.* 65 *Egon illam, quae illum, quae me, quae non?*, *Ad.* 539 *nusquam tu me*.

636 **charity begins at home**: lit. 'I'm my own nearest relative'. The expression has a proverbial ring, though the (mainly Greek) passages assembled at Otto, 289 do not have quite the same form of words.

637–38   The thought here may well (as commentators have noted) have
been influenced by Pl. *Epid*. 166–68: 'Most people who feel shame when
there's no point are deserted by their sense of shame when there is something
to be ashamed of, when they ought to feel shame'.

637   *si roges*: for the generalizing second singular in the subjunctive see
on 66.

638, 638a   *opust* = *opus est*: cf. on 102 *dictust*.

638   [*pudet*: Bentley proposed *pudent* on the grounds that the personal use
of *pudeo* was found in Early Latin, but the impersonal use is far commoner
in Terence. Victor 1993, 276 thinks the metre requires *pudent*, but the second
syllable of *pudet* would certainly be heavy in Plautus and could well be so
in Terence too; cf. Questa, 19, though he does not discuss this example. The
second syllable of *siet* at *HT* 1021 is another possible case.]

[K-L and subsequent editors read *hic ubi opus*, as does Questa, 440; the
manuscripts have *hic ubi opus est*. But Questa on p. 441 considers *hic ubi
opust* a serious possibility, and I see no reason not to read it.]

illi: the adverb, 'in those circumstances' (cf. OLD *illic²* 3; *illic* is *illi* with
the suffix *-ce*), contrasted with *hic*, 'in these circumstances' (OLD *hic²* 5); the
same contrast between *hic* and *illic* is found at 720. [The manuscripts here
have *illic*, but the reading *illi*, required by the metre, is attested by Donatus.]

638a   *uerentur*: cf. on 323 *uereor*.

639   *Adeon*: cf. on 315. Exactly as there, Charinus wonders whether to
approach Pamphilus directly. There Byrria replies to his question, here
Charinus imagines a reply.

640   **heap insults**: OLD *ingero* 2.b.

640 *promoueris*, **641** *fuero, gessero*: cf. on 381 *inuenerit*. For the intransitive
use of *promoueo* see OLD 5.

641   **I'll get it off my chest**: lit. 'I'll indulge my mind' (OLD *mos* 6).

642   Pamphilus, according to the text, showed no awareness of Charinus'
arrival at 625, and we cannot say whether he became aware of his presence
before addressing him here; that will be for the actor to decide. Davos takes
no part in the scene until addressed by Charinus at 665; he should probably
already be seen as trying to think up a new plan, a pose he resumes at 682.
Charinus has been entirely wrapped up in his own thoughts and has shown no
awareness that others are present until accosted by Pamphilus; cf. Men. *Samia*
641–57, where Parmenon has a 17-line monologue before being accosted by
Moschion (though in that case Moschion was aware of Parmenon's arrival),

and Frost 1988, 110 on the question of whether Moschion and Nikeratos are to respond in any way while witnessing Demeas' speech at *Sam.* 440–51.

show some care: OLD *respicio* 8; cf. 975 *me in tuis secundis respice*.

643 You've kept your word: OLD *soluo* 20 'To acquit oneself of, discharge, fulfil (a vow, promise, or sim.)', *fides*[1] 2 'A guarantee, promise, assurance'. Charinus is being sarcastic, an effect reinforced by the fact that after the first word there are no resolutions in this line and a high proportion of heavy syllables.

[**644 *Quid "tandem"?***: Victor 1999b, 270–71 finds these words absurd in Pamphilus' mouth and prefers to make them a continuation of Charinus' speech (without the quotation marks round *tandem*), but the absurdity he detects is not striking.]

644 *ducere*: cf. 180.

postulas: OLD *postulo* 4 'To look for as due, expect'.

646 Look what I suffer: lit. 'Alas! Wretched me!' (accusative of exclamation; cf. on 240).

spectaui: OLD *specto* 6.c 'to look at, judge (in a particular light, by a particular standard)'.

647–48 Charinus' reproach here combines the notions that his misfortune gives Pamphilus pleasure (*gaudium*, cf. 627–28) and that Pamphilus has led him on with false promises (cf. 629–38a), but without the accessory notion that Pamphilus' false promises resulted from embarrassment. (Cf. on 629 *Immo*.)

647 *Falsus*: OLD 2 'Deceived, in error, wrong, mistaken'.

solidum: OLD *solidus* 7 '(of qualities, conditions, etc.) Having substance, solid, real, lasting, etc.'.

[In place of *Non*, Victor 1999a argues for the reading *Numne*, found in one eleventh-century manuscript. However, this rare word is found 'in rhetorical questions to which a negative answer is assumed' (OLD) and is thus not appropriate here: the sense would require *parum* for *sat*. Nearly all manuscripts have *Nonne*, which also gives the wrong sense. On a separate point, the manuscripts have *satis*, but it is doubtful whether Terence would have allowed himself the proceleusmatic sequence *tibi satis* in a trochaic line (Laidlaw 1938, 42); Spengel changed *satis* to *sat*.]

648 *produceres*: OLD *produco* 7 'To lead on, entice, induce, bring'.

649 *uorser*: OLD *uerso* 12 (among passive uses) 'To be involved (in a condition), be subject (to), etc.'.

650 **this man**: Pamphilus points to Davos.

[*conflauit*: the manuscripts all have *confecit* (see OLD *conficio* 4 'To bring about, produce, cause', and cf. 674 with *nuptias*), a reading clearly known to Donatus as well. But Donatus also knew of a reading *conflauit* (see OLD *conflo* 3 'To bring about, occasion, cause (usu. something undesirable)'); since that gives a more colourful metaphor (either from blowing on a fire to make it burn, OLD 1, or from fusing or welding, OLD 5.b), I think it was more likely to be changed by a copyist at an early stage of transmission to the more banal *confecit* than the other way round. For the change from subjunctive *uorser* in 649 to indicative *conflauit* here cf. 272–73 *credidit ... habuerim*, 967–68 *sim nanctus ... euenit*, Pl. *Most.* 199, *Persa* 514–15, *Ps.* 929–30; there is no clear reason for the change in any of these cases. For the indicative in an indirect question cf. on 45 *dic quid est.*]

651 **carnufex**: cf. on 183 'villain', though here (combined with *meus*) it conveys that Davos has destroyed Pamphilus.

de te: these words are given extra emphasis by being placed before *si*.

653 **dudum**: 'just now'; cf. 591.

655 **Immo etiam**: for this combination, with *etiam* reinforcing *Immo*, see TLL V.2.953.31–65, H. Thesleff, *Yes and No in Plautus and Terence* (Helsinki, 1960), 65–66. It recurs at 673 and 708, though in those cases, as at Pl. *Ba.* 316, it forms a self-contained utterance.

just to show how little you know my troubles: lit. 'by which you know my troubles less', *quo* being the ablative of measure of difference (GL 403).

656 **they weren't planning this wedding for me**: Charinus already knows this from 359–70 (Drexler 1938, 54), but Pamphilus has received confirmation of it from Simo indoors. [Donatus attests a reading *haec nuptiae* and says that *haec* was the ancient form of the feminine nominative plural (*Legitur et 'haec nuptiae'; sic enim ueteres dixerunt*). K-L, Thierfelder, and Posani all read *haec* here and at 438 and 700, but (for no clear reason) not at 328. I accept the argument of F. Schmidt, *Hermes* 8 (1874), 478–87 that Terence probably wrote *hae* before a consonant.]

657 **postulabat**: cf. 644.

658 **forced into it by your own free will**: a bitterly contradictory remark.

Mane: OLD *maneo* 3 'To stay one's hand, have patience, wait'.

661 **insisting**: OLD *insto* 7.

[Nearly all manuscripts have *me esse ducturum*. Either *me* or *esse* must be omitted to make the line scan. The lemma in Donatus omits *esse*, as do p and perhaps the Oxyrhynchus papyrus, and most editors have followed this; cf. 383 *Dic te ducturum.*]

662   *adeo*: OLD *adeo²* 2 '(w. *dum, donec*, etc.) To the point of time (when)'.

663   The rapid changes of speaker in this line combine with the return of the musical accompaniment to convey Charinus' astonishment and Pamphilus' upset. [I do not know why Victor 1999b, 271 finds them 'needlessly complicated'.]

Quis homo istuc: understand *fecit*.

Interturbat: this must here mean 'He's messing things up', with *inter-* as an intensifying prefix, just as *perturbaui omnia* at 601 means 'I've messed everything up'. The only other occurrence of the word before the fourth century AD is at Pl. *Ba.* 733, where it means 'interrupt', like *obturbat* at 926 below. [Thierfelder marks *Interturbat* as an aside and takes it to mean 'interrupt' here too. But why should Pamphilus complain in an aside rather than reproaching Charinus directly? And does Charinus really interrupt anything Pamphilus was going to say? Some editors, perhaps rightly, have followed Bentley in deleting *Interturbat*, making the line an iambic senarius, and also making the next line a senarius by deleting *satis scio*, which is not essential for the meaning, since *scio* can easily be understood (as at Pl. *Ps.* 106–107 *nescio, / nisi quia futurumst*).]

664   *nisi*: OLD 5 '(after *nescio* and other general neg. statements, introducing a modifying cl.) Only, except that, etc.'.

[**665**   The hiatus at change of speaker after *Factum* is probably acceptable (so Questa, 336). Alternatively we can read *factumst*, which is found in one of the manuscripts used by Bentley. At 747 there is no hiatus at change of speaker before *Hem*.

A few manuscripts, including the Oxyrhynchus papyrus, have *o scelus* at the end of this line, as had already been conjectured by Spengel to avoid the hiatus between *Factum* and *Hem*. But Terence normally has vocative *scelus* without *o*, as at 317. (*Oh scelus* at *Ad.* 768 is probably an exclamation rather than a vocative.)]

666   *At*: used to introduce a curse (OLD *at¹* 11.b).

duint: an archaic subjunctive form, found in Terence particularly in imprecations and regularly at the end of the line. The form is discussed by de Melo, ch. 9.

667   *Eho*: cf. on 88.

coniectum in nuptias: cf. 602, 620. Understand *esse*.

669   Davos makes no attempt to explain to Charinus what the point had been of his advice to Pamphilus; he now knows that it has been overtaken by events, and it would be tedious for the theatre audience to listen to his explanation.

disappointed: OLD *decipio* 2. Note the balance of *Deceptus* with *defetigatus*.

Scio: Charinus continues his sarcastic use of this verb from 653 and 658. [K-L, Thierfelder, and Posani follow D¹ and L in giving this word to Pamphilus, and Victor 1999b, 271–72 gives it to Davos with concessive force, linked to *Hac non successit*. But it seems most natural as Charinus' response to Davos.]

670   *Hac*: understand *uia* from the second half of the line.

successit: OLD *succedo* 7 'To turn out well, succeed, prosper'; here impersonal.

[*adoriemur*: this reading is attested only by Donatus; the manuscripts all have *adgrediemur*. Both words can mean 'To come to grips with (a task, etc.), tackle, set to work on, attempt' (OLD *adorior* 3; cf. *aggredior* 4), and both can also have military connotations (OLD *adorior* 1 'To attack, assault, assail'; cf. *aggredior* 3). However, as at 650, Donatus has preserved the verb more likely to be changed by a copyist to the other, since the non-military use of *aggredior* is commoner.]

uia: OLD 9 'A means of achieving some object, expedient', or 10 'A way of proceeding, method'; but in combination with *adoriemur* the metaphor of a 'path' can still be felt.

671   *nisi si*: cf. 249.

processit: this means the same as 670 *successit* and is likewise impersonal. In this line it is one of four words starting with *p*, with *posse* following in the next line; the alliteration perhaps adds a touch of scorn as Davos asserts himself.

673   *Immo etiam*: cf. on 655; here understand *potest*. Pamphilus takes over Charinus' sarcasm.

675–77   Davos readily accepts the owner's view of what is required of a slave, and it is true that he exerts himself on Pamphilus' behalf at some personal risk (cf. 196–200, 210–14). Of course his actual owner is Simo, to whom he clearly feels no such loyalty. (Kruschwitz 2004, 49 sees a metatheatrical reference to traditional comic roles in this passage.)

676   *manibus pedibus*: cf. 161.

678 *praeter*: cf. on 436.

679 *succedit*: cf. 670 *successit*; here *quod ago* is the subject.

680 **Or if you prefer**: OLD *uel* 1.

missum face: OLD *mitto* 3.b 'to dismiss from office or service, discharge'. Given what Davos has just said about his duty as a slave, there could also (rather absurdly) be a hint of 3.a 'To allow to go free, release, set free'. For the periphrastic construction with *facio* see OLD *facio* 17.c, and cf. 833. *face* is the archaic form of the imperative, used for metrical convenience at the end of the line; cf. 821, 833 (but in mid-line at 712, if the manuscripts can be trusted).

681 **I'd like to do that**: Pamphilus probably means 'I'd like to be able to think of something better myself', though he could mean 'I'd like to pardon you' (cf. 678).

take me back to square one; lit. 'restore me to the position in which you found me (before I agreed to the marriage)', *in quem me accepisti locum* being short for *in eum locum in quo me accepisti*.

682 **iam hoc opust**: again at 704. *hoc* in this expression could be either ablative (cf. 32 *arte*) or nominative (OLD *opus*[1] 13.b).

Here you are: Davos draws attention to the pose that he is adopting. He does not mean that he has already thought of something; it is only at 704 that he finally does that. A scene in which a slave thinks up a new plan on stage is another stock scene of Latin comedy, like the 'running slave' scene (see on 338–74); cf. *HT* 668–78a, *Ph.* 553–60, Pl. *Mil.* 196–228. [*Em* is the reading of two manuscripts; the others have *Hem* (cf. on 116), but it would not be appropriate for Davos to react to what Pamphilus has just said with surprise, alarm, or any similar emotion. *Hem* can be used to introduce a train of thought, as at 359, but trying to think of a plan is rather different; it is not clear that the word could be used like English 'Hmm' to convey that someone is thinking.]

mane: cf. 658.

a noise from Glycerium's door: the sound of a door opening is often the first sign that a character is about to come on stage from indoors, a device inherited by the Latin playwrights from Greek drama. The noise is presumably made by a squeaking hinge or by the rattling of bolts. See Duckworth, 116–17 and (for Greek comedy) B. Bader, 'The Ψόφος of the House-Door in Greek New Comedy', *Antichthon* 5 (1971), 35–48.

a Glycerio: 'from Glycerium's house'; cf. 226 *ab ea*.

683 *Nil ad te*: understand *attinet*.

  Hem: here expressing impatience.

  nuncin = *nuncne*; cf. on 186 *hoccin*.

  inuentum dabo: a periphrasis for *inueniam*; see OLD *do*[1] 24.b '(w. pred.)
to render, make, cause to be', Bennett, I.438.

684–715 Mysis tells Pamphilus that Glycerium is keen to see him and
upset to have heard about his impending marriage. Pamphilus assures her
that he will stand by Glycerium and resist any pressure from his father.
(When he last saw Mysis she was on her way to fetch the midwife, but he
has more urgent things on his mind than to ask about the progress of the
birth.) Davos finally declares that he has thought of a new plan but does not
reveal what it is. He sends Pamphilus and Charinus away and tells Mysis to
wait outside while he goes into her house.

  The scene requires four speaking actors; cf. on 404–31. In this case
the presence of Charinus continues to complicate Davos' life. As noted
by Glücklich, 68, the complications of the situation are made clear to the
audience visually at this apparent climax of hopelessness.

  Metre: iambic septenarii, the longest run of this metre in the play. T.
J. Moore, 'Terence as Musical Innovator', in Kruschwitz, Ehlers, and
Felgentreu, 93–109, at p. 104 argues for a particular association of this
metre with Glycerium.

684 Mysis enters talking back into the house to reassure Glycerium; cf.
on 490–91.

  inuentum tibi curabo: similar to 683 *tibi inuentum dabo*; OLD *curo* 6.b
(a very rare use with this verb). Mysis gives an assurance to Glycerium, just
as Davos gave one to Pamphilus in the previous line.

[**685** *modo tu*: this is Bentley's correction of the unmetrical *tu modo* of the
manuscripts.]

686 *Ehem*: cf. 417; often used to express satisfaction at meeting someone,
and accepted here by editors as more appropriate than the *Hem* of the
manuscripts.

  good! I wanted to meet you: lit. 'you present yourself to me excellently'.

[*Quid id est?*: *id* has been added by editors for the sake of the metre. It is
missing from all manuscripts here, from nearly all in the same expression at
449, and from PC at 116.]

688 *Vah*: cf. on 589.

This trouble: Pamphilus probably refers to Glycerium's anxieties.

integrascit: this word is found only here.

689 *Sicin* = *Sicne*: cf. on 186 *hoccin*; the suffix *-ne* is regularly used in indignant statements couched in the accusative + infinitive (OLD *-ne* 1.c). [The manuscripts have the archaic infinitive *sollicitarier* (cf. on 203 *deludier*), making the line a solitary iambic octonarius. Since the line refers to Davos' responsibility for the state of affairs, that is perhaps not impossible: see the end of the note on 625–83. But editors except Marouzeau have preferred to maintain an unbroken run of iambic septenarii by reading *sollicitari*.]

690 she's heard about the preparations for my wedding: Mysis confirms at 692–93 that this is the case. At 300 Pamphilus urged her to say nothing to Glycerium about it, but it would be futile to speculate on whether it is Mysis or some other member of the household who has told her. Glycerium was in any case troubled by the fact that today was the day previously fixed for Pamphilus to marry Chremes' daughter (268–69); perhaps Mysis (who does know about the new wedding preparations) is here a little imprecise about what Glycerium knows. There is no reason to suppose that anyone in that house knows of the more recent development of Pamphilus' promise to his father.

691 *Quibus*: refers to *nuptias* in 690.

potuerat: cf. Pinkster, 441: 'The pluperfect indicative ... is found in the apodosis with conditional subordinate clauses in the subjunctive to underline that something had almost become reality.'

quiesci: cf. 598 *Quiescas*, 604 *quiessem*; here impersonal passive infinitive. The construction with the ablative (*Quibus*) is unusual; editors suggest it is analogous to the use of the ablative with *uacare* ('to take a rest from').

692 *Age*: OLD *ago* 24.a (*age* with another imperative) 'as a summons or exhortation to action'; here sarcastic.

edepol: see on 305.

694–701 Pamphilus' assurances are similar to those he gave Mysis at 270–98. He is doubtless trying to bolster his own confidence, and this time his speech has the additional function of reassuring Charinus that Pamphilus will on no account marry Chremes' daughter; at 702 he invites Charinus to comment on his performance.

694 *omnis*: for the lightening of the first syllable cf. on 391, though here it would be possible to lighten the first syllable of *adiuro* instead.

696   to hell with: OLD *ualeo* 3.d.

698   [I breathe again: the manuscripts make Charinus say this (cf. 333), and some editors have followed them. But his next remark at 702 suggests that Pamphilus' words have not made a strong impression on him. It was Bentley who gave this to Mysis. Her relief is, however, short-lived: cf. on 716–20.]

Apollo's oracle: the oracle of Apollo at Delphi on the Greek mainland was the most famous of all Greek oracles. It is also referred to at Pl. *Men.* 840 *Ecce, Apollo mihi ex oraclo imperat* ('Look, Apollo's giving orders to me from his oracle').

   atque = *quam*: OLD 15.

699   *ut ne*: cf. on 259.

   per me stetisse: OLD *sto* 22 '*per me*, etc., *stare* (w. *quominus*, *quin*, *ut*, *ne*), To be due to me, etc., my fault (that)'.

701   *in procliui*: OLD *procliuis* 2.b 'requiring no effort (i.e. helped by a downward slope), easy'.

702   *Forti's* = *Fortis es*: cf. 202 *locutu's*. *Fortis* as at 445, but perhaps with a hint of OLD 7 'courageous, brave, bold, resolute'. [The manuscripts give this to Charinus, as do some editors.]

703   [I know what I'm aiming for: I have accepted the suggestion of Victor 1993, 274–75 to read *coner* for the *conere* of the manuscripts and to give the whole line to Davos.]

   Hoc: emphatic first word in its sentence; Davos promises to get it right this time.

   effectum reddam: like 683 *inuentum dabo*; OLD *reddo* 17. Note the repetition of sound in *profecto effectum*.

704–706   Davos, having announced that he has thought of a plan, toys with both Charinus and Pamphilus, first telling Charinus that his new plan is exclusively for Pamphilus' benefit, then telling Pamphilus that he has no time to spare for explaining it to *him*. As a result the audience too have no idea what his plan is or what is in his mind when he goes indoors at 715. There is a similar effect, with an added wink at the audience, at Pl. *Ps.* 387–88: 'What are you going to do?' 'I'll make sure you know in good time. I don't want to go over it all twice: plays are quite long enough as it is.' Sharrock, 149 also refers to Pl. *Epid.* 376, 665, *Ps.* 720, and *Mil.* 810 for similar remarks; and cf. *HT* 335–36.

705   *Sat habeo*: cf. 335, again in Charinus' mouth, and 710 *satis habes*.

cedo: cf. 150. For its scansion here see Introduction, the end of section 8.5.

706   *ad agendum*: placed emphatically at the start of the line.

I've got time: OLD *uacuus* 11.

708–14   Davos and Charinus round off the scene with dialogue similar to that with which they rounded off the scene at 370–74 (Gilula, 89).

708   Where are you off to?: OLD *ago* 3 '(refl., also pass.) To betake oneself, come, go'.

uis dicam: cf. on 388 for *uolo* with the subjunctive.

Immo etiam: cf. on 655; here understand *abi*.

709   *incipit … initium*: the pleonasm underlines Davos' impatience.

me: ablative, as with *faciam* at 614.

710   you shameless man: striking rudeness from a slave to a citizen, emphasizing how much Charinus depends on Davos to help him. At 707 Davos has been rude to both Pamphilus and Charinus, but not with such an insulting term.

711   *quantum*: 'the amount by which'.

promoueo: only here in the sense 'put off', like 313 *prodat*, 329 *profer*.

712   *Ut ducam*: cf. 409 *ut possim*.

face: cf. on 680.

713   *Quid*: as in 322 *Quid ita?*.

Age: cf. on 310.

716–39   After five lines of reflection from Mysis, Davos reappears from her house carrying Glycerium's new-born baby and tells her to put it on the ground in front of Simo's house (we had better not ask what explaining he had to do to Pamphilus and Glycerium indoors). Before he can explain further to Mysis he sees Chremes returning to the stage from the right and decides on a change of tactic: he himself will go off to the left and immediately pretend to be arriving from that direction. Mysis is again left briefly on her own as Chremes approaches.

Metre: iambic senarii, the start of the last long run of this metre in the play (716–819). The onset of the new metre marks the start of an important new phase of the action.

716–20   Mysis has evidently not been entirely reassured by Pamphilus' words at 693–97, in spite of her 'I breathe again' at 698.

716   *Nilne*: cf. on 689 *Sicin*.

proprium: OLD *proprius* 1 'One's own absolutely or in perpetuity'; cf. 960 *propriae*.

Di uostram fidem: again at 744, in origin an appeal for the protection or help of the gods but effectively an intensifying exclamation, often expressing surprise or bewilderment, similar to 237 *Pro deum fidem*. The fuller form *Di obsecro uostram fidem* is found at Pl. *Amph.* 1130, *Cist.* 163, *Truc.* 805.

718   her husband: cf. on 295; here forming the climax of a tricolon.

721   *Mi homo*: 'found 4 times in Plautus [...] and 4 times in Terence, always in the mouths of women' (Adams, 71). 788 *mi senex* is another example of the characteristically feminine *mi*- address, again in the mouth of Mysis.

obsecro: used parenthetically as an interjection (OLD 3). Adams, 55–58 discusses its use as a marker of female speech in comedy, noting on p. 57 its combination here with *Mi homo*; he also notes on p. 56 that *obsecro* with a question or an imperative 'is used by [male] slaves in Terence only at *Andr.* 785, 861 [both times in the mouth of Davos]'. It is also used by young men, e.g. Pamphilus at 955. Barrios-Lech, 123–27 confirms Adams' findings.

722–23   *opus est tua ... exprompta malitia atque astutia*: for the construction of *opus est* with a noun in the ablative and a participle in agreement see OLD *opus*[1] 12.b; for *exprompta* see OLD *expromo* 2 'To bring into play, put to use'. [Most of the main manuscripts read *memoria*, which is supported by Donatus' commentary; a small number, supported by Eugraphius, read either *malitia* or *militia*. In the event, it is presence of mind rather than memory that Mysis will have to display in the scene that follows, and *malitia* and *astutia* make a natural pairing; see Lefèvre, 119–20, and cf. on line 164 'An evil mind, an evil heart'. It could be argued in defence of *memoria* that the plan in Davos' mind at this point might well have required Mysis to remember some instructions: he is about to expound it to her at 731–33 when he sees Chremes approaching and decides to abandon this plan altogether. But that would probably be too subtle a defence.]

724   *ocius*: OLD *ociter* 2.b '(compar. used much as positive)', found particularly with imperatives. At 731 it is probably a true comparative, as Davos is there impatient for Mysis to act more quickly.

725   *Obsecro*: cf. on 721.

726   the altar: see the note on the stage setting at the beginning of the play. Donatus here quotes Menander fr. 44 K-A. The text is very uncertain, but Menander appears to have specified that the 'foliage' consisted of branches of myrtle; as at 484, Terence has used a more general term than Menander.

728–29   Because ... so that: Davos changes the construction of his sentence. We might suspect that his real motivation for giving orders to Mysis is simply that he likes to be in charge.

[**728** *iurato*: Bentley's conjecture for the manuscripts' unmetrical *iusiurandum*; for the ablative participle with *opus sit* cf. 490, 523, 715. Donatus evidently had *iurandum* in his text; this would have to be understood as meaning *iusiurandum* (an unparalleled use) and as being in the nominative (cf. 337).]

729   adposisse: cf. 742 *posisti*, 763 *adposisti*. Ritschl, IV.118–21 argued that this was the only form of the perfect of *pono* and its compounds known to Plautus and Terence, although the manuscripts of Terence have only the later forms *adposuisse* etc. Here *adposisse* = *adposiuisse*.

730   scruple: OLD *religio* 2.

[*in te ... incessit*: Bentley doubted if *incedo* could be used thus in such a context, but see OLD *incedo* 6.b, TLL VII.1.857.18–20.]

Give it here: OLD cedo[2] 1.

732   Pro: cf. 237.

733   I must reject the first plan I was laying: of course we cannot say what this first plan was; at 507–16 Davos predicted that Simo would see the baby lying in front of one of the houses, but at 704 he appeared to have hit on a new plan altogether (cf. Introduction, pp. 24–25). The effect of his words here is to show his skill in improvising and adapting to a new situation, as Pseudolus does at Pl. *Ps.* 601–602, 667–86.

intenderam: OLD *intendo* 7.b 'to direct, aim (an action, policy, etc., against)'.

734   narres: cf. on 367.

from the right: i.e. from the audience's left; see the note on the stage setting at the start of the play.

736   ut quomque: cf. on 63, OLD *utcumque* 1 'In whatever manner or degree, according as'.

uide: OLD *uideo* 17 'To watch out, take care, see (that, or that ... not)'; cf. 456 *uidero*.

738   quod: accusative of respect.

opera opus sit: a common play on words, as at (e.g.) *Ph.* 563 *Numquid est quod opera mea uobis opus sit?*

[*ut* is Guyet's conjecture for the manuscripts' *aut*, which makes little sense.]

740–95 Davos stages a drama which enables him to let Chremes know that Glycerium has had a baby by Pamphilus and also that she claims to be an Athenian citizen. Mysis is an increasingly bewildered and enraged participant in his drama, since she has no idea why Davos openly denies Pamphilus' parenthood and Glycerium's citizenship – the main aim of which is to plant the ideas in Chremes' mind. Davos had asked her at 735–36 to 'make sure your story backs up mine'; in the event she is so perplexed that she cannot be said to carry out this instruction, but her presence is nonetheless crucial to the success of Davos' scheme. Davos uses her for his own purposes, of which she would of course be entirely supportive if she knew what he was doing. The scene has its desired effect on Chremes, who storms into Simo's house to break off his daughter's betrothal to Pamphilus; Davos is finally able to explain to Mysis what he has been up to.

At 751–53 Davos gets Mysis to move to one side so that he can whisper an instruction to her; at 760 he whispers a further instruction flatly contradicting the one he has just given her openly. This is similar to the tactic employed by Phaedria at *Eun.* 706–708, 712, 715; there the eunuch Dorus has little choice but to obey Phaedria's instructions, one of which is that he should deny what he knows to be the truth. Here, by contrast, Davos' aim is to get Mysis to declare the truth openly.

The scene is enlivened by asides from Davos to the audience (746), Chremes to the audience (750, 756, 766, 775, 780, 782), and Davos to Mysis (751–53, 760). But the bulk of it consists of dialogue between Davos and Mysis intended by Davos to be overheard by Chremes, who of course does not realize that Davos is aware of his presence. Play-acting scenes of this kind are discussed by Bain, 171–77. At p. 174 he mentions *Ph.* 348–77, where Phormio and Geta stage a quarrel to be overheard by Demipho; the difference between that and this scene is that both Phormio and Geta know what they are doing.

Davos' ploy is entirely successful. It is possible that Simo would again have won Chremes round on their next appearance if their dialogue had not been interrupted at 842 by news of a startling development, but at least for the time being Davos succeeds in putting Chremes off the idea of marrying his daughter to Pamphilus. Mysis' bewilderment adds considerably to the entertainment for the audience, and the presence of the baby is a striking visual element; the *Illustrated London News* chose its illustration of this scene in the Westminster School production for its front cover on Saturday,

December 30, 1871, and *The Graphic* also chose this scene to illustrate its review of another Westminster School production on December 18, 1880.

Did he but know it, Chremes is here on stage with his own grandson, and Glycerium is not only a citizen of Attica but his own daughter. Terence's audience are in no position to appreciate the irony of this situation, even if they may reasonably expect Glycerium's citizenship to be confirmed by the end of the play. If Menander's *Andria* had a divine prologue (see Introduction, p. 16), it may well have enabled his audience to enjoy the irony; cf. Act II of *Epitrepontes*, where Smikrines unwittingly arbitrates the fate of his baby grandson, who is on the stage, and it is widely believed by scholars that a prologue had made the situation clear to the audience. The presence of the baby on stage is also crucial in Act IV of that play, and *Samia* is another play by Menander in which a baby is an important focus of interest, visible to the audience at crucial points in Acts III and IV.
Metre: iambic senarii.

740 *Reuortor*: cf. on 404 *Reuiso* for a character's explanation of his reason for returning.
   quae opus fuere: cf. on 337.
741 **for her to be fetched**: cf. on 546.
742 *posisti*: cf. on 729.
   illic: the pronoun, formed of *ille* with the deictic suffix *-ce*; cf. on 458.
744 *homo*: OLD 3.b 'the person or individual concerned, the man in question', functioning essentially as a demonstrative pronoun (W. M. Lindsay, *Syntax of Plautus* [Oxford, 1907, repr. New York 1936], 45).
   Di uostram fidem: cf. 716.
745 *turbae, hominum*: partitive genitives with *quid* (cf. 600n.). *Quid hominum = Quot homines*; hence the plural verb *litigant*. cf. Pl. *Poen.* 619 *Sed quid huc tantum hominum incedunt?*
   illi: the adverb, as at 638, though here purely local in meaning. [As at 638, the manuscripts have *illic*, but *illi* is required by the metre and is attested by two manuscripts of Priscian III.187.]
747 *obsecro*: cf. on 721.
   hic me solam: understand *reliquisti*, a characteristic Terentian ellipse; cf. on 635.
   what's this performance?: in using the word *fabula* ('play') Davos purports to regard the baby lying on the ground as part of a piece of play-acting – as indeed it is, but Davos does not want Chremes (his intended

audience) to realize that he himself is behind it. OLD *fabula* 2 lists further occurrences of the expression *quae haec est fabula?* (add Pl. *Most*. 937), but the suggested translation 'what's that you say?' is not always appropriate: here and at Pl. *Persa* 788 it is not a response to anything said. For *fabula* see also 224, 925. Davos' pretended reaction here reminds us of Simo's reaction to the birth of this same baby at 469–77.

749   Satin = *Satisne*; cf. on 256 *Censen*.

750   I can't see anyone else here: Davos affects not to notice Chremes' presence until 783.

751   Au: an exclamation used by women to express consternation or astonishment; see Adams, 54. Again in Mysis' mouth at 781.

753   faxis: an old subjunctive form of *facio*, rarer in Terence than in Plautus, formed like the future *faxo* at 854 by adding *s* to the stem. There is a full discussion in de Melo, ch. 7 ('The Sigmatic Subjunctive in Archaic Latin'). It is not clear why Terence here makes Davos use a form which was obsolescent already by the time of Plautus.

754   Are you insulting me?: this is probably in response to 752 'You're crazy'.

   Speak up: Some editors have followed Donatus in taking this to be a further instruction given aside.

   A nobis: cf. on 226 *ab ea*.

756   meretrix: given extra force by coming at the end of its sentence, separated from *mulier*, and at the beginning of a new line. [Line 756 as transmitted in the manuscripts, with *Ab Andriast ancilla haec*, is too long: either *meretrix* or *ancilla* must be deleted to make it scan. Most editors delete *ancilla*, which perhaps crept in as a reminiscence of 461. *meretrix* certainly has more point and perhaps serves to make Chremes aware of the baby's origin, which he was wondering about at 750; hence his immediately following remark.] There is of course no reason to suppose that Glycerium has in fact ever worked as a *meretrix*, as Chrysis had done; indeed Pamphilus' words at 274–75 and those of Chrysis reported at 286–88 make it clear that she has not.

757–58   the sort of people you can play tricks on: Davos echoes the complaints of Simo against himself at 492–93.

   in quibus: only here in surviving Latin is *illudo* found with *in* + ablative of the person tricked or mocked. Elsewhere in Terence it has the accusative (*HT* 741 *Dignam me putas quam inludas?*, *Ph*. 915) or *in* + accusative (*Eun*. 942). Later the dative is also found.

759   adeo: cf. on 440.

760 *caue*: cf. on 403.

quoquam: 'To any place, in any direction, anywhere' (OLD).

excessis: another sigmatic subjunctive; cf. on 753 *faxis*.

761 Damn and blast you: lit. 'May the gods tear you up by the roots'; again at *HT* 589.

763 *Cedo*: as at 150.

quoium: OLD *cuius*[2] 'Of whom, whose?'; again at 932.

adposisti: cf. on 729.

764 *Mitte*: OLD *mitto* 5 'To pay no heed to, pass over, disregard, say nothing of'.

765 *Quoius*: cf. on 336.

766 all along: Chremes forgets that the wedding had been his idea in the first place (cf. 99–101).

767 *animaduortendum*: 'deserving punishment' (OLD *animaduerto* 8). This line is remarkable for having no canonical break in the middle of it, perhaps giving extra emphasis to Davos' simulated outrage. [The line was omitted by the first hand in D and L, perhaps a sign that at some stage of transmission a copyist's eye jumped from *nuptias* at the end of the previous line to *clamitas* at the end of this, as suggested by K-L in their apparatus.]

768 *Quem*: the relative pronoun; understand *puer* as its antecedent.

769 *Verum*: understand *est*.

Canthara: presumably another slave in Glycerium's household, mentioned only here. A female slave of this name appears in *Adelphoe*, and another is addressed offstage at Pl. *Epid.* 567. The name evokes *cantharus*, a large drinking vessel, and thus suggests that Canthara is a suitable colleague for the boozer Archylis (cf. 232).

with a bundle stuffed under her cloak: cf. on 507 and 515.

770 *pol*: cf. on 229; again in Mysis' mouth at 778, 788, 790, 803, 817.

[*gratiam* is the reading of manuscripts D and p; the others have the plural *gratias*. The singular is idiomatic with *habeo*, as at 42, *Hec.* 346, 653 (both with *dis*), and elsewhere; the plural is idiomatic with *ago*. *Ph.* 894 has *Dis magnas merito gratias habeo atque ago*, where the solemnity of the expression and the addition of *atque ago* may account for the use of the plural. The idiom is discussed by P. Langen, *Beiträge zur Kritik und Erklärung des Plautus* (Leipzig, 1880), 11–15.]

771 respectable women: literally, 'women of free birth', whose evidence will count for something against Davos' wild allegations. We cannot say who these women were, or how they came to be in Glycerium's house; the only woman we have seen coming or going is the midwife. Donatus notes that the point of Mysis' remark is that the evidence of free-born witnesses will outweigh that of a slave (lit. 'free-born evidence against a slave', *testimonia libera contra seruum*), and he adds: 'this is Terence's own way of putting it, since he said this in accordance with Roman custom' (*et hoc proprium Terentii est, nam de Romano more hoc dixit*). He perhaps has in mind that women at Athens did not appear as witnesses in court, whereas women at Rome could do so at least in some circumstances. But women at Athens could in fact make deposed statements, and male relatives could present their evidence (Scafuro, 49 n. 81). Some commentators have thought that Donatus was referring to a Roman rule requiring between five and ten free-born women to be present to establish the legitimate birth of a child (*Digest* 25.4.1.10); but that was required only as part of a rather elaborate procedure to be followed when a woman whose husband had died claimed to be pregnant. Others have thought it relevant that the evidence of slaves was more readily admitted in Athenian than in Roman courts, but the distinction between Athenian and Roman practice is not clear-cut, and in the Athenian context it is not implausible that Mysis should think the evidence of free-born women will be particularly helpful. In both societies the evidence of slaves was admissible only when obtained under torture, so Mysis has good reason to be grateful to the gods if she will not be required to undergo that; but that seems unlikely to be the primary meaning of her remark. Whatever supposed difference between Athens and Rome Donatus had in mind, he seems to have been missing the point. However, the presence of the women remains mysterious (it does not seem likely that Mysis has simply invented them), and perhaps the true explanation of Donatus' words remains to be found.

772 *Ne*: cf. on 324.

quoius: cf. on 336.

773–74, 780–81 Davos quotes the alleged thoughts of those in Glycerium's household; cf. the start of the note on 151–53.

775 *ut tu sis sciens*: cf. on 508.

777 *prouoluam … peruoluam*: the variation in prefix enables Davos to elaborate his grotesque threat.

778 *Tu pol homo*: *Tu homo* is a contemptuous form of address, here and elsewhere; cf. *HT* 1003; *Ad.* 111 *tu homo adigis me ad insaniam*.

This seems an appropriate point for Mysis to pick the baby up, in response to Davos' threat, though there is no indication in the text of her doing so. She presumably carries it indoors at 818. Wherever it is on Crito's entry at 796, he takes no notice of it.

778–79   One trick follows another: OLD *trudo* 4 '(of something following in temporal, etc., sequence) To drive on'.

780   a citizen of Attica: see on 221. At 220–25 Davos expressed great scepticism about this claim. Ostensibly he does so again here, calling it a *fallacia* at 778 just as he did at 220. But the important thing for his immediate purpose is that Chremes should get to hear of it; it is the detail most calculated to discourage him from allowing Pamphilus to marry his daughter.

780–81   forced by the laws to marry her: it is likely that an Athenian boy who had got a citizen girl pregnant could be threatened with serious consequences (both legal and extra-legal) by her family if he did not agree to marry her (and if she were known to her family, as Glycerium is not at this stage); 'forced by the laws' is a loose way of conveying this. Cf. Scafuro, 241–43, also discussing similar remarks at Pl. *Aul.* 793, Ter. *Ad.* 490. There is in fact very little evidence for relevant laws at Athens, still less for Rome: full discussion in Scafuro, 193–231, with summary at 229–31.

781   *Au obsecro*: cf. on 751, 721; the combination is frequent, and 'obviously a female phrase' (Adams, 54). [The manuscripts have *Eho*; *Au* was restored by K-L from Donatus.]

783   *Quis hic loquitur?*: cf. on 267; as Bain, 159 says, 'this passage is a piece of 'play acting', but it exploits the same convention'.

784   *Anne*: this form for *An*, used before a vowel, was restored here by Bentley for the sake of the metre; it comes again at 851.

785   *obsecro*: cf. on 721.

785–86   *Em scelera*: cf. 604 *Em astutias*; for *Em* at the end of the line cf. on 248. [*Em* is clearly required here for the manuscripts' *Hem*. Luck, 67–68 claims that *Em scelera* must come at the start of 786, like *Em astutias* at the start of 604, and adjusts the text of 786 to make that possible. Victor 1993, 275, not following Luck, suggests *Hanc oportet iam cruciatum hinc abripi* (with *cruciatum* as the supine) for *Hanc iam oportet in cruciatum hinc abripi. in* is omitted or deleted by a corrector in some manuscripts, but Victor gives no reason for preferring *cruciatum* to be the supine rather than the noun; it is clearly the noun at *Hec.* 773 and nineteen times in Plautus.]

786   to be tortured: as elsewhere, the physical punishment of slaves is taken for granted, even by another slave.

787   This is the man: i.e. 'the man we were talking about' (at 773–74). Mysis is perhaps too flustered and confused to grasp whom Davos means; at any rate he spells it out for her at 792 when Chremes has left the stage. (He had already made it clear at 732, but he was there perhaps talking to himself as much as to Mysis, and Mysis was already starting to feel bewildered.)

Non ... credas: for *Ne ... credas*; cf. Pinkster, 682–83: this use of *Non* is rare in Early and Classical Latin but came to be the norm later. [Three manuscripts have *Non ... credes*, and Priscian II.206 quotes this passage with *Ne ... credas*.]

788   *mi senex*: cf. on 721 *Mi homo*.

789   *attigas*: an old form for *attingas*, restored here for the sake of the metre; the manuscripts have *attingas*. This and related forms are discussed by de Melo, ch. 10 ('The Type *attigās* in Archaic Latin'); they were obsolescent already by the time of Plautus, but de Melo suggests that *attigas* in prohibitions is 'stylistically neutral' (p. 298).

790   *sceleste*: a common term of abuse in Plautus and Terence.

Si pol Glycerio non omnia haec: Davos interrupts Mysis before she can add the verb or the main clause.

793   You should have warned me: Davos had in fact identified Chremes on his arrival (cf. on 787), but Mysis probably refers not so much to that as to his extraordinary behaviour in the subsequent scene. Davos could point out that he had not had time to explain everything to her, and that is perhaps implied in his response at 794–95 (see next note), though he seems there rather to suggest his control of the situation.

794   whether you do everything instinctively and naturally or according to a careful plan: 'you do' is a generalizing second person. Davos is probably suggesting that he deliberately concealed his aims from Mysis so that her reactions would be more effective (cf. Bain, 174: 'her bewilderment ensures that she gives a more authentic performance'), though it is not impossible that he has his own performance in mind (since Chremes' unexpected arrival had forced him to make a rapid adjustment to his plans). In either case, see Introduction, section 6.6, p. 29.

According to Donatus, Terence has here turned into a question what had been a statement in Menander (*haec sententia a Terentio* ἐρωτηματικῶς *prolata est, quam Menander* ἐπιδεικτικῶς *posuit*). He does not say how faithfully Terence has otherwise followed Menander in this scene.

796–819 Davos and Mysis are still on stage when an entirely new character enters, looking for Chrysis' house; he has heard of her death and quickly reveals himself to be her closest surviving relative. Mysis recognizes him as Chrysis' cousin Crito, and he is disappointed to learn that Glycerium has not yet discovered her family. All go into her house, leaving the stage empty for the first time since 171. The effect of Crito's entry is thus similar to several scenes in Menander where there is a striking new development shortly before the end of an act; such scenes are discussed by Handley, 11–18. The audience may well guess that Crito's arrival will lead to a satisfactory outcome for Glycerium and Pamphilus, but they cannot tell how this will be achieved; there is no reason to think that Crito himself is in a position to help Glycerium find her family.

Metre: iambic senarii. Although Crito's arrival is totally unexpected, it is not marked by a change of metre; the resumption of musical accompaniment is saved for the lively altercation at 820ff.

797 to acquire wealth here by less respectable means: contrast Simo's account at 70–79. Crito, her closest relative, gives no hint that Chrysis had 'been forced to leave home by poverty, and because her relatives had failed to look after her' (70–72) or that her drift into prostitution had been gradual (74–79). We could of course choose to believe Crito rather than Simo, but Crito is the one who has an interest in presenting the story the way he does. Evidently word has reached Andros that Chrysis had done well for herself (cf. on 123 'the accompanying slave-girls'); that is why Crito has thought it worth his while to come to Athens to collect her property.

ditias = *diuitias*, restored here and elsewhere in Terence (*HT* 194, 527) for the sake of the metre; the manuscripts have the full form every time.

[**798 *in patria honeste***: this is the reading of the main manuscripts. Some later manuscripts have *honeste in patria* (see Victor 2007, 4), a reading also found in two ancient grammarians and preferred by some editors.]

799 *ea ... bona*: it seems to have been idiomatic to use *ea* rather than *eius* in this context; cf. *Hec.* 172 *ea ad hos redibat lege hereditas*, where no property has previously been mentioned but only the relative who had died.

reverted: OLD *redeo* 12.

by law: this makes it clear that Crito is Chrysis' closest surviving relative; the laws of Athens and Rome (see MacDowell, 98–99; F. Schulz, *Classical Roman Law* (Oxford, 1951), 222–25) are assumed, no doubt correctly, to obtain on Andros as well.

803   *Itan Chrysis?*: Crito avoids using a verb to refer to Chrysis' death.

***Hem*:** the tone of this at this point has been debated, but Cicero's usage at *ad Fam.* XIV.2.2 supports Donatus' interpretation of it as representing a groan or some such expression of grief (*magis gemitu significat quod minus dixerat*, 'he conveys more strongly with his groan what he had understated in words'): Cicero, writing in exile to his wife at Rome, says *Hem, mea lux, meum desiderium, unde omnes opem petere solebant! Te nunc, mea Terentia, sic uexari, sic iacere in lacrimis et sordibus!* ('What, light of my life, the one I long for, the one to whom everyone used to turn for help? To think that you, my darling Terentia, are now being harassed like this, that you are reduced like this to tears and mourning!'). Luck, 42 interprets *Hem* as a noise conveying to Mysis that Crito wishes her to complete his sentence for him, and Victor 1999b, 272–73 suggests that *Hem* should be given to Mysis, conveying that 'she is momentarily taken aback when Crito raises the subject of her mistress' death'; more plausibly, Müller, 122 argues that *Hem* is more flexible than Luck allows. There is no doubt a touch of hypocrisy on Crito's part here: he expressed no sympathy for Chrysis at 796–99, and 807–16 below show that he is concerned about the impression that he will make.

804   *Quid uos? Quo pacto hic? Satine recte?*: a succession of elliptical questions for which it is easy enough to supply the verbs. cf. on 635, 747 *hic me solam. Satine* = *Satisne*; cf. 749 *Satin*.

So-so: OLD *sic* 11.c 'expr. mediocrity'; so at *HT* 458 and perhaps *Ph.* 145. Donatus takes *Sic* thus, though some editors link it closely with *ut quimus*.

805   as they say: Mysis quotes a proverbial expression found in both Greek and Latin; cf. Otto, 285, Headlam-Knox on Herodas 2.9, and the similar remark of Byrria at 305–306. One formulation of the proverb as an iambic trimeter has been assigned by some scholars to Menander's *Andria* as the original of this passage: ζῶμεν γὰρ οὐχ ὡς θέλομεν, ἀλλ᾽ ὡς δυνάμεθα ('for we live not as we wish to but as we can', Menander fr. *47 K-A).

***quando*:** OLD 3 'In view of the fact that, seeing that, since, as'.

806–807   It is not explained why Glycerium has failed to find her parents. She knows that her name was originally Pasibula (cf. 946), and presumably also the details about her uncle that Crito knows at 928–32, and she has been in Athens for at least nine months and perhaps as much as three years (cf. on 70). But her pregnancy has doubtless made it hard for her to seek out her family in recent months: an Athenian citizen family would be unlikely to welcome a pregnant girl turning up out of the blue and claiming to be a family member.

807   an unlucky landfall for me: Crito has just arrived from Andros. The translation assumes the nautical sense of *appello* (cf. on 1 *animum ... adpulit*), though Maltby 1979, 138–39 at 139 n. 27 disputes this on the ground that the verb here has *me*, not *nauem*, as its object. He suggests that *me appuli*, 'like *tetulissem pedem* in the next line, is simply an elevated way of saying "I came"'; he sees these expressions, together with the one-word ablative absolute *auspicato* and the fullness of expression in 809 *dictast ... atque habitast*, as contributing to the characterization of Crito.

808   *pol*: cf. on 229; here unusually in the mouth of a man. As at 320 and 866, it is not clear that any particular effect is achieved by giving a man a characteristically feminine oath.

   tetulissem pedem: according to Donatus, 'critics note that *tetulissem pedem* is too lofty for the style of comedy' (*critici adnotant altius esse charactere comico "tetulissem pedem"*). The critics probably had in mind the reduplicated form *tetulissem* (for *tulissem*), found in Terence only here and at 832, though it is standard in Plautus. Karakasis, 95–96 suggests that the circumlocution *pedem ferre* is also high-flown; see also Maltby cited on 807.

809   She was always said and believed to be her sister: the circumstances of Glycerium's arrival on Andros were well known there (cf. 930–31 'Many others on Andros heard the same story'), but that does not diminish the truth of what Crito says here or the weakness of the position he finds himself in *de facto*.

   eius: for the scansion with a light first syllable see on 93.

810   *illius*: this form is regularly disyllabic in Plautus and Terence; see Lindsay 1922, 64–70, Questa, 72.

810–12   I'm a stranger ... to court: an outsider was bound to be at a disadvantage in an ancient court. Cf. on 817 for the meaning of *hospes*. Admittedly Glycerium too counts as an outsider at this stage, but Crito immediately goes on to deal with that point. [I cannot see why Victor 1993, 275–76 prefers the reading *me hospite* (found in manuscripts A and G) to *me hospitem*.]

811   *id*: taking up *me hospitem litis sequi*. [There is some manuscript evidence for *hic* ('here') in place of *id*; that provides a more straightforward construction and is accepted by some editors.]

812 **Besides**: OLD *simul* 5.b.

[**814** *grandicula*: the manuscripts have *grandiuscula*, which became the commoner diminutive form by the time of St Augustine but is here unmetrical; *grandicula* (a form found otherwise only at Pl. *Poen.* 481 in Early or Classical Latin) is found in an early medieval glossary, cited as *gl.I* in the apparatus of K-L and Posani.]

815 **swindler**: Crito uses the Greek-derived word *sycophanta* (from συκοφάντης, of which only the ending has been Latinized), which had evidently become embedded in Latin, at least in the world of the comic theatre (with some fifteen occurrences in Plautus), and appears at *HT* 38 in a list of stock comic characters. Crito's fear is realized at 919, where Simo uses the word against him, though not in the context that he foresees here.

817 **What an excellent stranger you are**: Spengel was surely right to give these words to Davos. *hospes* in this play always means 'stranger' (OLD *hospes*[1] 4; cf. 810, 843, 914, all referring to Crito); it would be a very odd word for Mysis to use of Crito, whom she knows well.

antiquom: OLD *antiquum* 'An old or long-established practice'; cf. Pl. *Most.* 789 *Antiquom obtines hoc tuom, tardus ut sis*.

obtines: OLD *obtineo* 2 'To maintain, keep up, persist in (an action, state, attitude, practice, etc.)'.

818 *quando*: as at 805.

Maxume: OLD *maxime* 7 '(colloq., as a reply) By all means, certainly'.

819 *nolo ... uideat*: see OLD *nolo* 2.b for *nolo* with the subjunctive.

the old man: Simo. Davos in fact gets out of the way with little time to spare; there is no need for a long pause before Simo enters with Chremes.

820–41 Just as the last act of Menander's *Dyskolos* opens with a lively altercation between two characters who enter in mid-conversation, so here the closing sequence of scenes is initiated by the entry of Chremes and Simo in mid-argument: Chremes has told Simo what he saw and heard at 740–89, but Simo is convinced that that whole scene had been staged to deter Chremes from marrying his daughter to Pamphilus (as indeed it had) and urges Chremes to let the wedding go ahead as planned. The scene is thus in some ways a reenactment of the earlier confrontation between the two fathers at 533–74, though this time it is interrupted by the new development at 842.

Metre: trochaic septenarii, the new metre with musical accompaniment marking both the start of a new sequence of scenes and the liveliness of the dispute between the two old men.

820 made enough of a test: OLD *specto* 6.b.

821 *face*: cf. on 680.

822 *inlusi*: OLD *illudo* 3 'To fool or trifle away'.

823 *enim*: cf. on 503.

now more than ever: see OLD *maxime* 6.b for this use of *nunc quom maxume* (= *nunc cum maxime*). [The manuscripts have *quam maxume* ('as much as possible', OLD *maxime* 1.b), which is less appropriate; Donatus preserves the better reading.]

[*postulo atque oro*: the major manuscripts have *oro atque postulo*, resulting in a breach of Bentley-Luchs' Law at the end of the line (see Introduction, section 8.4). The reading *postulo atque oro*, long accepted by editors, has been found in an eleventh-century manuscript: see Victor, 1999a, 81 n. 6.]

824 *initum*: OLD *ineo* 7 'To embark on, begin (an activity, undertaking)'.

825 *prae studio*: OLD *prae*^{2} 5 'In the face of, under the pressure of'.

[*lubes*: this text is proposed by Victor 1993, 276 to account for the fact that Donatus (at least in some of his manuscripts) says that *iubes* was known as a reading; one manuscript of Donatus has *iubet*, on the strength of which K-L and Thierfelder read *lubet* in Terence's text here. All manuscripts of Terence have *cupis* (the reading accepted by most editors), and the lemma in Donatus has *uelis*. Victor's reading restores a personal use of the verb found occasionally in Plautus and in manuscript A of Terence at *HT* 643; it is the reading most likely to have provoked explanatory glosses which would then have crept into the text as readings in their own right.]

827 *remittas*: OLD *remitto* 10.c '(w. inf.) to leave off'.

830 *ut*: repeated from 828 for clarity, because so much text has intervened.

831 The repetition and rhyme in *eius labore atque eius dolore*, and the position of *tuo* at the end of the line in contrast with *eius* at its beginning, make a punchy climax to Chremes' sentence, which was already notable for the balanced structure of 829 and the near-pleonasm of *seditionem* and *incertas nuptias* in 830. Shipp thinks the point of *incertas* is that the marriage might have to be annulled in view of the claim that Glycerium is a citizen at 780–81; but Chremes is here talking about a time before he had heard that, which he introduces as a new factor at 833.

832 *tetulit*: cf. on 808 *tetulissem*. As with Crito there, Maltby 1979,

139 sees this and the features discussed in 831n. as contributing to the characterization of Chremes.

fert: feras: the same verb in two different senses, respectively OLD 31 '(of circumstances, etc.) To prompt, suggest' and 20 'To put up with, endure, bear'.

833   *missos face*: cf. on 680.

834   *Per ego te deos oro*: for the word order cf. on 289. Simo is as insistent in pleading with Chremes here as he was at 538.

ut ne: cf. on 259.

animum inducas: see OLD *induco* 12.a on *animum induco* with infinitive 'To bring or prevail on oneself or find it in one (to do something)'; slightly different with accusative and infinitive at 572, 883.

836   because of the wedding: OLD *gratia* 7.

837   once they've been deprived of that motive: i.e. 'once they can see that they have failed to prevent the marriage'.

838   I know: Simo cannot possibly know this, which goes beyond what Davos had predicted to him at 507 and appears to be communicated to him here for the first time by Chremes. But he likes to give the impression that he is fully informed (cf. on 552), and he wants to sweep Chremes' objections aside. I do not know why some commentators have seen Simo as being sarcastic (Shipp) or speaking ironically (Kauer, followed by Barsby); if they are right, it cannot be the truth of Chremes' report that Simo doubts but the wisdom of Chremes' accepting what he has seen at face value.

At: cf. on 226–27 *ut* for the monosyllable at the end of a line preceded by an elision; again at 840 with *et*. [The word was moved here from the start of the next line by K-L for the sake of the metre; many editors omit it altogether, but it appropriately adds emphasis to Chremes' point.]

839   they weren't acting: lit. 'with a genuine expression'.

neither of them had realized I was present: Chremes had tried to catch Mysis' attention at 742–43, but he had no reason to think that she knew who he was at that stage or that she was putting on an act for his benefit.

[*praesenserant*: one would normally expect the singular *praesenserat* after *neuter* as the subject, but the plural is a natural colloquialism, introduced here by K-L because a note in manuscript D says that it was attested by Donatus, even though it is not in Donatus' commentary in its current form, nor in the manuscripts of Terence; K-L cite Pl. *Men.* 785 *neuter ad me iretis* as a parallel using the second person plural, though in that context we should not have expected the second person singular. The fact that D has the impossible *praesenseram* may be a clue to the correctness of K-L's reading, and it is easy to suppose that the plural was changed to the singular at an early stage of transmission.]

840 Davos told me earlier that the women would do this: by 'would do this' Simo means 'would bring a baby out in front of the house', which is what Davos predicted to him at 507. Evidently Chremes had told Simo something of what he had witnessed before they reached the stage at 820.

[*et*: most manuscripts have this at the start of the next line, which is possible metrically, but A appears not to have done, and Terence likes to have such a word at the end of a line; cf. on 226–27 *ut*.]

841 *nescio qui* = *nescio quomodo* (cf. on 6 *qui*), for which meaning 'somehow or other' see OLD *nescio* 7.c.

[*qui id*: a correction of the manuscripts' *quid*, required for the sense.]

hodie: see on 196.

ac uolui: 'as I wanted to'; cf. OLD *atque* 14. As Shipp explains, it is as if Chremes had in mind something like *aliter feci ac uolui*.

842–65 No sooner has he been named by Simo than Davos enters talking back to Glycerium and Mysis inside the house (cf. on 490–91). Simo is astonished to see him coming from there and appalled at 851 to learn that Pamphilus is there too. When Davos tells him that an old man has turned up who claims to know that Glycerium is an Athenian citizen, Simo orders another slave, Dromo, to carry him indoors and tie him up; Dromo takes Davos into Simo's house.

This and Pl. *Capt.* 721–50 and 1028 are the only places in Roman comedy where a slave is actually sent off for punishment; elsewhere punishments are regularly threatened and feared (cf. on 179, 199) but never carried out, though various beatings and brutal inquisitions do take place on- and off-stage in Plautus (see Richlin, 90–93). At Pl. *Most.* 1094 the slave Tranio comes close to being caught and punished, but he takes refuge at the on-stage altar; at 1114 his master threatens to pile up brushwood round him and set fire to it to force him to move, but at the very end of the play he is persuaded to let Tranio off. On the similar scene in Menander's *Perinthia* see Introduction, p. 20.

By making Dromo utter a few words in 861–62 Terence requires four speaking actors to be on stage at that point. It is a reasonable guess that Menander made Dromo a non-speaking extra, if Terence is otherwise following him faithfully; so Lowe, 160. In a three-actor company (with a silent Dromo) the actor playing Davos would reappear from Glycerium's house as Pamphilus at 872 after being carried into Simo's house at 865; but Terence was not writing for a three-actor company.

Metre: trochaic septenarii to 860, continuing from the previous scene, then, to mark the appearance of Dromo from Simo's house, four lines of iambic octonarii interrupted by one trochaic septenarius at 864 (though see the note there). Cf. Moore 2013, 109 on the last five lines: 'The echo of the meter associated with Davos' deception throughout the play [cf. on 575–604] increases the irony of the fact that he is actually telling the truth here, but Simo does not believe him. One trochaic septenarius interrupts the iambic octonarii, as Simo cuts Davos' arguments short musically as well as in content.' Moore 2012, 128 suggests that Dromo dances during these lines, but that is fanciful.

842–43   *impero* and *praesidio* could both have military connotations ('I command' and 'garrison' respectively), evoking the way in which some of Plautus' slaves represent their deceptive schemes as a military campaign (see Fraenkel, 48–49, 159–65), but they do not inevitably do so, and Davos is not here talking about trickery. If there is an echo of Plautine imagery, it is very faint. On the other hand, 'put your trust in me' is the language of the characteristically self-confident slave.

842   *Animo ... otioso*: ablative of quality (GL 400, Pinkster, 782–83).

   There's Davos for you: the fact that Davos enters from Glycerium's house offering words of comfort to those inside suggests that he is in league with that household; hence Simo's astonishment in the next line and his cross-examination of Davos at 849–50. Chremes himself has no reason to expect Davos to support Glycerium, after seeing how he treated Mysis at 747–87 (and cf. 838), but he can see at a glance that Simo was wrong to put any trust in Davos, as his most recent remark at 840 suggests that he did.

   Em Dauom: cf. on 604 *Em astutias*.

843   *Quid illud malist?*: an expression of astonishment found again e.g. at *Eun.* 547.

844   *hominem, aduentum, tempus*: for the tricolon cf. on 18 *Naeuium, Plautum, Ennium*.

   Scelus; cf. on 317 'you villain'.

845   **has reached shallow waters**: similar in effect to 'safe in harbour' at 480, though shallows and harbours are different things; as Shipp says, the

metaphor here is from swimming rather than sailing. The same image at Pl.
Aul. 803 *Haec propemodum iam esse in uado salutis res uidetur.*
    Cesso adloqui?: cf. on 343.
846   **bone uir**: cf. 616.
    Ehem: cf. 417.
    noster: OLD 4 '(attached to the name of a friend or relative) Our (my)
dear –; (often in addresses)'. Davos tries to be ingratiating.
847   **Everything's ready now indoors**: Davos tries to maintain the
pretence that he has been actively engaged in making preparations for
Pamphilus' wedding to Chremes' daughter in Simo's house, as he had been
instructed to do at 523; cf. also 581. After his exchange with Chremes at
783–89 he is doubtless (once again) confident that the wedding is no longer
planned; but he is in any case trying to talk his way out of an embarrassing
situation, having just been seen coming out of Glycerium's house.
848   **Fetch the bride whenever you want**: cf. on 546.
    sane: OLD 4 '(qualifying adjs. or advs.) Very, decidedly, quite'.
849   **Etiam**: OLD 2 '(w. pres. ind., expr. an impatient command) Will
you…!' The idiom is discussed by Barrios-Lech, 82–83. [Donatus preserves
the indicative; the manuscripts have the imperative *responde*.]
    Yes: OLD *ita* 11.
850   **ergo**: OLD *ergo*[2] 3.c '(used in echoing a word or idea) indeed, yes'.
    [*introiui*: K-L and some other editors accept *introii* from the main
manuscripts, but that requires a hiatus after *modo*. Victor 1993, 277 proposes
Iui modo intro for *Modo introii*, but it is simpler to change *introii* to *introiui*
(a reading found by Bentley in one Cambridge manuscript), with the first
syllable lightened by iambic shortening and *-oi-* scanning as one short and
one long vowel. Bentley claimed that Terence always treated *introeo* as
two words, with elision of the final vowel of *intro* (as at 363 and 590), but
Hec. 332 and 787 are possible counter-examples; in the latter case K-L and
Goldberg 2013 also accept lightening of the first syllable of the verb. Plautus
has the scansion of *-oi-* suggested here at *Ba.* 907 *introibis* and *Trin.* 10
introierit.]
851   **together with your son**: this is not strictly true, but it is perhaps (as
Donatus suggests) an attempt by Davos to shift the responsibility on to
Pamphilus, while also conveniently letting Simo know where Pamphilus is.
    Anne: cf. 784.
852   **didn't you say they'd broken up**: cf. on 552.

carnufex: cf. on 183.

853 ***Quid illum censes?***: understand *hic esse*. For *quid* meaning 'why' see OLD *quis*[1] 16.

He's having a row with her: cf. Charinus' similarly sarcastic remark at 653–54.

854 ***Immo***: the first syllable of *immo* is lightened here and elsewhere in Plautus and Terence, a puzzling phenomenon discussed (though not explained) by Lindsay 1922, 256–57; the light first syllable lightens the second by iambic shortening.

I'll tell you something scandalous: Davos of course does not regard Crito's arrival as scandalous, but he is keeping up the same pretence before Chremes as at 778–87. He has now regained his confidence and feels he can enjoy himself by putting on this act.

Indignum ... facinus: the same expression at 145, *Ph.* 613 and elsewhere; see OLD *indignus* 6.

facinus faxo: although *facinus* is not here the object of *faxo*, the sound effect is similar to that of *facinus facere* (a *figura etymologica*) at *Eun.* 644.

faxo audies: lit. 'I'll make you hear', with the future *audies* in parataxis after *faxo*, for the form of which cf. on 753 *faxis*; the use of a form probably felt to be archaic in Terence's time may add a touch of solemnity to Davos' utterance, though de Melo, 298 regards this use of *faxo* (as he also regards that of *attigas* at 789) as 'stylistically neutral'.

855 *ellum* = *em illum*, similar to *eccum* (cf. on 532); this form is found only in Plautus and Terence and then in later grammarians and commentators.

confidens, catus: the alliteration reinforces the negative sense of these words in Davos' mouth here (part of the act that he is putting on).

856 *uideas*: for the generalizing second person in the subjunctive cf. on 66.

quantiuis preti: genitive of quality (cf. on 608 *nulli*). For the first word see OLD *quantusuis* 'Of whatever size, amount, degree, etc., you wish, no matter how great'.

857 *tristis*: OLD 4 'Stern, solemn, austere'.

ueritas: OLD 6 'Disposition to speak the truth, truthfulness, frankness' (as at 68), or 7 'Adherence to standards of honesty, uprightness, sincerity'. [J. D. Craig, 'Terence Quotations in Servius', *CQ* 24. 3–4 (1930), 183–87, at p. 184 offers good reasons to doubt the authority of *seueritas* in one manuscript of Servius on *Geo.* 3.37, which he supposes to have influenced the manuscripts of Terence. *ueritas* is the reading before correction of three Terence manuscripts; the others all read *seueritas*. Craig compares 839 *uero uoltu*.]

858 [*adportas* fits better with Davos' reply than *adportat*, the reading of the first hand in *p* and accepted by K-L and Thierfelder; the manuscripts otherwise have *adportas*.]

859 *tandem*: cf. on 492.

860 **Dromo**: Simo is convinced that Pamphilus and Davos are hatching a plot of which Crito is part; for him, this is the last straw, and in his impatience he calls for Dromo four times by name in one line. The second syllable of the name is lightened by iambic shortening in its first occurrence, which helps to convey the urgency of Simo's summons. Comparable, though different (and for different effect), is the variation in the scansion of the second syllable of the vocative of Hylas at Virgil, *Ecl.*, VI.44 *Hylā, Hylă*; cf. also the variation in the scansion of the first syllable of the vocative of Ares at Homer, *Iliad* V.31 and 455 Ἆρες, Ἄρες. (Admittedly it is possible to take this line as an iambic octonarius if the second syllable is not lightened, and a few editors have done so.)

According to Gellius 10.3.19 the term *lorarius* ('flogger') was used of a character in a play who administered punishments; that would clearly be appropriate for Dromo here, though the word is not found before Gellius, and we need not suppose that Dromo is kept in Simo's household exclusively for that task. However, he is doubtless much stronger than Davos, capable of lifting him from the ground and carrying him indoors (as instructed in 861). On *lorarii* in Plautus see Richlin, 452–54.

If you add a word: for the uncompleted threat cf. on 164.

861 *obsecro*: cf. on 721.

quantum potest: cf. on 577. Here *potest* is impersonal.

862 [J. Andrieu, *Étude critique sur les sigles de personnages et les rubriques de scène dans les anciennes éditions de Térence* (Paris, 1940), 54–55 gives *Quam ob rem?* to Dromo; more tentatively he changes *Quid feci?* to *Quid fecit?* and gives that too to Dromo. But it is unlikely that Dromo would query an order from his own master in this way.]

Quia lubet: Donatus cross-refers to 213 *si lubitum fuerit*.

863, 865 *occidito, constringito*: the only two occurrences in this play of the future imperative in *-to*, which is discussed by P. Barrios-Lech, 'The Imperative in *-to* in Plautus and Terence', *CQ* 67.2 (2017), 485–506.

occidito is an example of the permissive use that he discusses on pp. 492–93 (hence the translation 'you can kill me'); it is capped by the direct command *constringito*, which has future reference since its fulfilment will not be quite as immediate as the response to the repeated present imperative *rape* at 862–63. *Cura* at the beginning of 865 could also appropriately have been the future *Curato*, but the present imperative form too is often found in commands with future reference, e.g. *Dic* at 383, 394. In fact the *-to* form was probably declining in usage by the time of Terence.

864   I'll stir you up now: a vague threat, with *commotum* probably similar in meaning to *Commoui* at 456 (Davos on Simo!); cf. OLD *commoueo* 12 'To make anxious, trouble, worry, upset, frighten'. [K-L give these words to Dromo, but they fit better as part of a dialogue between Simo and Davos. A few editors scan this line as an iambic octonarius, giving *Ego* a long second vowel in the first foot; see note 86 attached to Introduction, section 8.8 (a).]

865   tie his hands and feet together: this is how *Quadrupedem* ('four-footed') has been generally understood here, evoking the image of a hobbled horse or other animal. Commentators refer to *Odyssey* XXII.173–74, 189–91, where Melanthius is punished for his treachery partly by having his hands and feet tied together behind his back, but that is a refinement of torture that perhaps goes beyond what Simo has in mind; it will be painful enough if Davos is forced into a sitting position with his hands and feet tied together in front of him. [Kruschwitz 2010, 373–75 takes *quadrupes* to be used as a noun (as it commonly is), referring to Davos as 'the beast'. However, Simo has already said 'Make sure you keep him tied up'; *Quadrupedem constringito* must add a further detail to his instruction, and it must be *Quadrupedem* that supplies it, since *uincire* and *constringere* amount to the same thing. In addition, there is no evidence that *quadrupes* can be used as a noun to refer to a person, although *belua* can be.]

866–903   After shouting threats against Davos and Pamphilus as Davos is carried into his house, Simo summons Pamphilus from Glycerium's house and, convinced that Glycerium is not really an Athenian citizen, denounces him for his shamelessness in trying to pass her off as one. Then, however (at 866–92), he withdraws into a resigned acceptance of the situation. Pamphilus confesses his love for Glycerium but submits himself to his father's authority. None the less he manages to persuade Simo to hear what Crito has to say; he goes into Glycerium's house to bring Crito out.

On 891 Donatus writes 'The sense is heightened with striking solemnity; this is not reproduced from Menander but is Terence's own contribution' (*Mira grauitate sensus elatus est; nec de Menandro, sed proprium Terentii*). It is tantalizing that we do not have Menander's Greek to compare with Simo's rant from 876 to 892.

The metre changes to iambic senarii while Simo vents his anger and grief, changing again to trochaic septenarii at 896 when Pamphilus submits himself to Simo and persuades him to give Crito a hearing. cf. Moore 2013, 110: 'The meter changes to trochaic septenarii as Pamphilus confesses to his father that he is in love with Glycerium (896). This confession allows father and son finally to end their mutual deception and is thus an especially appropriate beginning of the play's last music.' Before that, just as Simo went into senarii at 196 for the start of a threat against Davos, so here he again threatens him in senarii at 866–67; but this time he continues in the same metre.

866 *Age*: OLD *ago* 24, here expressing anger.

hodie: cf. on 196.

si uiuo: an expression found several times in Plautus and Terence to reinforce a threat.

868 *ne saeui*: cf. on 384 *Ne nega*.

869 *pietatem*: accusative of exclamation; cf. on 145.

870 *capere*: understand *me* as the subject of this infinitive; accusative and infinitive of exclamation, with the accusative understood. Cf. on 245, and 879 below.

871 *Age*: cf. on 692, though not here sarcastic.

872 *Quid ais*: cf. on 184.

873 *mitte*: OLD *mitto* 4.b '(w. inf.) To forbear, avoid, stop (doing something)'; cf. 904.

874 *possiet*: cf. on 234 *siet*.

875 *Ain* = *Aisne*: OLD *aio* 2 '*ain?* (form of interrogation, expr. doubt, surprise, etc.) what's that? indeed! so! you don't say?'. This form regularly scans as a monosyllable.

tandem: cf. on 492.

So they say: Pamphilus is temporarily disconcerted by having to confront his father in a towering rage and probably also taken aback by the fact that Simo knows about Glycerium's claiming to be a citizen; Pamphilus does not know that Davos has told Simo about Crito's arrival. He has not yet worked out how most effectively to broach the subject with Simo, and he here stalls for time. Büchner, 107 n. 110 notes the parallel with Pamphilus' 'So they say' to Charinus at 321, but the context and tone are different there.

876   **'So they say'**: characters who are worked up often repeat the words that have angered them in this way; cf. 890, 900 below. For a similar repetition expressing a different sort of strong feeling cf. 282, 649.

ingentem confidentiam: accusative of exclamation, as at 869. OLD *confidentia* 2 'Audacity, temerity'.

877–81   A further sign of Simo's anger is that he speaks of Pamphilus in the third person throughout these lines instead of addressing him directly.

878   *Vide*: probably addressed to an imaginary representative of the world at large rather than to Chremes in particular; cf. on 588.

color: OLD 3 'The colour of the skin, esp. of the face, complexion [...] **c** (as a sign of fear, guilt, modesty, etc.)'.

indicat: for the indicative in an indirect question cf. on 45 *dic quid est*.

879   [*Adeo*: the manuscripts have *Adeon* (= *Adeone*), which would be idiomatic but is metrically impossible.]

inpotenti esse animo: understand *eum*; as at 870 this is an accusative and infinitive of exclamation with the accusative understood. *inpotenti animo* is ablative of quality; for the meaning see OLD *impotens* 3 'Lacking in self-control, headstrong, wild, violent, intemperate, etc.'.

praeter: cf. on 436.

879–80   **In spite of the traditions and laws of his city**: Simo believes that Pamphilus is planning to pass off a non-citizen woman as a citizen so that he can live with her as if they were legally married (exactly what Stephanos is alleged to have done in [Demosthenes] 59). That would be against the law, as it would entail claiming, for any offspring of their union, citizenship rights to which they were not entitled.

882   **I'm in a mess**: lit. 'Wretched me!'; cf. on 240 *miseram me*. Pamphilus cannot see how he will be able to win his father round in his current mood.

sensti = *sensisti* (the reading of the manuscripts, metrically impossible).

883   *Olim*: picked up by *eodem die* in 885.

ita: explained by 884.

animum induxti: see on 572.

884   *efficiundum*: understand *esse*.

885   *accidit*: OLD *accido*[1] 8.a 'To be applicable (to)'.

886 *quid ego?*: the elliptical expression conveys Simo's overwrought state, as do the three *Quor* questions that follow it, of which the first two say the same thing with different verbs, while the third amplifies the point and thus makes a fine emotional climax in a self-contained line.

889–92 J. F. Gaertner, 'Law and Roman Comedy', in Fontaine and Scafuro, 615–33, at p. 626 suggests that Simo tries to discipline Pamphilus by disinheriting him, but neither part of this seems right. Simo certainly washes his hands of his son, and he reacts strongly to being addressed as 'dad', but effectively he ends up saying 'I give up; have it your own way'; these lines represent an emotional outburst, not a formal act.

889 *ualeat*: cf. 696. For the tricolon here and at 891 see on 18 *Naeuium, Plautum, Ennium*.

890–91 Note how Simo rams his point home with his repeated use of Pamphilus' word 'dad'. For Donatus' comment at this point see on 866–903.

891 *liberi*: this could be taken as a generalizing plural, like *adducti qui ... dicant* referring to Crito alone in 892, but in fact *liberi* (of which there is no singular form) can be used with reference to a singular child, as e.g. at Pl. *Truc.* 384, 516, 858. The phenomenon is discussed by Wackernagel, 129–30; see also TLL VII.2.1303. 41–64.

891 *inuenti*, **892** *adducti*: understand *sunt* in each case.

892 *uiceris* (**'you've won'**): more precisely, 'you can be the winner'; *uiceris* is perfect subjunctive (either jussive or permissive). See (e.g.) Bennett, I.176, translating it as 'have your way', and cf. Pl. *Men.* 295 *perieris*, *Trin.* 1054 *amiseris*. Less probably it could be future perfect indicative.

893 **may I say something**: Simo's last speech has made it clear that he knows about Crito's arrival. That finally gives Pamphilus his cue to steer their confrontation in a new direction. (With *licetne pauca* understand *dicere*.)

895 *Chreme*: for the hiatus at change of speaker see Introduction, section 8.7, though it could be avoided here if the vocative form *Chremes* were used (see on 247 *Chremetis*).

tandem: cf. on 492.

Age: cf. on 310.

897 *oneris*: partitive genitive, dependent on *quiduis*.

898 Pamphilus' professed willingness to abandon Glycerium and comply with his father's wishes may seem like a betrayal of his assurances to Mysis at 270–98 and 693–701. That would be consistent with the anxiety he showed about disobeying his father at 260–64. However, now that Crito has turned up, he can be more confident than before of being able to establish Glycerium's citizenship (even if he cannot yet know just whose daughter she will turn out to be). He can thus risk the tactic of diplomatically submitting to Simo's control as a preliminary to getting him to agree to meet Crito (so Penwill, 144 n. 30). He may also calculate that after Chremes has heard him declare his love for Glycerium in 896 he will not be keen to marry his daughter to him, as noted by Donatus.

[*mittere*: the manuscripts have *amittere*, which can mean the same thing but is metrically impossible here. Understand *me* as the subject of *mittere*.]

899   *ut ne*: cf. on 259.

adlegatum: OLD *allego*[1] 2 'To employ (as one's agent for any purpose), commission, put up, suborn'.

this old man: Simo has not explicitly referred to an old man, but Pamphilus knows from 892 that Simo will know whom he means.

900   *sine me expurgem*, 901 *sine ... exorem*: cf. on 622. *sine te hoc exorem* means 'let me persuade you to agree to this', *exorem* being followed by two accusatives.

901   *ueniam*: OLD *uenia* 1.b 'a favour consisting of permission to do something'.

902   *cupio*: understand *sinere*, or perhaps *facere* (I'm happy to do anything'), as at Pl. *Epid.* 270 *Facere cupio quiduis dum id fiat modo* ('I'm happy to do anything, just so long as that gets done').

as long as I don't find that I'm being tricked by him: Simo has expected to be plotted against from the start of the play and has prided himself on being able to detect the plot (cf. on 459–80). He is now at such a low ebb that his main concern is that he should not be outwitted by his son.

ne: the regular negative with *dum* meaning 'provided that, as long as'; see OLD *dum*[2] 2.

comperiar: deponent; if it were passive, one would expect *falli* without *me*.

903   Chremes' sententious utterance is not very apposite as a response to Simo's last remark but is consistent with his attempts to calm Simo down and get him to behave reasonably at 868, 872–73, 893–95, 901. At 868 Simo appeared to contemplate punishing Pamphilus in some way, and since then he has harangued him forcefully, reducing him to a jelly-like state in which he says 'I'm in a mess' (882) and 'Dad, please' (889). Chremes perhaps means that that was enough by way of punishment; so Donatus:

'he refers to the accusation itself as a punishment' (*supplicium dicit ipsam accusationem*). [Victor 2015, 303–304 gives the line to Simo, claiming that his speech at 901–902 otherwise ends abruptly and that 903 explains why he has changed his mind and agreed to hear Crito out. This could be right, though I am not convinced that Simo needs to add any such explanation: he agrees because Pamphilus and Chremes have worn down his resistance with their pleading; cf *Ad*. 944–45, where Micio agrees to a more extraordinary request after much longer resistance.]

As Donatus notes on 901, Chremes is not angry at Pamphilus' attitude to his daughter and does not storm off back home; Terence wants him on stage for the next scene.

904–56   Pamphilus reappears with Crito, who is immediately recognized by Chremes as an old acquaintance (it is not explained how they know one another). In spite of having to submit to stinging abuse from Simo, Crito tells Glycerium's story: she had been shipwrecked off Andros as a small child together with her uncle, an Athenian citizen called (as far as Crito can remember) Phania, who died on Andros. Chremes recognizes the name as that of his brother and realizes that Glycerium must be his own daughter; the identification is confirmed when Pamphilus is able to supply the information that she had originally been called Pasibula (940–46). Nothing now stands in the way of her formal betrothal to Pamphilus as the daughter of Chremes, after which Chremes and Crito go into her house to see her (947–52). Simo suggests to Pamphilus that she be moved to their house and goes indoors to release Davos from his bonds so that he can see to the move. Pamphilus is left briefly alone on stage.

This is the last scene of the play that requires four speaking actors. The least essential character in the scene is Pamphilus, and it is possible that in Menander's *Andria* he did not reappear with Crito at 904 (cf. Lowe, 160); the actor playing him would then have had the two lines 902–903 to change with remarkable speed into the costume and mask of Crito and reappear at 904–905 talking back into the house to Pamphilus (if Terence is otherwise following Menander very closely and has not abbreviated 902–903). Terence has given Pamphilus an important part to play in supplying the name Pasibula when Crito's memory for names proves even shakier than in the case of Phania, but the scene could easily have been constructed without that complication. However, it also adds to the overall effect to have Pamphilus present when the truth about Glycerium's parentage is established and to have him commenting on the action in a series of asides. In addition, he is instrumental in securing Davos' release from his punishment at 953–56.

Plautus made much comedy out of a character's inability to remember a name at *Trin.* 906–27, and Terence did so again at *Ph.* 386–90. There are also moments of tension over the ability to supply a name at Pl. *Persa* 623–26, *Ps.* 984–91.

Metre: the trochaic septenarii continue until 928, then the metre changes to iambic octonarii from the point at which Crito stumbles over the name of Glycerium's uncle. cf. Moore 2013, 111: 'Terence thus sets aside the actual *anagnorisis* [= recognition] and resolution as a separate metrical unit, in the same meter associated throughout the play with Davos. Davos' hopes are fulfilled, though in the end through no action of his own.' [The change to iambic octonarii comes at 928 if, with Marouzeau, we move *is* from the start of 928 to the end of 927 and keep *tibi* after *cito* with all manuscripts except the Oxyrhynchus papyrus; the second syllable of *cito* will then scan long, as in 474, *HT* 375, rather than short as in *Ad.* 443. That is entirely possible.]

904   *Mitte*: cf. 873.

   harum: the three *causae* are listed in the following line.

905   *cupio*: OLD 3 '(w. dat.) To be well disposed to, wish well to, favour'.

907   *Quid tu Athenas insolens?*: understand *uenisti. Quid* = 'why'; cf. on 853. *insolens* OLD 1 'Unaccustomed (to), unfamiliar (with)'.

   It turned out that way: as noted by Donatus, Crito does not wish to admit that he has come legacy-hunting.

   hicinest: cf. on 478 *hicin*, though -*ne* is here interrogative.

[**908**   Editors have differed over whether to give *Men quaeris?* to Simo or (with most manuscripts) to Crito, making him address Simo with *Simo, men quaeris?*. Simo has not in fact sent for Crito, whereas Crito has come out hoping to meet him. *Men quaeris?* thus makes more sense in Simo's mouth.]

909   *paratus*: OLD *paro* 6.b 'to prepare mentally, school, prime'.

   Qua re: i.e. 'Why do you ask?' [Victor 1993, 277 thinks this ellipse is impossible and proposes giving Crito *Qua re rogas?*. That could be right, but *Rogas?* as the indignant reply to a question is idiomatic (cf. on 163), and I cannot see that the ellipse is difficult; *Eun.* 369 *Qua re, Parmeno?* is similarly elliptical.]

910–13   Once again (as at 892) Simo resorts to generalizing plurals, a sign that he is still worked up.

910   *hic*: 'here in Athens'.
911   **respectable**: lit. 'free-born', i.e. 'appropriate for boys of free birth'. Cf. on 330 'a man of free birth'.

in fraudem inlicis: OLD *fraus* 7 'A snare for the mind, an illusion; only in such phrs. as *in fraudem illicere, incidere*, etc.'.
912   *Sollicitando et pollicitando*: the jingle helps to convey the strength of Simo's feeling.

[*Iactas*: restored from Donatus; the manuscripts have *iactas*, which makes little sense.]

Sanun = *Sanusne*, the reading of the manuscripts; the form is restored here by editors for the sake of the metre.
913   *meretricios amores*: cf. on 756.

conglutinas: on the metaphor of gluing together see Fantham, 47–48.
914   *noris* = *noueris* (perfect subjunctive); cf. on 10.
915   *arbitrere*: second person singular, present subjunctive of *arbitror*. Terence uses only *-re*, not *-ris*, as the ending of the relevant deponent and passive indicative and subjunctive second person forms.
916   *adtemperate*: this adverb is found only here in Early and Classical Latin.
916–17   **turned out ... turned up**: Simo picks up the word Crito had used in 907 and makes a scornful pun on it. As at 469–506, Simo is wrongly suspicious of the neat coincidence; cf. Introduction, section 6.6, pp. 29–30.
918   **If I wasn't ... meet that point**: Pamphilus perhaps means that his father is the one who has really been up to tricks on this very day.
919   **Swindler**: this is exactly what Crito had feared he would be called at 815, though he did not foresee this context.

That's how he is: Donatus quotes Menander's Greek at this point (Menander fr. 48 K-A οὕτως αὐτός ἐστιν). This means essentially the same thing (though the force of αὐτός is uncertain), and it is not clear why Donatus quotes it. But it does support the idea that Chremes, Crito, and Simo took part in this scene in Menander's play.

mitte: cf. 764.

Videat: OLD *uideo* 16 'To pay regard to, look at, consider'.

qui = *qualis* (OLD *qui*¹ 2).
921   *istaec*: here with very clear second-person reference; cf. on 28 for the form.

moueo: cf. on 516.

aequo animo: cf. on 397.

[*feras* is the reading of A, labelled by Shipp as a potential subjunctive; the other manuscripts have *feres*. J. N. Grant, *Studies in the Textual Tradition of Terence* (Toronto, 1986), 89 suggests taking *non* as Crito's own answer to the preceding question, followed by *tu ... feras* as a jussive subjunctive, but this feels strained. If the subjunctive is felt to be awkward in *non ... feras* as a question, it would be preferable to read *feres*. K-L's punctuation of *non ... feras* as an exclamation is strange.]

922 *Nam*: used to support an affirmation (OLD 1).

ego: emphasized by coming outside the clause *quae dico*, contrasting with the second-person pronouns in the previous line.

923 **off the coast of Andros**: OLD *ad* 13.d. Crito's story confirms what the audience have heard from Davos at 221–24, though Davos was sceptical of it.

924 *una*: the adverb.

924, 926 *Tum*: 'next'. At 924 this could well be taken in a temporal sense, but at 926 (and again at 936) it simply introduces the next item in the narrative (OLD 8.c). [I do not share the feeling of Victor 1996, 375–76 and 2010, 49–51 that the transmitted text suggests two benefactors in turn for the shipwrecked man, nor that *Ibi* in 927 is in any way difficult, and I see no need for his suggestion in the later article that Terence has misunderstood Menander's Greek in 926–27. We can easily understand 'the man who took him in' in 927 to be the father of Chrysis (whom we know to be related to Crito) and *Ibi* in that line to mean 'in his house'. (*primum* ['first'] in 925 need not suggest that there was a second person to whom the shipwrecked man applied for help, nor does Victor suggest that it does.)]

925 **He's making it up**: lit. 'He's starting on a story'. Simo's word *fabulam* echoes Davos' *Fabulae* at 224 with reference to the same story; cf. on 220 and 747 for the theatrical associations of the word, a point already noted by Donatus here.

Sine: OLD *sino* 2 'To let (a thing) pass; (esp.) *sine* never mind!'.

927 *sese*: the reflexive pronoun is used as if Crito had said *ille mihi dixit* rather than *audiui ex illo*.

928 *mortuost* = *mortuos est*; cf. on 102 *dictust*. The death presumably followed quite soon on the shipwreck; otherwise it would be strange that Phania had not succeeded in getting a message to Chremes before he died. But he did survive the shipwreck, contrary to what we might have thought on hearing 221–23 (see on 221–24).

928–29 **Phania**: the name of a deceased character also at *Hec.* 458 and of an offstage character at *HT* 169. The Greek equivalent Phanias is the name of a character in Men. *Kitharistes*. [There has been much debate over who says what in these two lines; see Victor 1996, 374–75. The arrangement in the text is that of K-L. On the text of 928 see also the end of the note on 904–56.]

930 **Rhamnus**: a district of Attica, on the north-east coast opposite the island of Euboea.

Iuppiter: on the scansion of the final syllable, followed by change of speaker, see Introduction, the end of section 8.3 (b), though it is possible that the vowel here retains an original long quantity (see Introduction, section 8.6 (v), and cf. below on 950 *pater*).

930 *aiebat*, **932** *aibat*: see on 534 *ait*.

931 [The main manuscripts have *tum* after *in Andro*; the word was deleted by Bentley for metrical reasons; he claimed that it was omitted by a Cambridge manuscript.]

932 *quid eam tum?*: cf. 804 *Quid uos?*, 806 *Quid Glycerium?*. *eam* is in the accusative because Chremes already has the next sentence in his mind.

Quoiam: cf. 763.

933 *Quid tu ais*: a stronger version of *Quid ais?*

934 *Qui*: 'How'; cf. on 6.

illic = *ille*, as at 742.

935 **to avoid the war and follow my tracks to Asia**: according to the version reported by Davos earlier, Phania appeared to have been travelling on business, as perhaps Chremes too had been; see on 221–24. Terence's audience presumably did not ask themselves what 'the war' referred to, but it may have had a specific reference for Menander's original audience, probably reminding them either of the disastrous Lamian War of 323/2 (so Mazzarino, 29–32) or (if Menander used a slightly different word) of the years of internal dissension at Athens that followed it. 'Asia' means Asia Minor.

936 **he was afraid to leave the girl here**: we must suppose that Chremes had left Phania in charge of his daughter. We learn nothing about the girl's mother, just as we learn nothing in the play as a whole about whether Chremes or Simo has a wife living, except for the hint at 364 that Chremes does not.

936–37 **this is the first person I've heard from about what became of**

him: we cannot tell what enquiries Chremes made on his return from Asia (whenever that was), but he may well have had no idea where to start.

hinc: 'from him', i.e. from Crito. This personal use of *hinc* is found also at *Ph*. 604, *Hec*. 246, *Ad*. 361 (the latter two cases both with *scire*). [*hinc* was read by F. Nencini in his edition of the play (Rome and Milan, 1905) and also proposed by Victor 1993, 277–78. A originally read *hunc*, corrected by a later hand to *nunc*, the reading of the other manuscripts; *hunc* makes no sense, and *nunc* spoils the metre of the line. It is only slightly awkward that *hinc* has been used in a different sense in 935. Other attempts to cure the metre of the line have included reading *hoc* (Kauer) or changing *Postilla* to *Postibi*, *Postid*, or *Poste*.]

937   *illo*: cf. *me* at 614, 709 for this ablative.

apud: cf. on 408 'keep your wits about you'.

939   *Ne*: cf. on 324.

I'm sure you are: Pamphilus takes Simo's congratulations to have been addressed to himself, though they must, if the text is correct, have been meant for Chremes. [Bentley changed *tuam inueniri* to *ciuem inuentam* and made Simo address his remark to Pamphilus.]

940   **one detail**; *scrupulus*, the diminutive of *scrupus*, 'a sharp stone', is regularly used to mean 'a source of uneasiness or misgiving, a worry, headache' (OLD).

[*At scrupulus mi etiam unus*: the manuscripts have *At mi unus scrupulus etiam*, breaking Hermann-Lachmann's law in the third foot (cf. Introduction, section 8.4). Ritschl, II.271 n.** transposed the words to avoid this.]

941   *religione*: similar to the use at 730, here implying an excessive fussiness over details.

you boring man: *odium* can mean 'boredom' (OLD 5), and it can be applied to a person who induces a negative feeling (OLD 4).

looking for a knot in a bulrush: looking for something that does not exist; a proverbial expression for looking for difficulties where there are none (see Otto, 312–13).

[*istud*: restored for the sake of the metre; the manuscripts read *istuc* (as at 186, etc.), but that has a heavy second syllable, impossible at this point in the line, unless Lindsay 1922, 138–39 was right to think that it could be lightened. Admittedly, Terence elsewhere uses only the form *istuc*, though A has *istud* (accusative) at *Ph*. 524.]

942   **she had a different one when she was little**: it is not explained when or why she changed her name, presumably before she came to Athens (since Crito at 806 refers to her as Glycerium and here has some difficulty in recalling her original name). We know of one case in the Greek orators where a woman is said to have changed her name at some stage since early childhood, at [Dem.] 59.50 (Neaera's daughter), and it has been claimed that a similar name-change would account for the discrepancy in the names of a woman at Isaeus 3.30–34. D. Noy, 'Neaera's Daughter: a Case of Athenian Identity Theft?', *CQ* 59.2 (2009), 398–410 argues that both of those were cases of identity theft, with the woman in question taking the name of a girl who had died in childhood. Others have suggested that they were girls who had been given a pet-name as children, which is likely to be the explanation in Glycerium's case (so Austin, 75). At Pl. *Capt.* 984 we learn that the slave Tyndarus had previously been called Paegnium; K. Philippides, 'Tyndarus' Past: The Name Paegnium in Plautus' *Captivi*', *Class. et Med.* 62 (2011), 99–112 suggests that Paegnium itself had been a pet-name.

[**944** *egomet*: this is the reading of some manuscripts, including the Oxyrhynchus papyrus; the others, including A, have *ego*, which requires prosodic hiatus of *quom*. Either is possible. Recent editors except Marouzeau have read *ego*, but Bentley preferred *egomet*.]

945 **Pasibula**: this name is not otherwise attested; as Austin, 75 says, it should mean something like 'having or giving counsel in all things or to everybody'. [Unless this line is to be a solitary trochaic septenarius – which would perhaps be appropriate to mark the point at which Pamphilus supplies the crucial information – the second syllable of *Chreme* must be lightened by iambic shortening and something must be missing at the end of the line in the manuscripts, which follow Pamphilus' *Pasibulast* with one speaker saying *Ipsa est* and another *Ea est* (though V has *Ea est* followed by *Ipsa est*). Thus I have followed Dziatzko in making Chremes say *Pasibula? Ipsast.* (The first and third vowels of *Pasibula* are long.) Alternatively we could follow those manuscripts (all except A) which start the line *Non patiar. Heus, Chreme* (without iambic shortening) and read *Ipsa east* at the end of the line (so Bothe and Thierfelder, giving the last two words to Chremes and Crito jointly). But *Non patiar* is clumsy after 943 *Egon ... patiar*. Victor 1993, 278–79 offers a different solution, keeping the line as a trochaic septenarius.]

946 *hoc*: probably accusative, like *id* at 362.

946–47 **I'm sure you realize that we're all delighted**: Simo alludes to the formula of congratulation found at 939.

947   *Ita me di ament*: lit. 'so may the gods love me'; see OLD *amo* 8.c for this common asseveration.

As for the remaining matter: Pamphilus starts to raise the question of his relationship with Glycerium but does not need to complete his sentence.

948   **Circumstances**: OLD *res* 17 'The state of affairs, situation'.

lepidum patrem: accusative of exclamation.

949   **my wife**: strictly speaking, of course, Glycerium has not yet achieved this status, though we have seen at 273 that Pamphilus has regarded her as having done so; cf. also 295.

given that I've taken possession of her: lit. 'just as I have taken possession of her'. Cf. Pl. *Truc.* 843–44 (the prospective father-in-law speaking): 'You didn't wait for me to give her to you: you took her for yourself. Now you can keep her just as you've taken possession of her (*Nunc habeas ut nactu's*).' Pamphilus alludes to a Roman legal formula, normally found in the context of property ownership, and reflected in the legislation known as the *Interdictum Uti Possidetis* (for which see A. Berger, *Encyclopedic Dictionary of Roman Law* [Philadelphia, 1953], 512), for which this passage may well be our earliest evidence; a formula from the same interdict is echoed at *Eun.* 319 *uel ui uel clam uel precario* ('whether by force or by stealth or on loan'). It is possible that *Causa optumast* ('Your case is very strong') reflects the legal concept *iusta causa* ('just cause'), which was 'particularly important in connection with *possessio*' (Berger p. 535), and just conceivably *nil mutat* ('doesn't want to change the situation') could reflect the dictum 'no one can change by himself the ground on which he obtained possession' (Berger p. 637, under *possessio*), though that may well not have been formulated until much later. In any case, 'just as I have taken possession of her', like the formula at *Eun.* 319, gives a distinctively Roman colouring to the passage which is unusual in Terence, though common enough in Plautus.

If Pamphilus was not on stage at this point in Menander's *Andria* (see on 904–56), there was probably no formal discussion of his betrothal to Glycerium at this point either, though 99–102 show that it was possible for Chremes and Simo to discuss such a matter in his absence. See also on 957–81.

950   *pater ait*: scansion: this breaks Ritschl's law in the fourth element (-*ter a*-: see Introduction, section 8.4), unless the second syllable of *pater* retains an original long vowel (see Introduction, section 8.6 (v)). The most plausible candidate for the long vowel otherwise in Terence is at *Hec.* 258, but the text there is uncertain.

According to Donatus, 'when they say "naturally" and "of course" they show by gesture or expression that they have the dowry in mind, which Chremes is quick to understand' (*'nempe' et 'scilicet' dicentes manu uel uultu dotem significant, quod mox intellegit Chremes*). This is quoted with approval by Kauer and Shipp but seems fanciful.

951 **Her dowry is ten talents**: cf. on 100–101. For Terence's retention of Greek currency terms see 369 *obolo*, 451 *drachumis*. One talent = 6,000 drachmas. Ten talents is a very large sum for a dowry, not unthinkable for the very wealthiest families at Athens, but considerably larger than most dowries mentioned in the remains of Greek New Comedy. However, Menander fr. 296.11 K-A (from *Plokion*) mentions a ten-talent dowry, and it is possible that the fragmentary line *Koneiazomenai* 3 refers to one of five talents; otherwise the largest is four talents at *Epitr.* 134. In Latin, a dowry of twenty talents is mentioned at Pl. *Cist.* 561–62, of ten talents at *Merc.* 703; at *Truc.* 844–45 the bride's father proposes to deduct six talents from a dowry of unspecified size in order to punish his prospective son-in-law. Elsewhere in Greek Comedy dowries of one, two or three talents are mentioned (see L. Casson, 'The Athenian Upper Class and New Comedy', *TAPA* 106 (1976), 29–59, at pp. 54–55), at *HT* 838, 940 a dowry of two talents. It has generally been assumed that Plautus and Terence nearly always inflated the figures they found in their Greek texts, but the example of *Plokion* gives pause for thought. The figures in Greek comedy have themselves been suspected of being unrealistically large, but Casson argues that we should rather accept them as evidence that some of the families portrayed in the plays are exceptionally wealthy. So too T. B. L. Webster, *An introduction to Menander* (Manchester, 1974), 25–31; at 26 he says 'Chremes in the *Andria* seems excessive, especially as he has two daughters to provide for. We know that he had gone to make his fortune in Asia when his elder daughter was lost. He presumably did well, came back and married and had another daughter but no son; this may be the reason why he can give so large a dowry.' One of the characters in Menander's *Aspis* is said at line 350 to have property worth sixty talents; such a character could easily afford a ten-talent dowry, or even two of them.

   Eho mecum: understand *i intro* or something similar.

952 **for her to be moved over to our house**: it is taken for granted that Glycerium will move into her father-in-law's house (cf. on 386), but she will be moved without the ceremony of a formal procession – luckily for her, since she has only just given birth. We might have expected Simo to wait a little longer before making this suggestion (allowing time for the reunion of Glycerium and Chremes), but he is doubtless keen to reassert himself; and Terence is keen to round things off at the end of the play.

954   *ex sese*: OLD *ex* 20 'In accordance with'.

955   **I didn't tell them to do it wrong**: Simo jokingly puns on Pamphilus' complaint, as if by 'wrong' Pamphilus had meant 'not secure', i.e. *Haud ita iussi* means *Haud iussi eum non recte uinciri*, and Simo takes *recte* in the sense of OLD 4 'as it ought to be or be done, properly, correctly' or 8 'properly, thoroughly, altogether, well', whereas Pamphilus meant it in sense 7 'with good reason, rightly, justifiably'. Some, however, have seen Simo as taking *recte* in OLD sense 1 'in an upright position, vertically', since he knows he had ordered Davos to have his hands and feet tied together; on this view, *Haud ita iussi* means *Haud iussi eum recte uinciri*. Less plausibly, Kruschwitz 2010 argues that Simo is not joking at all but admitting that he was wrong to order Davos to be tied up (i.e. *Haud recte iussi eum uinciri*, with *recte* qualifying *iussi* rather than *uinciri*).

obsecro: cf. on 721.

956   *Age*: cf. on 310 'All right then'.

fiat: OLD *fio* 15 '*fiat*, so be it, very well'. Simo is now in a mood to make a concession that he would not have made earlier.

faustum et felicem diem: accusative of exclamation; the two adjectives are often found together.

957–81   Pamphilus continues the monologue which began in the second half of 956, rejoicing at his good fortune and keen to find someone to share it with (957–62). He is delighted to see Davos come from his house, though Davos himself, having just been released from his punishment, is not wholly enthusiastic about Pamphilus' news. Their encounter is witnessed by Charinus, who had entered at 957 and gradually comes to realize that nothing now stands in the way of his own betrothal to Philumena. Pamphilus offers to put in a good word for him with Chremes, orders Davos to fetch people to move Glycerium from her house, and asks the audience for their applause.

Spengel, pp. XXIV–XXV finds the inclusion of Davos in this scene a fine dramatic touch, both because of the contrast between his mood and that of Pamphilus and because of the opportunity the actor has to entertain the audience with appropriate movements of his arms and legs to show that he has just been released from a very uncomfortable position. How entertaining an audience finds such movements will depend on how they are performed and how callous the audience feels about the punishment of slaves.

Pamphilus' celebratory monologue at 956–61 is similar to those at *Eun.* 1031–33 and 1044–49 in which Chaerea expresses his joy at how things have turned out; if Donatus is right to say that 959–61 have been imported from Menander's original of *The Eunuch* (see the note there), they could well have come from that point in the play, though there is a closer echo at *Eun.* 551–52, where Chaerea says 'now, now is the time when I could put up with death, so that life couldn't spoil this joy with any sorrow' (*nunc est profecto interfici quom perpeti me possum, / ne hoc gaudium contaminet uita aegritudine aliqua*). Lefèvre, 79 notes the recurrence of the terms 'joy' and 'sorrow' (*gaudium* and *aegritudo*), and also the fact that at *Eun.* 553–56 Chaerea remarks that there is no one present to ask him why he is so happy; this is comparable with Pamphilus' wondering at 962 whom he would most like to share his news with.

At *Eun.* 1031ff. the celebratory monologues precede a final scene to round off the play with a new development; at Men. *Dysk.* 860–65 Sostratos has a similarly placed monologue in which he boasts of how much he has achieved in a single day. The final scene of *The Eunuch* involves characters imported by Terence from a different Menandrian play. Here Charinus has been added, and the rounding off of his part in the play is very straightforward; if there was a substantial new development at the end of Menander's *Andria*, we can only guess at what it was – something involving mockery of Simo, perhaps (so, tentatively, Lefèvre, 162)? Otherwise Lefèvre, 161–62 suggests there may have been an eventual reconciliation between Pamphilus and Simo and also Simo's pardoning of Davos, as well as the formal betrothal of Glycerium to Pamphilus by Chremes (cf. on 949); he also thinks it likely that a husband was found for Philumena, even though Menander's *Andria* had not included Charinus.

Did Menander's audience see Glycerium at the end of the play? B. Victor suggests that they did, and that she was shown both being reunited with her father and being betrothed to Pamphilus; since she has just given birth, he argues that she must have been wheeled on to the stage in her bed on the *ekkyklema*, a wheeled platform available in the Greek theatre for the display of indoor scenes but not available to Terence ('Indoor and Outdoor: Observations on the Originals of Terence's *Andria* and *Hecyra*', *CQ* 67.1

[2017], 118–31, at pp. 123–25). However, I am not sure that Menander would have seen any dramatic advantage in showing the reunion of father and daughter on stage, and there was certainly no need for her to be present at her betrothal, as we can see from *Dysk.* 842–47 and perhaps also *Misoum.* 444–46 Sandbach = 974–76 Arnott (though the state of the text there is such that we cannot be absolutely certain). Those plays support the idea that Menander's play included a scene of betrothal towards its end (cf. also *Perik.* 1013–15, *Sam.* 726–29), but it could well have been a transaction between men, as in Terence's play at 949–51.

Metre: the iambic octonarii continue for (probably) two lines (see on the text of 957); the play then ends, as most Latin comedies do and all of Terence's will, with a run of trochaic septenarii.

957 *Prouiso*: cf. on 404 *Reuiso*. Charinus has been at home waiting for news since 714.

    eccum: cf. on 532.

[The final syllable of *Pamphilus* is a light syllable before the diaeresis: see Introduction, the end of section 8.5. The text follows G. Hermann's proposal to read *me forsitan* for *forsitan me* and to place *putet* at the start of 958 rather than the end of 957; the latter proposal has subsequently received support from the Oxyrhynchus papyrus. With this text lines 957–58 are both iambic octonarii, the trochaic septenarii starting at 959. Others have kept *putet* at the end of 957, adjusting the preceding words to make the line scan (e.g. by reading *fors* for *forsitan*, as Dziatzko and K-L do); 958 is then the first of the trochaic septenarii.]

959–61 The reason why … in my joy: Donatus tells us that Terence imported this passage from Menander's *Eunuch* (see Introduction, p. 19). Nothing exactly like this comes in Terence's version of that play, though there are places where a character could appropriately have said it (see above on 957–81). Donatus remarks that the view of the gods expressed here is Epicurean, and Epicurus certainly believed the life of the gods to be both everlasting and blissful. He also believed that it was possible for mortals to attain a similar state of bliss: see J. Warren, 'Epicurean Immortality', *OSAP* 18 (2000), 231–61.

960 *propriae*: cf. 716.

961 if no sorrow intervenes in my joy: Barsby 1999 on *Eun.* 552, noting that both Clinia at *HT* 679–80 and Chaerea at *Eun.* 551–52 contrast their present joy with the possibility of sorrow, suggests that 'the *gaudium* /

aegritudo antithesis was something of a commonplace in such situations'. Similarly at *Hec.* 843 the Pamphilus of that play says in his joy 'I'm a god, if that's the case (*Deus sum, si hoc itast*)', and Clinia at *HT* 693 says of himself and his beloved 'We've won the life of the gods (*Deorum uitam apti sumus*)'. P. Flury, *Liebe und Liebessprache bei Menander, Plautus und Terenz* (Heidelberg, 1968), 94–96 discusses Plautus' parody of the motif at *Curc.* 167–69, *Merc.* 601–607, *Truc.* 372, contrasting these passages with *HT* 693.

962   *potissimum*: cf. 454.

**   *dari*:** OLD *do*¹ 19.c '(usu. refl. or pass.) to put (before one), present'; cf. *HT* 758 *Te mihi ipsum iamdudum optabam dari.*

[I have printed the first half of this line as in A, the second half as in most of the δ manuscripts (with *quoi nunc haec* rather than *nunc quoi haec*). There are several disagreements in the manuscripts over the placing of *mihi* (after *potissimum* in the γ manuscripts, before *ego* in G, after *optem* in the Oxyrhynchus papyrus), and manuscripts other than A, the papyrus, and the first hand in L have *exoptem*. The papyrus places Charinus' remark in 963 at the start of 962.]

963   *mallem*: understand *uidere*.

964   *solide solum gauisurum gaudia*: cf. 647 *solidum ... gaudium.* Pamphilus' excitement is shown by the double alliteration and by the *figura etymologica* in *gauisurum gaudia*.

966   I know what's happened to *me*: at Pl. *Capt.* 998–1004 Tyndarus, still in shackles, is more expansive on what it was like to be sentenced to hard labour in a quarry. In his case that is the prelude to being reunited with the father from whom he had been kidnapped as a child.

969   That's good news: Davos uses the formula of congratulation that had been used unexpectedly by Sosia at 105. There is no hint here of the scepticism Davos had expressed about Glycerium's Athenian origins at 220–24.

970   a great friend: OLD *summus* 10.

[972   The manuscripts have *ea quae uigilans uoluit*. As pointed out by J. P. Postgate, 'Observations on Latin Poets', *CP* 10.1 (1915), 26–33, at pp. 26–27, *somniat uigilans* belong together in sense; this makes it awkward that *uigilans* comes in the relative clause, though Postgate was not sure that it was impossible. He tentatively proposed moving *uigilans* to come before *ea quae*. It is simpler to transpose *uigilans* and *uoluit*; it is then formally ambiguous which clause *uigilans* belongs to, but the sense resolves the ambiguity.]

as for the baby: the baby was not mentioned in the previous scene, but presumably Pamphilus would have said (if Davos had not interrupted him) that there was now no obstacle to their continuing to bring it up as a legitimate Athenian child.

973   Are you the only one the gods love?: Davos pleads with Pamphilus to stop being so self-centred, as if his good fortune were unique to him. [Subjunctive *diligant* as at Pl. *Curc.* 248 *solus hic homost qui sciat diuinitus* (Bennett, I.290). Nearly all manuscripts read *est*; editors are divided on whether to read *est* or *es*, on whether to punctuate as a statement or a question, on whether the words are addressed to Pamphilus or spoken aside, and on whether (with *est*) the reference is to Pamphilus or the baby.]

I'm saved if this is true: Büchner, 116 points out the contrast with Simo's remark at 465, 'It's all over, if she's telling the truth', also in an aside

975   *Bene factum*: the same formula of congratulation as at 969.

Age: cf. on 692, but not here sarcastic.

your good fortune: OLD *secundus*[1] 4.c for neuter plural *secunda* = *res secundae*.

respice: cf. 642.

976   *Tuos*: OLD *tuus* 6 'Friendly or devoted to you'.

977   *adeo*: cf. 532.

longumst: it is idiomatic to use the present indicative in this expression; see OLD *longus* 12 'it is too long a business (to)'.

979   fetch people to move her from here: Pamphilus' instruction is very brief, and Davos may well be puzzled by it as well as slow in his movements after his punishment; hence Pamphilus' further command to get a move on. But it is in any case a comic convention that slaves are rebuked for being slow to carry out orders; see *HT* 250, *Hec.* 360, 436, 814, Ar. *Lys.* 426–27, Men. *Dysk.* 441.

980–81   Don't wait … Please give us your applause: I have followed those manuscripts which make Pamphilus the speaker of the last two lines. The 'betrothal' is that of Charinus and Philumena. The appeal for applause is traditional at the end of Latin comedies (*Hec.* and *Ad.* also end *Plaudite*, Terence's other three plays *Vos ualete et plaudite*), but it is uncertain in whose mouth it should come. K-L make Davos the speaker of 'Don't wait … settled inside' and (influenced by the mysterious speaker designation ω in the manuscripts and by Horace, *Ars Poetica* 155) put the appeal for applause, in this and in all the other plays, in the mouth of a separate *cantor* ('singer'); see Moore 2012, 73–75.

With these words compare the closing speech of Pl. *Cist.* (782–87): 'Spectators, don't wait for them to come out here to you: no one's going to come out; they'll all settle their business indoors... And now, as for what is left for you to do, spectators, give us your applause in the traditional manner at the conclusion of the comedy' (*Ne exspectetis, spectatores, dum illi huc ad uos exeant: / nemo exibit; omnes intus conficient negotium. / ... / ... / Nunc quod ad uos, spectatores, relicuom relinquitur, / more maiorum date plausum postrema in comoedia*).

No doubt the party preparations (such as they are) have been progressing in Simo's house throughout the play. At the end of the play most of the main characters are in Glycerium's house (but not Simo, Davos, or Sosia). We can easily imagine that they will all move over to enjoy the party, together with Glycerium and the baby – and perhaps Chremes will even send for Philumena to join them – , but nothing is said about this.

980 *despondebitur*: impersonal passive.

977a–99a Some of the later manuscripts preserve part of an alternative ending to the play, probably written some 200–400 years after the time of Terence, in which Chremes reappears and betroths Philumena to Charinus on stage. This was apparently intended to replace the last five lines of Terence's play, and its function was to round the play off by showing on the stage what Terence had in any case assured his audience would take place indoors. The alternative ending was already known to Donatus, who tells us that it was 'judged not to be by Terence' and was 'not found in most good copies'. The Oxyrhynchus papyrus (roughly contemporary with Donatus) has, before it breaks off, what could be the opening of 977 (with Pamphilus saying 'I won't forget. And'), followed by indications that Charinus speaks at the start of two following lines; in other words, it did not at this point have lines 978–79 as they are found in the other manuscripts, and 977 itself did not necessarily continue as it does in those manuscripts after its opening words. F. Ritschl, *Parerga zu Plautus und Terenz* (Berlin, 1845, repr. Amsterdam, 1965), 598–99 had already conjectured that the author of the alternative ending must have rewritten 977–78 to show that Chremes was seen coming out from Glycerium's house at this point and that Charinus and Davos withdrew to one side of the stage. The tattered remains of the papyrus suggest that Ritschl was thinking on very much the right lines, and I have printed the text he suggested for 977a.

As it stands, the alternative ending appears to end the play with the betrothal of Philumena to Charinus; Davos is not sent to arrange the transfer of Glycerium from one house to the other, and there is no appeal to the audience for applause and no indication that any characters leave the stage (though there is no indication of that at the end of *Ad.* either). Possibly an abbreviated version of 978–81 was intended to complete the play.

The text as transmitted in the manuscripts is full of errors; there are detailed discussions by Skutsch and by Victor 1989. Victor 1989, 71–72 argues that a line has been lost after 983a in which Pamphilus named Charinus as the husband he had in mind for Philumena. The scene would certainly be more convincing if it included such a line.

The language of 982a is modelled on that of 571, 994a *animum ... applicaueris* on that of 56 and 193; 990a *bene factum* is found at 105, 969, 975; 996a *facere coniecturam* is found at 512.

Metre: the trochaic septenarii continue to 990a, followed by iambic senarii to the end (though Skutsch, 60–62 tentatively suggests rearranging 990a–92a as four senarii, with expansion of *quam id quod abs te expecto*; even if 990a is kept as a septenarius, he expands 992a to become two senarii). To end a play with senarii would be very unusual, paralleled only by the spurious lines which are designed to conclude Pl. *Poen.* at 1371 (how many of the preceding lines are spurious has been debated).

981a   *alterae*: this form of the genitive is found only here, though for the dative cf. Brothers on *HT* 271.

[**983a**   *nunc*: added by Guyet for the sake of the metre.]

984a   **What you propose is nothing new to me**: this and the following lines show that their author believed Charinus to have approached Chremes previously; cf. on 373.

986a   *Daue*: the second syllable scans as *breuis in longo* before a change of speaker, like the final syllable of *Pamphile* at 267.

[**987a**   *amicitia nostra*: one might expect these words to be in the accusative as the subject of *tradi* in the next line (accusative + infinitive after *studui*), and that is how Spengel printed them in his first edition (1875). As they stand, they are a hanging nominative, an entirely possible construction. Umpfenbach and Marouzeau read *amicitiae nostrae*, presumably as genitive dependent on *aliquam partem* in the next line; but *aliquam partem* is best taken as an adverbial accusative (OLD *pars* 2.b).]

989a   *copiam*: OLD 7 'The means, possibility, or opportunity of doing something specified or implied'. [*copiam hanc* is Skutsch's very tempting suggestion for *copia ac* of the manuscripts, since *copia* does not seem so appropriate as a subject in this clause.]

991a   For the nonsensical *mihi agissime* various suggestions have been made, listed in the apparatus at Victor 1989, 70: *amicissime, carissime, mi aequissime, antiquissime*. Whatever the reading, Charinus' greeting of Chremes is remarkably effusive.

[**992a**   The last words of this line are unmetrical and make little sense. We can only guess at what the author wrote.]

994a   *quod ad cumque*: tmesis of *quodcumque*, as at 63, 263, with *ad* postponed to follow *quod*; Skutsch, 63 cites as a parallel Cic. *Leg.* 2.46 *quod ad cumque legis genus me disputatio nostra deduxerit.*

995a   *exinde ut*: OLD *exinde* 3 'In the same measure as, according as'.

[*existimaberis*: this is Skutsch's correction of the manuscripts' *existimaueris* and seems to be required for the sense, since we need a passive here.]

997a   *alienus*: OLD *alienus*[1] 7 'Unfriendly, unsympathetic, unfavourable, estranged'.

quis = *qualis*, as at 702.

999a   **six talents**: cf. on 951.

INDEXES

Index rerum